FRASER
OF
NORTH CAPE

Fraser as Commander-in-Chief, British Pacific Fleet, 1945

FRASER

OF

NORTH CAPE

THE LIFE OF
ADMIRAL OF THE FLEET
LORD FRASER
[1888–1981]

Richard Humble

ROUTLEDGE & KEGAN PAUL
London, Boston, Melbourne and Henley

First published in 1983
by Routledge & Kegan Paul plc
39 Store Street, London WC1E 7DD,
9 Park Street, Boston, Mass. 02108, USA,
464 St Kilda Road,
Melbourne, Victoria 3004, Australia, and
Broadway House, Newtown Road,
Henley-on-Thames, Oxon RG9 1EN
Set in 11/12pt Sabon by Input Typesetting Ltd,
London SW19 8DR
and printed in Great Britain by
Hartnoll Print, Bodmin, Cornwall
© Richard Humble, 1983

Library of Congress Cataloging in Publication Data

Humble, Richard.

Fraser of North Cape.

Includes bibliographical references and index.
1. Fraser, Bruce, 1887–1981. 2. Admirals—Great
Britain—Biography. 3. Great Britain. Royal Navy—Bio-
graphy. I. Title.
V64.G72F73 1983   359'.0092'4 [B]   83–8723

ISBN 0–7100–9555–4

By the special request of
Lord Fraser
this book is dedicated in gratitude and pride

God Save the Queen

Contents

CONTENTS

Illustrations

Foreword

ADMIRAL SIR HENRY LEACH

This book is about a great man: a great sailor, a great gentleman, and, to so many, a great friend.

It is difficult to do justice to an Admiral of the Fleet whose life covered such a tremendous range. Bruce Fraser first went to sea in the pre-Dreadnought Navy and rapidly made his name as a gunnery specialist, winning the Admiralty's favourable attention while still a young Lieutenant on the eve of the First World War. It was supremely fitting that his matchless talents as a gunnery expert earned such a unique reward: designing and putting into production the Royal Navy's last generation of battleships, then using that weapon of his own forging to fight and win the Navy's last battleship action.

Yet Bruce Fraser's service through both world wars was never restricted to the field of gunnery alone. He witnessed the birth of naval aviation with the Grand Fleet in 1917–18, was a highly successful aircraft-carrier Captain in the middle 1930s, and ended the Second World War in command of the strongest carrier fleet which Britain has ever sent to sea.

He spent eight months in a Bolshevik prison but twenty-five years later he received the Order of Suvorov from Stalin himself; he commanded three fleets in war; he was Controller of the Navy and First Sea Lord, and a member of the House of Lords; he made no mistakes nor great enemies; and he was loved and respected by all with whom he came into contact.

It would be hard to find a man of Bruce Fraser's talents and position who was so totally lacking in pretension or pomposity, so very human and endowed with the common touch. He never boasted of anything or sought publicity, but when it came his way he would use it to promote the Navy, never himself. For the Navy was his whole life and he was a true professional, ever receptive to new technology and new ideas to make the Navy a more effective Service.

Richard Humble has written a very shrewd biography of a remarkable person. Among all the history and anecdotes of a crowded and inspiring career he has rightly allowed a single theme to transcend all others: Bruce Fraser the man.

Acknowledgments

My first thanks are due to the two ladies who brought about my introduction to Lord Fraser and the ensuing writing of this book. Sister Gladys Duval of the Royal Masonic Hospital, where Lord Fraser regularly attended for checkups on his heart 'pacemaker', is, as a prewar nursing colleague of my mother, an old family friend. It was Gladys Duval who first urged me to write 'our Admiral's' biography and referred me to Lord Fraser's secretary and most trusted friend: Mrs Renée Duncan.

Without Renée Duncan's devoted help and solicitude, Lord Fraser's long retirement could hardly have enjoyed the comfort and serenity which were its most evident features. Without her encouragement and enthusiasm, which finally persuaded Lord Fraser that the telling of his life story was long overdue, this book would almost certainly never have seen the light of day. Seldom has any author been sustained by a more wonderful ally; any form of thanks for Renée Duncan's endless help, with documentation, references and introductions to vital *dramatis personae*, seems most wretchedly inadequate. The lion's share of any credit and approval which this book may attract is due to Renée Duncan. Her brother-in-law, Mr Ronald Duncan, also gave inestimable help in checking the many drafts through which the manuscript passed before Lord Fraser's high standards were met.

As Lord Fraser's longest-serving Flag Lieutenant, Captain Vernon Merry was an ever-prolific mine of information and insight on Lord Fraser's professional *modus operandi* and criteria, and I am deeply grateful for his help and encouragement. No less is due to Captain Richard Courage. As with Captain Merry, his papers include a wealth of documentation which has not survived the pernicious 'weeding' of our public records by civil servants, and these papers were unhesitatingly placed at my disposal. I am particularly grateful to Captain Courage for lending me the manuscript of his unpublished memoirs, which yielded much new material on the North Cape battle and the formation of the British Pacific Fleet.

With regard to the intricacies of the North Cape action I was very greatly helped by the generosity of Patrick Beesly, author of the definitive study *Very Special Intelligence*. He most kindly lent me the English manuscript of his lucid article 'Special Intelligence and Convoy Routing: JW.55B and the Destruction of the *Scharnhorst*', written in collaboration with Dr Jurgen Rohwer and published in *Marine Rundschau* (October 1977).

Many hands helped in unravelling the complex story of the British Pacific Fleet for me, but in addition to Captains Merry and Courage I owe a special debt to Mrs Nancy Chaplin (formerly 2nd Officer Bond, WRNS) for her generous loan of a wealth of material, especially on the historic mission to Pearl Harbor in December 1944; and Commander Charles Sheppard, whose extensive knowledge of the Far East was yet another gold-mine.

My thanks, too, to Vice-Admiral Sir Peter Gretton, Naval Assistant to Lord Fraser when First Sea Lord, for his concise guide to the problems besetting Lord Fraser in his last months of office.

I would also like to thank the by no means 'forgotten army' of helpers, ex-Navy and civilian alike, who corresponded with me and, in addition to reminiscences and anecdotes, lent me photographs, cuttings, letters and other invaluable items of documentation. Theirs was an essential contribution. They will, I hope, understand that it was impossible to include every story or photograph I received. Quite apart from considerations of space, Lord Fraser remained adamant that his biography should not be open to dismissal as a mere bouquet of admiring reminiscences, no matter how sincere. But my correspondents may rest assured that every item sent to me was shown or read to Lord Fraser; and in at least four cases out of five, the familiar disclaimer that 'I'm sure the Admiral won't remember me' was triumphantly proved wrong by Lord Fraser's piercing memory.

In expressing my lasting gratitude to these individuals I have pleasure in listing their names in alphabetical order, under the appropriate subject-heading.

(a) *HMS Minerva*, 1914–16
    Hawkins, Lt-Col. G. R., OBE, RM; Parkes-Buchanan, Capt. M. J.
(b) *HMS Resolution*, 1916–20; captivity at Baku, 1920
    Howard, Alfred H.; Richardson, R. D.; Wakeham, P.G.
(c) *HMS Excellent*, 1921
    Chandler, Cdr R. B., OBE
(d) *HMS Effingham*, 1929–32
    Bruce-Kingsmill, Cdr N.; Drage, Cdr C.; Goodwin, Cdr A. J. H.;

Ingleby-Mackenzie, Lady Violetta; Tapper, Capt. C. A. L.
(e) HMS *Glorious*, 1935–7
Hague, F.; Langley, Lt-Cdr P.G.O.; McCahon, Capt. J.
(f) HMS *Anson*, Home Fleet 1942–3; 'Pedestal' Malta convoy (HMS *Rodney*)
Eliot, Cdr C. J.; Forbes, Cdr J. G.; Freaker, R. C.; Hall, B. L.; Holby, G.G.
(g) Home Fleet, 1943–4, and *Scharnhorst* action
Bennett, R. M.; Cawood, E.; Coney, Capt. G. D.; Meyrick, Cdr M.; Nash, R. A.; Powell, Lt-Cdr E. S.; Quicke, Cdr J.; Uniacke, Col. J. A. C., RM; Wace, Mrs Marjorie; Waterfield, C. A. G.; Welby-Everard, Capt. P. H. E.; Wright, Desmond.
(h) HMS *Duke of York*, Home and British Pacific Fleets, 1943–6
Bayly, Lt-Cdr D. L.; East, Cdr R. D.; Godden, Cdr D. J.; Landon, L. E.; McGregor, J.; Morris, C. S.; Mortimore, F. J.; Mugford, K.; Nesbit, J. d'A; Paterson, Cdr C. J.; Vincent, Capt. P. M. C.; Waterhouse, D. R.; Wintle, K.
(i) Eastern and British Pacific Fleets, 1944–5
Barham, J. P.; Bartley, J.; Bird, P. B.; Bradnum, F. M.; Duncan, H. R.; Dunn, Mrs Brian; Fearnehough, G.; McCall, the late Admiral Sir Henry; Murphy, D. D.; Parkes, Mrs Olga; Pattison, M.; Pearcy, Arthur, Jnr.; Race, G. B.; Reid, C. E.; Rundle, J. S. E.; Short, J. R.; Stamps, Mrs Cora; Trumble, D.; Walker, J. E. T.
(j) Commander-in-Chief, Portsmouth, 1946–8
Beckwith, Cdr C. E.; Cogswell, Lt C (RNVR); Hill, D.; Norris, A.; Scales, Miss A. C.; Tate, W. K.; Tunbridge, P.
(k) First Sea Lord and retirement, 1948–81
Backhouse, T. A.; Bence-Trower, P.; Collier, Major H. V.; Crawford, Capt. J. S., DSO, OBE; Guild, Lt-Cdr J. M. C.; McLanachan, Cdr W. Y.; Perry, M. F.; Simpson, L.; Stoughton, B. M.; Streatfeild-James, Cdr C.; Wallas, T.

I would also like to thank the following for their kind assistance in supplying photographic material: R. D. Richardson for plate 11; Cdr A. J. H. Goodwin for plate 12; Lt-Cdr P. G. O. Langley for plate 14; Novosti Press Agency for plate 20; Mrs N. Chaplin for plate 22; US Navy for plate 24; F. J. Mortimore for plate 26; *Evening News and Hampshire Telegraph* for plate 28; Lady Violetta Ingleby-Mackenzie for plate 30; BBC Television Services for plate 38. Plates 16 and 21 are Crown copyright. All other plates used in the book come from Lord Fraser's private collection (Fraser Papers).

My special thanks to Jerome Dessain (Newton Abbot) and the Mall Studios (Ealing) for their sterling help with the photographs for this book.

Part One

The making of a Gunnery Officer
[1888 – 1920]

· I ·

'A most promising boy'
[1888–1904]

Bruce Austin Fraser, the man who was to become Admiral of the Fleet Lord Fraser of North Cape, victor of the Royal Navy's last battleship action and Commander-in-Chief of the most powerful fleet Britain has ever sent to sea, was born in London on 5 February 1888. And ninety years later, during his long and happy retirement from active service, it amused him to think that the advance of his name to the head of the Navy List began largely because he was a second son.

'My father', he told the author, 'was the old-fashioned sort. He told my brother, who was the older one, "You will go into the Army", and I would go into the Navy. It was a very good thing really, you know,' added Lord Fraser through a cloud of pipe smoke, 'because you then don't have to sort out anything else. No wondering about what you were going to do next – whether you should become a lawyer, or a doctor, or' – the inimitable Fraser grin – 'a scurrilous journalist.'[1]

When General Alexander Fraser, CB, gave his young sons their marching orders for the Army and the Royal Navy, in the year of Queen Victoria's Diamond Jubilee, it was the concluding act of service to his country in a long and highly distinguished career. This had been spent in the Indian Service, but the General's fame had not been won in battles and campaigns against the enemies of the Raj. General Fraser was a superb architect and engineer, a builder of public works intended to be 'pukka' – permanent. He typified all that was constructive and enduring in the British imperial dream, and left monuments to his formidable talents across the map of the Raj from India and Ceylon to the coasts of Burma.

Alexander Fraser first went to India in 1843 under the East India Company's regime as a subaltern in the Bengal Engineers. Born in 1824, he had been educated at Addiscombe, the Company's training college for gunners and engineers destined for the Indian Service. In the old days before the Cardwell Army reforms of the 1870s, Addiscombe was second to none in the field of military education and produced what were probably the best-trained specialist officers in the entire British Service:[2]

> By 1830 it was also generally conceded that officers should have special training; cadets for the Engineers now went to Addiscombe, the East India Company's College for gunner and engineer officers, where they received a special education. When they reached India they were required to pass, within six months of joining the corps, an examination of logarithms, practical geometry, plane trigonometry, the use of chain box, sextant and theodolite, and to be able to make a 'route sketch'. Fourteen months after joining, the young officer must be able to show a well-finished plan of a system of fortifications drawn by himself.

In General Fraser's case these skills had first been given full scope during the planning of the Company's early railways, of which the first line was opened in 1853; but opening up what was to become far and away the best railway system in Asia was only the beginning. When the Great Bengal Mutiny exploded in May 1857 Fraser was not in India. He was touring the English coastline with a special mission: to look at lighthouses.[3]

> 'They had told him', recalled Lord Fraser, 'to build a lighthouse on the Alguada Reef, which is at the entrance to the Irrawaddy. He said, "Well, I don't know anything about lighthouses," so the Company sent him home to England to look at every lighthouse in the country, which he did. And that's how he missed the Mutiny. He was home when it happened, and volunteered to go back, but the East India Company said the lighthouse was more important!'

The Mutiny ended the rule of the East India Company but the lighthouse project survived, and General Fraser duly returned to build the Alguada Reef Lighthouse. When finally completed in early 1865 this fine structure earned Fraser the warmest official praise from the governments of India and Burma – praise that was crowned by the following golden letter:[4]

Balmoral
Oct. 14 1865

Dear Sir,
I have had the honour to present to Her Majesty the Queen

the photographs of the Lighthouse on Alguada Reef, which accompanied your letter of the 10th Inst., and which have been very graciously accepted by Her Majesty.

In thanking you for your attention the Queen directed me to say that you may very well feel proud of the testimony to your merits borne by the Governor General of India in Council; not only because that praise is of an unusually strong character, but because it appears to have been fully deserved.

The work was evidently one of very uncommon difficulty and you will feel a satisfaction throughout your life in looking back at the boldness, perseverance, and skill which overcame such formidable obstacles without the sacrifice of a single life.

Believe me dear Sir,
Yours truly,
Col. B. Phipps

The railways of India are Alexander Fraser's first memorial; the lighthouses which he surveyed and built – on Alguada Reef, then Galle in Ceylon, and the Oyster Reef, Krishna Shoal, Akyab and the Rangoon River estuary in Burma – are the second. Last but not least came his layouts for wharfs, docks, and cantonments at Moulmein and above all at Rangoon, the latter being a truly pukka street plan where 'Fraser Street' still keeps his name in remembrance.

General Fraser ended his career in 1886 with the post of Chief Engineer of India on the Viceroy's Council. His professional achievements spoke for themselves; his personal qualities had won him the trust and friendship of Lord Lytton, Viceroy in 1876–80. On 2 July 1880, as Lytton prepared to embark for home on the expiry of his term as Viceroy, he found time amid the hurly-burly of departure to get off a grateful note:[5]

Good bye, my dear Fraser, good bye, and God bless you! I cannot leave India, without one last word of affectionate farewell to the friend and colleague, whose sympathy has never failed me, and whose help has lightened so much of my labour.'

Family life and children came late to Alexander Fraser, after he had retired to England to live in the south-east. Although thirty-seven years his junior Monica Stores Smith, whom he met in 1883, made him a devoted wife; their first son, Cecil, was born in July 1886 and Bruce followed in February 1888.

The boys enjoyed a happy and affectionate childhood, a lot of it spent in the open air with pets and horses under their father's enthusiastic but never compelling encouragement. To modern eyes this comes as something of a surprise, for Alexander Fraser's portrait photograph, with his beetling eyebrows and formidable moustache, suggests that archetypal, iron-hard Victorian *paterfamilias* – hardly the type of father who could write the following letter to his sons at their first school:[6]

29 February/98

My dearest Boys,
I have Cecil's letter of 27th this morning and will send him my stamp album as he desires. I hope you will take care of it, for it is rather a nice one and will become valuable in the course of time.

Cecil's writing case is all ready and no doubt Mammie will send it together with the 2/6 she owes Cecil when she is able to do so. He says he has no place to keep his 'notepapper' but I don't know why he spells paper with two p's!

I am very glad his watch is going well – how does Bruce's watch go?

The cow, calf, geese, dogs, cats, jackdaw, canary, horses, pigs, chickens and ducks are all well – and the cats are also I should think as they are pretty lively at night. They have taken to ringing the front door bell at night!

Jim the pony is however still a little lame. Mammie says she won't be able to send Cecil's half-crown until Monday or Tuesday, or the other things either as she is not going into Rochford or Southend today and tomorrow is Sunday, while it is possible that on Monday we shall be going over to Hill Farm – or 'Downham Grange' as it is to be.

On Tuesday we go to Town and stay till Thursday so I am not sure whether you will get the things till end of next week! I hope Bruce is going to treat us to a letter now and then? Why, you will have been gone a week next Monday – a week off the time to Easter so it will soon pass. Better not think of it too much but stick to your studies and the time will pass all the quicker the busier you are.

Good-bye old chaps, and with Mammie's best love joined with my own,
    Believe me always
        Your fond Daddie
        Alex Fraser

'Prep.' school for the boys was Elsted Rectory at Petersfield in Hampshire – a pleasant place, run by the inevitable clergyman, where the boys settled in well. They both turned in promising reports when their first half-term ended in October 1898, with Bruce 'doing nicely' in religious knowledge, 'diligent and accurate' at mathematics, 'making a distinct advance and always preparing his work very well' in Latin, 'making an excellent start' at French, 'a wonderfully correct speller' in English, and 'a very careful little player' in music. All in all, as his headmaster summed up, 'a most promising boy'.[7]

Eighty years later Lord Fraser looked back on Elsted Rectory with affection. 'The Rector took in about twelve boys, and used to get some students as assistant masters; they never stayed for longer than their summer vacations. Big house, great big barn; then they put in a cricket ground. There were horses – he hunted himself, the Headmaster – and we used to go for rides across the Downs.' And the Fraser brothers were still enjoying these surroundings when their father died in 1898.

Mrs Fraser never dreamed of altering her late husband's choice of the Army and Navy as careers for her sons. After completing the family move to Downham Grange in Essex, the problem she had to solve next was which schools the boys should go to after the Rectory to prepare for cadet-hood. In Cecil's case it was easy: most Victorian public schools had 'Army Classes' for polishing up candidates for Sandhurst or Woolwich. But comparatively few offered similar specialist facilities for boys wishing to enter HMS *Britannia*, the Navy's floating academy at Dartmouth in Devon. In her search for the right school for Bruce, Mrs Fraser wrote to Lady Lytton, now a lady-in-waiting to Queen Victoria, for advice; Lady Lytton consulted Admiral Fullerton, also attached to the Court. He in turn referred Mrs Fraser to the Admiralty, which solved the problem by recommending Bradfield College.

Bradfield was for Bruce Fraser what Westward Ho! was for Rudyard Kipling – a new school, whose headmaster, Dr Gray, was also the founder – but without the loneliness that the young Kipling knew. As Bradfield had an Army as well as a Navy Class, Cecil and Bruce could go through public school together, though Cecil went to the senior school and Bruce to the junior. 'We were allowed to go out for walks together on Sundays, the one time brothers met.'[8] Bruce started at Bradfield in 'Navy Class II' but after his first term was promoted to 'Navy Class I', whose pupils were exempt from 'fagging' for senior boys.

'First class' was how Lord Fraser recalled his schooldays at Bradfield, with particular respect for his headmaster's assessment of form. As the *Britannia* examination loomed over the horizon in 1902, Mrs Fraser anxiously asked Dr Gray how Bruce would do. He should pass in the first five, was the comforting prediction, and the headmaster's forecast was sound. The results placed Bruce fifth, and on 15 September 1902 he became Cadet Fraser in HMS *Britannia*.

In 1902 HMS *Britannia* had only four more years left to her as a training-house for Royal Naval officers; but during Fraser's time in her she was still a picturesque sight, the floating symbol of a conservative Navy destined, over the next ten years, to be swept from stem to stern by a torrent of controversial change. HMS *Britannia* was really two ships: the linked, built-up hulls of the old 'wooden walls' *Britannia* and *Hindustan*, which served as living quarters for the cadets. The latter were organised in four 'terms' or classes of 60–65 cadets, with each term supervised by a lieutenant. Fraser's term instructor was Lieutenant Chetwoode, later Captain of HMS *Queen Elizabeth* in the 1920s when Fraser was Fleet Gunnery Officer, Mediterranean Fleet. From among the cadets the term instructor appointed a class captain and Cadet Moore, Fraser's class captain at *Britannia*, would in time become Fraser's Second-in-Command, Home Fleet, in the Second World War.

The teaching year at *Britannia* was made up of four calendar terms of three months each. By far the most important member of the teaching staff was the instructor in trigonometry and navigation, invariably a university mathematics graduate. Taking his charges through plane and spherical trigonometry to celestial navigation, his task was to turn out junior officers who could work a ship's reckoning by the sun while still in their fifteenth year. Civilian teachers instructed in French and drawing, and once a week there was a divinity class with the chaplain. Seamanship was taught by petty officers, with basic instruction in a well-stocked model room before going on to the real thing: handling small boats under oar and sail.

Lord Fraser looked back on his time at *Britannia* as 'very nice — very austere. We had to get up at 6.30 every morning and go through a cold bath, then pull ashore in a big launch — enormous oars, you know', sketching in the air, from heartfelt memory, gigantic oars reaching above head height. A Navy tradition, dating back long before Nelson's day, was that the smartest and most able hands were designated 'topmen' and assigned to the uppermost masts and yards, and this tradition was maintained at *Britannia*. Having passed in fifth, thereby being ranked with the 'so-called cleverest' (as he typically put it), Fraser was assigned to the topmost yards, the royals, when the cadets went to sea for their sail training.

Fraser and his 'term' had their main training cruise in the old cruiser *Isis* in November-December 1903: a run down from Plymouth to the Spanish coast, with an introduction to the Bay of Biscay at its most irate on the voyage home. Leaving Vigo Bay for Devonport on Saturday 28 November, *Isis* ran straight into heavy weather, rapidly worsening into a storm so bad that it attracted the attention of the newspapers back home and gave Mrs Fraser some anxious reading. 'For three or four days the lads had a very uncomfortable time,' announced the *Daily Telegraph*. 'Our cruiser was at times rolling 45 deg., she was washed continuously fore and aft, the whole of the after accommodation, including the ward-room and officers' quarters, were continuously flooded.'[9] On Sunday the 29th the port boom was carried away and the port sea boat was stove in and left hanging from the falls. By Monday the gale was still raging unabated and *Isis* had put her head to the sea, reducing speed and struggling through repeated hailstorms with all on board feeling the cold.

The storm did not blow itself out without a resounding finale. The gale was already starting to slacken when 'a peculiar phenomenon was witnessed about half-past nine on Monday night. There was a crash, resembling an explosion. Several on board for an instant imagined something had gone wrong in the magazine, but the real fact was that a meteorite had descended and burst. An eye-witness states: "There was a terrific din, then a blaze of light, and afterwards numberless small lights all round. The spectacle, awe-inspiring, was of short duration." '[10] The storm-beaten *Isis* eventually reached Plymouth with her cold, damp, but exhilarated cadets on the morning of Tuesday 1 December. It was one of the worst storms Fraser was ever to experience at sea (he reckoned that the worst one was while coming back from Iceland in HMS *Anson* to take over the Home Fleet from Admiral Tovey in 1943). 'Of course,' he smiled, looking back to the earlier adventure, 'we all thought it was *wonderful.*'

The *Isis* cruise brought Fraser's year at HMS *Britannia* to a close, for 16 December 1903 was Prizegiving Day. With deep pride, Mrs Fraser added the printed results to the meticulous photograph album-cum-scrapbook she was keeping as a record of her sons' careers. Fraser had passed out joint first with six other cadets in all three classes – Mathematics, Extra Subjects, and Seamanship. Lord Selborne, First Lord of the Admiralty, presented the prizes. Fraser received a gold chain for his first place in 'Study'; he collected a fountain pen for his second place in 'Charts and Instruments' and another for his second in Physics.

He came out of *Britannia* with the white collar patches and dirk of a midshipman, his name on the Navy List, his career as an officer open before him. And on 15 January 1904 Midshipman Fraser joined his first ship: HMS *Hannibal*, a battleship of the Channel Fleet.

. 2 .

Sea legs:
Hannibal and *Prince George*
[1904–7]

It was a daunting prospect, abandoning the status of a seasoned *Britannia* cadet to become a very small cog in a battleship's complement of over 750. But Mrs Fraser was at her son's side as he travelled down to Portsmouth in mid-January 1904; the role of escort helped Bruce forget his qualms and concentrate on not cutting an unmanly figure when joining his first ship.[1]

> 'We stayed in a little hotel on the front, and in the evening we got a hansom, and my big sea chest was hoisted on top; and we drove into the dockyard. I told my mother on no account was she to come alongside the ship to see me go on board, so the hansom was stopped about 30 yards away, and the poor old cabby had to carry my sea chest up to the gangway, and my mother had to stop behind in the hansom. I walked up the gangway, and there at the top was an enormous Marine – he was one of the corporals of the gangway, of course. He gave me a big salute – I was very impressed – and then I was sent down to the Gunroom. I don't think at that moment I got a whack on the bottom, but I did, probably, later!'

A midshipman's life in a warship's Gunroom was tightly disciplined by the overlord of that cramped world: the Sub-Lieutenant of the Gunroom, or 'Snottie's Nurse'. His main role was to teach the midshipmen their place in the Navy's pecking order which was, effectively, nowhere: neither a rating nor an officer. A midshipman was precisely what his name implied: a 'midship man' who did not mess forward with the ratings, nor aft with the officers of the Wardroom. And the first thing he had to learn was total respect for his seniors, obeying their orders like greased lightning, with apparent laggards being smartened up by the sub-lieutenant's cane.

All this came naturally after public school and HMS *Britannia*, as did the endless penalties imposed by Gunroom etiquette. There was, for instance, 'scuttle drill', essential for regular ventilation when the ship was at sea. The Gunroom was so close to the waterline that the scuttles could only be left open in a flat calm. When a sea was running a junior midshipman would be set to opening the scuttles on the upward roll of the ship and closing them on the downward roll. Mistakes would inevitably result in a torrent of seawater coming inboard, the resultant discomfort being avenged by the sub-lieutenant's cane. Quick reactions at all times were encouraged by a senior jamming a fork into an overhead beam and shouting 'Fork in the Beam!' – cue for junior midshipmen to leave at the double, with a cut from the cane awaiting the last one out. Decorum was preserved (nominally at least) when a senior wanted to tell a questionable story. On the command 'Breadcrumbs!' juniors had to clap hands to ears – though 'of course, we always listened.' Another punishment was 'Mastheads', the victim being sent to roost up one of the ship's mastheads until told to come down. At best silly, at worst unthinkable to modern-day 'progressives', it all seemed right and proper to the Edwardian Navy. 'Just like public school, really,' was Lord Fraser's verdict, looking back, 'all friends afterwards.'[2]

Even at its most demanding, Gunroom discipline was only supplementary to the midshipman's most important task: learning to command men, most of whom were far older and more experienced than he was. Fraser had been three weeks in HMS *Hannibal* when he was put in charge of one of the ship's boats, the third whaler: five men with an able seaman coxswain – 'my first command' as he always called it. Lord Fraser never forgot his first order. 'The crew were expected to sit in the bottom of the boat; but as there was a lot of water in the bottom of the boat I was too frightened to tell them to sit down until I saw the officer of the watch looking at me through his telescope, and *then* I said "Sit down in the boat!" And they all sat down. This gave me a great deal of confidence.' But it was not long before he began to learn that the Navy has its own ways of getting things done, even when it comes to delivering a fleet's letters:[3]

'In those days the flagship generally used to make a signal "No steamboats allowed", and at about 11 o'clock "Send boats with letters"; and so about thirty sailing boats appeared off the stern of the flagship. Of course, as the junior midshipman – I'd only been three weeks at sea – I had to get out of the way of all the senior midshipmen; and so we went on sailing about behind the stern of the flagship, when I suddenly noticed that although everyone was trying to get to the port side, nobody was going to the starboard ladder. I said to my coxswain, who of course I thought was a very old man – he was about twenty-five – "How ridiculous that only one ladder is being used when there's another one quite free; I think I'm going alongside the starboard one." He was rather nervous about this but he agreed, so we set off. Then, just as I was getting towards the ladder, my foresail didn't come down properly and I went full tilt into the ladder with a tremendous bump, with everybody looking out of the scuttles and watching, and my crew frightened out of their lives, of course. Then a big man, full of gold lace, looked over the side and said "Come up here, young man!" So I rushed up the ladder, carrying the letters which I'd brought with me. He looked at me, and just said "How long have *you* been at sea?" I said, "Three weeks, sir." He said "You'll soon learn," and sent me down the ladder again. My crew at the bottom were overjoyed, and I thought they were praising me for coming back – but really it was because they'd feared they were going to be told to pull round the Fleet!'

A petty officer (PO) coxswain would probably have had the presence to explain to Fraser that a flagship's starboard gangway is *always* kept free for the Admiral and his staff. But Fraser did learn fast, moving on from *Hannibal's* third whaler to command the first picket-boat. 'This was a tremendous advance. I now had a PO coxswain, an engine-room rating, three seamen and a sparkling brass funnel.'[4]

The Channel Fleet's title was misleading, because for two-thirds of the year it never saw the Channel. Its 'beat' extended west and south to the coasts of Ireland and Spain, and the men of the Channel Fleet were almost as familiar with Queenstown, Vigo and Gibraltar as they were with Plymouth, Portland or Portsmouth. But when the Fleet was cruising in home waters one of its regular ports of call was Portland, where there was a coaling station, with the fleshpots of Weymouth close by. And it was during one of these visits to Portland that Fraser and his 'second command' came literally within feet of disaster.[5]

'Many nights we had to go into Weymouth at 11 o'clock to pick up the officers and bring them back. There was great competition to get to the first place along the side, cutting corners on the leading lights into Weymouth. And one night, just as I was nearing Weymouth, the forward lookout called "Sail right ahead!" I ordered "Hard-a-starboard", whether by good luck or good management I don't know: it was the end of Weymouth breakwater, not a sail. I stopped engines, and we all came on deck breathing very heavily. I said "I'll never cut corners again." If I'd turned the other way I should have been on the rocks at Weymouth and finished for life. But not a word of reproach from the Lower Deck, which shows their tremendous loyalty.'

Though barely appreciated at midshipman level – 'we were all too busy, steering our steamboats about'[6] – great events were afoot in the spring and summer of 1904. On 8 April Britain and France signed the *Entente Cordiale*, a formal reconciliation between the two nations after decades of tension, which deleted France from the list of Britain's most likely adversaries in a sea war. The *Entente* had been brought about largely by the personal charm of King Edward VII on his state visit to Paris in May 1903, but he was also anxious to preserve the best possible relations with his nephew, Kaiser Wilhelm II of Germany. So it was that in June 1904 the King visited Germany for the Kiel Regatta, escorted in state by a squadron from the Channel Fleet, including HMS *Hannibal*. The ensuing meeting of the British and German navies was Fraser's first chance to observe the Navy in action as a medium of international goodwill; it gave him one of the biggest frights of his career; and it clinched his respect for the Royal Navy's Lower Deck.[7]

'One night we had to take the officers to dinner in a German ship. There was a custom that when you were waiting alongside you were invited on board; and when we went alongside to pick them up later a chap leaned over the side and said "Come up, young man!" I said to my coxswain "Well, you'd better come up, too"; but he said "I'll never set foot in a German ship, because we'll be at war with them in four or five years." What commonsense comes from the Lower Deck. When I got into the junior officers' mess – I was only sixteen and a half – they plied me with so many drinks that I was sick all over their Mess. But after that you felt better, and so I was able to go down to my boat and take charge again. But as we went off I was terrified. I thought perhaps the Captain would be told to come on board and apologise, or I might be court-martialled. If I confided in the sub-lieutenant he would probably give me six strokes with the cane; if I confided in the Commander he might stop my leave for a month, perhaps. So my one hope was to confide in my coxswain, which I did, and told him how terrified I was and what I thought was going to happen. He was a very laconic man, and all he said was "Serve 'em right." I was so thrilled with this that I forgot all my terrors; and of course nothing happened. What a wonderful thing it is, the commonsense and foresight of the Lower Deck; I've never forgotten his name: Petty Officer Drage.'

The impeccable turnout and drill required for a royal visit came naturally to the Navy of 1904, because for decades it had been concentrating on these virtues above all else. The will to perfect the Navy's function as a fighting machine had atrophied because there was nobody to fight: no British fleet had seen action since the Crimean War half a century before. Admittedly, in those fifty years steam power, armour plate, and heavy-calibre breech-loading guns in rotating turrets had ousted sail, wooden hulls and batteries of squat muzzle-loaders mounted in broadsides; but no serious effort had ever been made to train the Navy for maximum efficiency with the new ships and the new weapons. Smart paintwork and gleaming brass came far higher up the list of priorities than smart manoeuvring at full speed, or scoring maximum hits on a moving target at long range during gunnery shoots. One reason for this was the fact that the Navy was still a coal-fired Navy. High speeds meant denser smoke and more soot; higher coal consumption meant more frequent repetitions of the Navy's filthiest job: coaling, with grit and coal dust spreading everywhere as the bunkers were refilled. As for gunnery practice, the concussion of the guns seemed to conjure up dust and dirt from one end of the ship to the other.

The obvious deficiencies of other navies naturally contributed to British complacency in Service as well as civilian circles. One episode which certainly strengthened the Royal Navy's feeling of superiority at this time was the notorious 'Dogger Bank incident' of October 1904. This was a bizarre offshoot of the Russo-Japanese War of 1904–5. In a desperate bid to recoup a string of humiliating defeats by the Japanese the Russian Baltic Fleet was sent out to steam round the world and tackle the Japanese fleet in its home waters. As the Russian Baltic Fleet traversed the North Sea on the night of 22 October 1904, its panicky gunners opened fire on British fishing boats in the belief that (by some miracle of geography) they were Japanese torpedo-boats. The incident soon blew over in a welter of Russian apologies, but Fraser always remembered going to his battle station – *Hannibal*'s maintop 3-pounder – as the keyed-up Channel Fleet, ready for action, ushered the Russian warships out of British waters. British reactions were as much derisive as indignant, with the British *Naval and Military Record* sneering at Russia's 'fleet of lunatics'.

The day before the Dogger Bank incident – 21 October 1904 – the man who was to do more than anyone else to sweep away the Navy's post-Victorian complacency became First Sea Lord. Admiral

Sir John Fisher (later Admiral of the Fleet Lord Fisher of Kilverstone) placed fighting efficiency above all else. As Commander-in-Chief, Mediterranean Fleet in 1899–1902, 'Jacky' Fisher had insisted on fleet manoeuvres at full speed – 15 knots then being the best speed that the most modern battleship could make – instead of the traditional drillbook minuets at more leisurely speeds. Fisher had also insisted that gunnery practice be carried out at long range – 6,000 yards instead of the virtually point-blank range of 2,000 yards. But Fisher was as concerned with the Navy's weakness in strategic deployment as with its lack of tactical efficiency. It was Fisher who persuaded the Admiralty to send the Channel Fleet down to the Mediterranean for regular joint manoeuvres with the Mediterranean Fleet. The first of these was held in 1901 and the practice was continued after Fisher became First Sea Lord in October 1904. As the Commander-in-Chief, Channel Fleet, Admiral Sir Arthur Wilson, was a hard taskmaster (his dour persistence with any problem until the job was done had earned him the Service nickname of 'Tug'), 1905 promised to be a busy year for the Channel Fleet.

For Fraser the year began with a transfer from *Hannibal* to another Channel Fleet battleship, HMS *Prince George*, which he joined with fifteen other midshipmen on 27 February. His new surroundings were familiar because *Prince George* was a sister-ship of *Hannibal*: the fourth of the 'Majestic' class, completed in 1896. The promise of a busy year was abundantly fulfilled. In July the Fleet was due to celebrate the first anniversary of the *Entente Cordiale* with a pair of exchange visits with the French Navy, the first at Brest and the second at'Portsmouth. Before that, however, *Prince George* had to join the Fleet for another cruise and joint manoeuvres in the Mediterranean. By 3 March Captain Stokes had *Prince George* ready for her shakedown cruise and speed trial. Her new complement had already come aboard from shore barracks, and on 23 March she arrived at Gibraltar with the Channel Fleet.

The next four weeks saw intense activity throughout the Fleet, concentrated on weaponry (guns and torpedoes) in a manner that would have been unthinkable before the advent of Fisher. *Prince George* and her sister 'Majestics' carried the motley collection of guns typical of British battleships before the launch of Fisher's 'all-big-gun' *Dreadnought* in December 1905. In *Prince George*, the primary armament of four 12-inch guns was positioned directly over the appropriate magazines fore and aft; but ensuring an uninterrupted flow of ammunition to the smaller guns was any gunnery officer's nightmare. The secondary armament of twelve 6-inch guns was interwoven with a tertiary armament of sixteen 12-pounders, and as if that were not enough there were twelve 3-pounders for really short-range work. When her guns were firing, *Prince George* presented the frantic activity of a kicked-open anthill, with human-chain ammunition parties strung all over the ship. The torpedomen led a less frenetic existence; *Prince George* carried four submerged 18-inch torpedo tubes, with another above the waterline in the stern.

The labour of gunnery drill at Gibraltar was momentarily broken on 31 March by what was, for Fraser, his second encounter with the Imperial German Navy, though considerably less traumatic than the first. *Prince George* emerged an easy winner from a collision with the German armoured cruiser SMS *Friedrich Karl*. The German captain's zeal in observing the activities of the British fleet while on an ostensible goodwill visit led him into a gross error of judgment while passing *Prince George*; and the hasty recall of *Friedrich Karl*, very much under a cloud of imperial displeasure, caused much amusement in the British ships. After incessant run-throughs of the drill at Gibraltar, the Fleet paid a series of visits to Tetuan Bay for shoots and test torpedo firings before sailing for the rendezvous – Marmarice Bay, south-west Turkey – on 20 April. The outliers of the Mediterranean Fleet were sighted on 27 April and five days of joint exercises began after a final coaling on 1 May, the Channel Fleet then parting company and sailing for Gibraltar, via Malta and Barcelona, on the 6th.

There was no let-up when the Channel Fleet returned to Gibraltar, just another month of drills and cruises over to Tetuan for the Fleet's own schedule of quarterly tests, the second of the year. The 12-pounders had their quarterly firing on 5 June and on the 10th the gunlayers had their test, which amounted to individual target-practice for every gun in the ship. Then, on 19 June, it was back to Tetuan yet again, this time for Fleet torpedo practice. But this particular evolution brought four months of gruelling hard work to a close. It was time for the Channel Fleet to return to home waters for the ceremonial meeting with the French Fleet at Brest – time to scrape, scrub, paint and polish from stem to stern.

Prince George's log, therefore, took up a new refrain on the voyage north to Brest, a daily repetition of 'Hands engaged cleaning & painting ship'. This was accompanied by another entry cropping up from day to day: 'firework drill',[8] in preparation for the Fleet's special tribute to the *Quatorze Juillet*. The resplendent Channel Fleet anchored at Brest on 10 July and lay, dressed overall, for a week of junketings and goodwill visits amounting to a unique and cheering milestone in Anglo-French history. On the 14th the guns of the British warships thundered out in a 21-gun salute to France's national day, and the carefully rehearsed 'firework drill' at last bore fruit in a splendid massed display. On the following day 120 French seamen dined aboard *Prince George* as guests of honour, similar hospitality being extended throughout the Channel Fleet. Never, it seemed, had the Royal Navy's role as the joint symbol of Britain's might and goodwill been more perfectly carried out.

Mrs Fraser had crossed the Channel for the celebrations, and mother and son enjoyed a wonderful lunch together in the forest near Brest. Fraser came home from the Brest festivities with two souvenirs: a photograph of himself in dress whites, basking in French hospitality, and a copy of the special ode written for the occasion by Edmond Novince, Academician and City Councillor of Brest. M. Novince did not stint himself, being swept to heights of poetic emotion dangerously approaching bathos; but his ode deserves remembrance as testimony to a moment of harmony which the navies of France and Britain had certainly never enjoyed before, and would never quite reach again. Roughly translated, the first and last verses ran as follows:[9]

> Hail, sons of Albion, and your gallant fleets
> Bearing to us wondrous hopes of a new, eternal Peace!
> Hip! Hip! Hurrah! All Frenchmen, rejoicing, ready stand
> On this happiest of days, to shake you by the hand!
>
> And when these blissful days are o'er, and France's sons
>   prepare
> To go to Portsmouth, and in turn enjoy this dream so rare
> May all the winds be fair for them! O'er London may there
>   rise
> A rainbow touching Paris, to gladden all our eyes!

The Channel Fleet returned the compliment at an equally splendid review at Spithead between 7–14 August 1905, in turn playing host to the French fleet. But the return visit of the French was only the prelude to a goodwill cruise which took the Channel Fleet to Ijmuiden in Holland, Swinemünde in Germany (the German Baltic Fleet) and Copenhagen, a tour extending throughout August and September. The Fleet came home north-about round Scotland – Fraser's first experience of northern waters – returned to Berehaven on 12 October and immediately began preparations for fleet gunnery calibration five days later.

Such was Fraser's introduction to active Navy service, which he experienced – though at the time too junior to appreciate it – in one of the most constructive periods the Navy has ever known. He was learning that Service life was more than spit-and-polish one moment and drills and exercises the next; more than grinding hard work,

Gunroom rules and the sub-lieutenant's cane. Fraser was now finding his feet as a member of the ship's community, holding down a place on the hockey team from *Prince George* which triumphantly defended the Fleet cup in the 1905–6 season.

Above all, Fraser was learning that pride in the ship is an all-round experience, aimed at the constant improvement of performance. This the men of *Prince George* experienced to the full when their ship emerged as the best in the Fleet after battle practice in September 1906. *Prince George* scooped the pool with a total of twelve 12-inch hits out of sixteen rounds fired. 'Magnificent shooting by the *Prince George*,' enthused *The Times*. 'The ship has received many congratulations on her excellent firing. When she had finished her practice one target sail was missing, and very little of the other three could be seen.'[10]

There have been worse apprenticeships. When Fraser left *Prince George* in March 1907 he could indeed look back on a rich and varied initiation.

· 3 ·

The Dreadnought Navy
[1907–12]

Nineteen years old, Fraser left *Prince George* on 15 March 1907 as a senior midshipman with three years' service behind him. He was now about to pass through a chrysalis-period extending over the next four years, taking him from midshipman to lieutenant. By the end of this time of transition he would have selected the branch of the Service in which he was going to specialise: navigation, gunnery, mines or torpedoes. And this formative period in Fraser's career can only be partially understood without reference to the changes which were simultaneously transforming the Navy, its ships and their deployment.

By 1907 the gaudy obsession of the Victorian Navy had already been swept away by the gales of Fisher's energy as First Sea Lord. To take one superficial but very noticeable example, when Fraser had joined *Hannibal* in January 1904 she was still resplendent in Victorian livery: black hull with a red stripe or 'boot-top', white upperworks, yellow-ochre masts, funnels and ventilators. A year later, when he went to *Prince George*, these splendours had been replaced by a sombre but functional sea of battleship grey. Instead of having to retain large stocks of four colours for the interminable chore of painting ship, the paint store now only needed grey; and painting ship was now a straightforward job instead of a finicky one.

Fisher's white-hot crusade for efficiency naturally aroused bitter opposition from the conservatives and romantics who had never understood Kipling's warning, in *Recessional*, against excessive faith in 'all our pomp of yesterday'. Resistance to Fisher and his fellow-reformers had been put into words by Admiral Sir Frederick Richards back in 1900: 'You have got an established system and a time-honoured one, so why alter it?'[1] To these diehards Fisher's determination to scrap every warship in active commission which, as he put it, 'Could neither fight nor run away', seemed insane. The old ships and gunboats alone made possible a constant British naval presence in every corner of the planet. But Fisher bulldozed these objections aside in contempt. He wanted powerful fleets of efficient modern warships, backed by a reserve of older but still serviceable ships which could be brought to fighting readiness at a moment's notice.

The first blast of Fisher's scrapping policy was certainly dramatic: a total of 154 warships removed from the effective list. Of these no less than ninety were written off as floating junk fit only for scrap – or sale, if buyers could be found. The other sixty-four were to be laid up in home waters without crews. The officers and men thus released could either be distributed through the Fleet or drafted into 'nucleus' or caretaker crews for the ships of the overhauled reserve. The scrapping policy meant more berthing-space: it meant less pressure on dockyard facilities; and, as Fisher triumphantly showed, it saved the Navy an annual repair bill of £845,000 for ships that had added precisely nothing to the Navy's fighting qualities.

The scrapping policy went hand-in-hand with an important series of shifts in British foreign policy that made it no longer essential to dispatch squadrons and flotillas to the ends of the earth. The Japanese alliance of 1902 gave Britain an ally in Far Eastern waters; the *Entente Cordiale* with France, two years later, gave Britain an ally in the Mediterranean. All this helped Fisher in his determination to build up maximum naval strength in home waters with which to counter the steadily growing menace posed by the Imperial German Navy. The old Home Fleet became the new Channel Fleet, reinforced by four battleships brought home from the Mediterranean; the old Channel Fleet became the new Atlantic Fleet, based on Gibraltar and poised to reinforce either the Channel Fleet or the Mediterranean Fleet in the event of war. All this reshuffling of the fleets, which were still to carry out regular joint exercises, meant that three-quarters of the Royal Navy's battleships could be concentrated in home waters to deter the German Navy, which was what Fisher wanted.[2]

But Fisher's most audacious *coup* was his introduction of a totally new breed of battleship: the 'Dreadnought', whose be-all and end-all was high speed and the heaviest possible big-gun armament. And the audacity of the Dreadnought was not so much that it made every other battleship in the world obsolete, but that it made every other *British* battleship obsolete as well.

Put in its simplest terms, the Dreadnought cut through a tangle of problems which had complicated battleship design ever since the appearance of the self-propelled torpedo back in the 1870s. As the supreme instrument of sea power, the battleship had as its purpose the destruction of enemy battleships. But when the torpedo arrived on the scene this could no longer be done at point-blank range: no battle fleet dared manoeuvre and fight within range of enemy torpedoes. Hence the development of the big gun, intended to reach and destroy enemy battleships safely out of torpedo range. A new type of warship, the 'torpedo-boat destroyer', was developed to beat off torpedo attacks while making torpedo attacks of its own. To take care of any enemy torpedo-boats which might get past the destroyers, battleships now carried insurance in the form of secondary and tertiary armaments for short-range gun actions.

But the trouble with this three-level armament was that the battleship's real teeth – its big guns – had to be limited to one turret forward and one turret aft to fit all the other guns in. This made a nonsense of the battleship's original function: to land the maximum number of heavy shells on enemy battleships. The last and most sophisticated British pre-Dreadnoughts, *Lord Nelson* and *Agamemnon* (completed in 1907 and 1908) carried ten 9.2-inch guns but only four 12-inch; and the resultant torrent of shell splashes thrown up round the target made it virtually impossible to judge what was landing where.

HMS *Dreadnought* concentrated all on long-range hitting-power. Laid down in December 1905 and completed in the incredibly short time of ten months, she carried no less than ten 12-inch guns. Even when required to fire at a target on which the least possible guns could be brought to bear, *Dreadnought* could fire twice the number of heavy shells that any of her predecessors could manage. The characteristic pre-Dreadnought pincushion of secondary and tertiary armaments, with barrels bristling at all angles from armoured casemates and barbettes, was swept away, the only other guns carried being twenty-four 12-pounders. Equally revolutionary were her engines. *Dreadnought* was the first battleship to abandon the huge, thundering triple-expansion engines for the smooth and vibration-free efficiency of steam turbines, driving four screws to produce a top speed of 22 knots. *Bellerophon*, Britain's second Dreadnought, was laid down in December 1906 and two more, *Temeraire* and *Superb* in 1907. From then on they were to keep coming at a rate of never less than three a year.

Dreadnought was still being built when the first three keels of another totally new warship type were laid down. This was the battle-cruiser, envisaged by Fisher as a battleship-sized 'super-cruiser' with a battleship's armament, but lacking a battleship's weight of armoured protection in order to produce a turn of speed faster than any battleship. The battle-cruisers were to be the fast, hard-hitting scouts of the main battle fleet, able to overwhelm all lighter enemy scouts with their weight of shell but fast enough to keep out of trouble from enemy battleships. Fisher called them 'New Testament ships' because, he claimed, they 'fulfilled the promise of the Old Testament ships' – the Dreadnought battleships. But this, like his fallacious assertion that 'speed is armour', turned out to be false when put to the test in battle. It was to be terribly punished at Jutland in 1916 and again, twenty-five years further on, when HMS *Hood* was blown out of the water by the German battleship *Bismarck*.[3]

Two months before *Dreadnought* was completed, Fisher judged that his 'nucleus crew' system was sufficiently advanced to allow him to announce the formation of a new Home Fleet, based on the Nore. This caused yet another storm of controversy because it was a piece of deception, and the full truth could not be published. The new Home Fleet was presented as an extension of the reserve, its role being to reinforce the main Channel Fleet in emergencies. But in fact Fisher used it as a cover for the new Dreadnought battle fleet he was bringing into existence: it was an excuse to keep all the Dreadnoughts in home waters, against Germany. Fisher's opponents denounced this scheme as fraudulent, mad, a suicidal weakening of the naval defences of the British Empire; and the unfortunate result was a feud in the Navy's highest circles that rapidly became public property.

In April 1907 Admiral Lord Charles Beresford took over the Channel Fleet from Wilson and immediately began to denounce Fisher's new Home Fleet. Here, claimed Beresford, was a naked piece of political economy drawing off much-needed resources from his own command. For good measure he also attacked the Dreadnought concept and the scrapping policy for the damage he claimed they had done to Britain's naval supremacy. The Press took up the feud with gusto, largely siding with Fisher and his adherents – 'the Fishpond', as they were known. But it took until December 1908 before the Admiralty finally grasped the nettle. Beresford was told that the Channel Fleet was scheduled to be absorbed into the Home Fleet in March 1909 and he would then be required to strike his flag, a year before his Commander-in-Chief's term of three years was up.

Such was the momentous background to Fraser's advancement from midshipman to lieutenant. On leaving *Prince George* he had gone on to a third battleship, the 'Canopus' class *Goliath* (March–April 1907) before receiving his promotion to sub-lieutenant and going to the battleship *Triumph* (May–September 1907). From then on his career was a sandwich of specialist courses ashore and appointments afloat: Navigation School at Greenwich (September–December 1907), then the 'turtle-back' destroyer *Gipsy*; back to Greenwich in April–June 1908, then, promoted again to lieutenant, to the cruiser *Lancaster* under Captain Sydney Fremantle in the Mediterranean Fleet. The decisive appointment in this phase of Fraser's career came after his promotion to lieutenant. In 1910 Fraser was appointed to the new light cruiser *Boadicea*, flagship of Rear-Admiral Sir Robert Arbuthnot, Commodore of the Harwich destroyer flotillas.

Arbuthnot was a fascinating character, a bridge between the old Navy and the new. Short and spare, a fine athlete in the best Victorian tradition, he was a stickler for discipline and adherence to Navy regulations, particularly those referring to dress:[4]

'In those days we had to wear a stiff shirt all day, regardless of working conditions. Then we took to wearing what-do-you-call-'ems, dickies; but Sir Robert came out one day, looked at the first officer he saw — he was the Commander, too — and he went up to him, pulled out the dicky and threw it away over the side. No more dickies!'

Fraser found, however, that Arbuthnot's bark was worse than his bite:[5]

'One day we'd sighted something about 50 miles off; and when it was reported Sir Robert said "Why do you take this lying down — he doesn't know what he's talking about!" So I retired hastily. But the next thing I knew, Sir Robert came up to me and said "I'm very sorry — you were quite right."

At this time I had a friend called Coltart, a very humorous young chap. Every month we had to walk 20 miles and sign a chit to prove we'd done it; and this young chap went to a dance instead, which Sir Robert went to as well. So he came down early to get off to the ship. He found the Admiral's Barge waiting there, and said "The Admiral's still dancing; will you give me a lift off?" So they took him off, and when they came back they found that Sir Robert had *run* down, only to find no barge waiting. When he came off — I was officer of the watch — he said to me "Put this young man under arrest!" And he was put under arrest. Sir Robert let him off the next morning.'

Fraser's spell in *Boadicea* (1910–11) was his first real introduction to the role of the destroyer in the modern Navy, based as it was on the torpedo attack — a revelation after his years in battleships. He had the great good luck to serve under a Commander-in-Chief of the first rank, who kept himself aloof from the reverberations of the Fisher-Beresford feud — a lesson in professional deportment which

Fraser was never to forget. Arbuthnot was not a member of the 'Fishpond', but he was no reactionary either. In July 1914, when Fisher's Dreadnought Navy assembled in its full majesty for the Spithead Review, Arbuthnot went on record as saying 'All that is best and most modern here is the creation of Lord Fisher.'[6]

Another enduring lesson Fraser learned from Arbuthnot was the deep interest Sir Robert took in the qualities of his young officers, and the trust he put in officers who had proved themselves worthy of it. This could be embarrassing, as Fraser discovered when one of the destroyer flotilla commanders went sick and Sir Robert told Fraser to assume temporary acting command. The first lieutenant of the destroyer in question, who would normally have taken over, was barely a month junior to Fraser and was naturally deeply resentful. Acutely aware of this, Fraser asked the Commander-in-Chief to reconsider but Sir Robert merely repeated the order, and Fraser had to go. 'It was only for three weeks,' he recalled, 'but it was a most awkward position to be in while it lasted.'[7]

Arbuthnot was no destroyer fanatic; he did not preach destroyer gospel to the exclusion of all else. This was not always so: many officers who had specialised in gunnery or torpedoes emerged with a blind spot as far as other branches of the Service were concerned. But in Fraser's case, as he never forgot, 'Sir Robert was the one who recommended me to specialise in gunnery';[8] and in 1911 Lieutenant Fraser headed for the Navy's high university of gunnery, HMS *Excellent* at Whale Island, Portsmouth.

· 4 ·

HMS *Excellent*

[1912–14]

Considering that no other institution in the Royal Navy was to have such a crucial influence on Fraser's career, and that he was destined to be remembered with pride and affection among that institution's most distinguished alumni, it is a pity that there is no simple way of describing HMS *Excellent*. 'Gunnery school'; 'gunnery training college'; 'gunnery shore establishment' – no such phrase comes anywhere near to doing the place full justice. For HMS *Excellent* and her 'sister-ship' at Portsmouth, HMS *Vernon* (the torpedo and mining school) have played a special role in the evolution of the Royal Navy. They have formed an intensely specialist university for dedicated graduates – not merely teaching the intricacies of a uniquely demanding trio of sciences, but serving as research centres in the constant expansion of those sciences.

In addition to this role, HMS *Excellent* has always been to the Navy what Aldershot has been to the Army: the fount of authority in drill and ceremonial, demanding the highest standards in immaculate precision. The gleaming black gaiters which were a compulsory part of the rig at *Excellent* led naturally to the nickname 'all gas and gaiters', and became the establishment's most enduring symbol. Gaiters were to naval gunnery officers what bearskins were to Guardsmen; and in later years Fraser relished the memory of how the association had been given royal recognition. It happened after the Second World War, when he was due to meet King George VI after the royal return from South Africa. On being asked 'what rig Admiral Fraser should wear', the King retorted, 'Any rig so long as he doesn't wear his gaiters!'[1]

Fraser had had his first taste of *Excellent*'s discipline back in 1907, when he had undergone his basic gunnery course as a sub-lieutenant. He never forgot the irrepressible liveliness which the young officers brought to this most staid of environments, formerly reserved for

25

the ranks of lieutenant and upwards. The conservative element had had reservations about opening *Excellent* to sub-lieutenants. 'Everyone on the Staff,' recalled Fraser, 'was wondering how they were going to behave, but they were very good – livened the whole place up.'[2] Not that this had any chance of going unchecked at *Excellent*, as some of the sub-lieutenants going through the mill with Fraser discovered to their cost. 'At the end of term, in the middle of the night, they put gaiters on all the ornamental lions on the West Battery, which amused the junior staff very much. But the First Lieutenant, Sidney Bailey, took a rather poor view of this and sent half of them to the local battleship for the weekend instead of going home – we thought this was rather hard.'[3]

But that was basic Gunnery School. There was no time or inclination for skylarking when Fraser returned to *Excellent* as a lieutenant, five years later, to go through the forbidding Long Gunnery Course and qualify as a gunnery officer. There was nothing like the Long Course. Candidates were exhaustively examined on every topic connected with the science of gunnery, from ballistics and dynamics to personal marksmanship with rifle and pistol. A crucial part of the Long Course was the lecture which each candidate was required to deliver on a leading gunnery topic. And as a young officer keen on the future of his profession, Fraser was naturally intrigued by one of the most controversial topics in gunnery at this time: 'director firing'.

Conceived by Rear-Admiral Sir Percy Scott, the theory of 'director firing' offered a new solution to an old problem: how to get every gun in the ship which could be brought to bear opening fire on the same target at the same time. The traditional method left everything up to the individual gunlayers, who drew their own lines on the targets, estimated their own ranges, chose their own angles of elevation and did the firing. This was why the Gunlayers' Test was the most important element in the yearly round of gunnery practice: it was accepted as the shortest line between the loaded gun and the target. But director firing was so different as to seem dangerously outlandish and impracticable.

Part of the trouble was that director firing was a simple theory. Shells only hit the target when the range was accurately measured and the gun was fired at the correct angle of elevation. Mistakes naturally meant a miss, and an eight-gun broadside could, in individual gunlayers' firing, land eight shells in a bewildering cascade all round the target. But director firing amounted to one gunlayer perched in the director tower, passing on the same range and angle of elevation to every gun in the ship. If the director gunlayer made a mistake and the shells fell short, all he would have to do was to raise the angle a little, all the gunlayers would follow suit, and eventually all the shells would be hitting together.

But when Fraser went through the Long Course in 1912 he found that director firing was a dirty word at *Excellent*. 'Whale Island wouldn't look at it – it was the Commander, Reggie Henderson, later Controller of the Navy. He didn't allow director firing even to be mentioned – thought it was all wrong.'[4] The opposition to director firing was not merely due to the scepticism which greets every novel idea. A good deal of the trouble stemmed from Sir Percy Scott and his unfortunate habit of making enemies of high-ranking officers who, handled with tact, might have become his allies. Tetchy and contemptuous towards any criticism of or interference in his crusade to perfect naval gunnery, Scott was indeed his own worst enemy. And in 1912 the Navy had still not forgotten one of Scott's worst outbursts: the notorious 'paintwork' row of 1907–8, which in turn was bound up in the feud between Fisher and Beresford.

In November 1907 Scott had been commanding the 1st Cruiser Squadron under Beresford in the Channel Fleet, when the Fleet was due for a visit and inspection by Kaiser Wilhelm II. As the inevitable painting and polishing got under way, Scott requested Beresford's permission for the cruiser *Roxburgh* to finish her gunnery practice first; and Beresford refused. Scott promptly lost his temper and sent the following signal to *Roxburgh*:

SINCE PAINTWORK APPEARS TO BE MORE
IMPORTANT THAN GUNNERY YOU MUST REMAIN IN
HARBOUR AND MAKE YOURSELF LOOK PRETTY

– Knowing full well that this piece of tart sarcasm would be read in transit by the whole Fleet.[5]

The outraged Beresford's over-reaction was to treat Scott to a public humiliation in the eyes of the Fleet. He summoned Scott for a tremendous dressing-down on the flagship's quarterdeck, rubbed it in with a general signal to the Fleet, and finally ordered Scott only to communicate with him in writing from then on. Inevitably the Press seized on the 'paintwork affair' with gusto, lambasting Beresford for humiliating a junior officer before the whole Fleet without giving him a chance to reply. And Beresford's rage was increased by the Admiralty's contenting itself with a private rebuke to Scott for the offending signal, taking the line that Beresford's behaviour had already been punishment enough. Beresford interpreted this attitude as part and parcel of Fisher's vendetta against him, and intensified his attacks on Fisher's 'disastrous' policies.

The feud got worse in 1908. In May Beresford pointedly refused

27

to shake Fisher's hand at a Levée, under the eyes of the King, courtiers, ministers, and other senior naval officers. Then, in July, Beresford signalled a manoeuvre to Scott's division of the Fleet which would have resulted in a collision if Scott had not disobeyed it. Beresford demanded a court-martial for Scott, and again the Admiralty refused. The whole situation had become intolerable and the Board solved it with premature retirements for both Scott and Beresford in February and March 1909. But memories of the Scott-Beresford feud were still very much alive when Fraser went through the Long Course in 1912.

Though *Excellent* opposed the theory, Fraser believed in director firing and wanted to lecture on it, having consulted Scott himself. 'He told me all about the difficulties he'd had, and what you had to do for director firing.' In the end, however, Fraser lectured on fire control as instructed by *Excellent*, and did so well that he scored an amazing 99 marks out of 100 – which, he pointed out to the author, he would never have done by championing director firing![6]

When the Long Course results were published in October 1912, Fraser had passed out top of the course and carried off the Egerton Prize. The framed certificate of the latter distinction, bearing the signature of the new First Sea Lord, Prince Louis of Battenberg, remained one of Fraser's most cherished mementoes in later life. With a grand total of 1,858 marks out of 2,000, Fraser was an easy winner over Lieutenants Hughes (second with 1,811 marks) and Mathews (third with 1,806). The breakdown of Fraser's achievement, which incidentally shows the searching complexity of the Long Course, was as follows:[7]

Subject	Marks earned	Out of
General gunnery	80	90
Gun drill	115	125
Stripping	120	125
Sighting and range-finding	110	115
Turret	73	75
Ammunition	69	75
Hydraulics	125	150
Theory (ballistics, hydraulics, dynamics, strength of material, machine construction, mechanical drawing)	390	410
Chemistry	36	40
Fortifications	50	50

Field exercise, musketry and pistol	92	100
Battalion	35	40
Field gun and field battery	40	40
LECTURE	99	100
Shooting appliances	45	50
Control (practical & theory)	127	140
Calibration, range tables, etc.	70	75
Additional marks (minor subjects)	182	200
GRAND TOTAL	1858	2000

Fraser's superb performance in the Long Course made him a man of mark in the branch of the Service in which promotion was regarded as most certain, but it also made him far too valuable to be given a Gunnery Officer's appointment right away. He, Hughes and Mathews were immediately 'lent' to the staff at Greenwich for the Advanced Gunnery Course of October 1912.

Director firing did not stay in the wilderness for long. When Fraser passed out top of the Long Course Winston Churchill had been First Lord of the Admiralty for a year. Though Fisher remained in retirement, Churchill became a fanatical member of the 'Fishpond' and consulted Fisher at every turn, learning about Scott's newest theory in the process. And on 13 December 1912, while Fraser was still at Greenwich, director firing was given its first real chance in a trial at sea. It was a revolutionary experiment, fit to rank with the famous tug-of-war in March 1845 when HMS *Rattler* had towed HMS *Alecto* helplessly astern and demonstrated the superiority of the screw over the paddlewheel.

Two Dreadnoughts, the sister-ships HMS *Thunderer* and *Orion*, were selected for the test. *Thunderer* was fitted with a director; *Orion* relied on the old system of individual gunlayers' firing. The two battleships each fired for three minutes at a range of 9,000 yards and a speed of 12 knots – and *Thunderer* scored six times as many hits as *Orion*. The results spoke for themselves, but the test did not lead to director firing being adopted overnight. Many snags still had to be overcome, such as the difficulty of ensuring that the director and the guns were properly aligned. Other opponents argued that the *Thunderer-Orion* demonstration was all very well as a peacetime test, but that battle conditions would be another thing altogether – the electrical link between the director and the guns would easily be severed by a single hit, or even by splinters from a near-miss. Nevertheless the basic decision was taken to adopt director firing, retaining gunlayers' firing as the emergency system. But only eight battleships had been fitted with directors for their main armament by the time war broke out in 1914, and it took another two years to instal directors in all the capital ships of Fisher's Dreadnought Navy.

In the last twenty months before the war Fraser remained a gunnery instructor. In 1913 he returned to *Excellent*, this time as a valued member of the junior staff. 'One bad thing *Excellent* did at that time,' he told the author, 'was that they never taught us properly about ammunition.'[8] This manifested itself in an unbelievably cavalier attitude to high explosives, which extended to the Navy's Department of Construction and produced capital ships with not enough flash protection for the magazines. No less than three of Fisher's 'New Testament ships', the battle-cruisers, were to be blown out of the water at Jutland by exploding magazines. The touchiness of cordite was simply not appreciated before 1914 and Fraser vividly remembered being taken through a magazine by candle-light, with the flicker and glow of the naked flames caressing masses of cordite cases. On another occasion he saw cordite charges being dried in front of a galley fire.

Fraser's main task in 1913–14, however, was not connected with ammunition: he was one of the key men entrusted with the job of spreading the gospel of director firing. It was up to *Excellent* to produce the drill for the new system on which the whole director training programme would be based, and Fraser was the man who did it. When not up to his neck in a sea of technological problems, Fraser enjoyed brief periods of respite on leave. One of them in 1913 enabled him to get over to Paris and savour the fleshpots, returning with the programme from the *Chat Noir* nightclub in Montmartre as a souvenir. But another leave at this time handed him an experience in total contrast with the technicalities of his work at *Excellent*: a brush with the supernatural.[9]

'My mother was very interested in spiritualism, and a cousin of mine was very good with a planchette – ouija board. He invited me to try, but I was no good. Then he said, "Would you like to put your hands on mine?"

The first thing "it" wrote was "Charles R."
I felt it was a hoax, but asked why "it" had come. "It" said, "because you were the Duke of Buckingham", and then "A very cold day when I went to my execution."

Well, neither of us happened to know, so we went to the encyclopedia to find out. And of course Buckingham was the great favourite of King Charles, who brought up the children of

Buckingham; and it *had* been a very cold day – you know, putting on two shirts, and so forth – but we hadn't known.

And really I've often thought about it all; you know Buckingham was Lord High Admiral of England, and was assassinated at Portsmouth. And *I* went on to become Admiral of the Fleet and Commander-in-Chief at Portsmouth! I don't know; but what an extraordinary thing.'

By the summer of 1914 Fraser's work on the director firing handbook was complete and the fruits of his labours had been well received by the Admiralty. As the Royal Navy prepared for the biggest test mobilisation in its history Fraser received the following tribute from Whitehall:[10]

Admiralty
10th July 1914

'Sir,
I am commanded by My Lords Commissioners of the Admiralty to signify their directions to you to convey to Lieutenant B.A. Fraser, R.N., now serving in H.M.S. "Excellent", an expression of their appreciation of the care and trouble taken by him in the compilation of the Handbook for Director Firing.

I am, &c,
Wm. Graham Greene'

The Commander-in-Chief
H.M. Ships & Vessels,
Portsmouth

It was now time for Fraser to leave the teaching staff and take up his first appointment as a seagoing Gunnery Officer. Twenty-six years old, possessed of Their Lordships' warm approval, Fraser went to the light cruiser HMS *Minerva* to assume his new duties. Not three weeks before, the Austrian Archduke had been assassinated in Sarajevo. Already the ultimatums were flitting menacingly between the continental powers. The count-down to war had begun.

· 5 ·

The old *Minerva*

[1914–15]

When Fraser joined HMS *Minerva* in July 1914, the Navy was
preparing to put Fisher's reforms to their first exhaustive test: a trial
mobilisation of the Third Fleet to accompany the review of the First
and Second Fleets at Spithead. This mobilisation would prove
whether it really was possible to take ageing warships off the dockyard wall, add complements of reservists to the caretaker nucleus
crews, and produce efficient fighting ships virtually overnight. And
as HMS *Minerva* was a unit of the Third Fleet, all Fraser's talents
as a gunnery instructor would now be called upon to the full.

Like *Boadicea*, Fraser's last ship, *Minerva* was a light cruiser; but
there the similarity ended. *Boadicea* had been a spanking new ship,
turbine-engined with a speed of 27 knots. *Minerva* was nineteen
years old in 1914 – a long time in the life of a warship – and she
was looking her age. She had been launched in 1895, the third of
the nine 'Eclipse' class light cruisers, and the best speed her two sets
of clangorous triple-expansion engines could deliver was 19 knots.
As for her armament, now to be Fraser's special province, it consisted
of eleven single 6-inch guns with only one of them on the centreline
– a direct throwback to the days when a warship's hitting-power
had been calculated in broadsides. For the past year Fraser had been
immersed in the sophisticated details of director firing, the highest
level to which naval gunnery had then been raised. Now he had to
return abruptly to the basics of gunnery: training individual gunlayers and their crews to reach maximum efficiency in the minimum
time.

When he reported for duty at Portsmouth, Fraser found that the
spadework of preparing *Minerva* to join the Third Fleet was well
under way. She had been commissioned at Portsmouth with a reduced nucleus crew on 12 June, and coaled a week later. The last
dirty and exhausting job, ammunitioning ship, had been completed

32

by 4 July. The ship had been cleaned and painted, her machinery trials had been run by the time her ranks and ratings arrived on the 14th, and the Royal Fleet Reserve ratings and Royal Marines joined ship on the following day. The training of the gun crews and ammunition details began at once under Fraser's direction.[1]

The energy and enthusiasm radiated by Fraser was irresistible to the sailors and Royal Marines he trained and commanded. He was, writes Lt-Colonel Hawkins of the Royal Marines (in July 1914 a corporal, RMLI in *Minerva*), 'a ball of fire if ever there was one':[2]

'My earliest recollection of him was his drive and enthusiasm to make *Minerva* the most efficient gunnery ship in the fleet. He had a big job on his hands because some of the officers were RNVR or RNR, and a large number of the ship's company were reservists and rather rusty.

The officers were exercised at the spotting table until they were as efficient as it was possible to make them. The gun crews trained until they too knew their jobs to perfection. The 6-inch loaders were kept hard at it, with seamen and Marines working like demons to try and beat each other. Lt Fraser was a perfectionist and the whole ship's company worked with enthusiasm to try to attain his standards.'

On the 16th and 17th *Minerva* sailed for her sea trials and manoeuvres off the south coast; and on the 18th, dressed overall, she joined the Fleet at Spithead for the Royal Review. Fisher's work was gloriously vindicated by this breathtaking muster which, in Churchill's words, 'constituted incomparably the greatest assemblage of naval power ever witnessed in the history of the world.'[3]

On 21 July *Minerva* sailed for Torbay to complete her contribution to the test mobilisation: target practice at sea, carried out on the 23rd. Already the orders had gone out for the dispersal of the Third Fleet, and on the 25th the Royal Fleet Reserve personnel in *Minerva* were duly demobilised. Then, on the 26th, came the electrifying news that Serbia had rejected Austria's ultimatum over the Sarajevo assassination. The First Sea Lord, Prince Louis of Battenberg, took the momentous decision to stop the demobilisation and Churchill, still First Lord, approved the decision. Until the international situation had been resolved, none of the Royal Navy's warships was to pay off or return to mothballs.

For *Minerva*, however, the decision came 24 hours too late for her to retain the men who had already been trained: they had left the ship. Fraser kept his fingers crossed as the new drafts came on board. 'I was hoping it would be the same crew,' he recalled, 'but it wasn't – it was an entirely new crew, and I had to start all over again.'[4] The second mobilisation, from 1–3 August, saw frantic activity at Portsmouth as the new hands arrived and were set to work before they had time to settle in. 'Hands employed in preparing ship for war' was the bleak standing entry in *Minerva's* log during these three days. Fusing the shells was a top-priority job. The sound of guns was heard at sea. Every man expected to be steaming into action within days, if not hours; and in *Minerva* there was a good deal of premature clearing for action, as Fraser admitted:[5]

> 'The first thing we thought we'd do was to throw overboard everything inflammable – the armchairs, midshipmen's chests and so on. But fortunately we had a rather old-fashioned Commander who said "Look, we've got to live with this, maybe for the next few years, so don't let's do anything more like that." But we'd already thrown overboard the wooden doors from the loos, and that sort of thing, and so later we had to put up sailcloth in their place.'

Minerva's age and Third Fleet status made her unfit for duty with the newly-designated 'Grand Fleet', which was already on its war station at Scapa Flow in the Orkneys. But there was essential work for her to do in the Western Approaches. When the signal 'COMMENCE HOSTILITIES WITH GERMANY' was flashed to HM ships at 23.00 hrs on 4 August *Minerva* was already at sea, heading for Queenstown in Ireland. There Fraser supervised the installation of a crucial improvement to *Minerva's* gunnery control system: voice-pipe communication with the guns, his own idea and recommendation. By the 7th she was back at Berehaven, with Fraser testing the new communications, exercising the 6-inch gun crews and supply parties. From the 7th to the 15th she was patrolling the Channel and southern Irish Sea, checking out shipping and hungrily watching for any German merchantmen trying to make a run home to the Fatherland. From Queenstown she then went down to the Spanish coast, arriving at Vigo on the 29th before escorting a homeward-bound convoy back to Plymouth. But *Minerva* did not stay long in home waters. On 12 September she sailed again, this time under orders to join the Mediterranean Fleet.

Arriving at Malta on 23 September, *Minerva* was first detached to join the escort of a convoy carrying the Indian Division from Egypt to Marseilles, and she did not arrive at Port Said until 3 October. She was immediately ordered through the Suez Canal in order to patrol the Red Sea shipping route to Aden and India, now menaced by the increasing likelihood of Turkey's entering the war on the side of Germany and Austria. As Syria, Palestine and Arabia were all Turkish provinces, an invasion of Egypt was regarded as inevitable if Turkey did come in; and it was vital to keep the Red Sea open to Allied shipping. *Minerva* passed through the Suez Canal on 5–6 October and at once set to work patrolling the Suez-Aden sealane, a duty which she was still performing when the Allies finally went to war with Turkey on 30 October.

Minerva was thus uniquely placed – in the right place at the right time – to take part in one of the least-remembered episodes of the First World War: the Royal Navy's patrolling of Akaba at the head of the Red Sea.

Thanks largely to the compelling story told in *Seven Pillars of Wisdom*, Akaba and T.E. Lawrence have become synonymous. The capture of Akaba by 'Lurens' with Arab irregulars in July 1917, after an agonising approach march through the desert, is the first climacteric of that great book. But readers of *Seven Pillars* will search in vain for any mention of the fact that British sailors were playing football at Akaba two years before Lawrence even set foot in Arabia to see what could be done to assist the Arab Revolt. The sole reference to this early naval activity at Akaba comes at the beginning of Chapter LV in *Seven Pillars*:[6]

> Through the whirling dust we perceived that Akaba was all a ruin. Repeated bombardments by French and English warships had degraded the place to its original rubbish

and the first of those bombardments was directed by Lieutenant B. A. Fraser, R.N. on the morning of 1 November 1914.

Minerva arrived off Akaba on 1 November to find out what, if anything, the Turks were doing there, and so she came through the Tiran Straits and up the Gulf of Akaba at Action Stations. A fort covered the final approach to Akaba, and Fraser was ordered to put half a dozen 6-inch shells into it. This was the first time he had ever fired at a genuine military target and it was, to say the least, something of an anti-climax:[7]

> 'There was no reply, so we stopped; and the next thing that happened was a donkey, putting its head round the corner! This caused much hilarity throughout the ship.'

Minerva's log records that the sense of anti-climax was not dispelled by events on the 2nd:[8]

> Landed flag of truce to demand surrender of Akaba. No one met party who returned after waiting. 9.30 shelled fort and barracks with 6″ lyddite and demolished them.

On the 3rd, Fraser landed with a party of seamen and Royal Marines, with two machine-guns, to reconnoitre the surrounding desert.

They found nothing. With supreme irony, considering the agony that would go into capturing the place in 1917 and the role it was to play in dislodging the Turks from Palestine, Akaba was totally deserted in November 1914 and could have been taken with ease. The trouble was that there were no troops to spare. The British in Egypt were justifiably obsessed with the imminence of a Turkish attack on the Suez Canal and kept every available soldier for the defence of the canal. All the Navy could do was to set up a standing patrol off Akaba, periodically rotated to release as many warships as possible for convoy escort duties. And *Minerva* formed part of the Akaba Patrol from November 1914 to the end of January 1915.

Altogether *Minerva* paid eight separate visits to Akaba during this period and her officers and men became drearily familiar with the place, despite the light-hearted literary efforts of the *Akabarbarian*, a topical magazine printed aboard ship. *Minerva* shared the Akaba Patrol with the 'Basilisk' class destroyers HMS *Foxhound* and *Mosquito*, the period of each ship's stay at Akaba varying between two to five days before being relieved. This constant British naval presence at Akaba soon prompted the Turks to infiltrate riflemen, machine-gunners and light artillery units which sniped at the ships from concealed positions, thus putting an end to the football matches of the first week. In December 1914 *Minerva* repeatedly embarked a seaplane at Suez before setting off on the Akaba run, in hopes that the arc of reconnaissance could be pushed inland as far as Ma'an; but the primitive seaplanes of 1914 were unable to gain enough altitude to get over the coastal hills.

After several failures the seaplane problem was overcome at last on *Minerva*'s sixth visit to Akaba (29 December 1914 – 2 January 1915). At 09.45 hrs on the 31st the seaplane was hoisted out, took off, and soared confidently inland up Wadi Akaba in the direction of Ma'an. But pleasure in this success was short-lived. Five minutes after the seaplane's departure, Captain Sutt of the Royal Marines and his assistant, Private Ward, landed at the north-western corner of the Gulf to reconnoitre the beach. Almost at once they came under fire from a Turkish force which, unseen from the ship, had been lying in ambush in the sandhills. As Fraser recalled:[9]

'Our Captain of Marines landed with his assistant to have a look around and they were ambushed. The Captain was wounded and his assistant was shot dead. So we opened fire on where we thought the Turks were, and presently a lot of them rushed out and scampered up the hill. We tried to fire on them, but by the time we'd set the fuses and got the distance it was

too late. So then we landed a party to bring off the Captain of
Marines and his dead assistant.'

Lt-Colonel Hawkins of the Royal Marines remembered Fraser's performance during this landing for rather different reasons:[10]

Although the *Minerva*'s Marines simply adored Lieutenant
Fraser, I have heard them curse him under their breath. This
occurred when they were engaging the enemy with rifle fire at
close range, at Wadi Ithm island from Akaba town, and he
came too close. In those days the Marines only had white suits
for wear in the tropics, so we dyed our uniforms with a
decoction of coffee and Condy's Fluid, which made an excellent
camouflage. Absolutely fearless, Lt Fraser only wanted to see
what was going on – but as *he* was wearing white uniform the
Marines thought he might get too close and give their position
away!

Despite the recovery of Captain Sutt, the tension grew when it
became clear that the seaplane was not going to return. The Turks
were obviously still in the neighbourhood – at 15.00 hrs Fraser's
guns opened fire on Turks spotted in the hills to the north-west –
and if a search party went off to look for the missing seaplane pilot
and observer there was every chance of losing the whole force. Since
Minerva had come under surprise shrapnel fire by night on her last
trip to Akaba the week before, the new policy was to shift anchorage
repeatedly in order to deny hidden Turkish gunners a fixed line and
range. The ship weighed at 16.00 hrs and headed down the Gulf,
stopping at 17.00 hrs to bury the victim of the morning's ambush,
Private Ward. After dark *Minerva* came back up the Gulf to sweep
the shore with her searchlight – and there in the beam was the
exhausted figure of Captain Sterling, the seaplane's observer. Sterling
was promptly brought off and explained that the seaplane had
crashed 20 miles inland; he had left Grall, the French pilot, 15 miles
away. Grall, whose leg was slightly injured, was following at his
best speed.

The next day – New Year's Day, 1915 – saw *Minerva* repeatedly
cruising up to the head of the Gulf, but each time failing to sight
any trace of Grall; and the ship was due to return to Suez on the
following day. During the night Captain Warleigh took the decision
to risk a search party, which landed at 06.50 hrs on the 2nd with
Fraser in command:[11]

'I took 150 men with me, with rifles, and on landing formed
them up into a sort of square in case of attack. Then we
marched inland, together with a field gun, under orders to go

no further than 10 miles. When we'd covered 10 miles we stopped and blew bugles, but found nothing; and so we came back quite safely, having suffered no casualties.'

Minerva stayed in the area until 17.30 hrs and Captain Warleigh, hating the thought of abandoning Grall, refused to leave for Suez without heading back for one last try around midnight. This faith was amply rewarded. Grall *had* made it after all, and at half past midnight *Minerva*'s searchlight beam again found a waving figure on the shore. As soon as Grall had been brought off, the ship headed for Suez. Two generous slices of luck in as many days had helped to save the seaplane's crew, who also deserve all credit for their determination to get through and return to the ship – 'a wonderful adventure, really', was Fraser's verdict.[12]

Clearly the Turkish presence at Akaba, though elusive, was becoming stronger with each visit by the Royal Navy, but the Akaba patrols continued throughout January 1915. On the Suez Canal sector it was becoming more and more obvious that the Turkish assault would not be very long in coming. What headquarters in Egypt wanted to know was whether the attack on the Suez Canal was being planned for a narrow front – a head-on assault from across the northern Sinai – or whether the Turks had plans for operating from the southern Sinai as well. Hence the continued watch on Akaba and, as far as *Minerva* was concerned, additional patrolling and guardship duties off the west coast of the Sinai peninsula.

In the hopeful search for more shreds of evidence about Turkish movements and plans, *Minerva* was used for a little 'cloak-and-dagger' work, embarking a Dominican monk and two Arabs to be slipped ashore on the Sinai mainland to get the latest news. This was done after *Minerva*'s seventh trip to Akaba (10–16 January), and Fraser was in charge of the landing and recovery of the agents. On the night of 18 January, while the ship lay at Gubal Island opposite the western tip of the Sinai, Fraser and the agents embarked in the cutter to cross the Strait of Gubal to the Sinai mainland. It was quite a trip for a single ship's boat. 'We had to go 30 miles in the cutter to land them,' Fraser recalled. 'We stayed all night, and brought them off at dawn. 'I've never been quite sure what it was all about!'[13]

The day after this night excursion, *Minerva* moved up the west Sinai coast and from 19–24 January lay off Tor (El Tûr) as guardship to the small Egyptian garrison there. As at Akaba it became clear that the Turks were stepping up their presence on the approaches to Tor. The most that *Minerva* could do was to deny the Turks unrestricted freedom of movement by day – as on the 22nd, when Fraser opened fire with shrapnel (two 12-pounders and three 6-inch) at a party of fifteen to twenty Turks sighted to the north-east. Turkish movement by night was inhibited by keeping the searchlights sweeping along the shore and coastal hills.

In the last week of January, *Minerva* was recalled to the Canal Zone, after a final visit to Akaba on 25–26 January, to take on the role of canal guardship. As her 'beat' was south from the Great Bitter Lake (the only place, once in the canal, where it was possible for her to turn) to Suez, the port side of the ship was given as much protection as possible with rows of sandbags. Because of this station down in the southern sector, *Minerva* missed the clumsy Turkish attack which went in on 3 February against the Lake Timsah sector, and which was repulsed with little trouble. All her men saw of the Turks on the 3rd was a distant troop of cavalry, against whom Fraser ordered five 12-pounder rounds to be fired. But there was no way of knowing that the attack of the 3rd would not be repeated, and six tense days passed before land and air reconnaissance confirmed that the Turks were withdrawing. During these six days (4–9 February) *Minerva* remained at Suez, very much on the *qui vive* 24 hours a day, burning searchlights at night and remaining at night defence stations. Uncertainty over what the Turks were up to inevitably led to fusses about security and possible enemy spies; on the 9th *Minerva* stopped and boarded the passing SS *Matiana* to investigate a report that someone aboard her had been taking photographs in the canal.[14]

By 10 February, however, it was clear that the threat to the Suez Canal had receded, and *Minerva* was preparing to take part in a limited counter-attack. On that day she embarked half the battalion of the 2/7th Gurkhas and took them down to Tor to join the Egyptian garrison protecting the manganese mine there, then attack the Turkish force in the neighbourhood. Fraser took ashore a field-gun and a small party to hold a beach-head encampment until the troops returned. It was his first encounter with Gurkhas and he was deeply impressed. 'Delightful little men; when they came on board they had their own food to think of, but we just told them, when you're on a ship you have ship's food. And they were quite happy, though a little seasick.'[15] The attack at Tor went in on 13 February and was a resounding success: sixty Turks were killed and 102 captured for the loss of one killed and one wounded. Courteous to the last, the Gurkhas did not omit to thank their hosts when *Minerva* disembarked them back at Ismailia. 'They boarded a ship and came alongside,' recalled Fraser, 'and gave us a hearty cheer and a speech in Gurkhese (*sic*), which we didn't understand but thought was so nice.'[16]

When the Turkish attack was repelled in February 1915 the war was six months old. The general belief of August 1914 that this would be a short war was long since dispelled, but the initiative now lay with the Allies, who were determined to force a decision by the end of 1915. And as the armies in France gathered strength for their first attempts to break the trench deadlock on the Western Front, the Royal Navy found itself the spearhead of a new Allied assault in the eastern Mediterranean. For Fraser and *Minerva*, the next task after the defence of the Suez Canal was the Gallipoli campaign.

. 6 .

Gallipoli
[1915–16]

The Gallipoli venture had first been seriously discussed by the British
War Council on 25 November 1914, as an ideal way of defending
Egypt by dealing Turkey a paralysing blow in the vitals. The two
champions of the scheme were Churchill as First Lord and Lord
Fisher. At the age of seventy-four, Fisher had been called from
retirement on Churchill's insistence when Battenberg resigned with
great dignity at the end of October. (Battenberg had been the victim
of intense vilification, particularly in the popular press, on account
of his German birth.)

The whole point of the Gallipoli operation was that it should be
a *coup de main*, thrusting through the Narrows of the Dardanelles
to take Constantinople, knocking Turkey out of the war and bringing swift aid to Britain's Russian ally. The supreme objective was to
break, and at all costs avoid duplicating, the paralysed deadlock that
had gripped the Western Front. As the world knows, from this
grandiose vision the Gallipoli venture lapsed into an ordeal which,
as far as the hapless troops were concerned, lasted from the first
landings on 25 April 1915 to the last troop evacuations on 9 January
1916. Here we are only concerned with what Fraser saw of this
most melancholy campaign and what he thought about it. On the
latter point he always remained uncompromising. There was and
has always been, he would say, far too much tendency to put all the
blame on Winston Churchill. In Fraser's view the Gallipoli fiasco
was 'partly the fault of, I'm afraid, the Royal Navy and the Army'.[1]
In the first instance the Navy was at fault for not making it absolutely
clear that naval gunfire was incapable of destroying the Turkish forts
and above all mobile guns defending the Dardanelles. In the second
instance, the time needed to remedy the worst deficiencies in the
Army's preparations made it utterly impossible to launch a surprise

41

land assault on Gallipoli, giving the Turks sufficient respite to improvise the defence of the peninsula.

The plain fact was that in early 1915 the British Army and Royal Navy were quite incapable of launching a closely co-ordinated amphibious invasion. No joint planning staffs existed to mesh the two services together, and the result was the aimless whirring of vicious circles. The original naval Commander-in-Chief, Eastern Mediterranean, Admiral Carden (replaced by Admiral de Robeck on 15 March) first underestimated the difficulties of hitting shore batteries with naval gunfire, then over-estimated the danger to warships of plunging fire from the shore. In fact the biggest danger in the Narrows was posed by minefields, as the Anglo-French naval force discovered on 18 March when three of its eighteen pre-Dreadnought battleships were sunk by mines and four more were crippled. The only minesweepers at the Dardanelles in February-March 1915 were North Sea trawlers with civilian crews, who quite understandably shrank from sweeping under Turkish shellfire which the battleships could not silence.

It was all very well for Churchill to urge de Robeck that his old battleships were expendable; the Admiral knew very well that their crews, at least, were not. After the sobering losses on 18 March, de Robeck listened to Generals Hamilton and Birdwood, who advised him that they reckoned the time had come to call in the Army. But the troops of the Mediterranean Expeditionary Force had come out with their weapons and stores so lamentably packed that most of the Army's equipment was back at Alexandria, being sorted out and re-packed. Not only was an immediate follow-up impossible after 18 March, but it took until 25 April before the first troops were ready to land on Gallipoli.

Maid-of-all-work that she was, *Minerva* was intensely active during the weeks of build-up for the invasion. She made her first trip to Tenedos, the island chosen to be advance base for operations off the Dardanelles, on 25 February – the day that Carden's battleships silenced the outer Dardanelles forts at Kum Kale and Sedd-el-bahr. On 1 March she coaled at Tenedos, then took General Birdwood down to Port Said (2–4 March); then returned on the 7th to the island of Lemnos, selected as the main base in the Aegean despite the grossly inadequate port facilities in the harbour of Mudros. Coaling at Lemnos on the 10th, *Minerva* crossed to Tenedos on the following day and then set off on a four-day patrol in the Gulf of Xeros (Saros), north of the Gallipoli peninsula.

Over the previous fortnight Fraser had seized every opportunity to drill and lecture his crews. On 9 March he had made another useful improvement to *Minerva*'s armament, mounting a field-gun on the after capstan (a neat way of obtaining a 360° traverse) in order to 'see off' the Turkish spotter planes which had started to keep an interested eye on the mounting activity on Lemnos. During the Gulf of Xeros patrol (13–16 March) Fraser's crews got in some useful 'live target practice', though their victims were admittedly small fry: a Turkish lighter and two boats destroyed by gunfire east of Cape Tbrizi. After this patrol *Minerva* carried wounded and fleet mails from Tenedos to Malta (17–23 March), and, on the 28th, had the honour of flying Admiral de Robeck's flag while transporting the Commander-in-Chief from Mudros to Tenedos and back.[2]

As April began the motley armada of warships and transports continued to assemble and Fraser had the particular pleasure of seeing his former second, third, and fourth ships – *Prince George*, *Goliath* and *Triumph* – join the Fleet. Another new arrival was a converted collier rebuilt as a seaplane-carrier: *Ark Royal*. With one of *Ark Royal*'s seaplane pilots – a lieutenant by the name of Sholto Douglas – *Minerva* headed south and carried out a successful air reconnaissance of Smyrna on 12 April.

On the 16th – nine days before the landings on Gallipoli were scheduled to begin – *Minerva* was involved in the closing stages of an incident which shows what a total failure British security had been during the build-up, as well as the excellent fighting spirit of the Turkish enemy at his best. The troopship *Manitou* was approached by a torpedo-boat flying Greek colours which closed to point-blank torpedo range, hoisted the Turkish flag and gave the horrified men aboard *Manitou* 'Three minutes to clear your decks'. Three torpedoes were then fired at *Manitou*, whose men could do nothing at all as all their weapons were stowed in the hold. The torpedoes all passed harmlessly beneath *Manitou*'s keel, but pandemonium broke out as the soldiers abandoned ship in total confusion. They thrashed in the water alongside their undamaged ship while the Turks in the torpedo-boat roared with laughter. The Turks then made off at top speed and would have got clean away but for *Minerva*, which gave chase and forced the raiders to beach their ship in Kalamati Bay.

It was not the best of omens for the approaching campaign. Nor was the sudden onset of bad weather which forced a two-day postponement of the landings at the eleventh hour. Unfortunately no measures were taken to stop the supporting warships from taking up their positions 24 hours too early. At 23.32 hrs on the 23rd, *Minerva* weighed anchor and 'proceeded to inspect our position for forthcoming landing of troops'. At 15.00 hrs on the 24th *Minerva*, with HMS *Ark Royal*, *Talbot* and *Manica* in company, arrived off Gaba Tepe where the ANZACs (Australian/New Zealand Army Corps) were intended to make their landing. But the warships did more than inspect the beach. For 20 minutes (05.40 to 06.00 hrs) Fraser directed the shelling of a Turkish battery behind Gaba Tepe, with the fall of shot being observed by *Manica*. Considering the speedy Turkish reaction to the Gaba Tepe landings on the following day (the general reserve of the Turkish 5th Army lay less than 6 miles inland from Gaba Tepe) this premature disclosure of the attackers' intentions was unfortunate. It was, however, typical of the overall failure to integrate the roles of the Navy and the Army at Gallipoli.[3]

When the landings began at dawn on 25 April it was a dreadful object-lesson in how to misuse the fire-power of a large supporting fleet. In all fairness this was not entirely the Navy's fault, for its gunners were being asked to make bricks without straw. Radar gunnery and the TBS radio-telephone were not perfected until the Second World War; at Gallipoli in 1915 the supporting warships had no settled fire programmes, no accurate maps of the terrain ashore (nor did the troops – such maps did not exist), and no efficient ship-to-shore communication. Air spotting and artillery direction was still in its infancy. Even so, some attempt could have been made in the previous month and a half to give each army unit the assurance of permanent fire support from the sea, for an opposed landing and tough resistance ashore were anticipated. But no such Army/Navy tactical liaison had been arranged.

Remembering that the military pundits held that no attack had a hope of succeeding without preliminary bombardment (the more lavish the better), this is particularly hard to explain. Though he was an advocate of covering naval fire, Fraser admitted to the author that 'it was a matter of opinion whether to open fire before the troops got ashore, to cover them, or make a silent surprise landing.'[4] As the grim events on the Cape Helles beaches proved, what was needed was the prompt suppression of Turkish strongpoints which revealed themselves *after* the first troops had got ashore, and the constant vague movements of the warships made this impossible even where such strongpoints were visible. As a result *Minerva*'s role during the opening fortnight suggests nothing so much as an anxious bystander, hovering round the scene of a multiple accident and wondering how best to help.

The original support plan for the Gaba Tepe landing was disrupted at the outset by the troops being landed in error some 2 miles north of their designated beach. *Minerva* was ordered south from Gaba Tepe to bombard Achi Baba, the central height dominating the tip of the Gallipoli peninsula, around which five other landings were made in the teeth of terrible losses. After firing a few salvoes at Achi Baba *Minerva* was moved again, this time to reinforce *Goliath* off

Y Beach; then came back to resume the bombardment of Achi Baba, which remained her principal target for the next four days. In view of the agonised struggles of the troops to deepen their beach-heads, the concentration on this island target was a waste of time and ammunition. Fraser put it succinctly: 'We were told to bombard the back slopes of Achi Baba to catch the Turks as they were driven back; but of course they never *were* driven back.'[5]

On 29 April *Minerva*'s gunners began to work over a rough-and-ready grid of the Gaba Tepe area, but before any close links could be established between ship and shore she was moved again. Her new task was to head into the Gulf of Xeros and signal to the British submarines which had run the Narrows and broken out into the Sea of Marmara. The first submarines to accomplish this hazardous feat, news of which gave a tremendous fillip to Army as well as Navy morale, were the *AE.2* and *E.14* between 25 and 28 April. By the time that *Minerva* arrived in the Gulf of Xeros and began signalling on the 30th, *AE.2* had been attacked, scuttled and her crew captured on the 29th. *E.14* returned safely after recall on 17 May.

During this time of enforced ineffectiveness and frustration, Fraser had one comfort. The anti-aircraft gun which he had contrived on the after capstan had more than proved its worth, being highly effective in driving off enemy reconnaissance aircraft. On 30 April, 1 May and 2 May, after an expenditure of no more than six rounds each time, Fraser's gun drove off a Turkish spotter plane within five minutes.

Throughout the first half of May, with only one diversion to hit Achi Baba again on the 13th, *Minerva* operated off the Gaba Tepe sector, firing at Turkish batteries and trenches. On the 15th she was pressed into service as a supply ship, sending ashore water in response to appeals from the Army. By the middle of the month it was known that German U-boats were on their way out to the eastern Mediterranean, and the Navy at Gallipoli was experiencing an increasing 'submarine scare'. This took some time to reach full pitch. A seaplane pilot in *Ark Royal* noted that 'There is now a genuine submarine flap' as early as 10 May.[6] Two days later the Turkish destroyer *Muavenet-i-Miliet* (with a German crew) torpedoed *Goliath*, Fraser's old ship, at the mouth of the Dardanelles in a night attack. The speed with which *Goliath* turned turtle and sank only increased the sense of unease and on the 14th the super-Dreadnought *Queen Elizabeth* was recalled on Fisher's insistence.

As the gradual withdrawal of the battleships to Mudros got under way, *Minerva* remained in close support of the Gaba Tepe beach-head until the 21st, when she headed south for another air reconnaissance of Smyrna (carried out on the 23rd). By the time the seaplane had been recovered and the ship headed back to Mudros *Minerva*, too, was reacting to the submarine menace, zig-zagging for the first time and with lookouts briefed to keep a special watch for periscopes. It was in the last week of May that the submarine nightmare became reality at last. On 27 May the battleship *Triumph*, another of Fraser's old ships, was torpedoed by *U-21* while steaming slowly off the ANZAC beach-head, despite the theoretical protection of her torpedo nets and being at action stations. *Minerva* was close by and Fraser saw the whole thing: *Triumph* capsized and sank in 12 minutes with the loss of many lives, 'a terrible sight to see'.[7] As if to make matters worse, the disaster was witnessed from the shore by hundreds of soldiers. Some of them spotted *U-21*'s periscope from their vantage-point on the heights. But *U-21* got clean away from the scene of her victory, repeating it two days later by sinking the battleship *Majestic* off Cape Helles. By the time of this latest disaster the full-scale withdrawal of the Fleet to Mudros was well under way, with the hasty departure of the big ships inevitably making the troops on Gallipoli feel that they were being left in the lurch by the Navy.

With the retreat of the capital ships to Mudros it fell to the cruisers and destroyers to shore up Army morale by showing the flag as often as possible off the beaches. But this could only be fitted in amid constant anti-submarine patrolling, which for *Minerva* took up the whole of June and July 1915. Of this period when *Minerva* and her 'chummy ships' acted as Aunt Sallies for the capital ships, Fraser was later to content himself with the laconic comment: 'We came through it all right';[8] but two months of scouring the eastern Aegean for enemy submarines with only brief interludes for coaling was undoubtedly nerve-straining, and the solitary periscope sighting made by *Minerva* on 15 July snapped the tension with a welcome flurry of action.

When the periscope was sighted at 09.50 hrs on the 15th *Minerva* was zig-zagging on the starboard side of a supply convoy. In the days before 'Asdic', when it was quite impossible to track a submarine under water, all that could be done was to let fly at the enemy periscope in the hope of forcing the submarine to the surface, where it could be shelled or rammed. It came down to snap-shooting on hastily calculated ranges and bearings based on the reports of the lookouts. *Minerva* fired at reported periscopes at 09.53 hrs, 10.15 hrs and 10.20 hrs, but her log honestly records that the last target, fired on at 10.32 hrs, was no more than 'an object off the port beam'.[9] Looking back on the incident Fraser readily admitted that it had probably been a false alarm, though he could be well pleased with the speed at which his gun crews opened fire with each new reported sighting. If nothing else it made a heartening sight for the storeships in the old cruiser's care, all of which arrived safely at Mudros in the afternoon of the 15th.

After a final uneventful patrol in the last week of July, *Minerva* prepared for her role in the coming renewal of the land battle. Since the end of April the troops on Gallipoli had been penned in two narrow beach-heads, at Cape Helles and at 'ANZAC', north of Gaba Tepe. New divisions had come out from England to reinforce the Mediterranean Expeditionary Force; and now, at the end of the first week in August, they were to be bundled into the campaign. This was to be opened by an energetic holding attack down at Helles, then a night assault on the Sari Bair ridge by the ANZACs, who would be reinforced beforehand by the landing of 20,000 troops. The ANZAC thrust would be complemented by the landing of two new divisions at Suvla Bay, a mile and a half further up the coast. The Suvla divisions would form the extreme 'left hook' of a decisive advance across the central heights of the Gallipoli peninsula. And the role devised for *Minerva* in all this was to join forces with the destroyer *Jed* and land a diversionary force in the Gulf of Xeros, out on the left flank of the Suvla force.

When described like this the new plan sounds highly impressive, suggesting that all the errors and deficiencies of the April landings had been appreciated and rectified. It was a good plan, and it did take the Turks momentarily by surprise. But there was everything wrong with the way in which the inexperienced but enthusiastic troops were dumped ashore at Suvla on 6 August and virtually left to fend for themselves without clear orders or energetic leadership from their generals. Little or nothing had been learned since April about landing troops in battle order and maintaining a steady flow of essential supplies (particularly water) from ship to shore. The Navy's role at Suvla was very difficult. The cruisers and destroyers had to provide fire support without the help of the battleships, and it was impossible for them to do this *and* minister to the troops.

If the Suvla supply planners and generals were the wrong men for the job, so were the 'troops' embarked by *Minerva* and *Jed* for the feint landing in the Gulf of Xeros. These were 350 rowdy and undisciplined Greek irregulars commanded by a couple of French officers, and precisely what they were expected to accomplish remains one of the unsolved mysteries of the war. Launching a convincing diversionary attack is a fine art, requiring sizable numbers of sound troops; but it proved hard enough to coax the Greeks into the boats to make the landing, let alone persuade them to disembark on the shore. To make matters worse the landing was hotly opposed. As the officer responsible for getting the men ashore and bringing them off, Fraser did his best but it was a hopeless job. The first attempt, on the 6th, was abandoned, and after the wounded had been brought off the two warships bombarded the shore before a second attempt on the following day. This fared no better than its predecessor and the operation was called off. 'I took some time to make sure that the shore was clear,' recalled Fraser, 'then I opened fire with all our guns and we brought them off'[10] – for a total cost of forty-six killed, wounded and missing. The two warships then returned to Mudros with the wounded. Predictably, the whole abortive business failed to prevent a single Turkish soldier from containing the Suvla perimeter on 7 August.

For Fraser and *Minerva*, the Gulf of Xeros fiasco marked 'the end of the Gallipoli business'. On 8 August the ship sailed for Port Said, thence to embark a force of sailors, Royal Marines and a machine-gun crew, for the defence of Sollum on the Libyan border. This reflected fears of a threat to Egypt's western frontier posed by the pro-Turkish Senussi tribe of central Libya, which materialised as the protracted if lightweight 'Senussi War' (November 1915–March 1916). But by the time the Duke of Westminster's armoured cars chased the Senussi back into Libya in mid-March 1916, Fraser had left *Minerva*. Summoned home to join the Senior Staff at *Excellent*, he was sadly missed by the men of the old cruiser whom he had led and inspired since the outbreak of the war. And only four days before the British and German battle fleets clashed at Jutland, Mrs Fraser proudly added the following letter to the family archive:[11]

Whitehall
May 27th

Dear Mrs Bruce-Fraser (sic),
 I received a letter from my boy on the *Minerva* this morning & I am copying out a passage in it which refers to your son, as I thought you might like to see him as he appears to his 'mates'.
  'We have suffered an irreparable loss. On arrival here the Gunnery Lieutenant got a telegram ordering him home & he left here last night. I am left without a real friend in the ship. I never imagined I could feel the parting so much. It is astonishing what a good friend he was to me, considering he's streaks above me. A finer officer and gentleman never breathed, & I can only hope he'll get a job more worthy of his genius. I didn't have a chance to thank him for all he's done for me so I wrote him a note before his ship sailed & got such a nice reply. I hope I

shan't stay in the ship long now he's gone. He was the life
and soul of the ship.'
With kindest regards,
  Sincerely yours,
    Mary Shaw

· 7 ·

Battleship *Resolution*
[1916–19]

When the British Grand Fleet steamed out to intercept the German High Seas Fleet off Jutland on 31 May 1916 Fraser was back at Whale Island, serving with the Senior Staff of *Excellent*. His career was taking on something of a contradictory twist. Before the outbreak of war he had, by compiling the director firing handbook, proved himself a leading exponent of modern naval gunnery. Yet Fraser's appointment to the elderly *Minerva* had also taken him to one of the war's most frustrating sideshows: the Mediterranean, far from the key naval theatre of the war and the technical excellence of the battle squadrons massed in Scapa Flow.

When he left *Minerva* in 1916 Fraser had served for over twelve years, yet in all that time he had only known one short spell afloat in a modern warship, and that had been the flyweight cruiser *Boadicea* back in 1910–11. Nor could he, in 1916, reasonably expect any radical advancement when the time should come for his next seagoing appointment. 'I was expecting another cruiser,' he told the author.[1] But before 1916 was out, Fraser had joined the Grand Fleet in Scapa Flow as Gunnery Officer of the newest Dreadnought to join the Fleet: HMS *Resolution*, the last but one battleship (*Ramillies* being the last, in 1917) to join the Grand Fleet before the end of the war.

This magnificent appointment, certainly the most unexpected and in many ways the most crucial of Fraser's entire career, was a direct result of the Battle of Jutland. The Navy's losses at Jutland had been grievous. Out of the Grand Fleet's 60,000 officers and men, 6,097 had been killed, 510 wounded and 177 fished out of the water and taken prisoner by the Germans. These losses cut heavily into the promotional 'lines of succession' along which proven officers and ratings serving with the Grand Fleet would otherwise have moved on to appointments in new ships. In May 1916 the fourth of the

50

'Royal Sovereign' class battleships, HMS *Resolution*, was due to leave the builders' hands and enter service by the end of the year. Her gunnery officer-to-be had already been nominated, but he was killed at Jutland – and Fraser was taken from the Senior Staff at *Excellent* to fill the vacancy. It was, he admitted, very much a case of being at the right place at the right time. Nine years had passed since he had last served in a battleship, and that had been the pre-Dreadnought *Triumph* back in 1907.

Fraser spent the autumn of 1916 up at Tyneside, supervising the last hectic weeks of *Resolution*'s fitting-out at Palmer's Yard, Jarrow. This was a particularly testing time because he found himself properly 'in at the deep end', beset with a thousand unfamiliar technical details and problems. While familiarising himself with the ship as fast as he could, trying not to reveal that he was in many ways an innocent abroad as far as her gunnery details were concerned, Fraser found himself constantly being asked 'where to put something or what to do with something' by the builders. It was a heavy responsibility, for many of these decisions could have a profound effect on the time it would take *Resolution* to become an efficient fighting ship. Fraser had to decide whether or not the hoist mechanism, bringing the shells up from the magazines to the turrets, would operate fast enough for the demands of action. He had to pronounce on the arrangements in the Transmitting Station (TS), the complex 'telephone exchange' which controlled the flow of information and orders to and from all parts of the ship. No such refinements had existed aboard *Minerva*. And these were just two examples out of many.

By the beginning of December 1916 – just over three years after being laid down, and just under two years from her launch – *Resolution* completed her fitting-out. The crew joined ship on 7 December and the ship was commissioned on the same day, with Fraser setting his new department to work with little or no delay. Over sixty years later one of them, Alfred Howard of the Royal Marines, recalled:[2]

As a Band Boy of 16, I was a member of the Royal Marine Band, sent up to Hebburn-on-Tyne in December 1916 to commission HMS *Resolution*, a West Country ship manned from Devonport.

Our Gunnery Officer was Lt Bruce Fraser, and no doubt he had been 'standing by' the ship for months as she was fitted out, studying the guns and fire control system being built. His first job was to train and perfect the whole gunnery department to make her the fine fighting ship she became.

The R.M. Band's job was to man the Transmitting Station, and although we had been through a gunnery course at Whale Island, we were quite unused to the most modern equipment in the 'Reso'. In the early stages of our training he patiently and thoroughly took each of us through the jobs we had to do before handing us over to his second-in-command, Lt Jeans, to rehearse us over and over again in the drill to gain the necessary perfection to produce good gunnery.

Fraser's work during the fitting-out was now put to the test in earnest as his crews flung themselves into making their new ship fit to take her place in the Grand Fleet with minimum delay. On 14–15 December they ammunitioned ship, a fast piece of work whose speedy conclusion was specially gratifying to Fraser. 'Captain Bruen had asked me if we could do it in three days. Trying to hide the fact that I hadn't the least idea how long it would take, I told him that sounded about right. Actually we did it in two days.'[3] Gun cleaning followed, and then (21 December) Fraser began exercising the 15-inch turret control parties, all before *Resolution* had even moved from Palmer's Yard. And on 30 December, during the short run up from Jarrow to the southern Fleet base at Rosyth in the Firth of Forth, the 15-inch guns were fired for the first time. In the New Year of 1917, as Alfred Howard put it, 'after weeks of intense training and "working up", we were considered fit to join the other four ships of our battle squadron – a proud moment for Bruce Fraser (or "Guns" as he was known) for all his hard work in preparing both ship and men for battle.'[4]

But – supreme anti-climax – there was no battle. Jutland remained the war's only full-scale clash between the British and German battle fleets. Before Jutland Admiral Scheer, Commander-in-Chief of the German High Seas Fleet, had hoped to whittle down the British superiority in numbers by ambushing portions of the Grand Fleet, but at Jutland it was the Germans who found themselves ambushed. Skilful tactics enabled Scheer to extricate his battered fleet and lead it home, but the Germans had stared total disaster in the face at Jutland, and never forgot it. They noisily claimed a tactical victory because they had sunk more British ships than the British had sunk German ships, but the British had enough new warships being built to make good their losses at Jutland, and the Germans did not. The entry of the United States into the war, and the arrival at Scapa of an American battle squadron to form the Grand Fleet's 6th Battle Squadron, only put the Germans further and further behind. By January 1918 – eighteen months after Jutland – the Grand Fleet's advantage over the High Seas Fleet was unbeatable: forty-three

Dreadnought battleships and battle-cruisers to the Germans' twenty-four.

But if the Germans dared take no risks with their outnumbered battle fleet, the same applied to the British, despite their apparent security in numbers. Admiral Jellicoe was shrilly criticised for his 'caution' at Jutland. And so he had been cautious, knowing full well that one ill-considered manoeuvre on his part could expose his battle squadrons to decimation by German torpedo attacks. This possibility remained a nightmare for the British right down to the end of the war.

When Jellicoe went to the Admiralty as First Sea Lord (December 1916) and command of the Grand Fleet passed to the dashing and aggressive Beatty, there was no change in the underlying caution behind every move the Grand Fleet made. For Beatty was, as Churchill said of Jellicoe, 'the only man on either side who could lose the war in an afternoon'.[5] Together with every officer and rating in the Grand Fleet, Beatty never lost hope that Scheer might make some unaccountable blunder that would give the Grand Fleet the chance of a crushing victory, but Scheer did not. As a result, for twenty-three months after *Resolution* joined the Fleet, Fraser and his men were like perfectly trained athletes poised on the starting-blocks, waiting for the crack of the starter's pistol that never came; and this, as every athlete knows, plays hell with the nerves.

In these bleak months all Fraser's reserves of buoyancy and cheerfulness were needed, together with his knack of inspiring men to keep trying to improve on their previous best performance in their work. At this he succeeded wonderfully, and it was not forgotten. 'Eternally patient, absolutely unflappable, and with it all a perfect naval gentleman. His men would joyfully go with him anywhere', was Alfred Howard's verdict sixty years later. In addition to working out new schemes for scotching tedium and improving performance in his department, Fraser was also left with plenty of time – virtually for the first time since leaving *Britannia* – for *thinking* about his work. From the weary monotony of Scapa Flow between 1917 and the Armistice grew the quiet time for sitting and thinking which he deliberately built into his working day when he finally became a Fleet commander in the Second World War.

But service in the Grand Fleet was not all stagnation and boredom in the last two years of the war. Such a thing would hardly have been possible with a Commander-in-Chief like Admiral Beatty, a born leader for whom Fraser had the greatest respect and admiration. And it was during the regular North Sea 'sweeps' and exercises carried out by the Grand Fleet that the embryo Royal Naval Air Service succeeded, by the summer of 1918, in gaining air control over the North Sea from the watchful Zeppelins and seaplanes of the German Navy. This was achieved by the first true marriage between the warship and the aeroplane, with warships carrying aircraft to within range of their target, then retiring to safe waters when the mission had been completed. And Fraser, though trained as a gunnery specialist – a high priest, as it were, of the cult of the Dreadnought – was present at the result of this revolutionary union: the birth of the Fleet Air Arm.

From his time in *Minerva* Fraser was familiar with the clumsy embarkation of seaplanes which had to be lowered over the side to take off, then hoisted back aboard the 'mother ship'. But by the second half of 1917 the Grand Fleet was pressing ahead with experiments in flying-off aircraft from warships. On 2 August 1917 Squadron-Commander Dunning made the first successful deck landing on the converted light battle-cruiser HMS *Furious*. Though Dunning lost his life in an attempted repeat landing two days later, he had proved that aircraft could not only fly off but land on a moving warship at sea. The carrier age was born, but until the first aircraft-carriers had been built with safe, unimpeded flight-decks stretching the full length of the ship, the first 'carriers' were cruisers and capital ships fitted with launching platforms. Three weeks after Dunning's deck-landing feat on *Furious*, Flight Sub-Commander Smart was launched in a Sopwith 'Pup' from such a platform on the cruiser *Yarmouth*, and shot down the Zeppelin *L.23* over the Danish coast.

Though the new technique had made this spectacular debut, it nevertheless remained extremely risky as the pilot could not land on deck again. He had no choice but to 'ditch' in the sea, as close to a friendly warship as possible, and hope to be picked up. For all that, further experiments were made with platforms, which now took the form of turntables fitted on top of the turrets of capital ships, but still permitting the main armament to be fired. This enabled the aircraft to be faced into the wind for take-off without the warship having to make any drastic alteration of course. The first capital ship to be so fitted was the battle-cruiser HMS *Repulse*, from which the first Sopwith 'Pup' took off on 1 October 1917. With one platform forward and another aft, two aircraft could be launched by each capital ship. On 4 April 1918 the first two-seater aircraft, a Sopwith '1½-Strutter' was successfully launched from the battle-cruiser HMS *Australia*.

In due course the turret platforms and launching-skids running down the 15-inch gun-barrels were fitted in *Resolution*, under Fraser's critical eye; and on 19 July 1918 the ship took part in the first true air strike in the history of naval aviation. This was the famous raid on the Zeppelin sheds at Tondern in Schleswig, carried out largely by Sopwith Camels – one-seater aircraft dropping diminutive bombs. The raid was a resounding success: the bombers not only hit the target but destroyed the Zeppelins *L.54* and *L.60* as well. The significance of this early demonstration of naval air power was not lost on Fraser. Though twenty-seven years were to pass before he commanded the ten fleet carriers and nine escort carriers of the British Pacific Fleet, his observation of naval aviation during his time with the Grand Fleet in 1917–18 ensured that he remained one of the Navy's most 'air-minded' gunnery specialists.

The Tondern raid was launched during the last great crisis of the war. By the middle of June 1918, massively reinforced by troops withdrawn from beaten Russia, the German armies on the Western Front were once more driving for Paris, just as they had been four years before. But on the very day of the Tondern raid in July 1918 the French armies counter-attacked on the Marne. The tide rolled back, this time for good. In the exciting weeks that followed, as the Germans continued to retreat, the burning question for the Royal Navy was whether or not the High Seas Fleet would gamble all on a desperate sortie. In fact Admiral Hipper, who had succeeded Scheer as Commander-in-Chief High Seas Fleet, did order such a sortie but it never took place. Rather than face a second Jutland when the war was plainly lost, the men of the German Navy mutinied on 28 October 1918, and the mutiny spread over the following days. The naval mutinies triggered off the German revolution which toppled the Kaiser from his throne, and hastened the signing of the Armistice on 11 November 1918.

Under the Armistice terms the most immediate prize demanded by Britain was the surrender of the newest units of the High Seas Fleet. The German warships were to come out to surrender without ammunition and without breech-blocks in their guns, but from the Royal Navy's viewpoint there could be no guarantee that, after all, they might not choose to go out in a blaze of glory, preferring destruction in a last suicidal battle to tame surrender. As a result the atmosphere was electric when the Grand Fleet put to sea, every gun loaded and every man at battle stations, to receive the surrender of the High Seas Fleet on 21 November. There are many famous accounts of this breathtaking moment in naval history, but that written by Fraser in a letter to his mother is here given in full.

> The Fleet had orders to leave harbour at 1am on Thursday morning.
> This involved the 1st Division (including *Resolution*) in going ahead at 0350, as in the order of the Fleet leaving

harbour there are all the Light Cruiser Squadrons, destroyers, battle-cruisers, 1st B.S. and 6th B.S. to go first. Each admiral takes his own division out of harbour, and we were told to unmoor at 0230.

It was a beautiful still night with a little moon & as I assist the 1st Lieut. in unmooring was up on the F'c'sl.

The *Sphere* man also arrived & I expect has made quite a pretty picture of the operation, with the small electric lights moving about, hoses playing on the anchors & the great cables clanking, etc.

We were aweigh at 0330 & turned ready for going ahead by 0345 exactly to programme.

We then passed under the (Forth) Bridge, *Revenge* leading & ourselves second.

As there is 10 minutes between each Squadron going out we saw no more of the remainder of the Fleet until daylight, each division making its own way through the swift channels by different routes.

At daylight about 0700 the whole Fleet was out & commencing to form up on the *Queen Elizabeth* (Beatty's flagship), about 20 or 30 miles beyond May Island.

At 0800 the Fleet was formed, each division being in the reverse order to that shown in the diagram. NOTE: There are 2 divisions in each battle squadron, *Revenge* to *Royal Oak* being the 1st, & *Emperor of India* to *Canada* the 2nd (*Ramillies* was absent from our division refitting). Thus the order of 1st B.S. on its way to meet the Germans was:

> *Emperor of India*
> *Benbow*
> *Iron Duke*
> *Marlborough*
> *Canada*
> *Revenge*
> *Resolution*, etc.

By 0900 the visibility had decreased to the normal North Sea conditions – about 2½ to 3 miles – & about half the Fleet could not be seen.

The *Cardiff*, *Castor* & 3 destroyer flotillas were spread about 10 miles ahead to sight the Germans & report them, & the whole Fleet then went to action stations with guns loaded in case of eventualities.

About 0915, the first enemy report was received from the *Cardiff* by W/T & course was slightly altered to bring the

Germans, who were in line ahead, exactly between the two lines.

At 0945 the *Cardiff*, who had taken up her position ahead of the *Seydlitz*, hove in sight & shortly afterwards the German battle cruisers appeared.

They are fine looking ships & everyone marvelled that they should have come in so tamely.

They lacked paint, made a horrible smoke, such as we or any of our coal ships would have been hung for, but all the same looked workmanlike & were keeping good station though only going 10 knots.

When the *Seydlitz* was nearly abeam of the *Q.E.* the whole British Fleet was turned by signal, leaders of each division together outwards, the remainder in succession & the order as shown in the diagram was assumed [see diagram 1].

I was as usual up in the Spotting Top & had a splendid view, although it was rather spoilt by the low visibility, a large part of our Fleet not being visible. (Each line in the diagram takes up about 8 miles.) After the battle fleet and light cruisers came the destroyers guarded as shown.

The whole proceeding passed without incident and on arrival inside May Island, we hauled off, to allow the Germans led by the *Cardiff*, to take up their anchorage & watched the whole cortege go by.

The 1st B.S. with AC1 (Admiral Commanding 1st Battle Squadron) in charge was detailed to guard the German ships & to take them to Scapa after examination & therefore as soon as the Germans had anchored we did the same alongside them, forming a square completely surrounding them.

The ship detailed for us to examine was the *Grosser Kurfürst*, a battleship of the *König* class, their latest except the *Bayern*.

At 1400 we left the ship, the Commander in charge, the Eng. Cmdr., Lt (T) & myself with our assistants being the examining officers.

Thus each British Captain only sent his representative to meet the German one, & the Flag Captain as the Admiral's representative went to see the German Admiral von Reuter, flying his flag in the *Friedrich der Grosse*.

I had to make out orders for the inspections of which there were to be two: a cursory one on the first day, to see that they could take no offensive action, a more thorough one on the next day, when all their ship's company were to be on the

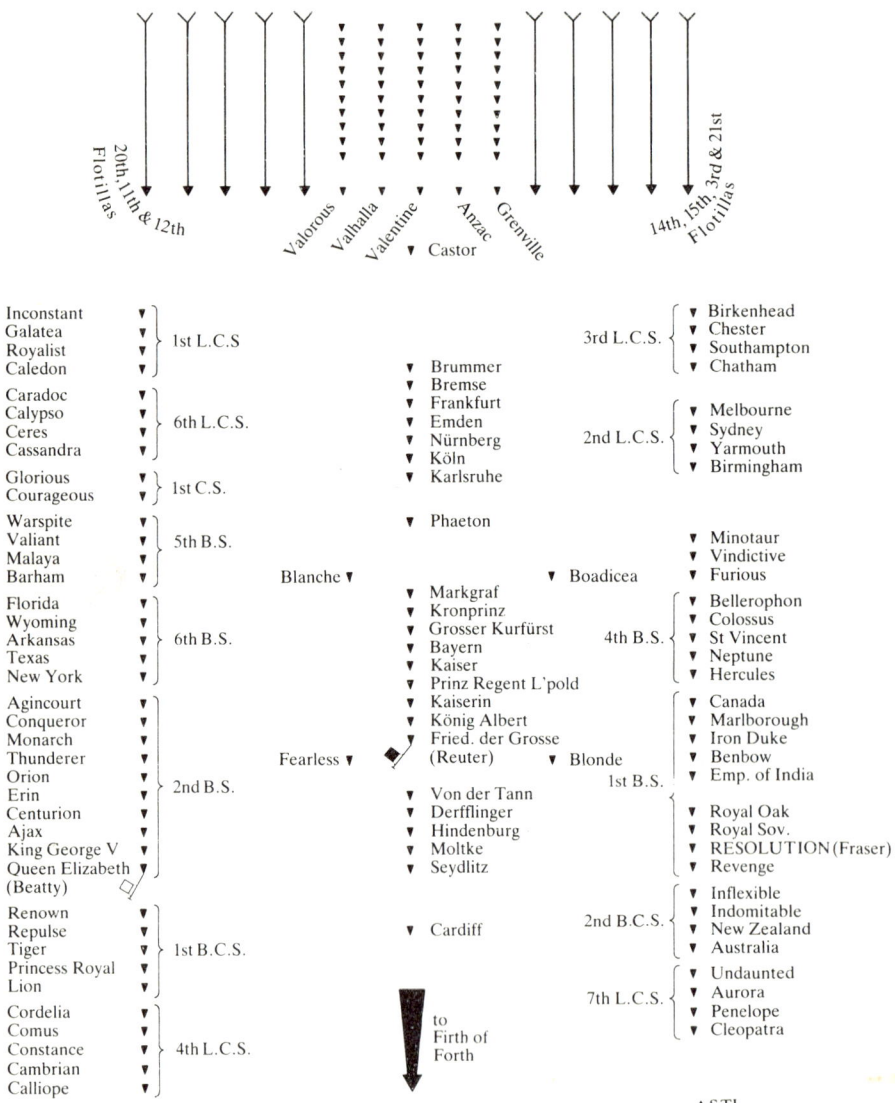

20th, 11th & 12th Flotillas

Valorous
Valhalla
Valentine
Anzac
Grenville
14th, 15th, 3rd & 21st Flotillas

Castor

Inconstant		Birkenhead			
Galatea		Chester			
Royalist	1st L.C.S	Southampton	3rd L.C.S		
Caledon		Chatham			

Brummer
Bremse

Caradoc
Calypso
Ceres   6th L.C.S.
Cassandra

Frankfurt
Emden   Melbourne
Nürnberg   Sydney   2nd L.C.S.
Köln   Yarmouth
Karlsruhe   Birmingham

Glorious   1st C.S.
Courageous

Warspite
Valiant
Malaya   5th B.S.
Barham

Phaeton

Blanche ▾   Boadicea

Minotaur
Vindictive
Furious

Florida
Wyoming
Arkansas   6th B.S.
Texas
New York

Markgraf
Kronprinz
Grosser Kurfürst
Bayern   4th B.S.
Kaiser
Prinz Regent L'pold

Bellerophon
Colossus
St Vincent
Neptune
Hercules

Agincourt
Conqueror
Monarch
Thunderer
Orion   2nd B.S.
Erin
Centurion
Ajax
King George V
Queen Elizabeth
(Beatty)

Fearless ▾

Kaiserin
König Albert
Fried. der Grosse
(Reuter)   Blonde   1st B.S.
Von der Tann
Derfflinger
Hindenburg
Moltke
Seydlitz

Canada
Marlborough
Iron Duke
Benbow
Emp. of India

Royal Oak
Royal Sov.
RESOLUTION (Fraser)
Revenge

Renown
Repulse
Tiger   1st B.C.S.
Princess Royal
Lion

Cardiff

2nd B.C.S.

Inflexible
Indomitable
New Zealand
Australia

Cordelia
Comus
Constance   4th L.C.S.
Cambrian
Calliope

to
Firth of
Forth

7th L.C.S.

Undaunted
Aurora
Penelope
Cleopatra

ASTI

Diagram 1 Fraser's diagram of the surrendered High Seas Fleet heading for the Firth of Forth, escorted by the Grand Fleet.
B.S. = Battle Squadron; B.C.S. = Battle-Cruiser Squadron; C.S. = Cruiser Squadron; L.C.S. = Light Cruiser Squadron. German destroyers flanked by British destroyer flotillas bring up the rear, at the top of the diagram.

upper deck, all hatches lockers cupboards to be open, plans of the ship available, & interpreters and guides to take us round.

On arrival we walked over the side, being piped & saluted & were received by the Captain to whom the Commander gave the orders.

The men were all strolling about the quarterdeck & smoking but otherwise quite respectful to us & their own officers & except for the fact that the ship was filthy dirty & that no one did anything, there was not much sign of the mutiny.

In some ships however the Captain was accompanied by a sailor with a white band: a member of the Sailors' Council.

The Captain was a funny little man not of the Prussian type & could speak fairly good English.

He detailed officers to accompany us & I went off with the Gunnery Officer round the turrets, magazines & shellrooms whilst my assistant with another officer went round the secondary armament.

All the magazines & shell rooms were empty, & the guns had had their breech blocks removed and left behind.

Most of the fire control, rangefinders & instruments had also been removed & they seemed to have carried out their instructions pretty thoroughly for which there must have been a certain amount of discipline still left in Germany.

We were generally disappointed in the sort of ship we expected to find, very far astern of us & our standard, except perhaps for their watertight subdivision which is good, & the large number of small compartments & doors probably accounts for the large numbers of men they carry (complement 1,400) & also the difficulty in sinking them.

Their turrets are on the American lines, all electric with hydraulic elevating only (12″ guns).

The men were quite ready to show us round & even explain things & in one or two cases stood up & saluted on (our) coming in to the turret, but everyone smoked. They seemed in quite good condition & well fed & clothed, the mail bags were the only things we saw made of paper fibre.

After we had been round, the Gunnery Officer took me down to his cabin, where he showed me the few private pistols & rifles they had which he asked me if they might keep & then showed me all the officers' swords which he said were also private property & asked if they might be kept, quite touching. The officers wore their ordinary uniforms but had removed their medals & the Gunnery Officer then told me that they were practically prisoners.

There was however little sign of this as all orders given were instantly obeyed without reference to anyone.

The inspection the next day was on much the same lines, only we took more people with us & carried it out more thoroughly, chiefly on a search for information.

We obtained most of the things we wanted to know, namely that they had a modified sort of director (*Richtungsweiser*), but in general they are very much behind us except for their water-tight subdivision, but I don't know that their ships would be possible for living in continuously like ours – too uncomfortable.

They undoubtedly as a general rule live ashore, manning their ships when required to go to sea, which possibly accounts for the mutiny & unwillingness to come to action.

On Tuesday we escorted them up to Scapa, where we are now, with no trouble.

On arrival they anchored inside the Flow & then we had to send navigating officers on board to take them to their final berths.

I went on board with the excuse of being bodyguard to the Navigator.

Their methods of navigation were more of the merchant service style than Royal Navy, i.e., they really had little idea of taking up an accurate billet.

They evidently are only used to going alongside walls. So here we are; the transports arrive tomorrow & take most of them except care & maintenance parties back to Germany.

To these reminiscences of the surrender Fraser appended 'A few anecdotes from the flagship', in which one of the most interesting points is the German reaction to the Zeebrugge Raid of 23 April 1918. This gallant but bloody failure to close the U-boat base at Zeebrugge with blockships must be accounted one of the most 'glorious failures' of the war – but it obviously impressed the Germans:[7]

The Chief of Staff went to see the German Admiral to represent our Admiral & informed him that the German flag was to be hauled down at sunset & not hoisted again without permission.

The German Admiral strongly objected & said that it had been flown with honour for 4 years.

Beatty replied that he didn't doubt that was the case in Germany but it wasn't going to be done here, & down it came & remained down.

The Captain of the *Bayern* also desired to make a statement & said that the Zeebrugge Raid had impressed them more than anything else during the whole war & was one of the finest things yet accomplished, perhaps however he desired to curry favour, but it undoubtedly made a great impression on their service.

At present there is little going on, we are at 6 hours notice & the Huns lie at anchor opposite us & the weather for the moment is beautiful.

No one knows what is going to happen next except that we do our next shoot on about the 13th & so presumably will still be up here.

C'est tout.

But *ça n'était pas tout*. Haggling over the terms of the definitive peace treaty dragged on over the next seven months at Versailles, and as the weary weeks passed the mood of the Germans interned in Scapa could be seen to change. On 31 May 1919 they celebrated the third anniversary of Jutland with red and white Very lights and hoisted the German ensign along with the red flag. Admiral Fremantle, commanding at Scapa with the five 'Revenge' class battleships, noted that the Germans 'appeared to be accepting their lot with submissive equanimity, but towards the end of some spirit of discontent' – if for no other reason that they were sick of being gaped at by swarms of sightseers in small boats. As the deadline approached for the expiry of the Armistice and the ratification of the draft Treaty of Versailles, Admiral von Reuter, consulting with Berlin, was preparing for the one course of 'offensive action' left to his disarmed and immobile fleet: suicide by scuttling.

Always aware that Reuter might be considering such a desperate move, Fremantle also knew that there was absolutely nothing he could do about it short of ejecting the Germans from their ships and interning them ashore. This was out of the question because it would have violated the terms of the Armistice and effectively reopened hostilities. But Fremantle was also under orders to complete a series of exercises at sea to prepare his ships for service with the Atlantic Fleet. On the morning of 21 June 1919 he took the squadron to sea, having told Reuter that the Armistice had been prolonged from noon on the 21st until 19.00 hrs on the 23rd. But at 11.45 hrs on the 21st, 4¼ hours after Fremantle had sailed, Reuter hoisted the prearranged signal for the scuttling aboard the German flagship.

Fifteen minutes later Fremantle's squadron was electrified by the frantic signal from Scapa: 'GERMAN SHIPS SINKING; SOME ALREADY SUNK'. Calling off the exercise, Fremantle ordered his ships to make full speed back to Scapa, but the return trip took 2 hours and by the time the squadron arrived it was all over. Of the six battle-cruisers, ten battleships, eight light cruisers and fifty destroyers under guard in the Flow, only the light cruisers *Emden*, *Frankfurt* and *Nürnberg*, the battleship *Baden* and a handful of destroyers were beached or saved from sinking by the furious British.

Baden was the last German battleship completed in the war, and it seems that her crew took comparatively token measures to scuttle her. When a salvage party from *Revenge* rushed on board, it was found that only one shaft gland had been eased free, the doors of the forward underwater torpedo tubes had been opened and the internal watertight doors had been lashed open. Had the main sea valves been opened as well she must have flooded rapidly, but it was found that she was only making water very slowly. The men of *Revenge* were able to close every scuttle, door and hatch in sight before handing over *Baden* to a party from *Resolution* commanded by Fraser. He in turn directed the raising of steam in one of the boilers to help pump out some flooded compartments, and the slipping of the anchor cables to enable the ship to be towed into shallow water and beached. There was, he admitted, little else that could be done. His description of what it felt like to tour the bowels of a flooded Dreadnought, not knowing if at any moment she might turn turtle, was 'a bit worrying' – an understatement if ever there was one.[8]

The British reacted to the scuttling with gusty outrage, making a great song and dance about German breach of faith. It was indeed galling for the strongest Navy on earth to be made to appear foolish, with the Germans scuttling their ships under the noses of their guards. One of the few high-ranking British naval officers to have shown any common sense about the scuttling seems to have been Admiral Wemyss, the First Sea Lord, who pointed out that the surrendered warships would mostly have been sunk anyway and that the scuttling was, as he saw it, a blessing in disguise. *Baden*'s fate certainly bears out that view. Though she was the most modern battleship to fall into British hands, and was raised with little trouble, she was merely used as a target ship before being sunk in 1921.

The surrender and scuttling of the High Seas Fleet brought the Anglo-German war at sea to a resounding close, but the Royal Navy still had plenty of work on its hands. In the Mediterranean and Black Seas, the problems of Turkey and of the anti-Bolshevik forces fighting the Russian Civil War called for considerable reinforcement from home waters. In the late summer of 1919, therefore, HMS *Resolution* headed for the Mediterranean. With her went Fraser, now sporting his 'third ring' as commander and the ship's executive officer. Though he relished the prospect of returning to the Mediterranean, he could not know that he was destined for the most galling period of his career: six months in jail as a captive of the Bolsheviks.

· 8 ·

Prisoner of the Bolsheviks

[1920]

When *Resolution* reached the eastern Mediterranean in the late summer of 1919 the international scene was, to put it mildly, fluid. While Turkey's peace settlement (the Treaty of Sèvres, eventually signed in August 1920) was being thrashed out in France, the Allies sat in Constantinople – not, technically, occupying the country, but determined to show that the victors had the upper hand. This was one of the main purposes of a march through Constantinople by *Resolution*'s ship's company, headed by Fraser. All such demonstrations really achieved was the alienation of every patriotic Turk, swelling the nationalist opposition led by Mustapha Kemal. The nationalists were also incensed by the claim of Greece to Smyrna (Izmir), a claim backed by the Allies, who gave the Greeks substantial aid when they landed at Smyrna and took it in May 1919. Thus began a vicious war in the interior of Turkey from which Kemal's troops emerged victorious in 1922, overthrew Sultan Mohammed VI and proclaimed a republic with Kemal as President and Soviet Russia as its first ally.

Meanwhile, north of the Black Sea, in August 1919 General Denikin's White Russian forces had advanced on Moscow along a hopelessly wide front from the Crimea to the Caucasus. They got as far as Orel, barely 200 miles from Moscow, before being forced to retreat in November-December 1919. As the beaten White Russian forces fell back to the Black Sea, the anti-Bolshevik regimes in Georgia and Azerbaidjan were increasingly exposed, while the White Russian forces operating from the eastern Caucasus and the Caspian Sea faced isolation and destruction.

As the Bolshevik counter-offensive went from strength to strength in the New Year and spring of 1920 a White Russian 'Volunteer Fleet' took shape at Enzeli (Bandar-e-Pahlavi) in Persia, on the southern shore of the Caspian Sea. Northern Persia had been so long subject to Russian influence that the country could offer the White Russians little or no effective aid. The question, therefore, was how long the Volunteer Fleet could hold out at Enzeli and the answer was not at all, if the Bolsheviks attacked Enzeli from the sea. Hence the British decision of April 1920 to send a small force via Batum and Baku to the aid of the Volunteer Fleet at Enzeli.

By this time the prospect of peacetime service in *Resolution* was appealing less and less to Fraser. He had had the bad luck, after serving under a captain whom he liked and admired, of finding himself as Commander under a new Captain with whom he found it hard to get on. Such incongruencies are frequently the fault of neither party – certainly not in Fraser's case, as no more loyal officer ever served – but they inevitably make for frustration and unhappiness. 'I was too long in *Resolution*, really,' Lord Fraser told the author; 'four years, going from "Number Three" to Commander. And after the war, when the new Captain joined, he wanted everything done his way – changed all the watches round – and I got rather downhearted; we didn't get on at all well. And then fortunately a new admiral joined, and he must have sensed the situation because he asked me to go ashore with him; and he and I went over the side with the new Captain saluting us, looking very black. But I was just about at breaking-point, then, to tell you the truth; and when volunteers were asked for to go to Baku I volunteered, you see.'[1]

The small British Naval Detachment with which Fraser set out for Baku and Enzeli in April 1920 would, in modern parlance, be called a 'team of foreign technical advisers'. As Fraser put it in his official report, their objective was threefold:[2]

(a) to place the ships of the Russian Volunteer Fleet, then at Enzeli, in a fit state to defend the port or to mount guns from them as seemed most desirable to resist attack from the sea.
(b) To mine the entrance.
(c) To assist the Military Authorities in any manner which would enable them to resist attack.

All in all it was a tall order for twenty-six ratings and five officers. The biggest worry was whether they would ever reach Enzeli at all, for this involved traversing Georgia and Azerbaidjan from Batum on the Black Sea to the Azerbaidjanian capital, Baku, on the Caspian. Nobody had a clue where the nearest Bolshevik Russian forces were, but it was unlikely that they would not intervene to stop the anti-Bolsheviks from opening a new supply-line between the Black Sea and the Caspian.

Fraser and the Detachment left Constantinople on 19 April and landed at Batum on the evening of the 21st, completing stores and receiving their final instructions on the following day. Any hopes of a swift and unobtrusive train journey to Baku were dashed at the outset. When a train was finally procured, delay followed delay: faults in the line, the Georgians wanting to detach their engine at the Azerbaidjanian frontier; and Fraser was obliged to send repeated telegraphs to clear the way for his party. When the Naval Detachment finally reached Baku at 1630 hours on the 27th, Fraser was met at the station by the head of the British Military Mission, Major Connal Rowan, and the British Acting Vice-Consul, Mr T. Hewelche. They had ominous news. Bolshevik forces had encroached on the frontier about 120 miles to the north; no steamer was leaving for Enzeli that evening; and the British officials had so far failed to obtain a permit to charter a special vessel. They added that the Azerbaidjanian Government was moving troops north 'to defend their country at all costs', and that a meeting had been arranged with the Governor-General of Baku that evening in hopes of getting a special permit for the Naval Detachment to leave the next morning.

Fraser's instinctive reaction was that not a moment more should be lost in getting clear of Baku. He suggested grabbing a ship, 'either by bribery or by force', and sailing that very night; but Connal Rowan and the Vice-Consul talked him out of it for fear of diplomatic repercussions. 'I decided,' continues Fraser's report,[3]

> to await the result of the interview with the Governor-General. I therefore left Chief Gunner Norman in charge of the train and proceeded with 3 officers to the British Mission, subsequently in company with Major Connal Rowan and the Vice-Consul obtaining a permit from the Governor-General at the Hotel Metropole at about 2300.
>
> At midnight I in company with my officers left the Hotel in a Motor Car to return to the station.
>
> Everything appeared to be quiet, and the British Vice-Consul after his interview with the Governor-General seemed to be satisfied that there was no danger for at least 3 or 4 days.

In fact, unknown to the British and other foreign missions in Baku, a Bolshevik *coup d'état* was taking place that very night. In return for a promise that they alone would be allowed to escape with intact skins, the Azerbaidjanian ministers had done a deal with the pro-Bolshevik leaders, agreeing to hand over power without resistance and lull the foreigners into remaining until they could be rounded up. The interview with the Governor-General, for all its fair seeming, had been a treacherous farce. When Fraser and his officers got back to the station they were stopped by a jabbering party of Azerbaidjanian soldiers and taken to a small waiting room. There they found the petty officers of the Naval Detachment, already under guard. Glumly, Chief Gunner Norman told Fraser 'that he had observed a large number of troops with machine guns in occupation of the station.'[4]

> A Russian Commissar of the worst Bolshevik type then appeared and covering us with a revolver demanded through my interpreter that we should submit to be searched and that we should give up any firearms or weapons on our persons.
>
> I asked the reason for this treatment of British Officers and he stated that the Government had fallen and that a Soviet Government had been established. Further that we were to consider ourselves prisoners and that I was to order my men to surrender all arms, weapons and ammunition.

At pistol-point though he was, Fraser refused to be cowed and flatly rejected the surrender demand. He told the commissar 'that we were only passing through Baku', adding that Britain and Azerbaidjan were not at war, but that the commissar's actions could change matters dramatically. Thus outfaced, the commissar retired, coming back with the information that Fraser and his men were not allowed to carry arms in a neutral country. Fraser hit that one straight back over the net, informing the commissar that he already had permission from the Azerbaidjanian Government to travel with arms. Now thoroughly confused, the commissar disappeared again. In his first encounter with the Bolsheviks Fraser was winning on points, but after further negotiations with an 'extremely courteous' Turkish officer was soon forced to accept that he and his men were in a hopeless corner:[5]

> Realising that the station was occupied by a large number of troops, that resistance would mean much bloodshed, and that even if we succeeded in leaving the station there was nowhere to go, I reluctantly consented to surrender asking at the same time if he could arrange to send us away after giving up our arms.
>
> He stated that he would endeavour to do so but could give no undertaking.
>
> I then proceeded under guard to the train and having assembled the men, explained the situation, whereupon the arms were collected and handed over.
>
> The Turkish Officer was most polite throughout and took my word that all arms had been surrendered without any search.
>
> A guard was then placed on the train and at 0400 on the

morning of the 28th April, H.M. Naval Detachment were prisoners of the Azerbaidjan Government.

Four hours after the surrender a Russian armoured train rumbled into the siding beside the train in which Fraser and his men were held under guard, and the Bolshevik occupation of Baku began in earnest. 'They were mostly dressed in British uniforms', as supplied to the White armies and eagerly stripped from White prisoners by the threadbare Reds, 'and were quite friendly, expressing their "thanks to Mr Lloyd George" for clothing them.'[6] But it took five days before the British were moved from their train, taken to the 'Commission for arresting counter revolutionaries and preventing sabotage', and subjected to a search concentrating (unavailingly in the face of the British sailor's ingenuity) on removing all knives, razors and scissors. Then:[7]

> At 1400 on the 2nd May, I was informed that we should be taken to a house in the town and subsequently we were marched under guard and carrying what we could of our baggage, to the Bailoff Prison, a march of about 2 miles in the hot sun. At the prison we were again searched and told to give up all valuables, but the party managed to retain most of their English money.

On the morning of the 3rd, after another meagre issue of black bread, the party was moved again, having been told that the new quarters consisted of 'three nice rooms'. These turned out to be:[8]

> 3 cells about 12 ft. square each with a small barred window high up on one side. The cells were in a corridor of about 25 other cells which were all occupied by the convicts of the town, murderers, thieves, pickpockets, and all the worst of humanity, suffering from disease and vermin. I protested to the Commissar who was Russian and apparently just taken charge, but he quite politely stated that there was nowhere else and we should have to stay.
> We were then locked in, a small hole existing through the door through which we could be watched, and through which presently a packet of lice was pushed as a welcome.

This was home for the next fifteen weeks, throughout the stifling heat of high summer. Conditions in the prison were appalling: three latrines, seldom cleaned out, for 350-odd inmates, and every corner of the building alive with bugs and fleas. The cell doors were only unlocked for half an hour in the morning and half an hour in the evening. A solitary tap with a trough – the only washing facilities

– stood in a courtyard about 40 yards square where the prisoners took what exercise they could in their brief periods of release from cells. Summary arrests of 'counter-revolutionaries', the unlucky ones being shot and the lucky ones released after brief spells in jail, kept the prison packed.

As senior officer of the biggest British contingent – the Naval Detachment – Fraser threw himself into the task of maintaining the morale of his men and fighting a succession of hostile commissars for better conditions and fairer treatment. The battle of morale was fought on two levels. It was not hard to feel contempt for the brutality and stupidity of their jailors, and Fraser's men collaborated magnificently in showing the Bolsheviks that British sailors obeyed their own officers, not unwashed thugs. But the prisoners' inevitable tendency to feel that they were the 'forgotten men of Baku' was much harder to fight.

Back in Britain Mrs Fraser and Lord Strabolgi were tireless in their efforts to remind the government of the prisoners' plight, but the Lloyd George Cabinet was determined to keep the 'Baku incident' in low key. The position of the British captives was anomalous, for if Britain and Soviet Russia were not at war Fraser and his men had undoubtedly set out to help the anti-Bolshevik cause; and they were fortunate to have been captured at a time when Allied intervention in Russia was already dead on its feet. Though Britain did not formally recognise the Soviet Republic until 1924, Lloyd George was determined to lead the way to formal diplomatic relations and regular trade with 'Bolshevik' Russia (soon to receive diplomatic promotion to 'the Soviet Union') despite the diehard resistance of his interventionist Cabinet colleagues.

To Lloyd George the Baku incident was a thorough nuisance but it was easy to 'play down' the affair, which could easily have been waved like a crusading banner by the interventionist lobby. To name just three absorbing news topics there were the Greco-Turkish War, the Russo-Polish War, and the conclusion of the last peace treaties. At home there were strikes, mounting unemployment and the unanswerable popular clamour for 'No More War'. Thus there was hardly any need to urge editors to keep the Baku incident in low key and refrain from inflammatory demands for the release of the prisoners. Such references to them as did appear between May and October 1920 were diminutive snippets tucked far down the page.

All this obliged Fraser and his men to rely almost entirely on their own reserves of physical and moral endurance, with intermittent help from foreign diplomats and individuals treated as *persona grata* by the Bolshevik regime. The latter were supremely important in helping with the overriding food problem. By the middle of May, albeit at an exorbitant rate, Fraser had managed to change some of the party's precious hoard of English pounds, which helped a lot:[9]

> From a shopkeeper who was allowed in the prison and was in league with the Commissar, I was allowed to buy a little food for the party each day after waiting in a queue with the various convicts for 2 or 3 hours.
>
> The food consisted of a little tea, sugar and onions and some salt fish. On the 18th May the Dutch Consul (Mr D Manassen) arranged for one meal to be sent in each day for all the party consisting of meat and potatoes and this was continued through the medium of Mr A. Seaman, a British subject, who was not arrested and who obtained the necessary funds from the various sources arranged by us. About this time the prison regulations were gradually relaxed for all prisoners, the time allowed for going out of our cells being longer and longer until we were allowed in the courtyard all day from 0830 to 1900.
>
> For the purposes of washing, exercise and latrine this was a great relief, though the courtyard was not pleasant with the hot sun, vermin blowing about in the wind and the chance of what remained in one's pocket (being) picked.

More exercise time gave Fraser's men·a chance to show the Bolsheviks that here, at least, was a bunch of rather special prisoners. The first demonstration of British morale, however, succeeded rather too well. The men started a game of leap-frog, a spectacle which almost certainly had not been seen in a Russian jail since the time of the Crimean War, if then. The other prisoners loved it. 'We organised a sort of field day in the prison yard,' Fraser recalled; 'all the old camel drivers and so on, they joined in – until we found that all the fleas and things were coming off them on to us, so we gave *that* up!'[10] A hilarious crowd gathered, but the horseplay was short-lived. Fearing that the prisoners were about to stage a counter-revolution right in the middle of his prison the commissar panicked, ordering all prisoners to be hustled back to their cells, locked in and the guard doubled. It was a palpable hit for the Royal Navy. 'From then on,' commented Fraser with satisfaction, 'the Bolsheviks certainly respected the British.' Two days later, to celebrate Empire Day (24 May) a Union Jack which the Detachment's signalman had brought along was cut up and made into red, white and blue rosettes which the party proudly wore.

But the political situation remained highly volatile and the Bolshevik authorities were as nervy as cats, constantly on the lookout for insurrection and counter-revolution. On 27 May news that a counter-revolution had broken out at Elizabethpol, only 200 miles away to the west, caused instant panic security measures at Baku. The prison guard at the Bailoff was doubled and martial law was proclaimed. Daily visits by the local storekeeper had already ceased; he and the deputy prison commissar had been arrested for fraud and put in with his former prison customers. Unfortunately for the prisoners the evidence of fraud – the storekeeper's food stocks – had been solemnly impounded and placed under seal, so for five days the staple prison diet reverted to black bread. In addition to severe food shortages during the crisis the prison's only drain became blocked and the mounting stench from the flooded latrines was appalling. Fraser went to the commissar and asked for tools so that the prisoners could clear the drain themselves; but it took two days of official prevarication and repeated requests on Fraser's part before the tools were finally produced and the latrines were cleared at last.

The crisis ended on 2 June when it was announced that the Elizabethpol revolt had been crushed, but that negotiations were being opened with the anti-Bolsheviks in Georgia. In the Bailoff, searches, with or without advance warning from affable guards or fellow prisoners, remained a serious nuisance; but at least they could be foiled by contriving ingenious hiding-places for the party's surviving knife and razor. ('It is curious,' reported Fraser, 'that on no occasion did it ever occur to the prison officials to enquire how we shaved.'[11]) Far more depressing was a new accompaniment to life in the Bailoff, which also began on the evening of 2 June:[12]

This evening the first of the shootings at the prison commenced and lasted off and on for the remainder of the time we were prisoners.

The condemned cell was next to ours and the condemned men were generally brought up in the afternoon. A priest who was under arrest for being anti-Bolshevik would bless them and the other prisoners crowded around kissing him and saying goodbye.

About 2300 a guard came to take him out. Most of the condemned men were brave to the end and generally made a short speech in the corridor stating their innocence.

He was then taken outside the prison under the window of our cell and placed against the wall. A motor car drove up, the shooting Commissar got out, 12 or 13 shots rang out and the car drove away, the dead body being thrown into the sea.

This towards the end rather got on our nerves and was most unpleasant.

As June dragged by conditions for Fraser and his men improved slightly; the convicts in the part of the prison occupied by the British were finally cleared out and replaced by more congenial company: political prisoners. 'These consist of all the so called bourgeoisie, hotel proprietors, photographers, railway officials, generals, oil merchants, &c.'[13] But other conditions remained as bad as ever and the strain gradually began to tell. The nights were particularly bad. 'There is only just room in the cell for all to lie down, six a side with feet touching and two feet breadth space. We generally have to block up every ventilation coming in from the corridor on account of the smell and one really dreads the sound of the door bolt shooting home.'[14] Health was another worry, of course. On the 11th Fraser recorded that:[15]

Nearly everyone is suffering from stomach troubles, two or three from malaria and we have no medicines. The smell still continues, but we have nearly all got used to it; flies are a scourge, but all have been impressed with the necessity of carefully covering up all food.

Boredom remained the most nagging mental discomfort, and Fraser was tireless in thinking up new diversions. 'The authorities got used to our amusements,' he wrote, 'and with a ball made of old clothes we managed to play a little football and a game of rounders for the sake of exercise, which our fellow prisoners afterwards adopted.'[16] Fraser also tried to draw on his formidable talents as lecturer and teacher – but with little success, for the most popular 'requests' were trigonometry and navigation, and he had no tables, books or writing materials. At least he, as senior officer, was able to relieve his feelings by pestering a succession of prison commissars to the best of his ability. 'The process of getting to the commissar is quaint', he noted:[17]

There are three doors one to each courtyard to pass through, each one guarded by a warder and finally the difficulty in getting into the Commissar's office.
　　At the first gate the warder says you can't go through. After protesting for some time the gate is probably opened to allow some prison official through and on pushing through after him the warder says you can go through. The same thing happens at the 2nd gate. At the third gate one asks to see the Commissar. The warder states that he is in the town. You tell him that you have seen him through his office window. The warder then says 'Come back in an hour's time.' You say that the Commissar has sent for you. He then lets you through. At the office door the guard states that he will not be free until the evening. The last card is played by 100 Rs and the Commissar is reached.

Conditions eased a little more after the political prisoners were joined in July by one Raboff, a former Bolshevik commissar who 'had apparently refused to work with them again, saying that he would have nothing further to do with a gang of thieves, murderers and robbers.' Raboff was a welcome arrival because he retained a good deal of influence in the prison and won a number of concessions. On 8 July:[18]

> everyone in the prison signed a paper stating that each person would be responsible for each other and permission was then given to leave the cell doors open at night, the corridor still being locked up. This is a tremendous relief, as the conditions at night are really becoming almost unbearable. Also in a similar manner and by the help of a little bribery we all obtained a hot bath. The cauldron in an old cook house was filled with water and heated up and we managed to obtain a bucket of hot water each which one poured over oneself.

At last, on 15 August, after a month of empty promises, the British contingent was moved from the Bailoff Prison to the town. The new quarters were rooms in the Polish Mission School, placed at the disposal of the British by request of their Polish fellow-captives in the Bailoff – a generous gesture by comrades in adversity. After the claustrophobic squalor of the Bailoff, the derelict building now taken over by Fraser and his men seemed almost luxurious.[19]

> 'One large and one small room were placed at our disposal and later a third was used as a sick bay and a fourth for two Frenchmen who joined up with our party on 26th August. A small galley was available which just sufficed for the fifty-three persons who were now prisoners.
>   Everything practically was broken down and had to be repaired. This was effectually done by the Naval element of the party. The galley was converted to burn oil fuel by ERA Grundy, the windows were repaired, the waterpipes mended, wooden beds were made upon which hammocks and bed covers could be stretched as mattresses. Two sailors carried out the cooking, another cut our hair, the Chief Gunner arranged the supply of food bought from the Bazaar.
>   We were now unmolested and except for the fact that food was difficult to obtain, that the confinement was monotonous, that no communication was allowed with the outside world or with anyone in town, and that we were allowed out in the courtyard for only one hour in the morning and one hour in the evening, we were fairly comfortable.

Of the last twelve weeks at Baku, Fraser bleakly wrote 'there is little to relate'. Despite their better quarters, the frustration of captivity remained as keen as ever. Fraser nursed the party's *esprit de corps* by encouraging little rituals such as the 'Entry of the Bread Pudding' for the Saturday evening meal, sugar and other painfully scarce ingredients being hoarded through the week for an extra-special ceremonial bread pudding. Diet and gastric disorders were always a major worry; there can be no doubt they were lucky not to have suffered worse from disease. 'I was taken ill myself at this time,' commented Lord Fraser, 'and moved into another room with one of my young sailors who had chest trouble. My Gunner, Mr Norman, who had always looked after me, managed to get the doctor to provide a bottle of brandy, and each day brought me lunch with a little brandy in it.'[20] The biggest scare came at the beginning of October, when three cases of typhoid occurred. But it was all too easy to administer the 'limited diet' prescribed by the Tartar doctor (also a prisoner) and the men duly recovered.

A permanent question-mark hung over the prospects of release. On 29 September, when the party had been prisoners for exactly five months, Fraser had to tell his men that he had just heard that all negotiations with the Georgians had fallen through and that there seemed little or no hope of an early release. 'This caused a great depression for a short time as we had been expecting good news and it was a difficult matter breaking it to my party. However, a little later I was delighted to hear a sailor start a mandoline and then a song. Nothing could break their spirit.'[21]

October dragged by, with the oncoming Russian winter staring the prisoners in the face as they shivered through increasingly bitter nights. And then, unbelievably:[22]

> On the 4th November at 2000 a Commissar came and said 'Pack up, the train leaves in two hours' time.' We hardly believed him but prepared to leave and an hour later he returned and said 'The train leaves tomorrow at 1530.' Eventually we got away under guard to the station and left Baku at 1600 on the 5th November. Two coaches were provided for us with no windows and as it was snowing the journey was most unpleasant.

True to form, the journey out of Azerbaidjan was as frustrating as the journey in had been back in April. There were repeated hold-ups due to vanishing guards, officious frontier authorities and the inevitable need for telegraphed confirmation of the exit permit. They finally crossed into Georgia at 17.00 hrs on 7 November and were taken down to the coast on a special train sent up from Batum,

74

where the battleship HMS *Centurion* was waiting to take them home.

The author could not resist asking Lord Fraser how he had felt when he set foot on a naval vessel again. Fifty-eight years had passed since the event, but the question still produced a slight frown of disapproval. 'Unfortunately,' he said, 'some of our civilians had too much to drink on the way down. That was most embarrassing, actually, because the poor old *Centurion* had prepared a big lunch for us on board; and we didn't know anything about that, so we had lunch on the way down. And I had to say "I'm awfully sorry but I don't think we can eat just at the moment", because of these few chaps – two or three civilians – who were too tight to appear. But I didn't come all the way home in the *Centurion*: I left the ship at Constantinople and came home on the Orient Express with Major Connal Rowan!'[23]

For his own men Fraser had nothing but praise, though he admitted, in the 'Recommendations' section of his report, that 'Where all displayed such spirit, set such a fine example to all Foreign subjects and never lost heart it is difficult to make any special mention.' Not that this kept him from mentioning Commissioned Gunner Norman, Leading Seaman Piggott, ERA Grundy, Leading Seaman Aspell, Leading Seaman Vidler, Leading Signalman Hutchins, and Petty Officer Morgan. 'When Officers and Men were living together in one cell, nothing could have been more happy than the relations existing between them,' he wrote.[24]

> Throughout the whole period of imprisonment, Officers and Men were always united in their common detestation of Bolshevik principle, contempt for their methods, indignation at their tyranny over all classes of their subjects, and sometimes pity for their ignorance.
> The men I think I may say never lost their respect for their officers, the officers never lost their admiration for their men, who by their cheerful spirit and bearing and their resource maintained the morale of the party.

Fraser might have added what he certainly felt: that it takes real adversity to bring out the best in any family.

Part Two
The making of a Sea Lord
[1920–1939]

· 9 ·

Fleet Gunnery Officer
[1921–9]

After the Great War, the grim reality of returning to the 'land fit for heroes' plunged hundreds of thousands of British servicemen into dismay, unemployment and near-starvation. Two years after the Armistice, when Fraser came home in the bleak winter of 1920, he was at least spared from these extremities but his future was far from secure. The coming of peace, the cancellation of warships under construction, demobilisation and scrapping soon reduced the Royal Navy to a shadow of its wartime greatness. The very ship which collected Fraser from Batum, the Dreadnought *Centurion*, was not seven years old – yet the voyage to the Black Sea to recover the Baku prisoners marked the end of her last commission. Out of thirty-four battleships and twelve battle-cruisers completed between 1909 and 1918, only ten battleships and two battle-cruisers built in that decade would still be in service at the outbreak of the Second World War. Certainly in 1920–1, with unrelenting demands for Service reductions filling the air and the notorious 'Geddes Axe' already sharpening, there was no promise of rewarding peacetime careers for Naval gunnery officers.

For Fraser, worries about the peacetime Navy and his role in it were only briefly set aside for a visit to the Palace to meet King George V. 'He asked me if I'd brought any stamps back with me; I said I was sorry, but I hadn't had the opportunity!'[1] The officers and men whom he had led and inspired in captivity clubbed together and presented him with a sword inscribed 'From the Enzeli Expedition' (which he finally presented to the Royal Naval Museum, Portsmouth, in 1980). This was a pleasant token of recognition for Fraser's services, but it did not compensate for more immediate problems. The happiness of his reunion with his mother was balanced by a pressing shortage of money, for Mrs Fraser's efforts to keep up Downham Grange had exhausted the modest family bank balance, and during Fraser's imprisonment at Baku she had been obliged to draw on her son's pay. As Fraser had been planning to use his accumulated pay as a reserve when he came home, this discovery came as a considerable shock.

For the next twenty-five years Fraser was obliged to monitor his mother's financial affairs and the first five years, on his Commander's pay, put the biggest strain on him. Fraser adored his mother and it pained him deeply to have constantly to admonish her on money matters. 'Don't think, little mum,' he wrote with affectionate concern in June 1922, 'that I grudge you the money & as to your success the position we are both in now speaks for itself. After all nearly all that you have spent has been on us. The only thing I feel is that you don't sufficiently disclose your plans or what the position is. . . . If one did it would be so much easier for us all.' And he added 'You will always be loved and admired not only by us but by those who know us all.'[2] This burden on his private life and the constant need to economise could easily have turned Fraser into an embittered and intolerant Spartan, but it did nothing of the kind. All it did was to confirm in him a lasting distaste for extravagance and excess, without in the least diminishing his natural generosity and understanding of the problems of others.

At least, during the demanding years of the early 1920s, he had work he understood and loved. HMS *Excellent* claimed his services again, this time as Commander (G) on the Senior Staff, 'Number Three' in the Whale Island hierarchy. In this post Fraser was the prime mover of daily routine at 'Whaley'. Commander R. Chandler, OBE, in 1921 a young Able Seaman going through the course for Seaman Gunner, remembered Fraser vividly half a century later. 'He was "God" as far as we young chaps were concerned. The appearance of his stocky figure on the parade ground meant that Battalion Drill might begin!'[3]

Chandler passed his Seaman Gunner's course and went on to reach commissioned rank under the controversial 'Mates Scheme' which Churchill and Battenberg had introduced back in 1912. During his time at Whale Island, Chandler qualified as a Staff Office Writer. 'So I found myself typing out letters, reports, etc, etc, for Commander Fraser and his Staff Officers.' Chandler remembered Fraser as 'a wonderful person to work for. Only the best would do. Every letter, etc. had to be perfect & no mistakes of typing or spelling were countenanced. I was nineteen and Commander Fraser was my ideal as a naval officer and a Commander (G) and always has been.'[4]

Fraser's postwar service at HMS *Excellent* (1921–2) was his last as a member of the Staff which, as ever, contained many talented officers destined to rise to high command. Foremost among these was Lt-Commander A. J. Power, like Fraser a future Admiral of the Fleet, who would command the East Indies Fleet at the end of the Second World War. Then there was Lieutenant (G) E. J. P. Brind, future Commander of the 4th Cruiser Squadron under Fraser in the British Pacific Fleet; Lieutenant (G) G. T. Philip, DSC, later Captain of the aircraft-carrier HMS *Furious* under Fraser in the Home Fleet; and Lieutenant (G) M. M. Denny, Captain of HMS *Victorious* under Fraser in the Home and British Pacific Fleets. This early association shows the immense value of *Excellent* as a focus for what might be called the 'Nelson's Band of Brothers' factor: a common training-ground for officers who in future years would serve together with the additional bond of *Excellent*'s unique 'old school tradition'.

Fraser's last 'term of office' at *Excellent* ended in 1922, but this time he did not get another seagoing appointment. Instead he was recalled to London and given a highly important Admiralty appointment: working on the team producing the new 'fire control table' for the Fleet.

The table took naval gunnery another long step forward, helping convert the warship from a vessel full of gunners to an automated *weapon system* under centralised control. It was a bank of instruments for sifting gunnery data and passing information on range and deflection to the guns. Like the human brain the table featured a left-hand side and a right-hand side working in harness, calculating the magic match of 'range' and 'line' which produced hits. Asked for his own summing-up of what the table did, Lord Fraser's reply was swift and simple: 'The right-hand side averaged out the range, the left-hand side averaged out the deflection.'[5]

Fraser's role in the table's development was twofold. First, his skills and experience as a gunnery officer were needed to see that the table accurately performed all the tasks required of it. Second, he had to see that the finished product could be installed in a battleship or cruiser with the minimum of disruption to the ship's layout, and with the minimum demands on the ship's manpower. These requirements could only be reconciled by constantly asking the question 'How will this work in practice?' And Fraser's adamantine practical sense was a tremendous asset to the design team.

The 'nuts and bolts' of the construction work was handled by Elliott Bros, whose experts were advised by Fraser and his colleagues (Commanders A. S. May and G. C. C. Crookshank, and Lt-Commander J. S. Dove) under Admiralty auspices. Liaison with Elliott's was good throughout, and it was one of their people who solved one of the most baffling problems encountered along the way. This concerned the choice of power to get the mechanism moving at the right speed, electric motors proving too slow. 'Suddenly Elliott's Under-Manager got the idea of using compressed air instead,' recalled Fraser. 'He said, "That's the system!" and we tried it, and it worked.'[6]

But that solved only one of a myriad problems. The perfection of the table took up two years of Fraser's life which he found strenuous but rewarding. He and his fellow officers were attached to that sonorous Admiralty body, the 'Fire-Control Section of the Department of The Director of Naval Ordnance'; but the wide-ranging technical demands of the job required Fraser to be nominally attached to the Department of the Director of Mines and Torpedoes as well. He found that this gave him freedom from being a cog in a single departmental machine, and relished the autonomy it gave him in practice: 'I used to play off one department against the other,' he recalled jokingly. Fraser also found his work surroundings, just off Whitehall, congenial. 'I was in what was supposed to have been "Nell Gwynn's Bedroom": 80 Pall Mall.'[7]

This first spell at the Admiralty – 1922–4 – opened the second phase of Fraser's rise from *Britannia* cadet to Admiral of the Fleet. Though he had first earned Their Lordships' approbation for his work on the director firing handbook back in 1913–14, it cannot be said that he had (to use a distasteful but useful phase) 'had a good war'. Fraser had missed all the major naval actions of the war; his appointment to *Resolution* had come about by a German shell not falling short at Jutland, while he was at Whale Island; his four years in *Resolution* had ended in frustration, unhappiness and the Baku fiasco. But after working on the fire control table his road ran steadily to the top, with no more detours. When Fraser had gone to the Admiralty in 1922 it had taken him fifteen years to rise from Sub-Lieutenant to Commander. But over the next fifteen years the Admiralty treated him as a senior officer selected, as the Service puts it, 'to go on', and go on he did: from Commander to Rear-Admiral, Third Sea Lord and Controller of the Navy.

From the fire control table and 'Nell Gwynn's Bedroom', Fraser went back to sea closer to the centre of a fleet command than he had ever been: as Fleet Gunnery Officer (FGO) in the Mediterranean Fleet. Between 1919 and 1939, with no opposition in home waters, the British Mediterranean Fleet remained the Navy's most prestigious as well as the biggest command. Significantly, with only one exception (the East Indies Squadron as Captain of HMS *Effingham*) virtually the whole of Fraser's sea time between 1919 and 1939 was spent with the Mediterranean Fleet. One of the minor ironies of his career is that though he successively commanded the Home, Eastern and British Pacific Fleets, the Mediterranean command in which he had served so often eluded him.

The post of Fleet Gunnery Officer was therefore Fraser's initial step up the final ladder of promotion, giving him an important share in the immense burden of work shouldered by a Commander-in-Chief's staff. The staff made the Commander-in-Chief's ideas work, and the FGO was the Commander-in-Chief's viceroy and trouble-shooter on all matters connected with Fleet gunnery. He was the focal 'communications number' between the Commander-in-Chief in his flagship and the individual gunnery officers of the Fleet. A good FGO was ubiquitous without being a pest, flexible and inventive in the face of unforeseen problems. He attended the Commander-in-Chief's staff meetings and was responsible for working out the fire programmes for the battle squadrons, cruiser squadrons and destroyer flotillas of the Fleet. Individual units would usually get the praise for particularly good shooting, but the FGO would invariably get the blame if the Fleet's gunnery was consistently poor.

In 1925–6 Fraser was FGO to two successive Mediterranean Fleet Commanders, the first being Admiral Sir Osmond Brock and the second Admiral Sir Roger Keyes, of Gallipoli, Dover Patrol and Zeebrugge fame. Captain Dudley Pound (afterwards Admiral of the Fleet and First Sea Lord from 1939 to 1943) was Chief of Staff to Admiral Keyes; and this was the first of four key associations between Fraser and Pound. Fraser was FGO when Pound was Chief of Staff (1925–6); he was Assistant Director of the Admiralty's Tactical Section when Pound was Assistant Chief of Naval Staff (1926–9) he was Chief of Staff to Pound when Pound was Commander-in-Chief, Mediterranean (1938–9); and he was Third Sea Lord when Pound was First Sea Lord. In the annals of the modern Navy the only precedents for this remarkable working relationship were the close associations between Jellicoe and Lord Fisher before 1914, and between Chatfield and Beatty from 1914 to 1927. As will be seen (p.176), in Fraser's case the association with Sir Dudley Pound nearly had a unique sequel in 1943, when Pound resigned and Churchill immediately chose Fraser as Pound's ideal successor as First Sea Lord.

In 1925, however, Fraser's recent work on the fire control table meant that the Mediterranean Fleet had a rather special FGO, and this was formally confirmed by Admiralty signal on 30 January 1925:[8]

Original to Commander-in-Chief, Mediterranean
Duplicate to Vice-Admiral, 2nd in Command, Mediterranean
Copies to Commanding Officer, H.M.S. "QUEEN ELIZABETH"
– do – H.M.S. "EMPEROR OF INDIA"
G.02137/25   30th January
Confidential
New Design of fire control table
   I am to acquaint you that Their Lordships have had under consideration the report of the trials of a new heavy ship design of fire control table.
2. Based on the recommendations of the Grand Fleet Fire Control Table Committee and built to the requirements of the Admiralty Fire Control Table Committee, the table has been manufactured by Messrs. Elliott Bros., after five years of steady progress.
3. In addition to the good work accomplished by Messrs. Elliott Bros., Their Lordships consider that the following officers largely contributed to the success so far attained, viz:
Commander A. S. May, M.V.O., O.B.E. – H.M.S. "WOOLWICH"
       "   B.A. Fraser, O.B.E. – H.M.S. "QUEEN ELIZABETH"
       "   G. C. C. Crookshank – ADMIRALTY
Lieut-Commdr. J. S. Dove, O.B.E. – H.M.S. "EMPEROR OF INDIA"
4. Their Lordships therefore request that you will convey to Commander Fraser and Lieut-Commdr Dove an expression of Their appreciation of the zeal displayed by them in the production of the table during the period they were serving at the Admiralty in the Fire Control Section of the Department of the Director of Naval Ordnance.
BY COMMAND OF THEIR LORDSHIPS

Looking back on his time as FGO, Fraser was particularly satisfied with two innovations made at his suggestion – simple and straight-forward in themselves, but effective in lightening the burden of staff work connected with the everyday running of the Fleet. He persuaded the Commander-in-Chief to allow the Fleet to return to harbour by squadrons, which took a considerable amount of strain off Fleet Gunnery services. And he suggested, also successfully, that routine administrative signals were the proper work of Staff officers and should no longer take up so much of the Commander-in-Chief's time. When Keyes replaced Brock later in 1925, Fraser remained on the Staff as a proven and hard-working FGO. He moved to the new flagship, *Queen Elizabeth*'s sister-ship HMS *Warspite*, and over the next year worked closely with Pound, Chief of Staff to Keyes.

Another notable member of the Fleet Staff was the Senior Operations Officer or SO(O): T.S.V. ('Tom') Phillips, later Vice-Chief of the Naval Staff when Fraser was Third Sea Lord, who went down with HMS *Repulse* and *Prince of Wales* off the Malayan coast in December 1941.

It was during this period, on the occasion of a Fleet gunnery shoot, that Fraser took his duties to a pitch not usually contemplated by even the most intrepid gunnery officers. He had himself landed on the target ship while the whole Fleet let fly at him. On being pressed for details by the author, Lord Fraser demonstrated his natural tendency to under-statement. The escapade was, he pointed out, very much off the record. 'I had a word with the Commander of a destroyer whom I knew quite well, and he took me across.' The target ship was none other than *Centurion*, the ship in which Fraser had been collected with his fellow-captives after their release from Baku in November 1920, On being left aboard, Fraser continued,[9]

> 'I must admit I felt a bit lonely. The battle fleet fired first, then a cruiser squadron, then a destroyer flotilla. I'd taken refuge in the conning tower. The battleships were all right – they fired very large shell, of course – and so were the cruisers, but I was worried that some of the destroyers' shells might come in. So before they fired I left the conning tower and finished up sheltering behind one of the turrets.'

Though he was taken off after the shoot none the worse for the ordeal, the incident remains a harrowing reminder of the lengths to which Fraser was prepared to go in 'seeing for himself'! It was a piece of nerve very much in the spirit of Keyes himself, a fire-eating admiral if ever there was one. Fraser remembered one encounter with Keyes on a calmer occasion, at the time of the Fleet musketry competition at Malta. 'Keyes came over, and I'd done him a little draft speech. I'd thought he'd probably tear it up, or something, but he was very grateful.'[10]

Fraser's working relationship with Pound continued when both officers returned to the Admiralty in 1926. By this time Fraser had been promoted Captain (30 June 1926). His first 'command' ashore was as Assistant Director of the Tactical Division at the Admiralty, with Pound becoming Assistant Chief of the Naval Staff.

Fraser's three-year sojourn with the Tactical Division (1926–9) came at a time when naval tactics were very much in the melting-pot, one of the biggest imponderables being the future role of the battleship. With the coming of peace in 1918 it was popularly accepted that the battleship was the most costly and destructive military status-symbol and that rival battle fleets must never be built again. The result was the first (and in many ways most successful) arms limitation treaty of modern history: the Washington Treaty of February 1922. This imposed a ten-year 'holiday' from battleship construction by the United States, Britain, Japan and France, and decreed severe tonnage and weapon restrictions for all new battleships, aircraft-carriers and cruisers built thereafter.

After the Washington Treaty it was virtually impossible to imagine a future fleet action in which more than about half a dozen battleships a side would be engaged. (As it turned out, the last battleship-versus-battleship engagement, Leyte Gulf in October 1944, was fought between six American battleships and two Japanese). The Washington Treaty signified Britain's acceptance of naval parity, rather than absolute supremacy at sea. It therefore demanded some drastic modifications in the Royal Navy's tactical planning, which since 1914 had reached its zenith (or, as far as simplicity was concerned, its nadir) in the intricate mass of Grand Fleet Battle Orders. With everything scaled down by the treaty, the 'battle fleet' of the 1920s, 1930s and the Second World War was a fraction the size of Jellicoe's Grand Fleet at Jutland.

It took time for the Royal Navy to adjust to this, and after 1918 the Service seemed to have plenty of time. Before 1914 the new Dreadnought Navy had been rushed into being, impelled by Fisher's obsession with Germany's growing naval might. But after 1918 there was no such urgency, no stampede to perfect the necessary tactical switch from giant *fleets* to small, balanced battle *groups*. This was approached leisurely, almost casually, the urgency only returning in abundance in the late 1930s. Battle groups rather than battle fleets won Cape Matapan, the *Bismarck* action and North Cape; and those momentous victories owed nothing to the leaden memory of Grand Fleet Battle Orders.

In the 1920s, however, the Royal Navy continued to draw heavily on the recent past, and Fleet exercises remained elaborate and ponderous to a considerable degree. This formality was of great importance in one respect: the stress placed on the proper role of each warship type. The cruiser's role was to scout for the enemy, feel out his strength, then either shadow him or lure him to destruction. The destroyer's role was to launch torpedo attacks, the battleship's role to carry the weight of the decisive gun action. At the Admiralty in 1926-9, Fraser began to apply his recent experience as FGO in the Mediterranean to the tactical problems of getting every element in the battle group into action at the right time, and in the most effective role. Long before *Scharnhorst* even joined the reviving German Navy in the late 1930s, the seeds of her destruction were already sprouting in Fraser's mind.

. 10 .

Captain of the *Effingham*
[1929–32]

Fraser's first seagoing appointment as Captain married him to the cruiser HMS *Effingham* for three years: 1929–32. It was an unusually testing first command; *Effingham* was flagship of the East Indies Squadron, based on Trincomalee in Ceylon (now Sri Lanka), and Fraser was doubling as Chief of Staff to the commanding admiral as well as acting as Captain of his own ship. From his time as Commander in *Resolution* and as FGO in the Mediterranean, Fraser had learned a good deal about how a captain should run his ship, and how a fleet chief of staff should run his staff. This knowledge served him well during his time in *Effingham*. Fraser served briefly under Admirals Sir Bertram Thesiger (1929) and Sir Dunbar-Nasmith (1932), but his longest association was with Vice-Admiral (later Admiral) Sir Eric Fullerton (1929–32).

Fraser had to travel out to Ceylon to join the East Indies Squadron – HMS *Effingham*, *Enterprise* and *Emerald* – at Trincomalee on 14 October 1929. Taking command of *Effingham* was a proud moment, though not unmixed with a slight apprehension. Lord Fraser readily admitted to the author that the prospect of taking his new ship smoothly out of harbour for the first time cost him some sleep the night before:[1]

'When I took over I spent half the night wondering whether I should take the ship out myself or leave it to my Navigator. In the end I decided to do it myself. I well remember weighing anchor – the first time I'd ever commanded a ship and a difficult harbour, lots of shipping. "Slow Astern Both", then "Half Speed", "Full Speed", and right down the line of merchant ships, then coming back again and so out of the harbour. At the end of it I asked my Navigator "Do you think that was all right?" and he drew breath and said "Well, sir I

87

don't honestly know whether you were commanding a destroyer before, or a battleship!" I didn't tell him that I'd never commanded *anything* before!'

Fraser's skill at handling ships was in fact one of his most impressive talents and he was justly proud of it. Many were the occasions over the next three years when his letters home mentioned some tricky piece of mooring, in which he had saved the day by personal intervention. He was particularly pleased when he had managed to insinuate *Effingham* into some unpromising anchorage where a big ship like a cruiser did not normally venture. Certainly the many and varied ports of call and coastal waters visited by the East Indies Squadron gave Fraser full scope for the exercise of this particular skill: coral atolls and reefs, East African estuaries bedevilled by tricky sandbars and anti-social tidal behaviour, and swarming international ports such as Bombay and Calcutta.

The vast East Indies Station was centred on Ceylon, reaching east past the Andaman and Nicobar Islands to the coast of Burma, then north and west round the Bay of Bengal. It included the entire coastline of British India, the Arabian Sea and the Persian Gulf as far as Abadan and Basra, and also took in the Gulf of Aden and the East African coast, south from Somaliland past Mombasa and Dar-es-Salaam to Cape Delgado and Kilwa Kisiwani in southern Tanzania. Finally it included all the major archipelagos of the Indian Ocean – the Seychelles, Mauritius, the Chagos, Maldives and Laccadives.[2]

To visit all these exotic places was a constant adventure for Fraser, who was probably the most enthusiastic and observant sightseer in the East Indies Squadron. Between cruising and exercises at sea there was plenty of time to indulge his natural eagerness to go anywhere, meet anyone and see all there was to be seen. As for the gruelling social round of receptions, formal calls, parties and dances which attended the showing of the White Ensign during the late afternoon of the British Raj, Fraser took it all in his stride and relished it all. Even when making some tart observation on the arrogance and insularity of the British community in India he had to admit to thoroughly enjoying himself, revelling in the luxury, colour and splendour which surrounded the rulers of the Raj.

A typical example is Fraser's account of Christmas in Calcutta in 1929. By this time Admiral Fullerton had succeeded Sir Bertram Thesiger (8 December 1929) and *Effingham* was already scheduled to sail for leave in England in the New Year of 1930.[3]

We were all day going up the Hoogli River in Pilot's charge & secured almost alongside the race course and Maidan, with a gangway out to the Governor's Houseboat from which we could walk ashore.

Had Xmas Day on board & went round the messdecks which were well decorated.

On Thursday 26th lunched with the Stewards of the Calcutta Turf Club at the Grand Stand & saw the big wheel from which the Calcutta Sweep draw takes place.

Wore my top hat, etc & afterwards went to the Governor's Box for the races – Viceroy's Cup day.

The Viceroy was not present & the Governor drove up in state with all his superb bodyguard in blue & gold.

The Squadron played host on the following day, with Admiral Fullerton lunching the Maharajas of Jodhpore and Trippura, and Fraser welcoming a party of ten Indian princes for a tour of the ship followed by refreshments. That night there was a State Ball at Government House – magnificence on magnificence, with the ornate bodyguard lining the walls and every Maharaja a blazing galaxy of cloth-of-gold and diamonds. Next day the social round continued with lunch at Government House, followed by polo – the 3rd Cavalry versus Jodhpore, victory going to the cavalry.

The New Year of 1930 came in with a march-past by the Squadron's sailors and Royal Marines, and Fraser added a personal touch to the celebrations. On the stroke of midnight a searchlight stabbed out from *Effingham* and illuminated the shining marble of Lord Curzon's Victoria Memorial for half an hour, to the delight and admiration of the watching crowds. This was an early example of Fraser's flair for impressive spectacle, displaying the Navy's resources and ritual to maximum effect, that reached perfection in the famous 'Sunset' parades held under his command in the Home and British Pacific Fleets.

On the eve of the Squadron's departure from Calcutta for Rangoon (2 January 1930) Fraser's hospitality was repaid by an unexpected invitation:[4]

I and three others were invited by one of the Princes of Mysore who had come on board to dine & dance at Firpo's, the big restaurant. There were about 20 Indians, some of the girls awfully pretty & nice, & I sat next to the Maharani of Cooch Behar; she is charming though not over beautiful, danced with her several times & had champagne – the biggest bottles you have ever seen. Afterwards we all went on to her house, very large & beautifully furnished, she has a polo ground & 6 or 7 tennis courts.

We had bacon & eggs & black beer & coffee & danced to a gramophone, finally leaving about 3 a.m.

She was very sorrowful at leaving England & was quite pathetic when she said she was not asked to private affairs in Calcutta. It is curious that the Viceroy & the Governor hold the view that people should mix as much as possible but do not seem able to impress these ideas on the rest of the community.

I think some people were quite shocked when I danced with an Indian at our dance, but I said that I didn't mind – what was good enough for the Viceroy was sufficient for me! & then they shut up.

Throughout the Christmas and New Year junketings at Calcutta, Fraser had been taking the measure of his new Commander-in-Chief. Admiral Fullerton had availed himself of the privilege afforded to the Commander-in-Chief, East Indies Station: that of taking his family to sea with him. Fraser developed a high regard for Admiral Fullerton, though confessing that he did not always find the Commander-in-Chief easy to work with, but the Admiral soon won Fraser's lasting gratitude. Fraser was naturally keen to visit the places and buildings with which his father had been associated, and foremost among these on the voyage down from Calcutta to Rangoon was the Alguada Reef lighthouse. Whether by accident or design (one suspects the latter) *Effingham* had 4 hours in hand when she reached Alguada Reef on the afternoon of 5 January 1930, and the Admiral generously suggested that they should anchor off the Reef and visit the light.[5]

'About 4 officers & I & Miss Fullerton sailed ashore in the gig & the Admiral & Mrs came in the galley.

It is a great long reef & the foundations are 30 ft deep. When we came ashore the Light Ho. keeper received us & we were hoisted on to the Pier in a sort of crane.

Then we all went up the Light Ho. which is beautifully & solidly built with graceful curved sides & just before the light there is a tablet with

CAPT ALEXANDER FRASER R.E.

Architect & Engineer

I had no films left for my camera but one of my officers very kindly took a photograph of it which I hope will come out. I was also taken standing in the door of the lighthouse.

The Light Ho. keeper was naturally very impressed: an old Scotchman who said that the Skerryvore Lt Ho in Scotland was built in the same style. The old records only go back to 1868, 3 years after completion, but there is an entry in that year that portions of the reef were to be filled in with Portland cement as recommended by Colonel Fraser.

I left a statement on cloth paper stating that I had visited my father's light ho & the keeper is going to have it framed & put alongside the original tablet.

All very interesting & it was so nice having sufficient time to land. I will send the photos when I get them.

From Rangoon their course lay southward to Port Blair in the Andaman Islands, 'a pretty little place whose inhabitants are nearly all convicts'. Fraser was always ready to joke about the fact that he was a former jail-bird himself: he experienced a distinct fellow-feeling when visiting the Andamans and cast a professional eye over the jail. 'We went over the prison which is rather like Baku,' he wrote to Mrs Fraser, 'except that it was clean & tidy but much the same sort of inhabitants.'[6] Then it was on to Car Nicobar, where two big native canoes came out to meet them and take Fraser and Commander Drage ashore in an exciting race, the Commander's canoe losing.

The Car Nicobar visit brought Fraser's first stint with the East Indies Squadron to a close, for within weeks *Effingham* was heading home to Portsmouth. His last letter to his mother from Colombo, bringing her up to date with his latest wanderings, stressed the particular pleasure of having been able to inspect his father's achievements for himself. 'We shall arrive at Portsmouth any time between 0600 and 1700 on Monday 24th Feb,' he wrote. 'I have sold my car in Rangoon – £145 – & I have also a photo of Fraser Str. I was talking to man who said the town had been awfully well laid out on the block system, so I was pleased.'[7]

Two months' leave in England flew and on 30 April 1930 *Effingham* was at sea again, returning East via Gibraltar, Malta and the Suez Canal. From the moment the ship weighed anchor at Aden (15 May) she was 'back on the beat', arriving at Trincomalee on 5 June. Fraser had made the most of the voyage to work *Effingham* up to full efficiency, but one of his impromptu exercises had unexpected results. 'It took us 7 days from Aden to Colombo as we were then going 13 knots,' he wrote. 'One night we were exercising night action, burning searchlights etc & I sighted a steamer ahead so we practised a night attack on her; afterwards I found she was an Italian & was quite alarmed! so signalled apologising for the inconvenience when she was quite happy again.'[8]

When *Effingham* rejoined the East Indies Squadron at the beginning of June 1930, the British authorities in India were taking stock after a winter and spring of violent discontent. In March Gandhi had led the first of his so-called 'non-violent' campaigns of civil disobedience, only to find 'non-violence' thrown to the winds by Indian extremism and British over-reaction. With violence still crackling since Gandhi's imprisonment on 5 May, the East Indies Squadron was kept in Indian waters for nearly three weeks before Admiral Fullerton was given the green light to proceed with his intended cruise to Africa. Much of the waiting period (5–24 June) was spent at sea on exercises: gunnery shoots, torpedo practice and power trials. As Admiral Fullerton stayed ashore with his family, Fraser was left in effective command and was happily busy. 'We have been doing a lot here & it is some time since I have been able to write,' he apologised to his mother on 23 June. 'Last week we did a full-power trial at 28½ knots & I spent about ½ an hour in the Engine Room.' This was a piece of typical Fraser; as he went on to admit, 'the temperature was about 128°. The E.R. people have to be relieved about every ½ hour.' But the African cruise, he added, was finally on. 'The Viceroy seems comfortable about India although the situation in Bombay is not very good & may necessitate martial law there. Ceylon is all quiet & they take no notice of Gandhi.'[9]

They sailed for Africa on 24 June via Mauritius and the Aldabra Islands, the first African port of call being Kilwa Kisiwani, the south-western extremity of the East Indies station; then northwards up the East African coast to Mombasa (20 July–31 August). Before this cruise all Fraser had seen of Africa had been the coastal fringes of Egypt and Eritrea – the Mediterranean, Canal Zone and Red Sea coasts – when serving in *Minerva* fifteen years before, and the African jungle with its teeming wildlife was a revelation. As ever, Fraser snatched every opportunity to get as far inland and see as much of the country as he could.

One of the highlights of the cruise presented just such an opportunity: a boat trip up the Rufiji River to visit what was, from the Royal Navy's point of view, one of the essential 'sights' of the East African coast. This was the wreck of the German light cruiser SMS *Königsberg*, which had fled up the Rufiji to escape certain destruction at sea at the end of October 1914. Her precarious existence up-river had been ended by the British shallow-draught monitors HMS *Severn* and *Mersey*, which pounded *Königsberg* to a wreck on 11 July 1915. Even Fraser's skill at manoeuvering *Effingham* in restricted waters was no match for the treacherous shallows of the Rufiji and the journey up to the *Könisgberg* had to be made in boats.[10]

Yesterday we went up the Rufiji, left the ship at 0600 & got to the Koenigsberg about 1000 – about 25 in the motor boat.

She is half submerged & lies alongside mangrove swamps. After she was destroyed the Germans formed a camp on shore, to which they had to wade through mud, & we did the same yesterday – got thoroughly dirty. They must have had a poor time.

I brought back a relic of wood.

Afterwards we went on, a procession of 3 motor boats up the river to look for hippos & crocodiles.

After another hour the water was quite thick with hippo heads disappearing & reappearing. Then we saw one old chap asleep on the bank & two shots were fired to wake him up as it was no good shooting him – not being time to get him. He got up in an awful hurry & lumbered down the bank into the water.

Then there was a baboon & monkeys, vultures, cranes & maribou storks, a couple of crocodiles who however slid into the water before we got very close.

Then a long green snake about 9ft swimming along the surface of the water.

We then had to turn & being low water, navigation was intricate & we all went ashore (involuntarily). However, after laying out anchors & on a rising tide we got off & proceeded, getting back to the ship about 7pm. A most interesting day.

From Mafia Island and the Rufiji River *Effingham* steamed north to Dar-es-Salaam, Zanzibar, Tanga and Mombasa, a quartet of visits which involved some hectic entertaining by, and on behalf of, the local British and African magnates. This lasted the whole of August, and when *Effingham* finally bid *au revoir* to the East African coast on the 31st everyone was glad of the day's rest called by the Admiral at Praslin Island in the Seychelles. *Effingham* then crossed to the southernmost end of the Maldives chain: Addu Atoll, which twelve years later would be pressed into service as an emergency 'Scapa Flow' for the British Eastern Fleet when the Japanese burst momentarily into the Indian Ocean. Fraser was in at the birth of the Addu Atoll base in September 1930, an unrecognised piece of history in the making. The base developed on the island of Gan would, thirty years later, be the subject of heated debates as one of the last British foot-holds east of Suez.

After her brief visit to Addu Atoll (10–12 September) *Effingham* completed her return journey across the Indian Ocean and on the 15th arrived back at Trincomalee. The Squadron went straight into autumn exercises, and it was not until 2 October that Fraser could put pen to paper and tell his mother of the gratifying results:[11]

Dearest Mum,

We have just arrived here (Colombo) & are now in dock for 7 days to scrape the bottom, etc.

Our fortnight at Trincomalee was a busy one. First of all we had to tow the target for the other ships to fire on two occasions (I was unlucky in the draw as to which of the three ships should do it) & then had to transfer it at sea to another ship while we fired.

A difficult job as the target is 150ft long & draws 15ft so not very handy.

We did well in the firing & won the Battle Practice Cup which the C in C presented to us in state.

Then we had Squadron football contests in which we were just defeated by a penalty goal unfortunately.

Then the pulling Regatta in which we won half the races (3 ships competing) but our cutters (14 oared boats) which count the most points were bad (the boat itself not the crew) so we didn't quite win this.

Then Squadron Boxing at the Canteen which we won easily so altogether came out pretty well.

Fraser then went on to outline *Effingham*'s odyssey for the next four months, a cruise to cover the north-western sector of the East Indies Station: Aden and the Persian Gulf. One of the first objectives was Djibouti in French Somaliland, where Admiral Fullerton and the Duke of Gloucester departed to represent Britain at the coronation of Emperor Haile Selassie of Ethiopia (2 November 1930). Then it was eastward round the bleak coastline of Yemen and Oman to Khor Jarama, Sur and Muscat, through the Strait of Hormuz and into the Persian Gulf, arriving at Basra – the furthest north reached by *Effingham* during the entire commission – on 29 November. After visiting Abadan, the Sir Bu Nasir Islands and Dubai, she left the Gulf on 19 December and sailed for Karachi to spend Christmas and the New Year. The cruise ended at Colombo on 2 February 1931 after *Effingham* had called at Bombay and Trivandrum on her passage down the Indian west coast.

Spring exercises (February–March 1931) were followed by a shortened cruise east to the Andamans and the southern coast of Burma, with the intricate navigation demanded by the maze of the Mergui Archipelago. This carried Admiral Fullerton to the south-eastern corner of his command, the last to be visited. Back at Port Blair (20–25 March) Fraser marvelled at the skill of the Andaman Islanders in fishing with bow and arrow. 'The Andamese run along about 11ft out from the shore & will shoot a fish 5 or 10 yards away about 2ft under water & swimming fast. They gave me the bow & arrows,' he added ruefully, 'but I haven't yet done the same.'[12]

From Table Island, northernmost of the Andaman chain ('Daddy's lighthouse', as Mrs Fraser was proudly reminded) *Effingham* headed north-east to Moulmein and the cruise down the Burmese coast, threading the Mergui Archipelago, to Victoria Point at Burma's southernmost tip. The Moulmein visit pleased Fraser on two counts. 'Daddy landed here in 1852 as Field Engr Officer for General Steele's force. We were the longest ship to go up the river which is shallow so everyone was pleased.'[13] Victoria Point was reached on 14 April and once again Fraser had a brush with history in the making, this time in the field of world transport:[14]

> Here we saw the first Imperial Airways machine to Australia alight & had a talk to the pilots. They unfortunately crashed later in the day. They were carrying I think too heavy a load of spares, etc. Imperial Airways do not organize sufficiently at the landing grounds. They arrived at dusk & spent most of the night in overhauling (there is no ground staff) & then have to go on the next morning; not a single fellow had been on this trip before.

After a refit in dock at Colombo which lasted until the end of June 1931, the next cruise (July–October 1931) repeated the East African itinerary of the previous year, minus the Rufiji River visit. For Fraser the unquestioned highlight of this return to Africa was his safari as a guest of C.J.P. ('Snake Man') Ionides, then an officer in the King's African Rifles. Fraser had a licence to shoot lion, but found the £100 range of the white hunters' fees too expensive for him until he had the luck to meet Ionides in Dar-es-Salaam. Ionides offered to take Fraser on safari free of charge except for expenses, and Fraser jumped at the chance to bag his lion. Accompanied by about fifteen African bearers the two officers pitched camp near Arusha, and Ionides soon had a likely quarry marked down.

'He said we'd got to put out a kill, and would I shoot a zebra. I said on no account would I shoot a zebra, so *he* shot one.'[15] The next morning at dawn, 'out came a great lion, silhouetted against the sunrise – a *wonderful* looking beast. He stood broadside on, looking in our direction. I thought to myself "I don't think I ought to shoot this magnificent animal", but after all that was what I had come up for, so I thought I'd better get on.'[16] Fraser was unhappy that it took him three shots to finish the lion – 'poor thing'. But there was an unexpected finale. Fraser and Ionides were walkng back to camp through dense bush, with no room for manocuvre, when a rhino calf trotted across the path, followed hot-foot by its concerned – and gigantic – mother. The cow rhino broke cover right on top of the two men and instinctively charged them. It was kill or be killed: Fraser shot first and Ionides swiftly added the *coup de grace*.

There now remained the problem of what to do with the 'disconsolate child': the rhino calf, pathetically nuzzling its mother's dead body. The calf refused to feed when the officers took it back to camp, but fortunately a German animal collector lived nearby. He took charge of the orphan, won its confidence and induced it to feed: 'a wonderful thing to see'. Somewhat cheered, Fraser returned from his safari to make preparations for shipping the lion skin home. Half a century later it was still to be seen glaring defiance at visitors to 'Moorcroft', Lord Fraser's home at East Molesey, dominating the hall; the rhino's feet were consigned to the dining room.

The 'safari cruise' of July–September 1931 was followed as usual by exercises, then a cruise up the west coast of India before spending Christmas, as two years before, at Calcutta. It was another winter of discontent for India with Gandhi, released from prison in January 1931, back at the political storm centre. The new Viceroy, Lord Willingdon, stood firm against any concessions to Gandhi and the Congress Party, and the programme of 'civil disobedience' was resumed. Fraser vividly remembered Lord Willingdon discussing the Gandhi problem at Calcutta during *Effingham*'s Christmas-New Year visit. 'He said, "I'll probably get the sack for it, but I'm going to have to send him to prison again." '[17] Gandhi was arrested on 4 January 1932, two days after *Effingham* had sailed from Calcutta for Rangoon.

Lord Willingdon made a deep impression on Fraser, who never changed his view that Britain's Viceroys could have done much more to alleviate social bitterness in India. One episode in particular failed to measure up to Fraser's standards of leadership and its responsibilities:[18]

'The Viceroy had asked a Maharaja to have dinner with him at the Bombay Club, but the Bombay Club said they didn't allow Indians in. So the Viceroy started a British-Indian Club, the Willingdon Club, which is still going. But Lord Willingdon should have sent for the Chairman of the Bombay Club, and said "If this is your rule, I shall close up the Bombay Club!" But he didn't. I think that sort of thing's the trouble with managers today – sometimes they won't take a firm line about anything.'

Never a man to conceal his feelings on the subject, Fraser mentioned to Lady Willingdon, at the Viceroy's Ball, that he had noticed that it seemed difficult to persuade Englishmen to dance with Indian girls. 'She must have told the Viceroy,' he recalled with satisfaction, 'because he shortly came across and said "I want to steal your partner for a few dances." Fraser's partner at the time was Miss Sen, one of the three beautiful Sen sisters whose portrait was hung in the Royal Academy.

By the New Year of 1932 Admiral Fullerton had entered the last six months of his time as Commander-in-Chief. He had cruised to every corner of his sprawling command but one stretch of coastline still had to be visited: the Arakan coast of Burma, covered by a short cruise in January 1932 before *Effingham* returned to dock at Trincomalee for refit. This was Fraser's last visit to Rangoon in *Effingham* and during it he managed to get away for a short holiday on his own: up to Mandalay by train, then a trip on an Irrawaddy stern-wheeler ('like Ole Man River') down river to Prome. On the boat he met a Burmese judge, who invited Fraser to stay the night at his home in Pagan. Fraser readily accepted, only to find that native officials could be even more pompous than some of the British ADCs and 'hangers-on' whom he found so irksome. Fraser horrified the judge by suggesting that the judge's down-trodden subordinates should be invited up for a drink, and was then coached in the colourful art of betel-chewing by the judge's wife. 'There is,' Fraser wrote to his mother, 'some difficulty in getting rid of it, however we made various visits to the side of the balcony & fortunately there was no one underneath.'[19] He arrived back at Rangoon on the morning of 25 January, the Squadron sailing that evening.[20]

> We had a big exercise on the way to Trincomalee, ourselves & our oiler *Slavre* who represented a monitor trying to meet before we could be intercepted by *Enterprise* & *Emerald*. I was C in C Pink, the *Enterprise* C in C Black, whilst our C in C took Directory Staff. We managed to accomplish our mission so (I) was very pleased.
>
> Now we are full of competition football, hockey, gunnery & so are pretty full up.
>
> In the football so far we have been winning so everyone in Effingham very pleased.

The command change-over finally took place at Aden on 12 June 1932. Admiral Fullerton's departure from Colombo, attended with all formal pomp and circumstance, was rendered positively deafening by the chance arrival of two warships (one French, the other Italian), each of which turned out to be a flagship. This saddled the British with additional courtesy visits to each flagship, quite apart from a seemingly endless series of reverberating gun salutes. 'Colombo harbour rang with salutes all day,' wrote Fraser. 'We sailed at 6.30 AM, both our ships cheering the C in C & the French & Italians did likewise which was really very nice of them.' And he commented, 'Admiral Fullerton has been strict, sometimes obstinate, but very good & kind & we have all learnt a lot from him.'[21]

Sir Dunbar-Nasmith began his command with a brief cruise down the African coast as far as Dar-es-Salaam, *Effingham* already being under orders to be back at Portsmouth by 12 September. While in African waters Fraser managed to include another solo trip up-country and made a point of calling on the German animal collector to see how the baby rhino was getting on. 'I don't think it recognised me,' he admitted, 'but it was quite tame.'[22] He kept in touch with the German and was grieved, about six months later, to hear that the rhino had died.

They sailed from Trincomalee for the last time on 13 August, coming home via Aden, Suez and the Mediterranean. Fraser had proved himself to be a highly efficient commander and chief-of-staff, and brought home a happy and hard-working ship. His experiences had confirmed a love of the East which he never lost, and which was to stand him in good stead when he returned twelve years later as a commander-in-chief. For the moment, however, very different but no less demanding duty awaited him in Whitehall.

Birth of the 'KG Vs'

[1933-5]

When he brought HMS *Effingham* home from the East Indies in autumn 1932 Fraser was still a cruiser Captain; seven years later, when the Second World War broke out, he was a Rear-Admiral, Third Sea Lord and Controller of the Navy. And the process of this transformation began when, in 1933, he returned to the Admiralty as Director of Naval Ordnance (DNO), one of the most important Admiralty appointments he ever held.

This was preceded by a brief interlude giving Fraser a chance to wear his 'other hat' (that of a commander afloat) for a little longer. When *Effingham* paid off at Portsmouth Fraser was appointed to HMS *Leander*, the first of five celebrated cruisers completed for the Royal Navy between 1933 and 1935. The 'Leander' class 6-inch gun cruisers included *Ajax* and *Achilles*, destined for fame and a special page in the Navy's history for their prowess in the River Plate action against *Graf Spee* in December 1939. The 'Leanders' were a notable addition to the Navy's armament and commanding the first of the litter, if only briefly, was a small but distinct feather in Fraser's cap.

Fraser's command of *Leander* was a temporary one ('Captain Meyrick hadn't got all his sea time in', he explained) and his job was to see the new ship through the hectic final stages of completion to the running of speed trials. To a certain extent he had 'been there before' when, as Gunnery Officer, he had helped prepare *Resolution* for service with the Grand Fleet in late 1916. With *Resolution*, however, he had largely been working in the dark, unused at first to the complexities of a modern battleship and teaching himself as he went along. In 1935 he went to *Leander* with his three years' service in *Effingham* still fresh on him, very much aware of the working needs of a modern cruiser, and he found the job much easier in consequence.

From dockyard clangour and the bridge of *Leander* as she notched up her first 32 knots over the measured mile, Fraser was recalled to the Admiralty as DNO. In 1913–14 he had produced the first director firing handbook. In 1922–5 he had helped perfect the new fire control table. And as DNO – 1933–5 – it was given to Fraser to devise the armament for the Navy's last generation of battleships, the 'King George V' class, the famous 'KG Vs'.

As a worthy effort in the cause of world peace – an international restriction of armaments by mutual agreement – the Washington Treaty of 1922 was a brave and highly effective experiment. This can be judged by the immense problems deliberately created for warship designers of powers bound by the treaty's terms.

The treaty ended ten years of unprecedented rivalry in naval armaments between the leading naval powers: Britain, Germany, the United States, Japan and France. In four frantic years – 1911–14 – battleship armament had leaped up from the 12-inch gun to the 13.5-inch, 14-inch and 15-inch guns. By the time the Washington Treaty was signed Germany had been bludgeoned out of the running by her defeat and the scuttling of the High Seas Fleet; but the Japanese, beating the Americans by a short head, already had their first 16-inch gun battleships in service (*Mutsu* and *Nagato*) and Britain was preparing to follow suit with four 16-inch gun 'super battle-cruisers' of her own.

The treaty had two obvious results, one of them short-term, the other long-term. It left a lot of 16-inch gun battleships uncompleted, the powers concerned having the choice of breaking them up or converting them into aircraft-carriers. And by laying down tonnage and weapon limitations, plus a ten-year ban on the building of more heavy ships, the treaty sought to hold down the fire-power of the next generation of battleships and battle-cruisers when the time should come for these to be built. Thus for every signatory power determined to abide by the Washington Treaty – Britain proving to be the most conscientious of them all – battleship design between the world wars concentrated on achieving the best possible blend of speed, fire-power and armoured protection permitted by treaty restrictions.

One dramatic outcome of the treaty limitations could certainly not have been foreseen. The Japanese converted two of their unfinished 16-inch gun giants – *Kaga* and *Akagi* – into large aircraft-carriers, both of which helped destroy the old battleships of the US Pacific Fleet at Pearl Harbor in December 1941. The British reaction to the same problem was very different. Instead of converting their first 16-inch gun ships to aircraft-carriers, they completed them but cut the hulls down like fence-posts. The result was the 'sawn-off' pair of battleships, HMS *Nelson* and *Rodney*, completed between

1922 and 1927. They featured three 16-inch gun turrets all grouped forward of the bridge and superstructure, with the after hull reduced to an ungainly-looking stump to comply with the treaty's tonnage ceiling.

Nelson and *Rodney* also adopted a device introduced by the Italians with their 'Cavour' class battleships (laid down in 1910): the three-gun turret. Multiple turret mountings had two advantages. They enabled heavier salvoes to be fired by each turret, and they could be fitted without unduly lengthening the hull. These benefits made multiple turrets an inevitable feature of heavy-ship design after the Washington Treaty. Before the treaty the heaviest British warship, the battle-cruiser HMS *Hood* (completed 1920) had a length of 860ft, an armament of eight 15-inch guns, and a displacement of 41,200 tons. But *Nelson* and *Rodney* were only 710ft long and of 33,950 tons displacement. They carried nine 16-inch guns each and were also better armoured than *Hood*, carrying a belt of 14 inches, 16 inches on the turrets and 6¾ inches on the deck. But their awkward derivation meant that the third vital ingredient, speed, was lacking: 23 knots was the best they could make.

One of the most dramatic experiments in triple-turret economy in these years was achieved by the tiny postwar German Navy, forced as it was to operate under the even stricter limitations of the Treaty of Versailles. Forbidden any new warship type bigger than a 10,000 ton cruiser, the Germans produced a 'super-cruiser' armed with battleship-sized (11-inch) guns in two triple turrets. These were the *Panzerschiffe* or 'armoured ships', sneered at by the British Press as 'pocket-battleships'.

The first of them, *Deutschland*, was launched in 1931 while Fraser was still in Ceylon with the East Indies Squadron; the second and third (*Admiral Scheer* and *Admiral Graf Spee*) took the water during Fraser's term as DNO, in 1933 and 1935 respectively. By the time Fraser left the Admiralty in 1935 the three 'pocket-battleships' had given German designers all the experience they needed to enlarge the type, adding another triple 11-inch gun turret forward and full armour protection overall. Such was the genesis of *Scharnhorst* and *Gneisenau*, launched in October and December 1936 and beating the first of Britain's new battleships – the 'KG Vs' – into the water by more than two years. But without the vital spadework carried out by Fraser and his staff during his time as DNO, the 'KG Vs' would certainly have taken even longer to build.

At the root of the problem lay Britain's adherence to the Washington Treaty and its successor, the London Naval Treaty of 1930, which extended the building 'holiday' by another five years. The decisive limitation imposed by these treaties was the maximum displacement of 35,000 tons for battleships. This seemed a hopelessly inadequate vehicle for 16-inch guns and sufficiently powerful engines to improve on the lumbering performance of *Nelson* and *Rodney*. No combination of double or triple 16-inch gun mountings seemed compatible with 35,000 tons displacement (until the Americans, with more time at their disposal, finally came up with the answer and launched USS *Washington* and *North Carolina* in June 1940). But by selecting the much lighter 14-inch gun, and mounting it in *quadruple* rather than triple turrets, the books could be made to balance: twelve 14-inch guns instead of nine 16-inch, a comparably heavy broadside for no additional displacement. And it was thanks to Fraser as DNO that the idea of mounting 14-inch guns in quadruple turrets was accepted as a practicable solution.

This was no easy project to 'sell'; as far as the British Service was concerned, it was a doubly outlandish concept. British yards had built 14-inch gun battleships for foreign powers, but none for the Royal Navy. To many influential laymen it also seemed insane, in the age of the 16-inch gun, to propose 'stepping down' to the 14-inch. Foremost among the critics was Winston Churchill. As late as August 1936 he was writing to the First Lord, Sir Samuel Hoare, that:[1]

> Nothing would induce me to succumb to 14-inch if I were in your shoes. The Admiralty will look rather silly if they are committed to two 14-inch gun ships and both Japan and the United States go in for 16-inch a few months later. I should have thought it was quite possible to lie back and save six months in construction. It is terrible deliberately to build British battleships costing £7,000,000 apiece that are not the strongest in the world! As old Fisher used to say, 'The British Navy always travels first class.'

Churchill, of course, was forgetting that Fisher never had to bother his head about international treaty limitations when planning the Dreadnought Navy before 1914. Nor was Churchill *au fait* with the suggestion to use quadruple turrets. Writing after the Second World War, however, Churchill did admit in *The Gathering Storm* that:[2]

> In my discussions with the Admiralty about battleship design I had not appreciated the fact that they had designed and were in process of drawing out quadruple turrets for the 14-inch guns, thus achieving a total of twelve guns. Had I realised this I should have been forced to reconsider my view.

As it happened, the British were not required to break totally new ground in adopting the quadruple turret: the French Navy was first in the field. France reacted to Germany's triple-turretted 'Deutsch-lands' by building two extremely unorthodox quadruple-turreted battle-cruisers. Laid down in 1932, *Strasbourg* and *Dunkerque* owed much of their design to Britain's *Nelson* and *Rodney*. All their 13-inch main armament was concentrated before the superstructure in two quadruple turrets. Later in the 1930s the French retained this layout for their 15-inch gun battleships *Richelieu* and *Jean Bart*.

Strasbourg and *Dunkerque* therefore served as timely models for the armament of Britain's new battleships, but the real reason for the adoption of Fraser's 'four-gun, 14-inch' layout was the time factor. At a second London Conference in 1935 it was agreed that the 14-inch gun should be regarded as the limit in future battleship construction – *unless* any of the signatories to the original Washington Treaty decided otherwise, in which case the 16-inch limit would be re-adopted. This was why Churchill wrote to Hoare that it would be a good idea to 'lie back and save six months in naval construction': he wanted to see what the other naval powers really had up their sleeves.

Unfortunately (as Fraser was to discover during the planning of Britain's last battleship, HMS *Vanguard*) Churchill never appreci-ated how much had changed since the time of Fisher's first Dread-noughts, and how much more time was needed to build a modern battleship. On the other hand, by the New Year of 1936 the Admir-alty was acutely aware that if the new battleships were to be in service by 1939–40, no further time could be lost. The Admiralty therefore plumped for the 14-inch gun and Fraser's recommen-dations in order to get started without further delay.

Thus Britain alone went ahead with building 14-inch gun battle-ships, while the French, Germans and Italians adopted the 15-inch ('Richelieu', 'Bismarck' and 'Littorio' classes), the Americans adopted the 16-inch ('North Carolina' and 'South Dakota' classes) and the Japanese broke all records with the monstrous 18-inch guns of the 'Yamato' class. As far as the British were concerned, the birth of the 'KG Vs' was a salutary example of honesty failing to be the best policy when faced with ruthless international rivalry.

As the plans of the 'KG Vs' took shape, a serious change was made to Fraser's original concept. The armoured protection was increased – or, as Lord Fraser later put it more succinctly, 'Chatfield (the First Sea Lord) decided to put on more armour.'[3] The heavier tonnage of armour made the planned format of three quadruple turrets excessive and the No. 2 turret was re-designed as an ortho-dox, two-gun turret. This was a considerable saving in topweight – each quadruple turret weighed 1,500 tons, while the twin turret only weighed 825 tons – but the time taken to design the new turret and its mounting inevitably caused further delays. HMS *King George V*, the first of the class, was not laid down until 1 January 1937; she was not launched until 21 February 1939; and she was not completed until 1 October 1940, by which time Fraser had been back at the Admiralty as Controller for seventeen months. So much for Churchill's breezy advice, over four years before, 'to lie back and save six months in construction'!

The quadruple 14-inch turret was the most notable contribution to the 'KG Vs' by Fraser and his Engineering Staff, but it was by no means the only one. Thanks largely to him, the 'KG Vs' were given a generous array of anti-aircraft guns (generous, that is to say, by 1939 standards). It was Fraser who introduced the dual-purpose 5.25-inch gun as the secondary armament of the 'KG Vs', instead of the traditional 6-inch. As well as serving as a conventional low-angle gun against surface targets, the 5.25-inch gun could be fully elevated to give the ship a high-altitude 'umbrella' of AA fire from sixteen guns in eight twin turrets.

The biggest problem posed by the 5.25-inch gun was its bulky ammunition. With calibres up to 4-inch it was possible to use 'fixed' ammunition, with the charge in its case attached to the shell and the whole thing loaded like a rifle bullet; but fixed ammunition for the 5.25-inch gun proved far too heavy to handle. Fraser's reaction to the problem was typically practical. 'I said, "Surely we can ram the shell home with the cartridge case?" So we sent down to Whale Island, and they tried it out, and it worked.'[4]

Before he left the Department of Naval Ordnance in 1935, Fraser had presided over several other important innovations with lesser classes of warship. One such innovation followed naturally from his work on the 'KG Vs': the adoption of the dual-purpose 5.25-inch gun for a new class of light cruiser, the 'Dido' class. Aware of the need for constant improvement in anti-aircraft defence, Fraser was also responsible for the introduction of AA fire control in destroyers. It should be remembered that in the 1930s the question of the vulnerability of warships to air attack was still an open one. There was a school of thought – to which Churchill and Admiral Phillips belonged – which believed that warships could beat off air attacks. Even when war came this belief died hard, surviving Norway, Taranto, Crete and the *Bismarck* action. It was finally dispelled by the terrible double lesson of Pearl Harbor and the sinking of HMS *Repulse* and *Prince of Wales* in December 1941.

Fraser however, had always believed in taking out insurance. When DNO he suggested to the Controller – 'Reggie' Henderson, Fraser's old commander at Whale Island and one-time foe of director firing – that small ships should be converted into specialised 'AA ships', with batteries of high-angle guns and pom-poms. Henderson agreed; Lord Chatfield, the First Sea Lord, gave his blessing to the idea; and the AA ships came into being. They put in sterling service in the war, helping to eke out the Navy's permanently over-stretched escort forces, but they were never any substitute for the air 'umbrella' that only escort carriers could provide. Fraser was the first to admit, looking back, that the AA ships never lived up to their prewar promise, though this was due in no little measure to the extremely rudimentary level of AA gunnery when the AA ships were conceived. 'We didn't get radar fire control or the VT (proximity) fuze until late in the war,' he reminded the author.[5] Indeed, the Admiralty had no specialised AA Warfare Division until one was set up in February 1940, when Fraser was Controller.

All Fraser's other achievements as DNO, however, came second to his work on the new battleships. Out of his long career, three years make that career unique. Two of them passed when, as DNO, he brought in the guns for the last generation of British battleships. And the third year was his time as Commander-in-Chief, Home Fleet (1943–44) when, after months of exhaustive planning by Fraser, those guns won the last battleship action in the history of the Royal Navy. Fraser's earlier work on the guns of the 'KG Vs' was triumphantly vindicated on 26 December 1943. On that day starshells from the 5.25-inch guns of his flagship HMS *Duke of York* lit up the unsuspecting *Scharnhorst*, and 14-inch shells from those quadruple turrets pounded *Scharnhorst* to a wreck. Fraser remains the only British admiral ever to have introduced an entirely new weapon system, then commanded in person while it won a famous victory.

But the biggest British warship in preparation while Fraser was DNO was a type with which he had had no experience at all: the aircraft-carrier. HMS *Ark Royal*, namesake of the sea-plane carrier with which Fraser had served at Gallipoli in *Minerva*, was laid down in September 1935. The new *Ark Royal* was the first big carrier to be 'custom-built' for the Royal Navy instead of being converted from another type. Displacing 22,000 tons, she was over twice the size of HMS *Hermes* (launched in 1919), the first ship built 'from the keel up' as an aircraft-carrier.

When *Ark Royal* commissioned in late 1938 her first Captain was A. J. Power, Fraser's former subordinate on the Senior Staff at *Excellent* in 1921. Power, however, had not beaten Fraser in reaching carrier command. When Fraser finally left the Department of Naval Ordnance in 1935 he had returned to sea – and the command of an aircraft-carrier. This he owed to the goodwill of the First Sea Lord himself, Admiral of the Fleet Lord Chatfield, who was deeply impressed with Fraser's work as DNO. 'Chatfield told me that I ought to have some air experience,' recalled Fraser simply.[6] For the man who would, within ten years, be commanding the biggest carrier fleet in Royal Navy history, this was a particularly timely appointment.

. 12 .

Carrier *Glorious*

[1935–7]

HMS *Glorious* was Fraser's second and last seagoing command as a Captain, and another decisive appointment during his rise to flag rank. It was a distinct mark of favour, for although the Royal Navy had six aircraft-carriers in late 1935 Fraser's experience in seagoing command was limited to his three years with the cruiser *Effingham*. As he approached the end of his tenure as DNO, he might therefore have expected to be given another cruiser, or a battleship. But by the middle 1930s it was already obvious that aircraft-carriers were going to play an important, if as yet undefined, role in any future naval war. Chatfield's sponsorship of Fraser to a carrier command therefore reflected a growing awareness in the Admiralty that the best admirals of the future were going to be those who understood aircraft-carriers and their potential.

For Fraser, going to *Glorious* demanded an even bigger mental adjustment than he had had to make when joining *Resolution* in 1916. In both cases he had to assume his new responsibilities in the giant confines of a capital ship, but in 1916 he had at least served in battleships before, if only in pre-Dreadnoughts; in 1935 he had no experience in aircraft-carriers at all. There was another important difference. *Resolution* had been a brand-new battleship, 'built from the keel up' to fulfil a specific role. *Glorious* was very different, the awkward-looking product of years of experimental conversion from a warship which had been laid down as a totally different type.

Glorious, *Furious* and *Courageous* had been completed as 'light battle-cruisers', the ultimate expression of Fisher's mistaken belief that 'Speed is Armour'. When completed it was impossible to find any kind of role for them. *Furious* was not even completed according to her original design; with her forward turret removed, she made a useful vehicle for testing the launching of aircraft from a ship's deck at sea (see Ch. 7, p.54). Further tests with a second, landing-on deck built aft confirmed that aircraft-carrying warships should have an unimpeded flight-deck from stem to stern.

By the time of the Armistice the first true aircraft-carrier was in service – HMS *Argus*, a converted liner – and work had begun on two more. These were the *Eagle*, converted from a battleship hull originally laid down for the Chilean Navy; and *Hermes*, the first aircraft-carrier to be designed as such. Neither of the latter two carriers had been completed before the Washington Treaty of 1922, by which time Britain had built up an impressive lead in the development and construction of aircraft-carriers.

By 'freezing' battleship construction for ten years, the treaty encouraged the international building of aircraft-carriers. As work went ahead on the Japanese *Kaga* and *Akagi* and the American *Saratoga* and *Lexington* (all four converted from the generation of capital ships banned by the treaty) it seemed that Britain would be left very much on the wrong foot. As the biggest British warship hulls were being completed as the 'sawn-off' battleships *Nelson* and *Rodney*, it was decided to convert the sizable hulls of the three light battle-cruisers into aircraft-carriers instead of scrapping them. With *Eagle* this gave the Royal Navy four 22,500-ton aircraft-carriers by January 1930 (when *Glorious* completed her reconstruction) plus *Argus* and *Hermes*. Apart from other considerations the conversion of *Glorious* and *Courageous* enabled eight 15-inch guns to be put into store, guns which subsequently formed the main armament of Britain's last battleship, HMS *Vanguard*.

If there was a failure to plan ahead, this lay in the inability to imagine, in 1924, the speed at which military aircraft would continue to develop over the next fifteen years, growing ever bigger, heavier and faster. As a result, thirty-six was the maximum number of aircraft which *Glorious* proved able to handle, instead of the fifty-two which had been optimistically planned for her when her conversion began in February 1924; and the same applied to *Courageous* and *Furious*. This tendency to operate far smaller air groups than in the Japanese or American fleets remained a British characteristic – and it had definite advantages. The British learned to handle less aircraft in greater safety and finally, with the 'Illustrious' class carriers, to give the aircraft hangars armoured protection.

After her Service rebirth as a carrier in 1930, *Glorious* certainly resembled the hybrid that she was. Her after two-thirds were all flight-deck and 'island' superstructure; from beneath the forward end of the flight-deck protruded the unmistakable bow of a battle-cruiser. Under the main flight-deck lay her two hangars, one above the other. The doors of the upper hangar opened on to a short flying-off deck with a pronounced slope down towards the bows.

She had a very good AA battery of sixteen 4.7-inch guns, a complement of 1,216, and her 4-shaft turbines could deliver a speed of 30½ knots. When Fraser went to the *Glorious* in 1935 the ship had just completed a refit which considerably eased the pilots' lot. This was the fitting of four arrester-wires, all linked to hydraulic cylinders, across the flight-deck. An aircraft coming in to land would lower a hook fitted beneath the tail; as the pilot touched down the hook would catch one of the wires whose 'give', smoothly controlled by the hydraulic cylinders, brought the aircraft to a rapid halt.

Old-style pilots complained that this invaluable aid lowered the standard of flying; all that mattered to Fraser was the increased efficiency in launching and recovering aircraft, the carrier's ultimate function. To this end all artificial aids and improvements were welcome, for few naval weapons were more dependent on the vagaries of wind and weather than the aircraft-carrier. Irrespective of the course steered, a battleship or cruiser could use its rotating turrets to keep the maximum number of guns bearing on the target; but a good stiff wind is essential for short take-off and landing runs, and an aircraft-carrier could only fulfil its role as a seagoing airstrip when steaming at full speed directly into the wind.

The flight-deck of *Glorious* was only 590ft long and too strong a wind could easily prevent naval aircraft from operating, especially in the biplane era. The dangerous rise and fall of the flight-deck as the carrier pitched to the waves could, in a gale, exceed 50ft at bow and stern, with extra-high wave crests breaking clean over the bow and flight-deck and making the latter as slippery as a skating-rink. Another gale hazard was the danger of aircraft being blown clean off the flight-deck. This meant that aircraft could not be left ranged on deck, which made launching and recovery a lengthy as well as an extremely hazardous process.

All this made excellent seamanship and an acute weather sense — for there was no point in launching aircraft if worsening weather conditions would make it impossible for them to return — essential qualities for carrier captains. These qualities Fraser possessed in abundance. 'He was,' writes Frank Hague, a young Leading Telegraphist in *Glorious*, 'the finest seaman I ever served with. His ship-handling was a joy to behold. Everyone who served on that ship with him must remember the incredible manner in which he manoeuvered *Glorious* into Malta's Grand Harbour, through a very narrow entrance in a slab-sided ship with a howling gale blowing, like one parking a bubble car. No buoy jumper ever received a wet shirt when Fraser was in command.'[1] But *Glorious* was not merely efficient and well-handled under Fraser: she was, Hague added, 'an extremely happy ship. Everyone in the ship would have been happy to give his right arm for Captain Fraser had he asked. Apart from being a *real* gentleman who never ever raised his voice regardless of the situation, his concern was always for the ship's company – liberty men were always piped to clean whilst the duty watch moored ship.'[2]

Running a happy ship was a particular achievement for a carrier captain in those years, when British naval aviation was still ruled by a temporary compromise between the Admiralty and the Air Ministry. Down to 1937 the Royal Air Force provided the Royal Naval Air Service (or 'Fleet Air Arm', to use its better-known title) with its aircraft, a high percentage of pilots, and the fitters and skilled maintenance staff. Though over half the pilots were naval officers, all held RAF rank. The Admiralty provided the funds for the Fleet Air Arm, specified the type of aircraft required, provided the ships in which they were embarked and the equipment with which they were serviced. When ashore, Fleet Air Arm crews came under RAF discipline; when afloat, they were subject to Navy discipline. Here was a rich seed-bed for petty inter-service rivalries, none of which were known under Fraser in *Glorious*. This was the first demonstration of his flair for generating enthusiastic co-operation between the Services, soon to be accepted as his greatest qualification for high command.

The art, as ever, lay in making it all seem easy and natural. 'I, too, look back to *Glorious* as my happiest ship', wrote Captain John McCahon, one of Fraser's pilots, to the author. 'With Captain Fraser at the top, "Wings" Jock Halley (RAF) i/c Flying, Cmdr Stevenson "Flight Deck" and Cmdr Crane executive officer ('Not forgetting the Navigator', added Lord Fraser, 'who fixed our position just as the aircraft left') everything "went" ':[3]

> At Sunday Divisions the FAA looked a motley collection. Half the pilots were RAF and half RN, with one RM officer at least in each squadron (Nos 812, 823 and 825). The fitters, riggers, armourers and some air-gunners were RAF; observers, telegraphist air-gunners, torpedomen and many aircraft hands were RN. They were all 'flat out' for their squadrons, regardless of whether they were light blue or dark blue, and that was the spirit throughout the ship.

Under Fraser's command *Glorious* served with the Mediterranean Fleet for two years (1935–7) under two Commanders-in-Chief: first Admiral Sir William Fisher, and then, from March 1936, Admiral Sir Dudley Pound. The first months in the Mediterranean were months of tension resulting from Mussolini's invasion of Ethiopia (October 1935), a move which had grave implications for Britain's tenure of the Mediterranean/Suez Canal/Red Sea route to India. Britain endorsed the League of Nations' imposition of trade sanctions against Italy (8 November) but opposed the all-important oil sanction for fear of provoking a war with Italy. But these half-hearted measures only left Mussolini's generals free to proceed with the conquest of Ethiopia.

Had the League of Nations decided to save Ethiopia (a League member) and stop Italy by force, the British Mediterranean Fleet would have been the instrument most ready to hand. The Ethiopian crisis therefore saw the Mediterranean Fleet preparing for possible war with Italy. As far as *Glorious* was concerned, this preparation consisted mostly of exercises to perfect the dangerous art of night flying and operations. The biggest problem, of course, was landing-on, for this could only be done with the ship burning the fewest and dimmest of lights. Illuminating the flight-deck for the benefit of returning crews was out of the question: it would have made the ship a splendid target for enemy air reconnaissance, surface forces, and submarines.

The full potential of night carrier operations was not revealed until 11–12 November 1940, in the classic carrier strike which crippled or sank most of the Italian battle fleet in Taranto. This triumph was the work of the new aircraft-carrier HMS *Illustrious*, but the groundwork had been done by Fraser and *Glorious* five years before. If the Ethiopian crisis had resulted in war with Italy, it would have fallen to *Glorious* to make history with the first-ever carrier strike. Certainly Fraser's men would have been ready; 'at the time,' asserts McCahon, 'we had no idea of this possibility, but were only too keen to demonstrate our capabilities night or day.'[4]

With Ethiopia and Libya both Italian provinces, the potential Italian threat to Egypt and the Suez Canal was obvious. The Ethiopian crisis was followed by a new treaty between Britain and Egypt (August 1936) which confirmed Alexandria as the main British base in the Mediterranean for the next eight years at least. But as the seat of British sea power in the Mediterranean shifted east, the focus of international tension shifted west with the outbreak of the Spanish Civil War. For the ensuing thirty-three months of that conflict Gibraltar, rather than Alexandria, was the main British naval base for defending the interests of British nationals and shipping caught up in, or forced to run the gauntlet of, the war zone.

The Mediterranean Fleet was not, of course, constantly at sea on exercises or police duty; the Fleet was Britain's foremost medium for showing the Flag, and the ensuing social programme was heavy. For this Fraser had been well trained by his time with the East Indies

Squadron and, as then, he thoroughly enjoyed it. In the Mediterranean he again showed himself as the host with the personal touch:[5]

'Sir Dudley Pound thought that the Royal Navy ought to make some demonstration of friendship to the Alexandrians both for their hospitality and their work. As *Glorious* was alongside and we had a big hangar, he suggested that we should give a cocktail party in the *Glorious*. I agreed and put my Navigating Officer in charge of making the arrangements; he was rather a gourmet. He immediately requisitioned a lot of wood to build all the bars in the hangar; I thought it was a bit too much wood, but he said he couldn't do with less.

I thought it would get frightfully hot inside the hangar with all those people on board, so I thought I'd have a try at helping. I raised the hangar lift half way, then put up the sail outside. A pleasant breeze then blew through the hangar for all the party, and I think it was the coolest place in Alexandria. Anyway, the party was a great success and I think everybody was very grateful – both to the C-in-C, who received all the guests, and to *Glorious*.'

In May 1937, however, the Royal Navy concentrated in home waters for a very special occasion: the Spithead Naval Review for the coronation of King George VI. And as *Glorious* prepared to take her place in the rigidly drilled line of warships assembled for the review, an incident took place which says a good deal about Fraser's personal qualities as a commanding officer.

Thanks to the fore flying-off deck there was very little space for the party working the anchors, and it was necessary to post a signalman on a small platform over the ship's side. His job was to relay orders from the bridge to the officer in charge of the anchor party. As *Glorious* crept closer and closer to her designated position in the line, Fraser and the navigator were conning the ship. *Courageous* was wearing the flag of the Rear-Admiral Aircraft Carriers, and had already hoisted the signal 'PREPARE TO ANCHOR'. Unfortunately this signal was also commanding the attention of the young signalman in *Glorious*. When the signal was hauled down in *Courageous* the signalman yelled 'Let Go!', although *Glorious* was not yet in her correct position; and down went the bow anchor. By dint of quick thinking and subtle manoeuvring Fraser managed to get the other bow anchor down and moor the ship in position – but certainly not with the same amount of cable out to each anchor.

Roasted alive by the Fo'c'sle Officer, the signalman was put in the Officer of the Watch's report before receiving another tirade from the Chief Yeoman of Signals. This left the horrified boy in no doubt that he was not only the most useless idiot in the entire Signals Branch: his stupid negligence had made *Glorious* the laughing-stock of the assembled Fleet, and might well have caused a serious accident. By the time he appeared before Fraser as a defaulter, the unfortunate boy was a nervous wreck.

'Off Caps!' and the charges were read; no doubt that the boy was guilty, only about the punishment. Fraser asked if the signalman had anything to say. 'No, sir,' stammered the boy, his mouth dry. Calmly, Fraser explained the heavy responsibility resting on all signalmen and the vital importance of being able to rely on them implicitly. It was obvious that the boy was most anxious to be helpful and had misread the signal from *Courageous*, which was to anchor *when in position*. Fraser then paused to let his words sink in before adding, almost casually, 'If you have any ideas about anchoring this ship, then I think that you should discuss them with me first.' He then gave the signalman a 'Caution', the mildest sentence possible – and easily the most appropriate.[6]

A trivial incident? Not, apparently, to the men who were serving under Fraser at the time, and who found it at the top of their memories over forty years later.

As the Fleet dispersed after the Coronation Review, Fraser seized the chance to do some good work for Anglo-American naval relations. The US Navy had been represented at the Review by the highly-respected Admiral Harold Stark, USN (Chief of Naval Operations at the time of Pearl Harbor, and afterwards Commander-in-Chief US Naval Forces in Europe). Fraser was taking *Glorious* down the Channel, heading for Falmouth, when he sighted Stark's flagship ahead. Here was the cue for a piece of courtesy which not every British captain would have extended in home waters. 'I asked Admiral Stark whether I could come under his command during the night, as we were both going down Channel, and he readily agreed. So I took station astern, and following his signals for altering course, etc., during the night. When I left his command in the morning to go into Falmouth he thanked me very much, saying he appreciated the gesture.'[7]

This pleasant episode was followed at once by a demonstration of the sharp-edged competence behind the ready courtesy:[8]

'After we left Admiral Stark, Admiral Binney joined *Glorious* at Falmouth. He was put in charge of *Glorious* and a cruiser, and we went out for exercises in the Atlantic to test the capabilities of an aircraft-carrier against two other cruisers. Our aircraft managed to find the two cruisers and "attack" them almost unnoticed, which proved the capability of naval aircraft. When we got back to Malta Admiral Binney wanted to stop on board, but as I was not under his command I asked him if he would move to another ship, and he did.'

When Fraser left *Glorious* in late 1937 he had added another resounding success to his record. Though a gunnery specialist of Fisher's Dreadnought Navy, the heyday of the big gun, Fraser had adapted with ease to the Navy's most modern branch, the Fleet Air Arm. He had also helped add a vital new dimension to British naval aviation, that of night operations. Ability in every branch of the Service to which he had turned his hand already entitled him to respect and further advancement; it was the human quality that made him unforgettable. Though a professional to the core Fraser was, as Frank Hague put it simply, 'a perfect Gentleman to the lowest rating and the highest Officer'.[9]

· 13 ·

Rear-Admiral and Chief of Staff

[1938]

On 11 January 1938, one month before his fiftieth birthday, Fraser reached one of the most desirable goals in the career of any naval officer: promotion to Flag Rank, with the broad gold cuff-band and ring of a Rear-Admiral. Seniority and previous experience made Fraser equally suited to take over an Admiralty department ashore or a cruiser squadron afloat. Instead his next appointment took him straight back to the Mediterranean, as Chief of Staff to Admiral Sir Dudley Pound.

With only a three-month interruption – March-June 1939 – Fraser was to work closely with Pound during the next five years, and he was always generous in admitting how much he learned from Dudley Pound in their long working relationship. Fraser, however, respected his chief without imitating him in every detail. Pound was the supreme centraliser, working long hours and poring over details which Fraser, the supreme delegator, regarded as the proper work for staff officers who knew their jobs. His deep and loyal respect for Pound was never in doubt and he worked hard and devotedly for his chief, but there were certainly times when he found the job frustrating. Pound's love of detail and reluctance to delegate the *minutiae* of the daily round were not easy qualities for an officer of Fraser's quality to work with.

As the Captain of the Fleet tended to support Pound, Fraser was often left unsupported when he failed to agree with the Commander-in-Chief, but he never let such occasions develop into the 'friction at the top' which could make life in a Fleet flagship tense and miserable. He knew that a Commander-in-Chief must not be saddled with additional burdens from his own staff. If the C-in-C wanted something done, the Chief of Staff's job was to get it done quickly and economically – maybe improving on the original idea with suggestions of his own, but taking no umbrage if the suggestions were turned down. This was Fraser's creed during his year as Pound's Chief of Staff, and the proof of the pudding was in the eating. Within three years Fraser could look at the superb wartime achievements of the Mediterranean Fleet under the leadership of Admiral Cunningham, Pound's successor, and reflect that as Chief of Staff he had helped tune the fine instrument which Pound handed over to Cunningham in 1939.

The year 1938 saw Nazi Germany swallow Austria in the *Anschluss* (12 March) and intensify the hate campaign against Czechoslovakia which culminated in the Munich Crisis of September. In the Spanish Civil War the year also saw a virtually uninterrupted run of success for General Franco, aided by German and Italian forces. To counter Italy's ominous alignment with Germany, Britain maintained a consistently amicable attitude towards Italy as a former ally. British policy was to indicate that Britain was prepared to recognise Italy's new empire in return for an Italian guarantee to maintain the *status quo*, and no increase of Italian forces in Spain. An Anglo-Italian agreement to this effect was signed on 16 April 1938, the month after the Austrian *Anschluss*.

Italy was certainly not ready for a naval war in the Mediterranean in 1938. Two of her four existing battleships were still undergoing extensive reconstructions begun in the previous year; her first two formidable new 'Littorio' class battleships (41,000 tons and nine 15-inch guns) were still far from completion. The prospect of Italian battleship parity with the British Mediterranean Fleet therefore lay comfortably in the future. Italy had made no experiments with aircraft-carriers and none were included in her new building programme. This failure to add the roving arm of naval aviation to Italy's impressive sea and air forces would in time prove one of the biggest nails in Mussolini's coffin – but this was not apparent in 1938. Against Italy's absolute superiority in land-based aircraft, the carrier-borne strike force of the British Mediterranean Fleet, which in the event of war with Italy would have to operate from Gibraltar and Alexandria at opposite ends of the Mediterranean, was a card of untested strength. Though its aircraft would clearly be no match for the most modern Italian fighters by day, the British trump was the Fleet Air Arm's ability to operate by night – an ability which Fraser had helped develop during his time in *Glorious*.

Despite these temporary advantages for the British over the Italians in the Mediterranean, the supreme crisis of 1938 was, of course, Munich, the results of Hitler's demands on Czechoslovakia to give up the ethnic German lands on Czechoslovakia's German-Austrian border. Ignorant of Germany's military unpreparedness for war, Chamberlain and Daladier let Britain and France be bluffed into acquiescence. Chamberlain came back from his meeting with Hitler at Bad Godesberg (22–24 September) claiming that 'It is up to the Czechs now.' He was impressed by Hitler's meaningless gesture in postponing the invasion of Czechoslovakia until 1 October – meaningless, because this had been the scheduled date all along.

Bad Godesberg left Europe with a count-down of seven days to war, during which time Duff Cooper, First Lord of the Admiralty in Chamberlain's Government, urged the Prime Minister to take the vital step of mobilising the Fleet. Unwilling thus to 'provoke' Hitler, Chamberlain demurred until late on the 27th and the actual orders did not go out until the morning of the 28th. This left the Fleet with a mere four days in which to prepare for the 1 October deadline – a mortifying comparison to the ten days it had enjoyed back in August 1914, even when the flying start conferred by the 1914 Spithead Review is taken into account.

So it was that in the Mediterranean Pound and Fraser were given four days in which to prepare for a war with Germany which hopefully would not, but probably would, bring in Italy on Germany's side. Though Britain's involvement in such a war would be the result of her obligation to support France, there were no Anglo-French contingency plans in September 1938: just the vague understanding that the French Navy would look after the western Mediterranean basin. Even if the unwillingness to provoke Mussolini had not existed, the British were in no condition to take the offensive in the Mediterranean. In Egypt stores and ammunition were way below the levels needed to sustain an offensive naval strategy. All things considered, the Munich Crisis offered the Mediterranean Fleet few alternatives to the defence of Egypt, the Canal Zone and the Red Sea approaches.

Within 48 hours of British naval mobilisation, however, the crisis was dramatically dispelled by the agreement of Britain and France to Hitler's demands at Munich, after a token 'mediation' by Mussolini. The end of the war scare caused popular jubilation, though Duff Cooper resigned in disgust from the Admiralty because of Chamberlain's claim to have returned from Munich bringing 'peace with *honour*'. But there was no euphoria in the British Admiralty after Munich. There the crisis inspired a far-reaching analysis of the Navy's readiness for war – no longer if it might come, but when. The most vital data in this analysis were the 'post-mortems' from the various Fleets and squadrons on how the Munich Crisis had found them. And the report sent in by Pound from the Mediterranean owed much to Fraser's work in sifting, collating and summarising the information from the ships and shore facilities of the Fleet.

Stressing the insufficiency of ships and ammunition, the report pointed out that the Mediterrean Fleet would have had to fight with its peacetime complements, for the mobilised men could never have arrived in time. The local defences of the Mediterranean station – such as existed in September 1938 – had never approached full readiness. Strategic deficiencies were as bad as the material ones. Joint planning for the future was essential: not only with the French but between the three British Services as well, to yield a cohesive war effort on land, sea and in the air. Attempts to cut Italy's communications with North Africa would expose the Fleet to losses and damage which the limited repair facilities in the Middle East would not be able to make good.

Pound's report also estimated that another two 6-inch gun cruisers, eleven destroyers and fourteen submarines would be needed by the Mediterranean Fleet, and stressed that excessive convoy duties would dissipate the Fleet's strength. (As it happened, Fraser had already suggested that more convoy exercises should be practised instead of traditional battleship-versus-battleship exercises, but Pound had not agreed.) The report finally asked for a clear decision on Malta: to defend the island in the event of war, or abandon it. The lack of a garrison or AA defences would make the former choice impossible, although the geographical advantages of Malta made the second choice unthinkable.

Fraser's hand in all this is unmistakable: insistence on essentials, rejection of irrelevancies, demand for a clear plan and the determination to stick to it. Pound expressed his gratitude to Fraser with a note in which appreciation and brevity were perfectly combined:[1]

> Commander-in-Chief,
> Mediterranean Station
>
> COS,
> I am very grateful for the magnificent work which you and
> COF and his Staff have done during the late crisis.
> The responsibility which you and COF have assumed and the
> initiative you have all shown has resulted in our preparations
> having progressed in the shortest time possible and has left
> me free to deal with major questions.
> D.P.

But to Fraser the 'major questions' were so vital that he could not rest content with this. After Munich he sat down to distil all the sobering experience of 1938 in a memorandum to the Admiralty. And the title he chose – 'War with Germany, Italy and Japan'[2] – was a telling commentary on the year of Munich, showing the gulf between Service concern and civilian relief after that traumatic crisis.

Fraser's deductions were as simple as they were lucid, and so were the solutions he proposed. 'Powerful forces are arrayed against us,' he wrote in his brief preamble, 'and the scale of our defences was not originally designed to meet the resultant scale of attack. For the successful waging of such a war, therefore, it is all the more necessary that our plans should be perfectly definite and the forces of all three Services who would co-operate should be practised in working together. With this object in view,' he continued:

'I. Grand Strategy should be formulated so that there is a common strategical plan for all three Services, for our Ally, and for the Dominions.

II. The execution of Grand Strategy should be centered, as set forth later, so that the questions arising can be immediately investigated and the common purpose of all the forces at our disposal can be maintained.

III. The Grand Strategical Plan should be designed so that our forces are disposed in accordance with the following principles:
(a) That offensive action be directed against the enemy's weakest and most vulnerable point.
(b) That in other areas our defences are such as to ensure our security.

IV. Training should be confined strictly to the requirements of the strategical plan.

V. Vulnerable points which are difficult to reinforce after hostilities have commenced must be re-inforced well in advance.'

It is profoundly depressing to find these fundamental points of strategic national security being spelled out, as if to a school class, a year before the outbreak of the Second World War. It is even more depressing that Fraser, still a comparatively junior Flag Officer, should have felt it his duty to do so. But it is most depressing of all to remember that it would take over two and a half years of virtually uninterrupted defeat – from September 1939 to July 1942 – before such a joint war-winning strategy began painfully to emerge.

In his 1938 memorandum Fraser's first concern was the lack of close co-operation between the Navy, the Army and the Air Force. 'The tendency with the present organisation is for each Service to prepare its own plans for opposing the greatest danger with which it is confronted and for the other Services to be asked to co-operate,' he wrote. Fraser suggested a team of experienced senior officers, drawn from all three Services, 'working in concert and entirely free from routine duties' to prepare the master plan of British grand strategy. This team should work out the basic plan, appropriate dispositions and initial plan of operations; see how these stood up to the acid-test of probable enemy strategy; and submit its recommendations and proposal to the Chiefs of Staffs' Sub-Committee.

> Such a body would be responsible for co-ordinating the strategical conduct of the war under the Chief of Staff's Sub-Committee and the operations in support of that strategy would remain the responsibility of the Services.
>
> I have in mind a case like the Dardanelles campaign, the undertaking of which would have been the responsibility of this authority to decide.

When he turned to the strategy itself, Fraser again began by stating the obvious. 'It is axiomatic to say that success in war depends upon a concentration of forces and strong offensive action at the enemy's vital points, whilst in other areas retaining sufficient forces only to assure our security.' He challenged one of the most pessimistic appreciations by the Chiefs of Staff before Munich: that war with Germany and Italy might oblige Britain to abandon the Mediterranean as a feasible theatre of operations. This, he submitted, was probably the result of excessive concern with the decisive Franco-German front – a distaste for sideshows elsewhere – but it was mistaken. 'It appears probable that the arguments contained in the appreciation are based more on the question of security than on the more important factor of taking the offensive at the outset of hostilities and securing the initiative.' In other words, nobody wins wars by being more concerned with the defensive than with the offensive, and in a war with Germany, Italy and Japan the Mediterranean was the natural place for Britain to launch an early offensive.

Fraser's blueprint for grand strategy against the triple enemy was as follows:

Action against Germany
(a) With the land forces at the disposal of the Allies, the German land frontier is probably too strong to warrant an offensive at the outset.

The French land frontier must be held and is vital to our security.
(b) The German Air Forces must be contained and prevented from doing vital damage.

With the present strength of German defences it will not be economical to carry the offensive far into German territory except as a retaliatory measure for the bombing of our towns and to assist in the maintenance of the French land frontier.

(c) German sea forces must be contained and destroyed as soon as possible since the security of our sea communications is vital to us.

The early destruction of German heavy ships which have a higher speed than most of ours is of first importance and if the enemy remain in harbour must be undertaken by air during the first phase.

If this is accomplished our cruisers and light forces will be enabled to operate freely and to counter the operations of surface raiders and submarines, whilst our capital ships can be freed to re-inforce other areas.

Action against Italy.
(d) On account of their geographical positions, and of the general state of the country, Italy and her possessions form the weakest opponents and are the most suitable object for concerted attack. An initial success in this direction would have far-reaching effects politically, embracing in its sphere of influence, opinion in Turkey, Greece, Bulgaria, Roumania, Egypt, and Arabia. In the case of the last named such influence would probably spread to Iraq, Persia, and India, freeing us from many anxieties.
(e) A favourable influence in the countries mentioned above, which are important as sources of supply to both Germany and Italy, might have an effect which could prove vital.
(f) Italy is vulnerable:
    (i) In her sea communications and (except via Germany) in her sources of supply – by means of naval forces. Any additional supplies required from Germany would necessarily weaken that country.
    (ii) In her industrial centres, which are mostly in the north – by air forces.
    (iii) In her railways, on account of their overhead electrical system, which can be reached by sea and air. The destruction of particular points might sever her communications between the north and the south.
    (iv) In Libya – by land and air forces.
    (v) In Abyssinia – by blockade.
The vulnerability of Libya and Abyssinia lies in the fact that further re-inforcements can be stopped on the outbreak of war.

Action against Japan.
(g) Japan is already heavily committed in China and is also the one country against whom we might hope for some assistance from America.

(h) Hong-Kong is surrounded and has no facilities for operating air forces. Thus in present circumstances there is little hope of either holding or re-inforcing this colony.

(i) Owing to the great distances involved, there is little chance, with the forces that could be made available at the outset, of a British offensive materially affecting our interests in China, which are already seriously inconvenienced.

(j) On the other hand, provided Singapore can be held and the strength of our naval forces is sufficient to threaten Japanese activities in areas far from her bases, it will be equally difficult for her to secure material successes except in that matter of Hong-Kong.

(k) It would therefore appear that our policy against Japan would be to hold Singapore and, until the European situation has been liquidated, to provide only a sufficient threat to prevent the Japanese from extending their efforts. The supply of armaments to China should be considered.

With the situation in Europe in hand the full strength of our land forces can be thrown against Japan with every chance of success.

For an outline of Britain's future strategy drawn at the close of 1938, this was not a bad forecast of how the Allies went about winning the Second World War after the turning-point of 1942. First came the domination of North Africa and the Mediterranean, then the defeat of Italy, then the liberation of North-West Europe, the invasion, overrunning and defeat of Germany; and finally the concerted offensive against Japan.

Fraser's 1938 memorandum envisaged war with the future triple Berlin-Rome-Tokyo 'Axis' and so did the Admiralty's own war plans, approved by the Board on 30 January 1939. These provided for a war against Germany and Italy, and 'the active intervention of Japan against ourselves and France'. This was the correct view of the 'worst possible case' that could confront the British Empire after Munich, but it was not endorsed by the British Cabinet and the Foreign Office, from which the Admiralty took its orders. As advised by their economic 'experts', Chamberlain and his political colleagues chose to believe that the dictatorships' economies were so weak that all France and Britain would have to do was hold the ring and wait for their enemies to collapse. As Fraser had feared, the strategic initiative was thus weakly yielded to the enemy, and the result was an unprecedented series of defeats from the fall of Poland in 1939 to the loss of Malaya, Singapore and Burma in the spring of 1942.

In the New Year of 1939, however, Fraser was about to reap the reward for his excellent work as Chief of Staff in the Mediterranean, his capable reaction to the Munich Crisis and the lessons it had taught him. In Whitehall, chronic ill health forced an early retirement and untimely death on Admiral Sir Reginald Henderson, Controller of the Navy, who had been Commander at *Excellent* at the time of Fraser's Long Course back in 1912. To carry on Henderson's outstanding work as Controller, Fraser stood out as the most promising candidate. His earlier work as DNO had already proved his ability at planning a better, stronger Navy, and in the aftermath of Munich his talents were needed in Whitehall as never before. Once again chosen as the right man for the right job at the right time, Fraser was appointed Controller of the Navy and Third Sea Lord, assuming his new duties on 1 March 1939.

Part Three

The making of
a Commander-in-Chief
[1939–44]

· 14 ·

Third Sea Lord and Controller
[1939–40]

Fraser became Controller fourteen days before Britain was finally jolted awake from the vain dreams of peace after Munich. On 15 March 1939 Germany occupied the defenceless core of the Czech lands and proclaimed an 'independent' Slovakia. Six days later Germany annexed Memel and began the now-familiar round of hectoring demands on Hitler's intended next victim: Poland. Then, on 22 May, came the signing of a new German-Italian military alliance. This was the 'Pact of Steel', in which the two Axis countries pledged each other immediate military support in the event of either 'becoming involved in warlike complications with another Power or Powers'.

The Pact of Steel confirmed the British Admiralty's determination to plan for a war against Italy as well as Germany, with the substantial aid of the French Navy and its bases. In Whitehall French naval collaboration was never considered as more than a welcome bonus: the Admiralty's war plans did not depend entirely on the French alliance. Clearing and defending the United Kingdom's maritime lifelines was still justly regarded as the predominant task of the Royal Navy; and from Munich to the German invasion of Poland on 1 September 1939 British naval planning proceeded without excessive reliance on the French Navy. This was to prove of vital importance in the catastrophic summer of 1940.

The Admiralty's most urgent task after Munich was to reverse the numerical depletion of the Fleet which had been an inevitable feature of the interwar years, and get the new ships built as quickly as possible. This job fell to Fraser, as Third Sea Lord and Controller. The enormous extent of his responsibilities has been succinctly defined by Captain S. W. Roskill in *The War At Sea* as:[1]

the design and construction of all warships and of all their machinery, weapons and equipment. . . every aspect of ship and weapon design and production, of scientific research and development, of naval construction, of marine and electrical engineering, of wireless and radar design and production was covered by one or other department of his vast organisation.

When Fraser became Controller, work on the new generation of capital ships was rapidly going ahead. Of the 'KG V' class battle-ships, HMS *King George V* and *Prince of Wales* had just been launched (February 1939) and *Duke of York*, *Anson* and *Howe* would follow between February and April 1940. Five new aircraft-carriers, improvements on the 'Ark Royal' type with armoured flight-decks, had also been laid down (HMS *Illustrious*, *Victorious*, *Formidable*, *Indomitable* and *Implacable*). As with the 'KG Vs', none of these new carriers would be ready before the end of 1940 apart from *Illustrious*. Meanwhile the Germans had launched their first battleship, *Bismarck*, a week before the first two 'KG Vs', and her sister-ship *Tirpitz* followed on 1 April 1939. The first German carrier, *Graf Zeppelin*, had been launched in December 1938 and a second was already under construction. Thanks mostly to Luftwaffe Commander-in-Chief Göring's refusal to co-operate in building a German naval air force neither of the German carriers was com-pleted; but they still represented a considerable future threat to Britain in 1939.

Yet though (numerically at least) the Royal Navy's superiority over Germany in battleships and aircraft-carriers had been preserved, capital ships were not the biggest worry. Far more serious was the lack of escort warships to protect the merchant convoys on which Britain would depend in war. On any one day in 1939, out of a total of about 4,000 vessels registered in Britain, the average number of British merchant ships at sea – coasters as well as deep-sea dry cargo ships and tankers – was 2,500. To protect these 2,500 ships the Royal Navy had about 150 fleet destroyers (with torpedoes) and escort destroyers (AA guns and depth-charges only). If the merchant ships at sea were sailed in convoys of thirty-five ships each, this yielded the meagre allocation of only two destroyers per convoy – and that was assuming that every single destroyer could be put on convoy escort duties, which was impossible.

To help fight the escort famine, a massive destroyer-building pro-gramme was envisaged. The 1939 Naval Building Programme yielded sixteen new fleet destroyers and twenty 'Hunt' class escort destroyers, raised by subsequent programmes to seventy fleet des-troyers (including six originally begun for Brazil) and eighty-six 'Hunts'. But building more destroyers could never be more than a partial solution to the escort problem. Not only did it take at least eighteen months to build a destroyer, but not enough of them could be spared for convoy escort: more destroyers would also be needed to screen the new battleships and aircraft-carriers when *they* joined the Fleet.

It therefore fell to Fraser to introduce a stop-gap escort warship, of a type that could be built in much larger numbers than were possible with destroyers. That stop-gap took shape as the famous 'Flower' class corvettes – the slow, miserably uncomfortable and unglamorous little ships without which Britain would certainly have lost the Battle of the Atlantic. And their introduction, plus the speed with which they were turned out in shipyards around the country, was Fraser's first great achievement during his three years as Controller. The corvettes (even their name was not settled until early 1940) were an emergency, workaday measure, but they formed by far the biggest element in the naval construction programmes on which Fraser worked in 1939.

There were two of these programmes: the 1939 Building Programme which would have gone ahead even if war had been avoided that year, and the back-up 'War Emergency Programme' put into effect on the outbreak of war. The 1939 programme included the last of the new carriers (*Indefatigable*), two cruisers, a fast minelayer, sixteen flotilla-leader and fleet destroyers and twenty 'Hunt' class escort destroyers. Then came an experimental pair of 'Black Swan' escort warships, followed by the first batch of fifty-six 'Flower' class corvettes. The 1939 programme also included twenty 'Bangor' class minesweepers and twenty converted trawlers, the latter a supplementary measure intended to eke out the deep-sea escort force a little further. Fraser's War Emergency Programme added another six cruisers, twenty-two flotilla-leaders and fleet destroyers, thirty-six more 'Hunts', and a second batch of sixty corvettes. Then came twenty-four new submarines, sixteen more 'Bangor' class minesweepers and thirty-eight more trawlers. (Programme figures are for ships actually completed and accepted into service.)

This was how Fraser, from the Controller's Office, prepared to remedy the years of peacetime neglect of the escort forces – and, it must be admitted, the Admiralty's own over-confidence as far as the submarine menace was concerned. As late as 1937 the Naval Staff had issued the unguarded statement that 'the submarine would never again be able to present us with the problem we were faced with in 1917.' This temporary euphoria was the result of the perfection, after years of trial-and-error, of 'Asdic': the sonic scanner for detecting submarines under water (nowadays known by the American name 'Sonar'). Asdic was indeed a revolutionary technical breakthrough, but it still had severe practical limitations. Many of the latter would not be revealed without the experience of combat, but the Admiralty was beginning to anticipate the most obvious weakness in 1939.

A convoy could easily take up 5 square miles of sea. Assuming a minimum escort of a destroyer leader in front and single corvettes to port, starboard and astern of the convoy, the area covered by the escorts' Asdic would amount to no more than four small, semicircular patches. Thus an approaching submarine would be able to close and attack, particularly from astern, before the escorts' Asdic had picked up any warning echo at all. Hence the desperate need for any escort vessel able to carry Asdic and throw depth-charges, and the disproportionate load thrown on the stop-gap solution, the corvettes. Fraser never regarded them as anything but a partial answer and worked flat out to bring in the next, improved generation of U-boat hunters: the 'River' class frigates, the first twenty-seven of which were completed after the 1940 Building Programme.

Fraser's ready grasp of the escort warship crisis was another example of his flexible approach to unfamiliar areas of the Service. He had made his name as a 'big-gun' specialist; nearly all his sea time had been spent in battleships and cruisers; his Admiralty duties in the 1920s had been mostly connected with the advancement of gunnery, and never with anti-submarine warfare. From this professional foundation he had successfully adapted to naval aviation and carrier command. Now, as Controller, he found himself planning warships for U-boat hunting, a role in which he had no experience of his own, or, for that matter, of anyone else. It took until the end of 1940 before the most dangerous U-boat tactics could be assessed, but Fraser had made the decisions that mattered eighteen months before. Thanks to the building programmes he set in motion in the summer and autumn of 1939, the first deadly offensive of the U-boats a year later did not succeed where the *Luftwaffe* had failed.

When Fraser had become Controller in March 1939 the First Sea Lord was Admiral Sir Roger Backhouse, who had replaced Lord Chatfield in 1938. Backhouse, however, was not only a sick man but a dying one, and his illness meant that the Admiralty was deprived of effective leadership at the top until Sir Dudley Pound replaced Backhouse on 12 June 1939. This came as a distinct relief to Fraser: 'It was good to have a First Sea Lord again.'[2] He had come to understand Pound well over the past fifteen years, and the feeling was mutual.

Throughout the mounting tensions of summer 1939 Fraser's hopes for close inter-Service collaboration remained largely unfulfilled, but he was comforted by at least one lesson taught by the Munich Crisis:

the need to bring the Fleet to war readiness as early as possible. Four days after Germany and Italy signed the 'Pact of Steel' the British Admiralty sent out the orders for 15,000 officers and men to be called up to man the Reserve Fleet, which was brought forward to readiness by 15 June. (The flagship of the Reserve Fleet, reviewed at Weymouth by the King on 9 August, was Fraser's old cruiser HMS *Effingham*.) Another measure taken in June was the creation of a special section of the Admiralty's Trade Division to prepare for arming the entire Merchant Navy with AA guns, low-angle guns for fighting submarines, and machine-guns for the fishing fleet.

Thus by 22 August, when a stunned world heard that Germany and Soviet Russia had signed a Non-Aggression Pact robbing Poland of any prospect of prompt military aid, the Royal Navy's war preparations were already well advanced. On the 23rd the Admiralty received Cabinet authority to institute an additional emergency measure: the requisitioning of twenty-five fast merchant ships for conversion as 'armed merchant cruisers', and of thirty-five trawlers to be fitted with Asdic. By 1 September, when the German Army invaded Poland, the British Home Fleet had mostly been concentrated at its war station in Scapa Flow and preparations were afoot for shipping a British Expeditionary Force across the Channel to join hands with the French.

On 3 September 1939 Chamberlain sadly informed the British people that they were at war with Germany – and the Admiralty signalled to the Fleet 'WINSTON IS BACK'. Churchill, that day appointed First Lord of the Admiralty in Chamberlain's War Cabinet, wasted little time: he arrived at the Admiralty at 6pm on the 3rd. He wrote in *The Gathering Storm* that 'I spent a good part of the night of the 3rd meeting the Sea Lords and heads of the various departments, and from the morning of the 4th I laid my hands upon the naval affair. . . in spite of certain serious deficiencies, notably in cruisers and anti-submarine vessels, the challenge, as in 1914, found the Fleet equal to the immense tasks before it.'[3]

But several weeks passed before the true nature of these tasks emerged. Prewar planning had envisaged Italy going to war as Germany's ally, thus permitting an early and heartening assumption of the offensive in the Mediterranean – as Fraser had outlined in his memorandum at the end of 1938. Instead, 'non-belligerent' Italy stayed out. This reduced the Royal Navy to hunting for the German surface raiders already at sea, trying to stop more from getting out, and hoping that the heavy units of the German surface fleet would be imprudent enough to come within range of the much slower Home Fleet. The official attitude, in Germany as well as Whitehall, was to contain the war, not extend it. Bombing attacks on civilian targets were forbidden for fear of retaliation by the other side, and the German U-boat commanders were under strict orders only to attack French and British shipping in accordance with international law: surfacing, making sure of the victims' nationality, and ordering the crew to take to their lifeboats before the victim was sunk.

Yet a spectacular incident on the first night of the war suggested that Germany had already embarked on unrestricted submarine warfare. The captain of *U-30* mistook the passenger-carrying *Athenia* for an armed merchantman, and sank her without warning. One hundred and twelve lives were lost, including twenty-eight Americans. German propaganda condemned the sinking as an act of *British* sabotage, claiming that a bomb had been planted aboard *Athenia* on Churchill's orders. 'This falsehood,' growls Churchill in *The Gathering Storm*, 'received some credence in unfriendly quarters'[4] – but Churchill does not include the intriguing tailpiece to the *Athenia* incident. This took place on the night of 4 September, and Fraser was a fascinated witness.[5]

> 'While the First Lord's room at the Admiralty was being got ready for Winston he asked me, as Third Sea Lord, to dine with him in the small flat he rented in Victoria. I took the DNC with me.
>
> The three of us had just started dinner when the telephone rang in the next room. Winston told the butler to take a message, but in a minute or two the butler came back and said "I think you ought to come, sir."
>
> We in the dining room could hear most of what Winston was saying:
> "Yes, sir."
> "Certainly, sir."
> "Not at all, sir."
> "No, sir."
> "Quite sure, sir."
> "Of course, sir."
> – and we wondered who on earth could be on the other end, to make the great Winston kow-tow!
> He came back and said:
> "I can hardly believe that it could be possible for the President of the United States to ring me up himself in my little flat in Victoria. How did he know I was here?"

Apparently Roosevelt, seeking a cast-iron reply to the Germans' accusations of British sabotage, had wanted to know if in fact any British submarines had been anywhere near the area where *Athenia* had gone down. As Fraser recalls:[6]

'Roosevelt had said, "If you say 'no', that's good enough for me." Winston told us, "This is very important. I must go and see the Prime Minister at once. Sorry to leave you" – and was off.'

Roosevelt's telephone call was not followed by any world-shattering moves by the United States, but it was most welcome proof that he was prepared to go a long way in bending American neutrality in Britain's favour. The conversation was followed within a week by a personal letter to Churchill in which Roosevelt said:[7]

What I want you and the Prime Minister to know is that I shall at all times welcome it if you will keep me in touch personally with anything you want me to know about. You can always send sealed letters through your pouch or my pouch.

Such early cordiality was an immense encouragement, offering hopes of more positive American aid in the future. If and when Roosevelt could persuade Congress that German control of the Atlantic would be as fatal to the United States as to Britain, the Royal Navy might be offered facilities to fight the U-boats from both sides of the Atlantic, even if Germany and the United States never went to war. To Fraser this was a prospect of the highest importance. One of his biggest problems as Controller was sharing out dockyard facilities for new construction and repairs between the Royal and Merchant Navies. If British warships and freighters, damaged in the Atlantic, could get their repairs done in the United States, the burden on Britain's grossly overloaded shipyards would be greatly reduced. When at last these facilities were granted in the spring of 1941, all preparations had been made to send the requisite British teams of builders and naval engineers across the Atlantic to liaise with their American counterparts. That not so much as a day was wasted in taking up the offer was the work of Fraser, who had been planning for this particular eventuality ever since his interrupted dinner in Churchill's flat on 4 September 1939.

To put it mildly, Churchill's performance as a war leader (both as First Lord and Prime Minister) has never lacked critics; but Fraser was never to join their ranks. During his two and a half years as Controller Fraser saw a lot of Churchill, in Whitehall meetings and numerous inspection trips about the country, and developed a great respect and liking for him. This was mutual, and Fraser certainly became one of the admirals on whom Churchill relied most. But the fact needs careful definition. Over the years many charges have been levelled at Churchill's relations with senior Service officers – 'ruthlessness', 'interference', 'impatience', 'capriciousness', and 'favouritism', to quote but a few. These accusations have often ignored or discounted Churchill's *modus operandi* as a war leader. It has been asserted (see Appendix 1) that Churchill resented criticism or opposition and always tried to surround himself with pliant favourites. By no stretch of the imagination could Fraser be described as a pliant favourite; like Montgomery, he had several choice clashes with Churchill during their association. But Churchill stuck to Fraser, despite the occasional heated exchange, because of the respect he had for Fraser's qualities, and foremost among those qualities was Fraser's sense of duty. Churchill himself acknowledged this in the couplet from Tennyson which he chose and repeatedly quoted as Fraser's personal 'signature tune':

> Not once or twice in our long Island story,
> The path of duty was the way to glory.

Churchill wrote these lines above his signature on the souvenir portrait photograph which he sent Fraser after the sinking of the *Scharnhorst* in December 1943, and quoted them yet again in *Closing the Ring* (p.146).

Fraser's interpretation and performance of his duty was innocent of any departmental touchiness and this naturally appealed to Churchill, one of whose pet hates was bureaucratic objection for the sake of objection. When Churchill was fired by an idea (not necessarily his own) which might or might not turn out to be useful, he had to get the experts busy at once and find out whether it would work. 'ACTION THIS DAY' demanded the distinctive red labels which Churchill used to get papers and questions back without delay. Fully aware of their potency in speeding paperwork as well as their historic role, Fraser cast a calculating eye over these labels as he stood one day beside Churchill's desk waiting for Churchill to finish some dictation. 'I saw these labels on the desk, pinched one, and have it to this day. I tried it once on one of my own papers in the Admiralty, and it worked!'[8]

While pressing a new scheme, as at all times, Churchill refused to respect parochial opposition from any department – Admiralty, War Office, Air Ministry or Civil Service. 'Power in a national crisis, when a man believes he knows what orders should be given, is a blessing,' he wrote. 'At the top there are great simplifications. An accepted leader has only to be sure of what it is best to do, or at least to have made up his mind about it.'[9] These sentiments were so nearly Fraser's own that he had no difficulty in respecting them. He rode the Churchillian stream of minutes, suggestions, complaints, and the famous 'Prayers' ('Pray let me have a time-table showing when *Hood* will be ready for sea', or whatever) without resentment at not being allowed to get on with his job in peace. 'That was *his* job,' Lord Fraser pointed out to the author; 'to push forward ideas – and it was up to us, the Service people, to turn them down when they weren't practical.'[10]

From the moment Churchill returned to the Admiralty in September 1939 until his departure on becoming Prime Minister in May 1940, much of the torrent landed on the Controller's desk. A typical example came on 11 September 1939: Churchill's reaction to the War Emergency Programme, 'First Lord to Controller, DNC and others'. Apart from containing a classic Churchillian error – 'all experience shows that a cluster of weak ships will not fight one strong one' (an assertion soon to be disproved by the Battle of the River Plate) the minute listed Churchill's complaints about the scheduled number of new escorts and argued for quantity above quality:[11]

> I would ask that a committee of, say, three sea-officers accustomed to flotilla work, plus two technicians, should sit at once to solve the following problems:
>> An anti-submarine and anti-air vessel which can be built within twelve months in many of the small yards of the country. One hundred should be built if the design is approved. The greatest simplicity of armament and equipment must be arrived at, and a constant eye kept upon mass production techniques. . .
> I hazard specifications only to have them vetted and corrected by the committee, viz.:
>> 500 to 600 tons.
>> 16 to 18 knots.
>> Two cannons around 4-inches, according as artillery may come to hand from any quarter, preferably of course firing high angle.
>> Depth-charges.
>> No torpedoes, and only moderate range of action.
> These will be deemed the 'Cheap and Nasties' (cheap to us, nasty to the U-boats). These ships, being built for a particular but urgent job, will no doubt be of little value to the Navy when that job is done – but let us get the job done.

Fraser was the man who had the job of killing this idea which, though superficially attractive, stemmed from Churchill's ignorance of small warships. These 'Cheap and Nasties' would have abundantly lived up to their name, though in the opposite sense to that fondly intended by Churchill. Though far smaller than the 'Flower' class corvettes (only a handful of which had been laid down at this time) they were supposed to be 3 knots faster and carry twice the fire-power. Building 100 of them before a scrap of experience had been gained from the 'Flower' class corvettes would have been a profligate risk. As for the idea of building them within a year, this was an obvious non-starter and showed up Churchill's constant tendency to forget how much warships and their equipment had changed since Fisher's day. (In fact it was Fisher himself who insisted that 'You cannot build ships in a hurry with a supplementary estimate' – and that had been back in 1902.) All these points gave Fraser more than enough ammunition to sink the 'Cheap and Nasties' idea at birth; and this he did (as Churchill had requested, 'point by point') within 24 hours of Churchill's minute landing on his desk.

Churchill's fertile imagination immediately produced 'Catherine' (12 September), a plan to force an entry into the Baltic in the teeth of the *Luftwaffe*, German surface craft and U-boats. 'Catherine' was a transparently desperate attempt to seize the initiative at sea, now that this could no longer be done in the Mediterranean. The idea was to take two, hopefully three, of the old 'Royal Sovereign' class battleships and make them immune to air and submarine attack by giving them extra deck armour and side-blisters. This would create 'a battle squadron which the enemy heavy ships dare not engage.'[12] The 'Catherine' fleet was to sail with fuel and supplies for three months, at the end of which time, hopefully, the Scandinavian neutrals would have been persuaded to join the Allies. Apart from forcing the German Navy to drop everything and defend its own back yard, the most important strategic prize of 'Catherine' would be the halting of imported German iron ore from Sweden and Norway. And the venture might even persuade Soviet Russia to reconsider its unholy alliance with Germany.

In purely abstract terms 'Catherine' was a daring and imaginative plan; in practical terms it was a wholly unwarrantable gamble. It threatened a hecatomb of light warships desperately needed elsewhere. Pound and Fraser were also obliged to point out that the specially modified battleships needed for 'Catherine' could not be completed ready for action when the Baltic thawed in March-April 1940 without shelving vital construction work already in hand. While the British would be working flat out through the winter preparing the 'Catherine' fleet, the Germans would be adding to their ocean-going U-boat fleet, and the Royal Navy must have the ships with which to fight the growing menace in 1940.

'Catherine' effectively died on 26 September when Churchill was bluntly told that the project must be shelved because of higher construction priorities. But Churchill doggedly kept trying to revive his stillborn brainchild. 'Pull the guns out,' he wrote to Pound on

21 October, 'and plaster the decks with steel. . . . These four-gun ships could be worked up into a very fine battery if the gunnery experts threw themselves into it. But above all they must bristle with A.A., and they must swim or float wherever they choose. . . . Remember no one can gainsay what we together decide.'[13] In the same letter Churchill naïvely asked, 'How are you going to get these ships into dockyards' hands with all your other troubles?' Thanks to Fraser, Pound had the answer to that one: the thing could not be done. The Navy was already at full stretch in the Atlantic, hunting for the *Graf Spee*, and the Fleet was beginning to suffer worrying losses in home waters.

The Navy's first attempt to clear home waters of U-boats, using carriers in collaboration with Asdic-fitted destroyers, had proved an excessive risk. On 14 September *Ark Royal* narrowly escaped a torpedo attack by *U-39*, which was then sunk by *Ark Royal*'s escorting destroyers. But three days later *Courageous*, hunting for U-boats in the Bristol Channel with two destroyers in company, was sunk by *U-29*. Painful though it was – 518 men and Captain Makeig-Jones were lost – this early lesson that Asdic did not spell automatic defeat for the U-boats was very necessary, and carriers were prudently withdrawn from the anti U-boat campaign. Meanwhile the Home Fleet was suffering for the prewar neglect of Scapa Flow's defences, which were so run down that the Admiralty ordered Admiral Forbes to take the Fleet to Loch Ewe on the west coast of Scotland. Scapa remained in use as an anchorage for isolated units of the Fleet. But on the night of 13–14 October the old battleship *Royal Oak* was at anchor inside Scapa Flow when she suddenly shook to violent explosions, turned over and sank with the loss of 834 officers and men.

Due to the darkness of the night and the sheer size of the Flow, nearly an hour passed before the first inkling of the disaster reached *Iron Duke*, the Scapa headquarters ship. The news reached Whitehall intermittently. 'I was sent for about 3am,' recalled Lord Fraser, 'and asked to explain what had happened. I didn't know. Shortly afterwards we heard that *Royal Oak* was sunk. I didn't think a submarine could get in; we all thought it [Scapa Flow] was properly defended.'[14] But the only alternative causes to U-boat attack were spontaneous internal explosions or, far more sinister, sabotage. The Admiralty immediately ordered a concentration of divers at Scapa and an enquiry was held under strict security, security which still pertains. Three days after the disaster, however, Goebbels's propaganda machine went into full cry, trumpeting the news of *Kapitänleutnant* Prien's daring penetration of the Flow in *U-47* and his attack on *Royal Oak*. Despite the obvious exaggerations and lies in Prien's

.story as published the attack itself, as Churchill admitted, 'must be regarded as a feat of arms on the part of the German U-boat commander.'[15]

Though the *Royal Oak* disaster naturally pushed Scapa Flow to the top of the list for urgent shore defence improvements, these could not be made overnight (though, ironically, one of the block-ships intended for·the Kirk Sound entrance used by Prien turned up the day after the sinking). The Home Fleet remained based on the Clyde throughout the winter, until Scapa was considered fit for its return. But the biggest menace in the first three months of the war was not U-boats, or German air attacks. The use of the first German 'secret weapon' of the war, the magnetic mine, was devastating. In September only eight out of fifty-three merchantmen were lost to mines; in October eleven out of forty-six; in November twenty-seven out of fifty. These were losses suffered in waters where conventional minesweepers were regularly at work. Clearly the Germans were using something much more subtle than normal contact mines; on 13 September, SS *City of Paris* was rocked by an underwater explo-sion without her hull being penetrated. They had to be magnetic mines.

The British had not only used magnetic mines themselves in the First World War but were preparing to use them in the Second. By the late summer of 1939 the British had devised a sweep capable of destroying British magnetic mines, but it was useless against the unknown German model. Shipping losses soared ominously, includ-ing the brand-new cruiser *Belfast*, repaired for a glorious career after having her back broken by a magnetic mine on 21 November. But two days later a magnetic mine was found on a mud-flat at Shoe-buryness and was most gallantly disarmed by Lt-Commander J. G. D. Ouvry. The information thus revealed enabled the production, master-minded by Admiral Wake-Walker, of the 'LL Sweep', a trail-ing magnetised cable.

Sweeping for magnetic mines, however, remained acutely hazard-ous until ships were given a means of reducing their own magnetic fields. This counter-ploy was 'degaussing', perfected in December 1939: fitting each ship with a girdle of cable through which electric current was passed to reduce the ship's magnetic field. More tem-porary immunity could be given to smaller ships by 'wiping' them as they lay in dock: running a cable along the hull from a shore generator, and switching on a powerful current for a few hours. The LL Sweep, 'degaussing' and 'wiping' together guaranteed victory over the magnetic mine, but the task of supplying and distributing the equipment, and juggling dockyard routines to get the work done, was enormous. It was even more daunting than the task of arming every ship in the British and Allied merchant navies, because HM ships had to be degaussed as well. Fraser, however, coped imperturbably with the challenge and was soon able to show gratifying results. By the second week of March 1940, 321 warships and 312 merchantmen had been degaussed and another 219 warships and 290 merchantmen were already in hand.

Another vital area in which Fraser was increasingly involved from the summer of 1939 was the development of radar for use in warships. Since 1934 British radar development had been the preserve of the RAF. But on 21 June 1939 Admiral Somerville, investigating the prospects for naval radar, was shown the first experimental gunlaying set at the Bawdsey (Suffolk) radar station. Churchill, then still a 'distinguished civilian', had been given the same demonstration the day before, and had come away convinced that 'we must have this on His Majesty's ships.' When Churchill returned to the Admiralty he pressed the further advancement of naval radar and found a ready ally in Fraser. The real breakthrough, both for location and gunlaying, did not come until the perfection of the cavity magnetron in February 1940, making possible the design of a 10cm radar for shipboard use. And that breakthrough only occurred when it did because the research scientists John Randall and Harry Boot, inventors of the cavity magnetron, were given the use of Navy transformers from Portsmouth, borrowed from the Service under Fraser's aegis.

So ended Fraser's first year as Controller of the Navy, which had begun in peacetime and ended in a war which was anything but 'phoney' for the men at sea. His work in that year enabled the Navy to weather the biggest crisis it had ever known, for by the spring of 1940 the first corvettes were fast approaching readiness for their vital work against the U-boats. Fraser had ridden the waves of Churchill's enthusiasms with skill and firmness, neither sinking nor allowing himself to be swept away, refusing to permit any tampering with the essentials of the building programme. He had coped and was still coping magnificently with the unexpected peril posed by the magnetic mine, and the Navy was about to enter the electronic era with shipborne radar. The Navy has had many great Controllers in its long history. But Fraser's achievements in his first year as Controller outshone them all.

· 15 ·

The Years of Crisis

[1940–2]

True to Fraser's worst fears, the passive abandonment of initiative by the Allies yielded bitter fruit between April and the end of June 1940. The Germans struck at the Allies on two fronts: Scandinavia and the Low Countries. By 25 June Germany had won the most resounding string of land victories in her history and controlled the coastline of mainland Europe from the North Cape to the Pyrenees. The maritime lifeline of a totally isolated Britain, now facing not only Germany but (from 10 June 1940) Italy as well, lay open to attack from the new bases gained for the German Navy on the Norwegian and Biscay coasts.

Yet the disasters of April-June 1940 yielded three unexpected advantages to Britain. The first was the fall of Chamberlain's government and its replacement by a national government under Winston Churchill – vital new leadership, boosting both national morale and the inception of a truly national war effort. The second advantage was the punishment suffered by the German Navy during the Norwegian campaign, which so reduced the German surface fleet that it was unable to play any decisive role in the projected invasion of Britain later in the year. And the third advantage was the concentration of U-boats in home waters during the battle for Norway, which took them out of the North Atlantic and into the confines of the North and Norwegian Seas. Fifteen U-boats were sunk in January-June 1940 and only thirteen new boats were commissioned. The expansion of the U-boat force was scotched for six vital months, during which time Fraser saw the first of his new escort warships entering the water at an increasing rate.

HMS *Gladiolus*, first of the 'Flower' class corvettes, was launched at Middlesbrough on 24 January 1940. By the beginning of the Norwegian campaign on 8 April another seven corvettes had been launched. Seven more followed in April, with 22 April a red-letter day on which three corvettes were launched, all in different yards (*Honeysuckle, Clematis* and *Anemone*). Another seventeen had been launched by the end of June, including the first corvette built overseas (*Trillium*, by Canadian Vickers). In the same period twelve new 'Hunt' class escort destroyers were launched. This promising start was soon followed by the first U-boat 'kill' scored by a corvette: on 1 July, when *Gladiolus*, helped by aircraft from No. 10 Squadron, sank *U-26* south-south-west of Ireland.

But acting as supreme 'trouble-shooter' for warship construction was only one of Fraser's duties. The Admiralty's wartime assumption of responsibility for merchant shipping repairs saddled him with another burden, but this, at least, he did not have to carry alone. On 1 February 1940 the Glasgow shipbuilder Sir James Lithgow joined the Board of Admiralty as Controller (Merchant Shipbuilding and Repairs). The close *rapport* which Fraser established with Lithgow was vital to the war effort, for the two men were tackling a problem unique in its complexity. This problem consisted of the increasing demands on the finite resources of dockyard time, space and labour being made simultaneously by the Royal and Merchant Navies.

Much resilience was demanded of Fraser and Lithgow because of Churchill's inevitable tendency to switch priorities from merchant to naval shipping, or vice versa, according to whatever report had impressed him last. Thus, 'Repairing ships is better than new building,' Churchill urged Fraser on 5 March 1940. 'A strong effort should be made to turn this 8,000-ton ship into an effective cargo-carrying bottom. . . .*There ought to be a tremendous move-on in the salvage and repair departments.* The tonnage working on any given day ranks above the rate of new merchant shipbuilding.'[1] By 1 April, however, Churchill was on the opposite tack. 'Where are the facts about the return of the 40 destroyers which are in hospital to their duty?' he demanded, of Fraser. 'And can anything be done to speed up new destroyers, especially those of the 40th Flotilla, by leaving out some of the final improvements and latest additions, which take so much time? The great aim must be to have the maximum number during these coming summer months. They can go back to have further treatment when we have a larger margin.'[2]

Fraser, of course, had to point out to Churchill that it was the 'final improvements and latest additions' which made a modern warship fully effective. The only advantage in sending ships to sea deaf and blind for want of their full array of electronic equipment would acrue to the U-boats.

Life was not made easy by the deep respect Churchill had for his friend Professor Lindemann (later Lord Cherwell) – 'the Prof', who headed Churchill's own statistical department. To many, Lindemann was cast in the exasperating role of *eminence grise*, vetoing good ideas or advising Churchill to do so because he, Lindemann, disagreed with them. This was not Fraser's experience: 'I liked the Prof very much. One evening he said "Come in here, I've got something to show you." He sat in his little room, and threw a matchbox across, and this *thing* went off – flashed a light. It was the start of the VT fuze.'[3] But when Lindemann's figures differed from those supplied by heads of department there was likely to be trouble from Churchill, and Fraser and Lithgow soon found themselves on the receiving end.

It happened after the Norwegian campaign, in which two of Fraser's former ships were lost: *Effingham* wrecked near Narvik, and *Glorious* sunk by *Scharnhorst* and *Gneisenau*. Fraser not only had to allow for the additional loss of an AA cruiser, a sloop, nine destroyers and six submarines: he had to cope with the rush of repairs needed by four cruisers, two AA cruisers, two sloops and eight destroyers. Churchill, however, now Prime Minister, was once more obsessed with merchant shipping statistics; and the result was a spirited clash with Fraser, with the rest of the War Cabinet as impressed spectators:[4]

> 'I remember that very well indeed. He [Churchill] had asked me and Lithgow to change over and put more men on merchant ship repairs. As we went over to the meeting we saw that the Prof's figures showed there had been no change, and I said "I think you and I are going to get into trouble over this." When Churchill looked at the figures he said "You've disobeyed my orders." I couldn't stand that, particularly as I heard "The Beaver" say "He's a mule!" So I spoke out. I said "Sir, you are being most unfair and unjust. We're carrying out your orders, but you can't take a cruiser out of dock with its bottom out. It's impossible to change over as quickly as that." And Churchill never said a word: he turned to some other subject.
>
> And then, after the meeting, all the ministers who were present came up to me and said "My goodness, you've taken a weight off our shoulders – not many people speak up to him like that."
>
> For the next meeting the following week I had to be away for some reason or other; I knew everything was all right – but Churchill sent across to know why I hadn't been there.

In *Their Finest Hour* Churchill claimed that, 'There was no division, as in the previous war, between politicians and soldiers, between the "Frocks" and the "Brass Hats" – odious terms which darkened counsel. We came very close together indeed, and friendships were formed which I believe were deeply valued.'[5] This was certainly true of Churchill's growing respect for Fraser, who so obviously worked as easily with politicians as he did with other Service chiefs.

A revealing tribute has been paid to this facility by Sir Harold Macmillan, in 1940 Parliamentary Secretary to the Ministry of Supply and Chairman of the Industrial Capacity Committee. This is how Macmillan and his colleague, Colonel J. J. Llewellin of the Raw Materials Allocations Committee, liaised with the Admiralty and the Ministry of Aircraft Production in 1940–2:[6]

Somehow or other the work of allocation between rival Ministries had to be carried out, and the instruments that we had were on the whole not unsatisfactory. . . . After a few months, I do not remember any case of an appeal to the Production Council, or afterwards to the Cabinet. This was partly because we relied in addition on personal arrangements made on an 'old boy' basis. It so happened that Sir Harold Brown, operational head of our Ministry, Sir Charles Craven at the Ministry of Aircraft Production, and Sir Bruce Fraser, the Controller of the Navy, were all naval officers and shipmates of old days. Associated with them was Sir James Lithgow, who was at the Admiralty in charge of merchant-shipping repairs, and was a member of the Navy by adoption. It was indeed fortunate that these men who, if they had quarrelled, could have wrecked the whole production effort, happened to be old and intimate friends, linked by the greatest of all ties – the tradition of the Navy. This group, known throughout Whitehall as the 'boilermakers', lunched together every week at the old Carlton Hotel.[7] Both Llewellin and I were co-opted and attended at fortnightly intervals, on the days our respective committees met. Many of the questions which would have been bitterly debated by these officers and their representatives in public were resolved in this genial manner in private. As their mutual confidence grew, they were able to adopt *ad hoc* arrangements. For instance, the Admiralty might be building a Bofors-gun plant to which a large number of machine-tools were allocated and some already delivered. But they admitted that the buildings would not be ready for at least six months; so by agreement and with the confidence that the tools would be given back when required, vital lathes or guillotines were made available by Sir Bruce to Sir Charles or Sir Harold.

It was the rule of the lunch that we all paid in turn. Sir James was very rich and very generous but, like many Lowland Scots, critical of unnecessary expenditure. When it was his turn to pay we always ordered the most expensive liquors and the finest cigars. Sir James duly paid the bill, sometimes with a wry smile.

This was how, with the minimum of jarring strain and an atmosphere of genial efficiency, Fraser kept his enormous Admiralty 'empire' smoothly meshed in to the national war effort. In so doing he won the respect of War Cabinet ministers on both sides of the political spectrum, including Ernest Bevin and Lord Beaverbrook, the dynamic Minister for Aircraft Production.

Beaverbrook developed a particular liking for Fraser and loved to tease him that the Navy was a gang of reactionary pirates. But after the great days of the Battle of Britain in August and September 1940, the air war developed into the 'Blitz', the German night bombing offensive against British cities. During the Blitz the Royal Navy fully repaid its debt to the RAF for the earlier development of radar, with a highly important contribution to the 'Battle of the Beams'. This was the successful attempt to deflect the signals guiding the German bombers to their targets. The splendid document recording this contribution and its sequel, the ensuing knockabout dialogue between Fraser and Beaverbrook, is not to be found in the Admiralty or public archives because it was kept by Fraser as a souvenir – Admiralty Docket S.D.O. 2247/40.[8]

Special transmitter made by H.M. Signal School (26/10/40)
It was recently discovered that the Germans were making use of W/T beams to guide their bombers on to their targets. The Air Ministry made an urgent unofficial request to the Signal Department for any transmitter which could be used to jam the German W/T beams. The wave frequency involved was very high and the only transmitter which could be made available was one in H.M. Signal School, and this required considerable modification.
The Experimental Department of the Signal School worked on the set night and day for several days, built two special silica transmitting valves, installed it in a lorry and turned it over to the Air Ministry.
Information has now been received that this set has proved very efficient on trial, and is likely to be of considerable value in the effort to reduce night bombing.
It is submitted that a signal of commendation may be made to the Captain, H.M. Signal School.

'Approved', noted Fraser when this docket landed on his desk on 28 October; and he added, 'After action this paper to be forwarded to

Lord Beaverbrook by hand to show that we are not always thieves.' Beaverbrook returned the docket on the 31st, having added his contribution: 'None the less you are thieves & it is my conviction that you would steal the Crown Jewels if it would help the Navy.' 'So little thanks from so few to so many,' appended Fraser in mock resignation.[9] Beaverbrook kept the 'thieves' joke going in his subsequent dealings with Fraser. When 'The Beaver' became Minister of Supply at the end of June 1941, Fraser sent him a congratulatory note. 'My dear Admiral,' replied Beaverbrook, 'thank you very much for your good wishes. Come and see me any time you like. I am always glad to see an Admiral. And as for thieves, I am Ali Baba. P.S. – I mean to work very closely with you for the glory of your Admiralty.'[10] From then on, Beaverbrook's nickname for Fraser remained 'Ali Baba'.

But there was little to laugh about in the ominous new pattern of the war at sea from June 1940 onwards. After their attempt to finish Britain by direct assault failed with defeat in the Battle of Britain, the Germans fell back on the indirect strategy of blockade and commerce warfare. For this they were now ideally placed, thanks to their recent conquests. Naturally enough, the *Luftwaffe* was ready for action from French airfields before the redeployment of the U-boats. From July 1940 a new and unexpected enemy to British shipping appeared in the Focke-Wulf Fw 200 Condor: a four-engined bomber with a range of 2,210 miles. The Condor could fly patrols from Bordeaux-Merignac out across the Bay of Biscay, circling right round the British Isles to land at Trondheim-Vaernes in Norway, operating far out into the Atlantic against convoys, stragglers and independently routed ships. In its first two months of operations, the Condor sank thirty ships (total 110,000 tons). Of the 109,611 tons of shipping sunk by the *Luftwaffe* in August and September 1940, 90,000 tons were sunk by the Condors of I/KG 40 from Bordeaux-Merignac.

The Condor menace could only be beaten by giving convoys their own aircraft cover as well as surface warship cover against U-boats and, when possible, battleship cover against surface raiders. But if battleship escorts were hard enough to find whenever a surface raider got out, providing convoys with instant carrier protection was a stark impossibility. Looking forward to 1941 and 1942, Fraser and Lithgow began to earmark suitable fast merchantmen for reconstruction as 'Woolworth carriers', fitted with simple flight-decks, no hangars and a handful of fighters kept on deck. A German prize taken in February 1940, the *Hannover*, was taken in hand and entered service as HMS *Audacity*, first of the escort carriers, in June

1941. But the time it took to build even escort carriers produced a desperate attempt at a short-term partial solution.

This was the CAM-ship, the 'catapult-equipped merchantman', with a solitary Hurricane fighter perched on a catapult stuck in the bows, the nearest the British came to adopting kamikaze tactics in the Second World War. When an enemy aircraft approached the CAM-ship's convoy the Hurricane would be launched; after the intruder had been shot down or chased away, the pilot would patrol over the convoy until his fuel ran out. He would then bale out and hope to land in the water close enough to a ship to be picked up before he died of cold. But although CAM-ships were quicker and easier to produce than escort carriers, it took until spring 1941 before suitable catapult equipment was perfected and ordered for installation in fifty merchantmen chosen by Fraser and Lithgow. The first successful launch was made on 31 May 1941, but the first successful interception of a Condor by a CAM-ship fighter did not take place until 1 November 1941. This was over a year after KG 40's most prestigious 'kill': the 42,000-ton liner *Empress of Britain*, sunk by a Condor off North-west Ireland on 26 October 1940.

Much invaluable experience for the CAM-ships and escort carriers was gained from the early conversion work on the *Pegasus*, *Maplin*, *Springbank* and *Ariguani*. *Pegasus* was an old seaplane-carrier of First World War vintage and the other three were merchantmen requisitioned for the Navy in September-October 1940, for conversion as 'fighter catapult ships'. All four were ready by April 1941; two went to the North Atlantic and the other two to the Gibraltar convoy route. *Maplin* downed the first Condor early in August 1941, proving that the thinking behind the CAM-ship idea was sound. The decision to accept the deliberate sacrifice of fighters at sea was a courageous one to take in September 1940, when every British fighter was worth its weight in gold; but it is hardly possible to over-state the importance of the timely pioneering work on escort carriers achieved by the Navy under Fraser's Controllership. All the groundwork on escort carrier development had been completed before the United States entered the war in December 1941. The experience thus gained enabled the massive resources of the American shipyards to embark at once on an enormous programme of escort carrier construction, assuring the decisive defeat of the U-boats in 1943.

Hardly less important than the escort carriers were two vital electronic aids developed under Fraser's Controllership: 10cm radar and 'Huff-Duff'. Throughout 1940 and 1941 the Fleet's warships continued to sprout strange aerials as they were fitted with 50cm gunnery radar: Type 282 for AA fire, Type 283 for long range, heavy-calibre AA fire, and Type 284 for surface fire. The cavity magnetron breakthrough in February 1940 yielded the new narrow-beam (10cm) radar – Type 271, capable of locating a U-boat's conning-tower in bad or zero visibility. Type 271 was tried out in the 'Flower' class corvette *Orchis* in March 1941. It proved such a success that twenty-five corvettes had been fitted with Type 271 by July, most of the sets being hand-built at the Admiralty Signal Establishment at Eastney, Portsmouth.

Type 271 radar gave the hard-pressed escorts a tool for locating U-boats attacking convoys at night *on the surface*, where Asdic could not detect them and where they were practically undetectable with the naked eye. Equally important was 'high frequency direction finding' – HF/DF, or 'Huff-Duff'. This electronic eavesdropper exploited the radio 'chatter' with which the U-boats kept in touch with each other and their HQ at Lorient. A U-boat would sight a promising convoy, shadow it and summon all available U-boats to form a 'wolf-pack' and attack. With 'Huff-Duff', skilled operators could pinpoint nearby U-boats at once, no matter how short the Germans kept their signals.

By late 1941 Asdic, Type 271 radar and 'Huff-Duff' had formed a potent trinity making it impossible for U-boats to approach convoys undetected; by the early summer of 1943 the addition of escort carriers had helped make it impossible for U-boats to operate in the North Atlantic with their former impunity. Lord Fraser was quick to point out to the author that this vital technology was the work of hundreds of scientists and technicians improving on earlier inventions and techniques, which he was lucky to have at his disposal. But the fact remains that the weapons which won the Battle of the Atlantic (with the exception of Asdic) were all perfected during Fraser's Controllership of 1939–42, when the foundations of victory in the future were securely laid amid the losses and disasters of the present.

It was also in this period that Fraser found himself opposing both Pound and Churchill on the subject of future battleship construction. This, of course, was because battleships had no part in the primary objective of beating the U-boats, and the 'KG V' battleships and 'Illustrious' class carriers still had to be completed anyway. But the fact that the Board of Admiralty's most senior gunnery specialist (Pound had been a torpedo specialist) set his face against even one new battleship showed how much had changed since August 1914.

The idea of building a super-battleship that would enshrine all the experience still to be gained from the 'KG Vs', and carrying this through into peacetime (whenever this was likely to come) was first raised by the Deputy Chief of the Naval Staff, Rear-Admiral Tom Phillips, late in 1939. He suggested that the four 15-inch turrets held in store since the reconstruction of *Glorious* and *Courageous* as carriers should form the main armament of a new 15-inch gun battleship. Churchill was immediately attracted by the idea, and on 3 December 1939 asked Fraser to draw up 'a legend with estimates in money and time' for a battleship 'of the battleship-cruiser type, heavily armoured and absolutely proof against air attack'.[11]

Fraser's reply was clear-cut: the overriding priority was the escort-building programme. A new battleship must be regarded as an unwarrantable luxury. But the seed had been sown, and it sprouted during the debate over the 1940 Building Programme in which it was decided to cancel the four projected 'Lion' class super-battleships (which would have had 16-inch guns). Churchill wanted work started on a new battleship, using the old 15-inch mountings, and was supported by Pound. Lord Fraser recalled that once again, 'I said "I'm very sorry, but we can't possibly build a battleship now, with all the new destroyers waiting to come out, and so on – it's quite impossible." That left the Board meeting in some disarray.' Fraser yielded so far as to admit that the spare 15-inch gun mountings did indeed offer considerable savings in cost and construction time, whereupon:[12]

> 'Churchill said, "It must be finished in a year." I said, "It'll take four years to build, sir." He said, "*It'll be finished in a year*", and again I said, "It'll take four years to build, sir." He stopped at that. Actually, *Vanguard* took five years to build.' [Laid down 2 October 1941; launched 30 November 1944; commissioned 25 April 1946.]

Fraser also drew fire from Churchill over the inevitable delays after the 'bases for destroyers' deal with the United States, settled after months of haggling between Roosevelt and Churchill on 5 September 1940. The fifty old destroyers handed over to the Royal Navy could not go straight into action against the U-boats; apart from anything else, they all had to be fitted with Asdic. It was largely due to Fraser's timely preparations that the old 'four-stackers' were able to enter service in late 1940–early 1941, but this did not stop Churchill fulminating over the time taken to refit the destroyers.

After the *Athenia* sinking (*see* p.132), Fraser had sent a dockyard party to the United States to assess American techniques and capacity, hoping for an early prospect of placing repair work west of the Atlantic. Since then, Fraser had kept an anxious eye on the cautious development of Anglo-American relations. In August 1940, while the 'bases for destroyers' deal was still being nursed through its final stages, Admiral Ghormley arrived in Britain with a US Naval Mission to glean all available data from the Royal Navy's war experience to date. This was generously supplied, Fraser naturally being one of the main donors; he saw a good deal of the US Naval Mission. 'They were allowed to see all our damaged ships and detected quite a lot – for instance, we'd been using cast iron as engine bases, and when a mine went up they'd crack. And then we'd often put the scuppers too low; the water would come in if the ship sank a bit.'[13]

Liaison work with the US Naval Mission accompanied Fraser's preparations for the vital milestones passed in March-April 1941. On 11 March Roosevelt gave his assent to the Lend-Lease Act, freeing Britain from the need to pay cash for war materials supplied by the United States. And on 4 April the United States agreed to repair British warships in American yards, a boon for which Fraser had been yearning since the outbreak of war. The personnel for the British liaison teams needed for such work had already been re-cruited and trained on Fraser's orders, and were sent across the Atlantic at once. 'From this time onwards,' as Roskill states in *The War At Sea*, 'it was rare for any American Navy Yard, and many private yards as well, not to have at least one British ship in its hands for refit or repair of action damage. The building of warships of many types and of merchant ships on British "Lend-Lease" account also dates to this time.'[14] But Lord Fraser recalled that:[15]

'When we sent our first ship to America for repair, Roosevelt wanted to see the estimates of everything to be done. When he saw them, he said "I see they have included the champagne glasses!" He crossed this item out, as he didn't think champagne glasses were needed at the time.'

In these dark months one of the happiest moments for Fraser came on 16 November 1940, when he stood proudly behind his mother as she launched the 'Fiji' class cruiser *Jamaica*. As he watched the new ship take the water he could not know that three years later she would be under his command, playing a leading role in the *Scharnhorst* drama. It is also pleasant to record that Fraser's out-standing services as Controller were recognised and rewarded at the time. He had been appointed Companion of the Bath in 1939, his first award since that of the OBE, twenty years before. Promotion to Vice-Admiral had come on 8 May 1940, and in the Birthday Honours of 1941 Fraser was knighted as a KBE.

Fraser's great Controllership ended on 22 May 1942, when he handed over to Admiral Wake-Walker. Though the Battle of the Atlantic was still rising to its climax when he left the Admiralty, Fraser had supervised the crucial transition of the Fleet from peace to war and its equipment with the weapons of victory. He now went back to sea, for the first time in over three years, and on 28 June 1942 hoisted his flag in HMS *Anson* as 'VA2 Home Fleet' – Vice-Admiral, Second-in-Command.

. 16 .

Second-in-Command

[June 1942–May 1943]

When Fraser went to the Home Fleet at the end of June 1942 he had been ashore as Controller for the past three and a quarter years and lacked any personal experience of Second World War conditions at sea, or of the working of a modern wartime fleet. As he was acutely aware, this was hardly the best preparation for a new Second-in-Command, joining the Home Fleet as the Allies were reaching the nadir of their fortunes in the war. By June 1942 the demands on the Royal Navy had never been more relentless and those demands bore down particularly hard on the Home Fleet, faced as it was by the overriding dilemma posed by the Russian convoys.

The last four Allied convoys to North Russia – PQ.13 in March, PQ.14 in April, PQ.15 and PQ.16 in May – had been fought through against increasing enemy opposition and in natural conditions which increasingly favoured the Germans as the Arctic summer drew on. The political decision to keep sending aid to Russia meant that there could be no question of suspending convoys for the summer months and the latest convoy, PQ.17, was already on its way to Archangel when Fraser joined the Home Fleet. It would have to run the gauntlet of air attacks by *Luftwaffe* units based on Bardufoss, Banak and Kirkenes airfields in the region of the North Cape. Poised to strike at the convoy under cover of this air umbrella were the battleship *Tirpitz*, pocket-battleships *Lützow* and *Scheer*, the heavy cruiser *Hipper* and twelve destroyers.

Meanwhile, everything had combined to sap the British Home Fleet's strength: accident, construction-time and the drain of heavy warships from home waters to the Mediterranean. *King George V* was still completing repairs to collision damage suffered on 1 May (when she sank the destroyer *Punjabi*). *Anson*, scheduled to wear Fraser's flag as VA2, had only just been commissioned and still had her working-up to complete. Admiral Sir John Tovey, the Commander-in-Chief, had only one British battleship ready for action (his own flagship, *Duke of York*); the only other British capital ship with the Home Fleet was the carrier *Victorious*. The Home Fleet would have been in poor case without help from the US Navy: the battleship USS *Washington*, cruisers USS *Tuscaloosa* and *Wichita*, and 8th Destroyer Squadron (Task Force 99, commanded by Rear-Admiral Giffen, USN).

But as the distances involved and the preponderance of German shore-based air cover kept the odds stacked against the Allies, not even this most welcome reinforcement gave Tovey a fleet which could tackle the German battle squadron with confidence. He first asked that PQ.17 be split into two sections, each of which, sailed independently, would be harder for the Germans to locate than the full-sized convoy of thirty-five ships; but this was refused. In a lengthy Admiralty signal on the eve of PQ.17's departure (27 June), Tovey was told that the Admiralty would control the convoy's movements. Tovey was 'not expected' to place the Home Fleet 'in a position where it will be subject to heavy air attack unless there is a good chance of bringing *Admiral von Tirpitz* to action'.[1]

All this meant that the Home Fleet's protection for PQ.17 (as indeed for all North Russian summer convoys) was 'more threatening than real', as Tovey put it. He detached Rear-Admiral Sir Louis Hamilton's 1st Cruiser Squadron to give PQ.17 close support as it entered the Barents Sea. If *Tirpitz* and her consorts did come out, the only heavy ship in the Home Fleet likely to get a crack at her was the carrier *Victorious*. In Fraser, Tovey had a new VA2 noted for his fine prewar work in carriers with *Glorious*; and no sooner had Fraser hoisted his flag in *Anson* than he shifted it to *Victorious*, in which he sailed with the Home Fleet on 1 July to cover the passage of PQ.17. Admiral Tovey's flagship was HMS *Duke of York*; Rear-Admiral Giffen's was USS *Washington*; Rear-Admiral Hamilton's was HMS *London*. The two American cruisers were attached to Hamilton's 1st Cruiser Squadron.

The PQ.17 tragedy may be briefly summarised. By 22.00 hrs on 4 July PQ.17 was well into the Barents Sea, with Hamilton's cruisers 5 miles ahead of the convoy and the Home Fleet patrolling its distant beat some 350 miles to the west. The convoy was in excellent heart, having lost only three ships to four air attacks during the day, and was magnificently holding formation as it stood on to the east with nearly two-thirds of its perilous voyage already completed. But in Whitehall Admiral Pound was deeply concerned: reconnaissance had yielded no confirmation of the German warships' position for the past 30 hours. (They were in fact still in Altenfjord, some 400 miles south of PQ.17.) Concluding that the Germans were already at sea, steaming north to assault PQ.17, Pound ordered Hamilton's cruisers to withdraw to the west and the convoy to be scattered at 21.36 hrs on 4 July. Though to the men at sea it came like a bolt from the blue, the order to scatter was promptly obeyed – in the natural belief that the Admiralty had discovered that a German surface attack was only minutes away. The German warships did put briefly to sea on the 5th, but by then their sortie was unnecessary: the ships of PQ.17, scattered all over the eastern Barents Sea, were already falling easy victims to *Luftwaffe* and U-boat attacks. In all, twenty-one out of the thirty-one well-ordered merchantmen scattered on the 4th went to the bottom.

Such was Fraser's harrowing introduction to service with the Home Fleet. Here was no ordinary defeat at sea: it was a military disaster as well because, as Admiral Schofield has pointed out,[2] the Russians could have equipped a complete field army with the weapons and equipment lost in the sunk freighters. But the circumstances were uniquely traumatic. PQ.17's escorting warships had been peremptorily ordered to leave the merchantmen to their fate, an 'informed decision' made in the absence of true information. Tovey, the 'man on the spot', was uncompromising in his report to the Admiralty: he stated bluntly that 'the order to scatter the convoy had been premature; its results were disastrous.'[3] The destruction of PQ.17 was – and remains – one of the most humiliating incidents in the history of the Royal Navy.

For Fraser, to whom pride in the Service and its tradition had long been bone-marrow deep, it was a grief too acute for words. Nearly forty years later, at the close of his life, he would still refrain from comment on the PQ.17 tragedy. 'There it was,' he told the author briefly: 'the Admiralty had decided, and that was that.'[4] Two reasons may be given for his reserve. One is Fraser's revulsion at postwar attempts to 'sensationalise' the PQ.17 story (the most notorious effort resulting in the legal case of Broome v. Cassell and Irving in 1970). And the second is loyalty to his old chief Sir Dudley Pound, under whom Fraser had served for so many years and whom he knew well, but who had been the man who gave the fateful order for PQ.17 to scatter. As Fraser saw it the real villain of the piece had been operational procedure, with its obsessive insistence on the maintenance of radio silence. Pound had intervened in the belief that Tovey, the Commander-in-Chief afloat, would be in no position to break radio silence at such a crucial moment. After PQ.17, Fraser privately vowed that if he should ever find himself in the same position he *would* break radio silence – as often as was necessary for the right hand to know what the left hand was doing.

Even if all had gone well and PQ.17 had arrived in the White Sea intact, convoy sailings to Russia would have had to have been suspended for a while. An even higher priority now dominated the strategic scene: the plight of Malta, whose sorely tried garrison and population would face certain starvation if another relief convoy could not be forced through the western Mediterranean in the month of August. Substantial warship detachments were demanded of the Home Fleet for this new Malta convoy, which was given the code-name 'Pedestal'.

As the German and Italian airfields in Sardinia and Sicily were far closer to 'Pedestal's' track than the German bases in Norway were to the track of the Russian convoys, the only chance of success was to give 'Pedestal' the strongest possible carrier escort. This, together with a battle group in case the Italian battle fleet came out, would accompany the convoy as far as the deadly bottleneck between Sardinia and Tunisia. At this point the carriers and the battle group would withdraw to Gibraltar, leaving a close escort to fight the convoy through the last quarter of its voyage to Malta. The strong carrier support was a luxury which, if all went well, would be extended to the Russian convoys. This made 'Pedestal' an experiment of the greatest interest to the Home Fleet, and Fraser asked for permission to go and see for himself as a strictly unofficial 'passenger'. As Home Fleet operations would be restricted to a minor key until the Fleet got its warships back from the Mediterranean, Tovey readily agreed; and Fraser quietly arranged his passage with the commander of the 'Pedestal' operation.

This was an old acquaintance: Vice-Admiral Sir Neville Syfret, a fellow gunnery specialist who had succeeded Fraser as Commander (G) at *Excellent* in 1922. It was agreed that Fraser would accompany neither Syfret in his flagship *Nelson* nor Rear-Admiral Lyster's carrier force (*Victorious*, *Indomitable* and *Eagle*). Instead, when Syfret's main body collected the fourteen merchantmen of 'Pedestal' off the Clyde on 3 August, Fraser embarked as the 'incognito' guest of *Rodney*. The plan was to penetrate as deeply into the western Mediterranean as possible before Axis air reconnaissance got wind of the operation, which ruled out a halt at Gibraltar. As luck would have it, the 'Pedestal' armada ran the Gibraltar Strait in thick fog early on 10 August and no enemy aircraft located the convoy until the morning of the 11th.

The two hectic days which followed gave Fraser his first taste of action in twenty-seven years; the last time he had seen a gun fired in anger had been in *Minerva* in 1915. As recalled by Commander J. G. Forbes, *Rodney*'s Navigating Officer, Fraser thoroughly enjoyed the experience:[5]

Admiral Fraser did not fly his flag, of course, but as *Rodney* was fitted as a flagship, he was given the Admiral's Bridge (a deck above the Navigating Bridge) from where he had a panoramic view of events. He was accompanied by a Royal Marine orderly and two Bren guns, and from accounts afterwards they had a grand time shooting at enemy dive-bombers, claiming at least one hit!

Fraser was most interested to see how the carrier air umbrella would work. No British wartime fleet had ever sailed with stronger carrier protection; the three 'Pedestal' carriers could put up a combined force of seventy-two fighters to keep off Axis aircraft. But this protection was drastically reduced at the outset. At 13.15 hrs on the 11th, *Leutnant* Rosenbaum's *U-73*, evaded the destroyer screen, worked its way under the convoy and put four torpedoes into *Eagle*. With her hull ripped open, the old carrier sank in 8 minutes. Fraser, his glasses glued to his eyes, watched her sink from his vantage-point. 'I saw her go down – she went very quickly. The Captain [L. D. Mackintosh] had been my Commander in the *Glorious*; I saw him slide down the flight-deck and on to the hawse-pipe.'[6] Prompt attendance by destroyers saved about 900 of her complement of 1,160 including, Fraser was happy to hear later, Captain Mackintosh.

For convoy and fleet the afternoon of the 11th passed without further incident, but as the sun was setting (20.45 hrs) thirty-six German bombers and torpedo-bombers attacked out of the darkening sky to the east. Fraser watched the awesome firework display as the massed guns of the fleet opened up in the dusk, shooting down four of the raiders and driving off the others without a single ship being hit. The night of 11–12 August carried the 'Pedestal' fleet 130 miles closer to Sardinia but by the morning of the 12th, as the standing fighter patrol went aloft from *Indomitable* and *Victorious*, the *Luftwaffe* bases on Sardinia were only 70 miles away. Luckily the first German air strike shortly after 09.00 hrs was of no great strength, six of the nineteen attackers being shot down and the others chased off by the sixteen British fighters in the air. The Italian Air Force took up the running with a series of attacks between 12.15 hrs and 13.45 hrs, some eighty aircraft in all, with eleven German bombers joining in as the Italians retired. These attacks were largely disrupted by the carrier fighters, the sole convoy casualty being the freighter *Deucalion*, damaged by bombs and forced to drop astern. (She was sunk at dusk close in to the Tunisian coast, still gallantly making for Malta on her own.) An Italian fighter-bomber attack on *Victorious* could have had disastrous results, as she was caught while her Hurricanes were landing-on. The only bomb to hit, however, broke up on the armoured flight-deck.

Fraser had missed none of these attacks. 'I had a cabin just down below,' he recalled, 'and when there was some action coming up I went up above with my Royal Marine, who was a very young chap of about 18 or 19, and a young Signalman.'[7] Their great moment came in the early evening of the 12th, as the 'Pedestal' forces came within range of the deadly Ju-87 Stukas based on Sicily. At 18.35 hrs twenty-nine Stukas and fourteen Italian dive-bombers attacked, concentrating on Syfret's warships. And it was during this attack that another addition was made to the Fraser legend – the widely-held belief that the Admiral was responsible for shooting down a Stuka.

As ever, Lord Fraser was quick to issue a disclaimer and give credit where credit was due:[8]

'It happened as *Indomitable* was about to be bombed – that was seen all round, of course. My Marine hadn't yet arrived and it was the little Signalman who turned his machine-gun and fired at this group of, I think, about six aircraft that were coming round in a tight circle over *Indomitable*; then all the pom-poms opened up. One aircraft came down almost straight at us, then swung off to one side, into the water. We *thought* we'd got it, but really you couldn't say for certain what had happened to it. . . . I was watching *Indomitable*. For a moment we thought *Indomitable* had gone; she disappeared in the splashes and explosions – and then, about five minutes later, up came her signal: "READY FOR 25 KNOTS." '

What had happened was serious enough: *Indomitable* had taken three heavy bomb hits which failed to reach her vitals, but which damaged her flight-deck too badly to operate aircraft. Those of her aircraft in the air had to land on *Victorious*, the only carrier now operational. By a miracle this damage was caused only minutes before, at 19.00 hrs, the time came for Syfret to order the covering force to withdraw and hand over the convoy to Rear-Admiral Burrough in the cruiser *Nigeria*. If 'Pedestal' had, by a similar misfortune, been deprived of its carrier protection 24 hours earlier, the convoy might well have been annihilated. As it was, eight ships of the convoy were sunk during the terrible passage of the Sicilian Narrows on 12—13 August – but despite this appallingly high price 'Pedestal' achieved its objective. The four surviving freighters and the tanker *Ohio* (the latter nursed into Malta with her back broken but her 10,000 tons of fuel intact) gave the Malta garrison the vital transfusion needed to survive until the tide of defeat was turned for good at Alamein.

Exhilarated though he was at having taken part in the venture, Fraser typically found time to leave a lasting memory with Commander Forbes when the time came to leave *Rodney*. 'I shall always remember,' writes the Commander, 'that on our return to harbour after the operation, Admiral Fraser came up to the bridge and thanked me personally for bringing him back safely.'[9] Much of what Fraser had learned by accompanying 'Pedestal' could never have been conveyed merely by reading reports of the action, or even by talking with participants. He had now seen, confirmed in action, the unique benefit conveyed by adequate carrier support. On the other side of the coin, 'Pedestal' had repeated the grim lesson that it was suicide to send a fleet within range of superior land-based air forces. And the latter point was particularly relevant when Fraser returned to the Home Fleet in late August 1943, for with *Victorious* repairing the damage suffered during 'Pedestal' the Home Fleet was left with no carriers at all.

Hard on the heels of Fraser's return to the Home Fleet came Churchill's return to London (24 August) from his journey to Cairo and Moscow. Churchill's sessions with Stalin had been stormy, beginning as they had to with Churchill confirming that there could be no 'Second Front' invasion of German-occupied France in 1942. Stalin bitterly accused Britain and the United States of going back on their word, and Britain in particular of failing to deliver all the supplies promised to Russia by the northern route. 'Has the British Navy no sense of glory?' sneered Stalin in a brutal reference to PQ.17. Though Churchill gave as good as he got he came away from Moscow, in his own words, 'with new resolve to aid Russia to the very limits of our power', urging the Admiralty 'to solve the problem of running convoys by the northern route'.[10]

Though the problem was beyond solution in the short term, Admiral Tovey did what he could to diminish it. He radically changed the dispositions of the attenuated Home Fleet for the passage of PQ.18 in September 1942. This time he planned to run the show from his flagship *King George V* (now back with the Fleet) in Scapa Flow – in direct telephone communication with the Admiralty. Fraser would command the Distant Covering Force in *Anson*, with *Duke of York*, *Jamaica* and five destroyers. Their base for the operation would not be Scapa but Akureyri in north Iceland. This convoy would not sail with a light-weight, 'detachable' escort: it would be driven through to Archangel with a fighting destroyer escort sixteen strong, every available long-range destroyer in the Home Fleet, along with one of the priceless new escort carriers,

HMS *Avenger*, carrying twelve Sea Hurricanes and three anti-submarine Swordfish.

Commanding the fighting escort was Rear-Admiral Robert Burnett, the Home Fleet's Rear-Admiral (D), flying his flag in the AA cruiser *Scylla*. As PQ.18 and the subsequent fourteen months were to prove, he was adept at handling the crucial 'flying switch' of the escort forces from outward-bound to homeward-bound convoys in the dangerous longitude of the North Cape. To help with the vital flow of signals between Burnett's flagship and the convoy and escort, Tovey 'lent' Burnett his Signal Officer, Commander Richard Courage. 'Bob Burnett made me an honorary member of his staff so that I could help his Signal Officer, Sandy Gordon Lennox,' writes Courage. 'Sandy told me to control the convoy R/T. . . . The use of R/T on previous Russian convoys had been discouraged because it was known that the Germans could not only listen to every word but record and analyse it afterwards. For this convoy it was decided that the benefit to be derived from rapid R/T communications during action outweighed the risk we were open to.'[11]

Forty ships strong, PQ.18 sailed from Loch Ewe on 2 September; thirteen of them were sunk before the convoy reached Archangel on the 18th, after epic battles between the escorts and the *Luftwaffe*. No previous Russian convoy had ever experienced air attacks of such intensity but the Germans failed completely in their bid to break up the convoy, as they mistakenly believed they had done with PQ.17, with U-boat and massed air attacks. Some forty-one German aircraft were shot down and three U-boats were sunk, with another five damaged. The Home Fleet's losses were gratifyingly light: the destroyer *Somali* and fleet minesweeper *Leda*, both sunk by U-boats. Despite its frustrating stand-off role, Fraser's covering force had played its part to the full, being located by German air reconnaissance on 8 September and helping influence Hitler to forbid a planned sortie by the German battle fleet.

But there was no chance of sailing another Russian convoy in October or November 1942. Once again the Home Fleet was milked of warships to meet the demands of the Mediterranean theatre, the cause this time being the 'Torch' invasion of French North Africa scheduled for November. Despite Stalin's protests the Russian convoys were therefore suspended for two months until the escort strength of the Home Fleet was restored. When they started again in December 1942 the convoys were given the new code-letters 'JW' (for security reasons), beginning with the number 51. Tovey's advice had finally been taken by the Admiralty and the new convoys were sailed in two halves, the second half sailing a week after the first.

By December 1942 the two best pieces of news for the men of the

Russian convoys were that *Tirpitz* had gone south for a refit (23 October) and that the *Luftwaffe's* strength in Arctic Norway was being considerably reduced as successive units were rushed south to the Mediterranean. But the pocket-battleship *Lützow* and heavy cruiser *Hipper* posed a most serious threat to the resumed convoys. As the Home Fleet now lacked any carriers at all, there could be no question of risking the priceless 'KG Vs' in the constricted sea corridor between the winter pack ice and the Norwegian coast. Each half-convoy would, however, have the now customary distant cover of a battle group. Because of the ever-present worry about a pocket-battleship breaking out into the North Atlantic, this necessitated Tovey putting to sea as well as Fraser.

On 15 December Tovey sailed in *King George V* with the cruiser *Berwick* and three destroyers, to give distant cover to JW.51A while Fraser in *Anson*, with *Cumberland* and three destroyers, moved up to Akureyri ready to cover JW.51B. The new system got off to a flying start, with JW.51A taking the Germans completely by surprise and reaching Murmansk without a single casualty on Christmas Day. Burnett, with the cruisers *Sheffield* and *Jamaica*, had accompanied JW.51A to Murmansk, whence he sailed on 27 December to come west and pick up JW.51B, which had been at sea for five days. But on the 27th JW.51B was disrupted by a great gale and driven 30 miles south and 60 miles west of where Burnett and Tovey expected it to be on the 30th – the day on which *U-354* sighted and reported 'six to ten ships steaming east at 12 knots with a weak escort'. Grand-Admiral Raeder at once ordered Vice-Admiral Oscar Kummetz to sortie from Altenfjord with *Lützow*, *Hipper* and six destroyers, and liquidate this tempting target. And the result, on 31 December, was the Battle of the Barents Sea.[12]

Kummetz had barely put to sea on the evening of the 30th when he received the paralysing signal, 'Use caution even against enemy of equal strength because it is undesirable for the cruisers to take great risks.' This order explains much of the hesitancy of the Germans on the 31st, when *Hipper* and *Lützow* closed in on JW.51B from north and south, only to be outfaced by the flimsy screen of five close-escort destroyers under Captain Sherbrooke in *Onslow*. *Hipper*, attacking from the north, had crippled two of Sherbrooke's destroyers when she was most gallantly brought to action by Burnett with *Sheffield* and *Jamaica*, steaming at full speed towards the gun flashes on the southern horizon. With *Hipper* reporting damage above decks Kummetz declined to intervene with *Lützow*'s powerful battery of six 11-inch guns and ordered a retirement instead, leaving JW.51B to reach Murmansk safely on 3 January.

For the Home Fleet this was a splendid start to the New Year, but by far the most dramatic consequence of the battle derived from the lamentable performance of the German force. This sent Hitler into a frenzy, raging that the German heavy ships were a waste of good men, guns and armour plate: they were to be scrapped forthwith. Raeder resigned in protest and was replaced by the U-boat Commander-in-Chief Karl Dönitz. But Dönitz soon managed to persuade a calmer Hitler that the German heavy surface ships still had a role to play and must be kept in being. While this furore was raging in the German camp the British Home Fleet successfully ran two more untouched Russian convoys: JW.52 (17–27 January 1943) and JW.53 (15–29 February). In the same period the return convoy RA.52 reached the United Kingdom with the loss of one ship out of eleven.

Fraser provided the distant cover for JW.52 and RA.52, but during the passage of RA.53 the effects of Raeder's replacement by Dönitz suddenly made themselves felt. On 8 March RAF reconnaissance noticed that the battle-cruiser *Scharnhorst* had left Gdynia in the Baltic. As at this time it was known that the return of *Tirpitz* to the Arctic was imminent, this move by *Scharnhorst* was deeply worrying and Fraser moved to Hvalfjord in Iceland with *Anson*. Three days later *Tirpitz* was sighted leaving Trondheim, and by the 14th *Tirpitz*, *Scharnhorst* and *Lützow* were all at Narvik. When all three moved up to Altenfjord on the 22nd the Home Fleet suddenly found itself confronted by the most powerful German battle squadron assembled since the outbreak of war – in the very month that the operational U-boat strength reached its zenith of 240 operational submarines, and the struggle for the North Atlantic lifeline moved to its climax. This time Tovey's advice that the Russian convoys must be suspended for the duration of the Arctic summer was unanswerable, and on 30 March Stalin was so informed by Churchill.

Throughout the desperate weeks of April and May 1943, when every available escort was thrown into the Atlantic battle, the Home Fleet necessarily reverted to a passive role. But for Fraser this was by no means a time of inaction. For the past ten months he had been devoting himself to absorbing the lessons learned from the PQ and JW convoys, and mulling over the opportunities they presented, but he was also developing his own unique style of what may be called 'admiralship': the art of being an admiral.

From his experience in *Resolution* with the Grand Fleet during the First World War, Fraser was already deeply aware of the threat to morale posed by the contrast between the soft life in the big ships, and the appalling strain put on the men of the destroyers and light escort forces. Fraser's determination to show his sympathy and understanding towards the officers and men of the little ships went naturally with his own gregarious, approachable instincts, developing a policy which he himself summed up as 'champagne for destroyers'. Once experienced this was never forgotten, as the following example shows. It will be noted that the officer concerned, Lt-Commander R. C. Freaker, RNR, was not even under Fraser's command:[13]

I did not serve with Lord Fraser at any time, but I had the pleasure of meeting him once during the war and have never forgotten the occasion. This was while, as a Lieut-Cdr RNR, I was serving as Commanding Officer of HMS *Jed*, a 'River' class frigate.

On 28 January 1943, while on escort duty in North Atlantic, *Jed* developed defects and was ordered into Iceland for repairs. At the time of our arrival in Iceland HMS *Anson*, the flagship of Admiral Fraser, was anchored in the same fjord.

The next day – a Saturday as far as I remember – I was having a late breakfast when I received a signal from Admiral Fraser which said that he would like to visit *Jed* at 1100, 'if convenient'. Naturally I replied that it *was* convenient, and we duly welcomed Admiral Fraser on board. He was wearing a naval raincoat, and apart from his cap there were no visible marks of his rank. He saw all over the ship and spoke to a number of the ratings. He even commented on the depth of our bilge keels. It was only afterwards that I learned that Admiral Fraser had been Third Sea Lord at the time the 'River' class frigates were ordered, and naturally was interested in the class.

On the completion of his visit he invited me to have lunch on board the flagship. I thanked him but explained that as we were in dry dock and our motor boat was not in the water I had no boat. He said that his barge would collect me. On arrival on board *Anson* I found that I was one of a number of guests at the Admiral's luncheon party. All the others appeared to be senior Army or Air Force officers. As a mere lieut-commander I felt very honoured.

After lunch various boats arrived to pick up these senior officers. I appeared to be the only one without his boat – but the Admiral's barge was called away for me! I felt a little embarrassed and I thanked Admiral Fraser very much for his kindness and all the trouble he was taking for me. He replied that 'nothing was too much trouble for a frigate'. I have never seen Lord Fraser since, but I have never forgotten his kindness – or the meaning of his last words to me.

But sometimes a firmer hand was needed. One such occasion, also in Hvalfjord during these months, featured an Allied destroyer captain (name and nationality withheld on Lord Fraser's insistence), understandably rendered 'tired and emotional' by a particularly demanding convoy run. Invited to dinner aboard *Anson*, the destroyer Captain regrettably measured his length on the Wardroom floor after an over-enthusiastic session with the port. In the words of Fraser's then Flag Lieutenant, Lt-Commander C. J. Eliot:[14]

> the party broke up in some disorder. Sir Bruce was one of the gentlest and kindest men I have ever served with, but for about the only time in my life I saw him really angry. He dictated a signal to me for ⸺ which simply said 'I SHALL INSPECT YOUR SHIP AT 0900 TOMORROW FRIDAY'. He also made another signal relieving ⸺'s Captain as senior officer of the screen and appointing the next in seniority, a British Commander.
>
> The next day, promptly at 0900, the Admiral accompanied by all his Staff went aboard ⸺. We were greeted by the Captain who, apart from the fact that he looked a bit white, was perfectly correct, very smart in his best uniform. The Admiral really put the ship through her paces. He inspected every inch: upper deck, mess decks, engine room, bridge, etc., all at breakneck speed. We on the Staff were quite exhausted, and I think the Admiral was tiring, but the Captain was as fresh as a daisy – and the ship was in tip-top condition. Considering that the ship's company had only had a few hours' notice, and that in the middle of the night; and that she had been at sea almost continuously for weeks on end, she was quite incredibly smart and neither the Admiral nor any of his Staff could find anything wrong. Furthermore, nobody could have been more on the ball than the Captain.
>
> When we got back, the Admiral sent for me and made another signal which simply said 'I WAS DELIGHTED WITH ALL I SAW IN YOUR SHIP THIS MORNING. WELL DONE.'
>
> We went to sea shortly afterwards. The ⸺ had been degraded to a wing of the screen and the RN destroyer was leading. The Admiral left it like that for the night but next morning, in his usual kindly way, he said me 'I think he has learned his lesson by now', and made a signal reinstating ⸺. He was right, too, for we often went to sea with ⸺ again, and a smarter ship and more alert Captain would have been hard to find.

Nor was the 'Fraser touch' – ever – reserved for officers only. Leading Signalman Hall of the VA2's communications staff, who kept his watches on the Admiral's Bridge, remembered Fraser as 'a man of great kindness, consideration and humour':[15]

> The Admiral would not tolerate inefficiency, and as soon as a signal was sent by lamp or flags he expected to be informed of its content immediately. He appeared interested in visual signals – particularly in a clean flag hoist!
>
> But he always seemed concerned with the welfare of the crews of the smaller ships, and nearly every day, during bad weather, signals would be made asking for reports of the conditions on board. As the only representative of the Lower Deck on the Admiral's Bridge, I was frequently questioned by him about conditions on our mess deck and whether or not the galley was able to prepare the food.
>
> During our time in *Victorious* a leading telegraphist and I asked for permission to fly from the carrier, which we did in Barracudas, and on our return the Admiral asked us how we'd got on. He took a great interest in individuals.

Such are the retentive memories of a very special commander in a time of preparation. On the purely professional level, by the spring of 1943 Fraser had proved himself an utterly capable and dependable VA2 to one of the country's foremost admirals of the Second World War. When the Russian convoys were suspended at the end of March 1943, Tovey's period of command was drawing to its close. For the Admiralty, for Pound, for Churchill, there was no doubt that Fraser was the right man to succeed Tovey in command of the Home Fleet when Tovey struck his flag on 8 May 1943.

Fraser was fifty-five years old when he took command of the fleet which, two years earlier, had won the most dramatic British naval victory of the war by sinking *Bismarck*. Now, though he had never commanded or even fought in a fleet action, he had to anticipate possible battle with a menace greater by far than that which *Bismarck* had posed. But amid all the handshakes and ceremonial of 8 May 1943 there was heartening encouragement in the following 'Naval Message' from Whitehall to Fraser:[16]

> TO: C IN C HOME FLEET FROM ADMIRALTY PERSONAL FOR ADMIRAL FRASER FROM THE PRIME MINISTER
>
> I SEND YOU MY CONGRATULATIONS IN YOUR GREAT COMMAND. OUR INTIMATE WORK TOGETHER AT THE ADMIRALTY GIVES ME THE UTMOST CONFIDENCE YOU WILL DISCHARGE IT WITH SKILL AND VIGOUR.

Commander-in-Chief Home Fleet

[May–December 1943]

Fraser's biggest asset on taking command of the Home Fleet was his previous ten months' service with the Fleet as VA2. He knew the job, and, no less important, the Home Fleet knew he knew the job. There was no need for Fraser to 'work himself in': he was thoroughly familiar with the Fleet's operational environment in all seasons, at sea and on shore, and with the problems faced by the men and ships of his new command. Another priceless asset for Fraser was the excellent Staff team he inherited from Tovey, a legacy better than much fine gold. (Among the gallery of talent on Fraser's Staff was the then Lt-Commander Michael Le Fanu, destined in 1961 to become the Navy's youngest Controller in seventy years, to mastermind the plans for Britain's Polaris fleet and, like Fraser, to rise to First Sea Lord and Admiral of the Fleet. Like so many others, Le Fanu took Fraser as his model in professional standards and deportment.) Thus there was no need for Fraser to institute any drastic 'house-cleaning' among the Staff when he took over, and the result was a reassuring sense of continuity in the administration of the Fleet.

Fraser's third legacy from Admiral Tovey was the soundness of the Home Fleet's morale. This had taken a severe blow with the PQ.17 disaster in July 1942, when 'What price the Wop Navy now? What about the *Jervis Bay*? Why did we come at all?' had been some of the most bitter Lower-Deck comments during the cruisers' retirement from the Barents Sea.[1] Repairing the Home Fleet's morale after PQ.17 must be counted among Tovey's last great achievements with the Home Fleet, which had defied the *Luftwaffe* to fight through PQ.18 and gone on to win a clear-cut victory in the Barents Sea battle of 31 December 1942.

In his first weeks as Commander-in-Chief, Fraser was also spared the unenviable task of trying to make naval reality prevail over political expediency, for the decision to suspend the Russian convoys during the summer months had been taken back in March. Desperate though the Soviet Union's position had appeared during the summer and autumn of 1942, it was obvious by spring 1943 that the picture had changed out of all recognition. At Stalingrad during the winter of 1942–3 the Russians had managed to wipe out the toughest German army on the Eastern Front, recovering all the ground lost in the German summer offensive of 1942. In Fraser's view, expressed to the Admiralty at the end of June 1943, the convoys could no longer be considered vital to the survival of the Soviet Union, and hence to the successful prosecution of the war. There could, he argued, be only one objective in resuming the convoys: to 'enable the German surface forces to be brought successfully to action'. But therein lay the rub: in the summer of 1943 such an achievement was utterly beyond the resources of the Home Fleet.

The German battle squadron in Arctic Norway was harder-hitting and faster than any possible concentration of British capital ships. *Tirpitz, Scharnhorst* and *Lützow* could fire a total main-armament broadside of eight 15-inch and fifteen 11-inch guns, while *Tirpitz* and *Scharnhorst* were capable of speeds of 30 knots and more. For the Home Fleet the old dilemma still applied; such a powerful force would be required to tackle the German squadron that the Germans would never dare come out. And in summer 1943 there was no chance of assembling such a powerful force anyway, because of another familiar incubus: the demands of the Mediterranean theatre. After the Alamein/'Torch' offensives of October-November 1942 had come the long battle for Tunisia, and when Tunis fell on 8 May 1943 work immediately began on the build-up for the invasion of Sicily, with every available capital ship in the European theatre of operations earmarked to protect the invasion fleet.

Fraser therefore found that his first task as Commander-in-Chief was to play host to the stream of warships which came up to Scapa, in May-June 1943, to exercise and work up efficiency for the coming assault on Sicily. This was by no means straightforward because, as Roskill points out in *The War At Sea*, 'the effective strength available to the Commander-in-Chief was in fact barely adequate to meet his responsibilities':[2]

New ships and those which had recently re-commissioned, or had completed refit or repairs, generally came to Scapa to 'work up' efficiency; but this placed an extra strain on the base, which had to provide them with targets, arrange exercises for them, and also give anti-submarine protection while they were at sea ... all the heavy ships of Force H (the battleships *Nelson, Rodney, Warspite* and *Valiant* and the fleet carrier *Indomitable*, under Vice-Admiral A. U. Willis) came from the western Mediterranean to Scapa during June to prepare for the invasion of Sicily and, in particular, to practise heavy gun bombardments in support of an army recently flung ashore on a hostile coast.

In June 1943 there could be no way of knowing how vitally important the 'big-gun' experience gained during the Mediterranean invasions would prove to the Home Fleet on 26 December. At the time it spelled weeks of hard work for Fraser's Staff and the Scapa base facilities. The Staff coped admirably with the additional load, most notably, perhaps, Le Fanu, with his legendary telephone-answering 'signature' of 'Scapa Services here: can we help you?' But it was only natural that Fraser should become somewhat irked by the stream of telephone calls from the Admiralty, from which there was only one escape: putting to sea. As recalled by the Chief-of-Staff's Secretary, Lt-Commander Selwyn Powell:

> I think the episode that sticks out most clearly in my mind is the 'trip to Glasgow'. Admiral Fraser had got fed up with constant telephone calls from the First Sea Lord's office – 'I must get the Flagship off the telephone buoy'. 'Where will you go, sir?' 'Let's go to Glasgow. I can inspect the Wrens.' So we went. Lovely weather, a very successful trip. On the way home Commander Thomas, the Master of the Fleet [the title borne by the Navigating Officer on the C-in-C's Staff], said, 'There seem to be U-boats about. Don't you think it would be a good idea if we went through the Sound of Mull, sir?' 'If you think there's room for us.' 'Oh, yes, sir, quite a few feet either side to spare.' 'Right.' From the quarterdeck you felt you could touch land on either side. A beautiful day – Oban on the starboard side in the distance, Duart Castle to port. Then we passed Tobermory with Admiral Sir Gilbert Stephenson saluting and dipping his Ensign as we passed.

Years later Admiral Stephenson, discussing the incident with Powell, admitted, 'I was never so taken by surprise in my life':

> 'I was having my afternoon nap when a signalman woke me. "*Duke of York* coming up the Sound, sir." "Don't be a bloody fool, lad. *Duke of York* is a battleship." "It *is* a battleship, coming up the Sound, sir." I sprang up, seized my cap and rushed outside. By the time the C-in-C came by all was in order, men lined up, the Ensign dipping in salute.'[3]

By the end of June 1943 the work of 'Scapa Services' was finished as far as the Mediterranean warships were concerned, all of which had returned south for the invasion of Sicily. But they took with them *King George V* and *Howe*, no less than 50 per cent of the Home Fleet's modern battleship strength. Fraser was left with no modern carriers at all (the old *Furious* was long overdue for refit) and only *Duke of York* and *Anson*. The only other battleship in home waters, the obsolete 'Queen Elizabeth' *Malaya*, was paid off and reduced to 'Care and Maintenance' in July 1943, releasing her crew for service in more modern warships. Given the fire-power of the German battle squadron, this left the Home Fleet even weaker than it had been in the previous summer. But, as in 1942, the balance was redressed by the US Navy. In July 1943 Rear-Admiral Hustvedt, USN, with the battleships USS *South Dakota* and *Alabama* and five destroyers, were transferred to Scapa from Argentia, Newfoundland. In the increasingly unlikely event of a German surface naval strike at the North Atlantic convoy route, Fraser would now be able to engage with his two 'KG Vs' reinforced by the two 'South Dakotas', with their combined main-armament broadside of eighteen 16-inch guns.

No one was more aware than Fraser that he was presiding over the end of an era: the last months of the war in which it would be appropriate for American heavy naval units to serve under British command. Fraser knew that if the time should come for the Royal Navy to participate in strength in the Pacific theatre, the boot would be very much on the other foot. This he accepted as quite natural: a case for courtesy, rather than the counter-productive chauvinism which has never been far away in Anglo-American strategic counsels. And courtesy remained the keynote in his dealing with the American warships:[4]

'They were very good. We asked them to change to British signalling, and they agreed right away. Curiously enough I said, "Well, one day we shall have to change to yours." And sure enough, when the time came to set up the Pacific Fleet, one of the most important things in our discussions with Admiral Nimitz was offering to change to American signalling – they were awfully pleased.'

Though the signalling hurdle was cleared with ease at the outset, it was soon clear that both navies had a lot to learn from each other:[5]

'When the Americans came over to join us they seemed to have no experience of submarines at all. They really didn't take many anti-submarine precautions – we had great difficulty making them take proper precautions. I took them up with me to Iceland, which was where we'd be restarting the convoys from.

We went out for a range-finding exercise as well, and I sent the Americans up north of me, and they disappeared over the horizon! I asked them afterwards why they had disappeared, and they said "Actually, we only wanted to make sure we'd cross the Arctic Circle." Then the fog came down; we'd come in two detachments, and all of a sudden we heard depth-charges going off left and right. Of course, we knew it had to be porpoises, or basking sharks, or something. Don't know *how* many depth-charges they let off!'

On the social level the fact that 'Uncle Sam's Navy' was alcoholically dry and the Royal Navy was not offered obvious attractions to the Americans, who soon learned to time their courtesy visits to British ships for the hour of the British 'sundowner'. Though ever the soul of hospitality, Fraser was bound to admit that:[6]

'At that time the Americans were always calling on us about 6 o'clock in the evening, and it did get to be rather a nuisance. The American Admiral used to make a signal: "Could I come and see you about 5 o'clock?" When the American Secretary of State, Knox, came up to see us (20–21 September) I remember telling him "I'm sure it's time you allowed alcohol in the US Navy," and he said "Actually, I'm in favour of this – it's the *admirals* who are all against it!" '

When visiting American warships Fraser's lack of pomp and generous interest in junior officers and ratings came as something of a shock to his American colleagues. His first visit to one of Hustvedt's battleships was typical: the result of a friendly request to be allowed 'to walk round your ship informally' around noon:[7]

The Admiral was conducted round the ship by a fairly large group of officers, but in the informal way that he had requested; and one can imagine the concern of the American officers when they realised, at one point in the tour, that their distinguished British guest was no longer with them, and a hurried search party had to be organised.

At this date the ships' companies of RN ships still had their separate messes, and the meals were brought to the messes by the 'cooks of messes' ten minutes before the meal was piped. But the US Navy had introduced a cafeteria system whereby the individual collected his own meal from a central servery and took it to a common mess. The Admiral was eventually discovered chatting to American sailors halfway up the queue to the servery – he'd wanted to have some first-hand information of the time it took for a sailor to collect his dinner.

As described by former Flag Lieutenant (afterwards Captain) Vernon Merry, visiting ships was one of the hinges of Fraser's working daily routine as Commander-in-Chief:[8]

'He didn't believe in getting up early. He'd appear in the Cuddy at about five past nine – quite late for a seagoing routine. By that time the rest of the Cuddy had had their breakfasts and disappeared; a good routine, no forced conversation at breakfast. The Admiral would always have an egg for his breakfast, and coffee; he used to eat his breakfast quickly, and I would have put his signals on his plate to read while he was having his breakfast. Then he'd go off for a turn on deck and the cabin would be cleared for the Staff Meeting, for which he'd appear at 9.30.

The Staff Meeting would last till about ten o'clock, after which the Admiral would spend a few minutes over special points with the appropriate Staff officers, and talking with his Secretary. By about half past ten he was ready to go off visiting.

He was so good at visiting the ships. He'd walk round taking everything in, and he would talk to anybody – just as happy talking with, say, an ERA down an engine-room, asking about his problems. And this way the Admiral got to know a lot of the details, particularly with radar. He'd ask 'Why isn't your set working today?' 'Well, sir, we're waiting for parts.' 'What sort of parts?', and so on. It might be an oscillator, or some kind of valve; but the Admiral would find out from a little exchange like this that there was a shortage of these parts throughout the Fleet. And he'd look at me, and I'd make a note to get on to the Fleet Radar Officer when we got back.

The Admiral would finish up with a glass of gin and a chat in the Wardroom; and then it was his habit, when we were back in the barge, to invite me to say what I'd thought of the ship. She might have looked a bit scruffy, and we'd discuss why. Between us we'd build up a useful memory of the ship – no knowing when we'd be visiting her next.

After each visit I'd contact the appropriate Staff officer and say, 'I think you ought to know the Admiral's concerned that there seems to be a shortage of spares for the Type 273', or whatever. And woe betide the Staff officer if he hadn't come back to the Admiral with a solution in a reasonable time – 'That trouble over the radar spares, sir – what it is is *this*, and I've done *that* about it.' There was one occasion, in Sydney, when the officer in question hadn't done the necessary and it didn't look as if he was going to; and the Admiral heard about it. He told the chap, 'You will go down to that ship *personally*, and you will *stay there* until she's been repaired.' Instant results. But that was an exceptional case.

Back from visiting by one o'clock; a gin in the Cuddy; then lunch, which would be over by about two. And then he used to sit on his settee and he'd like to be left alone until four, when Barnwell (Admiral's Steward) would take in his tea. Now, all the time I was with him I never found him getting his head down in the afternoon. He used just to sit and think. I'd often have to put my head in and see what he was doing; he was sitting and thinking about the readiness of the Fleet, working out what he'd do under any circumstances – just thinking it all over. I never saw him with his eyes closed. Not that he'd have minded anyone else getting their heads down – at sea you slept when you got the chance – but *he* wouldn't sleep then. Those two hours were dedicated to thought, and, of course, it paid off. Long before he fought the *Scharnhorst* he'd thought about all the difficulties and problems beforehand, and what he'd do about them.

Then he'd have his tea at four, and during the First Dog (1600–1800 hrs) he'd be prepared to see Staff officers; he might polish off the little bit of reading that his Secretary might have ready. A turn on the Quarterdeck for a bit of exercise, and then we'd gather in the Cuddy for a glass of gin at about quarter to eight; and more often than not there would be guests. The Admiral always kept a very good table; I think C-in-Cs' 'table money' at that time was £17 10s a day, and he'd never have seen any change out of that. When the guests included destroyer, submarine or carrier officers champagne was always served; battleship, cruiser or other big ship officers only got wine. There would be at least four courses, the conversation was always lively and everybody was soon put at his ease. Even when there were no guests, the regular members of the Cuddy (Secretary, Flag Lieutenant, Chief of Staff, Captain of the Fleet and Flag Captain) were always sure of a convivial evening at the Admiral's table.

I'd take the day's last batch of signals in to the Admiral between eleven and eleven-fifteen. As he got ready to read them he'd say, 'Have a nightcap, Flags.' I'd say, 'Thank you, sir', and he'd add, 'And pour me a Scotch.' He'd read the signals while I got the drinks, then I'd sit on the back of the settee, facing his desk, and he'd say, 'Right, Flags, what are we going to do tomorrow?' 'Well, sir, what about going to see *Onslow* at 1045, she's just back from her refit, then *Opportune* at 1115; then we could come back and see *Gambia* at 1145.' 'All right, Flags, that sounds fine.' Any other business we'd handle then, perhaps while drinking the 'other half'; and I'd leave him just after midnight, to go and write out the signals, which would be received in the ship concerned at about one in the morning. The usual sort of thing was, 'C-IN-C TO *SO-AND-SO*: IF CONVENIENT I WOULD LIKE TO WALK ROUND YOUR SHIP INFORMALLY AT 1045 TOMORROW, NORMAL ROUTINE TO CONTINUE.' He'd use this form because you couldn't turn out a ship's company in the middle of the night to start sweeping and cleaning.

The Admiral had a tremendous respect for the small ships, destroyers, frigates, submarines, and thought that serving in anything bigger than a cruiser was a pretty easy time. 'Champagne for destroyers' was one of his favourite sayings, the idea being that nothing was too good for the small ships. One of his specialities was to invite, say, a destroyer alongside *Duke of York* for the night and she'd be the flagship's guest, the Admiral turning over his sea cabin to the visiting Captain and the rest of us generally acting as hosts. Once he invited the submarine *Stubborn* alongside after she'd had a tough patrol; the Germans had bottomed her and she'd been unable to dive after getting away. When she slipped the next morning the Admiral signalled, 'C-IN-C TO *STUBBORN*: WELL DONE. IT WAS A GREAT PRIVILEGE TO HAVE LAIN ALONGSIDE YOU IN MY FLAGSHIP.'

How to sum it up? He didn't believe in putting in a long working day behind a desk, worrying over details. He devoted his time to thinking, to visiting, to showing himself to the Fleet. He had a good team of Staff officers to look after the details and he gave them full responsibility. He was a superb delegator.

I can't remember a happier 'flagship atmosphere'. It was understood by every officer in the flagship that there was to be no bickering, no moaning, no forming of factions. Any complaints between Staff and ship's officers were to be channelled straight through to the Admiral or to the Flag Captain without anyone putting their oar in along the line. Sometimes the Admiral would talk about this in the Cuddy. He'd seen quite enough of the other thing – friction between ship and Staff – during his earlier career, and had vowed that if he ever became an Admiral himself he would have peace within his flagship. And so it was.'

Nor was 'showing himself to the Fleet' confined to visiting seagoing warships. As recalled by the then Lieutenant J. Nesbit, RNR, a junior watchkeeping officer in *Duke of York*:[9]

> On several occasions, when *Duke of York* went to sea for a day's routine practice shoot (to calibrate guns & so on), the Admiral would shift his flag to one of the boom defence vessels which had the thankless job of working the defence nets, such as those at Hoxa Gate and Switha Sound. He'd spend the day with usually rather a scruffy crew (no one else seemed to care about them, so this was no wonder), yarning with them about their homes and their hopes, drinking cocoa out of pint mugs and partaking with relish of their cuisine – the latter definitely not up to *Duke of York*'s standard!

A keynote of Fraser's 'admiralship' was his interest in and encouragement of young and junior officers, and Nesbit remembered how this warmth was extended to the junior officers of the American ships:[10]

> The Admiral would sometimes invite young officers – sub-lieutenants and midshipmen – to the flagship for a cocktail party, to which two or three of the ship's company would be invited to help entertain. He was charming and friendly, and would take aside some young lieutenant for a long chat about his home in Wyoming, or somewhere. This of course endeared him to them all.

In August 1943 the two American battleships were replaced by the heavy cruisers USS *Augusta* and *Tuscaloosa*, plus the light carrier USS *Ranger*. The latter was particularly welcome because her arrival filled the gap left by the departure of *Furious* for refit. The old British carrier's last stint of sea time before her refit had come on 8 July, when Fraser had taken the entire available strength of the Home Fleet to sea on Operation 'Camera'.

The object of 'Camera', timed as it was for the eve of the Sicilian invasion (which commenced on 10 July) was to cruise off the Norwegian coast and hopefully persuade the Germans that the Allies were about to attempt a major operation against Norway. Fraser pugnaciously cruised to within 150 miles of the Norwegian coast, closer than the Home Fleet had ventured since Tovey's unsuccessful attempt to catch *Tirpitz* with a carrier strike back in 1942. The sweep never had much chance as a serious diversionary attempt: with so many Allied troops massed in North African ports the Germans were well aware that the next big Allied move would have to be somewhere in the Mediterranean, and Sicily was high on the list of probable targets. Yet Fraser's sweep of 8 July was certainly not a mere waste of fuel oil: it proved just how drastically the *Luftwaffe*'s strength in Norway had been reduced, for ten months before it would have been suicide to have cruised so close to the Norwegian airfields. The experiment was repeated at the end of July (Operation 'Governor') this time with *Illustrious* accompanying the Home Fleet. This famous carrier was now operating American-built Grumman F4F fighters, 'Wildcats' to the Americans, 'Martlets' to the British, and they shot down a heartening total of five German reconnaissance aircraft during the sweep.

It was galling for Fraser to have such a brief loan of a modern fleet carrier, but *Illustrious* stayed with the Home Fleet for barely a week. On 5 August she left, taking with her three of Fraser's cruisers and a destroyer flotilla, escorts for the *Queen Mary*, which was carrying Churchill and the Chiefs of Staff to the 'Quadrant' Conference in Quebec (19–24 August). It was, therefore, to a typically reduced Home Fleet that King George VI came for a visit and inspection (12–14 August). Britain's most recent 'sailor king' (who, as HRH Prince Albert, had served at Jutland) always found visiting his ships a bracing respite from the cares of state. Despite the necessary formalities the visit passed off happily, as much to the pleasure of Fraser as of the King. There was, however, a brief moment of awkwardness when Fraser had to tell the King that the scheduled day at sea with the Fleet should be postponed. Amid all the preparations no one had noticed that the King would be going to sea on that most ill-omened of days: Friday the Thirteenth.[11]

'It was Captain Denny who pointed out that the Fleet would be very worried about the King, so we changed it to Saturday. But the King wasn't very pleased at first. In the end it all went off all right, though the King was rather tired – he'd had a full day. As he came down from the Bridge the Master-at-Arms went on in front, with the bugle blowing as the signal for everyone to stand at attention; and the King said, "Who does he think I am – the Emperor of Japan?" '

The success of the visit may be judged by the King's letter to Fraser afterwards:[12]

BUCKINGHAM PALACE
August 17th 1943

My dear Fraser,
I must write & thank you very much for all your help & kind hospitality to me on my visit to the Home Fleet under your command. I did so enjoy my few days with you & I was so impressed with all you showed me especially the day at sea

& the gunnery practice. I thought the shooting very good by all the different types of guns you now carry. As you know I always appreciate the way you all treat me as a sailor & I do feel one of you when I am at Scapa.

Again very many thanks to you & I wish you the best of luck.

        I am
    Yours very sincerely
    George R.I.

The royal visit in mid-August was a most satisfactory conclusion to Fraser's first three months as Commander-in-Chief and a prominent milestone, for in the next six weeks a sequence of dramatic events transformed the prospects of Fraser and his Fleet, not to mention those of the entire Allied war effort.

In the Mediterranean Mussolini had already fallen from power (24–25 July), toppled by the invasion of Sicily. On 3 September, the fourth anniversary of the outbreak of the war, Italy signed an armistice with the Allies and although the Germans moved in fast to occupy southern Italy the Italians surrendered their battle fleet a week later. The surrender of the Italian fleet removed the most urgent motive for the Allies to retain a decisive naval superiority in the Mediterranean. The Allies proceeded with the invasion of Italy (3–9 September), their purpose now to pin down as many German divisions as possible before the great cross-Channel invasion scheduled for the following year. The Germans came perilously close to wiping out the Anglo-American beach-head at Salerno (9–16 September). But the Allied troops, thunderously supported by the fire of Admiral Cunningham's battleships, won through to enter Naples on 1 October: the first major city on the mainland of Europe to be liberated.

The second event in these six weeks occurred in northern waters. It was really a two-act drama: an unexpected sortie by *Tirpitz*, *Scharnhorst* and ten destroyers to bombard Spitzbergen (6–9 September), followed within a fortnight by the momentous crippling of *Tirpitz* by British X-craft (midget submarines).

The German sortie, a hit-and-run raid against the 100-strong Norwegian garrison on Spitzbergen, was insignificant in itself, though a timely reminder that Allied air intelligence was still, in the fifth year of the war, completely unable to keep a round-the-clock check on German naval movements in the Arctic. By the time news of the attack reached Fraser in Scapa and he put to sea with the Home Fleet, the German warships were already on their way home and there was no chance of intercepting them. But all was redressed on 22 September, when the British X-craft struck at *Tirpitz* in Ka-afjord. The cost was heavy: the single X-craft (out of the six committed to the attack) which returned in safety to her parent submarine had to be scuttled on the long tow back to Scapa. Yet two X-craft, though their crews were captured, successfully laid their explosive charges beneath *Tirpitz* as she lay at anchor, and the resultant blast ended the battleship's career as an ocean-going warship. Her engines and fire-control equipment were wrecked, two turrets immobilised and her port rudder twisted. Six months of intensive repairs were needed before *Tirpitz* would claim a semblance of seaworthiness.

The X-craft would probably have claimed *Scharnhorst* as well, had not her gunnery on the Spitzbergen raid been so bad that her captain had shifted berth in preparation for a much-needed practice shoot. The pocket-battleship *Lützow* also escaped the X-craft; but her immediate departure for the Baltic via Narvik and Trondheim (23–29 September) caught the British decidedly by surprise. Though she was sighted heading south from the Vestfjord approach to Narvik on the morning of the 26th, it took until the early afternoon before the Admiralty passed on the news, not grading the faithful Norwegian agent's report as very reliable. Another 22 hours elapsed before *Lützow* was sighted by air reconnaissance. This time-loss robbed Fraser of the chance to despatch USS *Ranger* to within extreme carrier strike range before *Lützow* could reach the safety of German waters. But it was almost entirely due to him that *any* effort was made to catch the pocket-battleship while she was still off the Norwegian coast.

As soon as the Admiralty's report was received on the 26th, Fraser had a Fleet Air Arm squadron of torpedo-bombers armed with torpedoes and placed at the disposal of RAF Coastal Command. This timely example of inter-Service generosity was jeopardised by repeated RAF objections about the unsuitability of the weather and the inadequacy of the Beaufighters escort available for the joint RAF/Fleet Air Arm strike force. Fraser, however, had no hesitation in forcefully reminding Air Vice-Marshal Ellwood of Coastal Command that the Fleet Air Arm was used to launching strikes from carriers in far worse weather and with no fighter escort at all. As a result of his urgings the strike aircraft finally took off at 12.16 hrs on the 27th. By then the last sighting report was 6 hours old and the mission was a very long shot indeed. Despite a gallant search off the Norwegian coast (with only half the fighter escort originally promised by the RAF, and without the safety factor of cloud cover insisted upon as essential by the RAF), the Fleet Air Arm men missed

Lützow by a narrow margin — as tantalising as it was final — of about 40 miles.

Thus by the end of September 1943 there was an entirely new strategic situation in Arctic waters. Fraser's acute frustration at failing to intercept *Lützow* as she was withdrawn from the board was offset by the knowledge that *Tirpitz* was crippled and *Scharnhorst* was (for the immediate future at least) on her own, bar the small German destroyer force at Altenfjord. Thus presented with opportunities which Tovey had never enjoyed, Fraser was already looking forward to the resumption of the Russian convoys, weighing the chances of bringing *Scharnhorst* to action, when totally different prospects were suddenly placed before him. At the beginning of October Fraser was summoned to Chequers, where Churchill offered him the supreme post of the Royal Navy, the ultimate dream of every serving officer: the job of First Sea Lord.

Sir Dudley Pound's health had been sadly deteriorating for many months before, while still in the United States with Churchill after the 'Quadrant' Conference, he had finally presented his resignation to the dismayed Prime Minister. When it came to selecting a new First Sea Lord Admiral Cunningham who had achieved wonders with the Mediterranean Fleet since June 1940, was — as Churchill says in *Closing the Ring* — 'an obvious choice, proposed by the First Lord, Mr. Alexander'. But Churchill argued that Cunningham could not be spared from the Mediterranean 'when so much was going forward and all operations expanding'; he wanted Fraser, not Cunningham, to replace Pound.

Cunningham certainly did have a formidable workload under Eisenhower as Naval Commander, Mediterranean; moreover, the recent crisis at Salerno argued that the Italian campaign was not going to be all plain sailing. But there was a little more to it than that. Churchill had worked closely with Fraser at the Admiralty when Fraser was Controller: he knew Fraser well and liked what he knew. Fraser had also served two previous long-term Admiralty appointments (as DNO and as Head of the Tactical Section) while Cunningham had only had a few prewar months as VCNS before going to the Mediterranean Fleet in 1939. And Churchill cites Fraser's Admiralty 'track record' in his account of how Fraser was duly offered the supreme opportunity of his career — and turned it down:[13]

> In Admiral Fraser, then commanding the Home Fleet, we had an officer of the highest seagoing reputation, who had also long experience of Admiralty administration and staff work. It was to him I first offered the post. The Admiral said that of course he would serve wherever he was sent, but that he thought

2, 3   Fraser's father and mother

4 'My dearest boys'–Cecil and Bruce (*not* in sailor suit), in 1896

5 *Britannia* cadet, 1902–'Bruce, the day he joined the *Brit.*'

6 *Prince George*'s triumphant hockey team, 1906; Fraser in back row, extreme
right

7 Lieutenants three, in full dress: *Boadicea,* 1908,
with Fraser on left

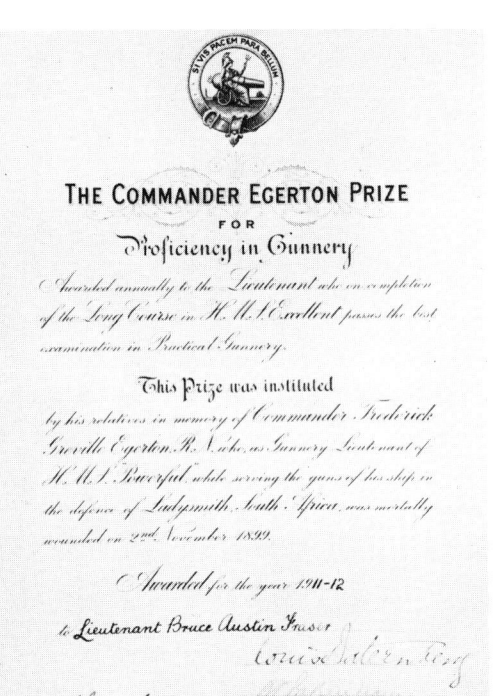

8 Fraser's Egerton Prize certificate, 1912, signed by Battenberg as First Sea Lord

THE COMMANDER EGERTON PRIZE

FOR

Proficiency in Gunnery

Awarded annually to the Lieutenant who on completion of the Long Course in H.M.S Excellent passes the best examination in Practical Gunnery.

This Prize was instituted by his relatives in memory of Commander Frederick Greville Egerton R.N. who as Gunnery Lieutenant of H.M.S. Powerful while serving the guns of his ship in the defence of Ladysmith, South Africa, was mortally wounded on 2nd November 1899.

Awarded for the year 1911-12

to Lieutenant Bruce Austin Fraser

9 The old *Minerva,* 1914: 'Guns', seated at right of breech, with one of his 6-inch gun crews

10   'Ah, happy days'–Fraser as Lieutenant-Commander and 'Guns' of *Resolution,* 1917

11   Release from Baku, November 1920: Fraser *(seated, hand to cap)* with the freed Naval Detachment aboard *Centurion*

12   Captain of *Effingham*, 1930–Fraser (*standing, fourth from right*) with Admiral Fullerton and East Indies Squadron staff officers relaxing up-country at Port Victoria

13   The proud son: Fraser visits his father's lighthouse on the Alguada Reef (*see p. 90*)

14   Carrier Captain: on the bridge of *Glorious,* 1935

15   The wartime Board of Admiralty, September 1939. *Clockwise, round table:*
Shakespeare (Parliamentary and Financial Secretary), Burrough (Assistant
Chief of Naval Staff), Ramsay (Fifth Sea Lord), Phillips (Deputy Chief of Naval
Staff), Pound (First Sea Lord), Hudson (Civil Lord), Churchill (First Lord),
Arbuthnot (Fourth Sea Lord), Little (Second Sea Lord), FRASER (Third Sea
Lord and Controller), Carter (Permanent Secretary), Barnes (Deputy
Secretary)

16　Fraser, as Third Sea Lord, escorts Sir Stafford Cripps on a visit to the Home Fleet

17　Fraser presents his Rear-Admirals to King George VI, 12 August 1943. The King is shaking hands with Rear-Admiral Burnett, victor of the Barents Sea action and Fraser's 'great lieutenant' in the *Scharnhorst* battle

18   Souvenir portrait of Fraser as Commander-in-Chief, Home Fleet, 1943

19 'I did so enjoy my few days with you'–the King with Fraser and Home Fleet officers, hugely enjoying one of the turns during a 'smoker' in *Duke of York*'s Wardroom

20 Russian congratulations on *Scharnhorst*'s demise: Fraser greets Golovko aboard *Duke of York*

21 Welcoming Montgomery (unaware that his visit to the Home Fleet is a useful dress-rehearsal for the King's visit in the following week) in the hectic weeks before D-Day, 1944

22 Fraser, commanding the as yet non-existent British Pacific Fleet, 'makes his number' with the famed American Admiral Spruance, Pearl Harbor, December 1944

23　Turning the first sod of the new Fleet Club in Sydney. 'Later
I went back to see how they were getting on. I found all they'd
done was fill in the hole I'd dug.'

24　Flanked by Fraser and Air Force General Spaatz, Admiral Nimitz
(unaware of his coming 'ordeal by grog'–*see pp. 276-7*) is invested with the
Order of the Bath

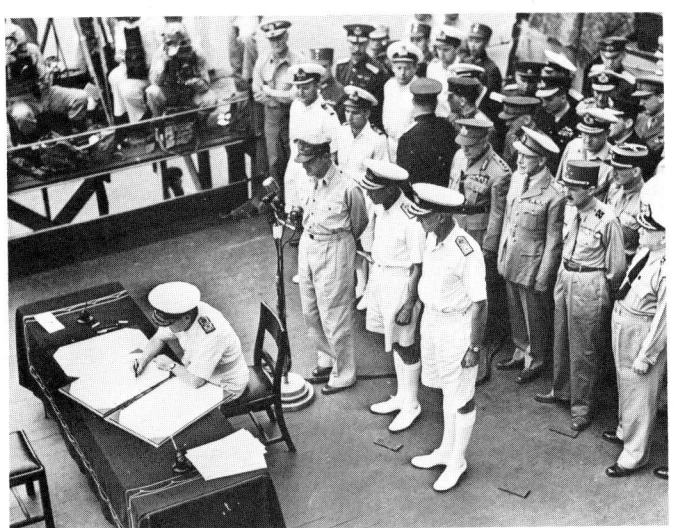

25   With MacArthur and the Flag Officers of the British
Pacific Fleet at his back, Fraser signs the instrument of
Japan's surrender for the British Empire, USS *Missouri, 2*
September 1945

26   Seen from *Duke of York* in Tokyo Bay: the massed fly-past by aircraft of
the Third Fleet to celebrate the surrender of Japan, 2 September 1945

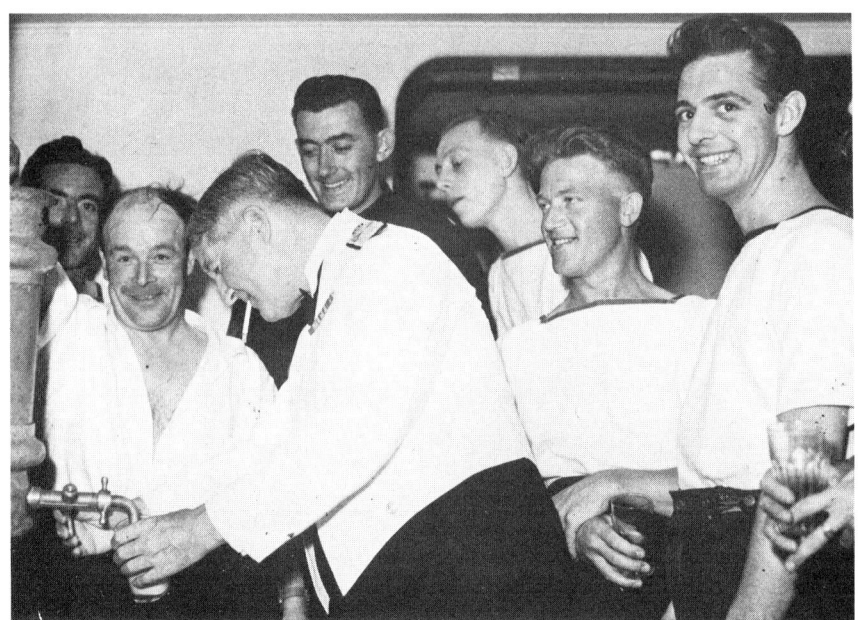

27   A rather special Commander-in-Chief relaxes with his 'family'. Fraser
draws the first pint of beer brewed in the Sydney Fleet Club

28   Commander-in-Chief, Portsmouth; Fraser chats with ex-Navy men
during his visit to Hilsea Gasworks

29 As First Sea Lord,
Fraser makes a new friend at
the time of the vital NATO
naval command talks, 1950.
The Americans loved it

30 St James's, Piccadilly, 1956. In retirement, Fraser attends the wedding of
his god-daughter–born on the East Indies Station and christened from the
ship's bell of *Effingham*

31 A joke with Douglas Bader at a Forces dinner

32 Memories of Home Fleet days: guest appearance on *This is Your Life* for John Mills, December 1960

Andrew Cunningham was the right man. 'I believe I have the confidence of my own fleet,' he said. 'Cunningham has that of the whole Navy.' He asked me to weigh the matter longer. I replied that his attitude was most becoming, and after further thought and consultation I took him at his word.

Lord Fraser's personal account of the exchange is slightly but significantly different:[14]

'I was summoned down from the Home Fleet by Churchill, who asked me to be First Sea Lord. He said the only reason why he didn't want Cunningham was that he didn't want to take him away from the Mediterranean, where he'd done such wonderful things. I told Churchill, "I think I have the confidence of my Fleet, but Cunningham has the confidence of the whole Navy. I haven't even fought a battle yet. If one day I should sink the *Scharnhorst*, I might feel differently." He more or less sat back at that, and said, "Thank you very much." And then he decided, when I wouldn't take it, that he would ask Cunningham.'

Admiral Cunningham's appointment as First Sea Lord was announced on 4 October, little more than a fortnight before Sir Dudley Pound died on the 21st – Trafalgar Day. In his farewell letter the Pound, which was published, Churchill paid tribute to Pound's 'vast and precise knowledge of the sea war in all its aspects', and concluded:[15]

'You leave us at a moment when the control of the Mediterranean is virtually within our grasp, when the Italian Fleet has made its surrender in Malta harbour, and when, above all, the U-boat peril has been broken in a degree never before seen in this war. These results have been of measureless value to your country, and your notable share in them sheds lustre on your name.'

The following day Churchill sent Fraser the following letter:[16]

Private and Confidential   10, Downing Street,
                                                          Whitehall
                                               October 5, 1943

My dear Fraser,
Now that matters have been settled in the sense you advised, I should like to tell you how becoming your attitude was, and how much I am obliged to you for it.

I wish you all success in your great Command.
    Sincerely,
      Winston S. Churchill

So it was that October 1943 opened with Fraser in the unenviable personal position of knowing that he had done his duty by the Navy and his country in stepping aside for Cunningham, yet also knowing that he had deliberately turned down the biggest professional opportunity of his career, which might well never be offered to him again. This inner knowledge, added to the frustration over *Lützow*'s escape, made him keener than ever to bring *Scharnhorst* to action, a dream which could be realised before the following four months were out. For on 1 October Churchill had cabled to Stalin that the convoy cycle was to be resumed, starting in November.

This meant that October in Scapa Flow was a month of busy preparation for the resumption of the convoys. During these weeks Fraser fought his first 'battle' as Commander-in-Chief. This was his celebrated clash with the 'Chief Wren', Dame Vera Laughton Matthews, resulting from his kindly instinct to encourage the lowliest ratings in the Service, many of whom had never set foot in one of HM Ships. Fraser saw no reason why he should not entertain Wrens and their escorts to tea aboard his flagship if he chose, and took it none too kindly when the senior Wren officers of Orkneys and Shetlands Command protested with threats of resignation. The subsequent 'state visit' to Scapa by Dame Vera ended in a mutually satisfactory solution to what Fraser always regarded as (literally) a storm in a teacup. But Fraser was surely the only Admiral in the Navy who could have charmed the massively indignant 'Chief Wren' into helping him stir the flagship's Christmas puddings!

It was agreed that the new convoys would retain the successful two-phase routine established with the first 'JW' convoys in the previous year, with the second half of each convoy sailing a week after the first. The first to sail (1 November) was convoy RA.54A of thirteen empty merchantmen homeward-bound from Murmansk 'collected' by nine destroyers, two minesweepers and a corvette sent out by Fraser. Shielded most of the way by fog, it escaped detection by the Germans. Though German intelligence suspected that the convoys were being resumed the first two outward-bound convoys, JW.54A (sailed 15 November) and JW.54B (sailed 22 November), of eighteen and fourteen ships respectively, also got through intact. Unloading at the Russian end of the route was such a slow business that only eight empty ships were available for RA.54B, which left Murmansk on 26 November, also arriving safely. Aided by unusually helpful if not exactly docile Arctic weather, the renewed convoy cycle had started well. By the second week of December thirty-two outward-bound merchant ships had reached Murmansk and another twenty-one had returned to the UK, without any damage or molestation by the Germans.

By and large, Fraser's dispositions for protecting the new convoys used the proven methods of the previous winter. Each convoy would have a close destroyer escort. Burnett's cruisers would provide close support for each outgoing convoy, then switch to the homeward-bound convoy. A battle group would provide distant cover. But there were two highly important innovations. First, Fraser was determined to break the sanctity of radio silence whenever he deemed it necessary that all elements at sea – convoy and close escort, Burnett's cruisers, and the battle group – should know precisely where they were in relation to the others. The primary objective was the safe passage of the convoys and the 'flying switch' between outward and return convoys must not be fumbled. Second, the improved facility of British Special Intelligence in decrypting German signals – particularly the now-famous 'ULTRA' decrypts from the German 'Hydra' code – was yielding much more reliable advance warnings of probable German naval sorties. This information, plus the reduced *Luftwaffe* strength in Arctic Norway, led to Fraser's decision to take his battle group right into the Barents Sea if it seemed that *Scharnhorst* might try to pounce on a convoy.

Everything about *Scharnhorst*'s record argued that she must surely come out. The battle-cruiser had always been one of the most active and successful heavy units of the German Navy. With her famed sister-ship *Gneisenau*, she had sunk the gallant but pitifully outmatched armed merchant cruiser *Rawalpindi* in November 1939, and eluded the battle-cruiser *Renown* off Narvik in the following April. On 8 June 1940 *Scharnhorst* and *Gneisenau* had surprised and sunk Fraser's old carrier *Glorious*, along with the destroyers *Acasta* and *Ardent*. In February 1941 *Scharnhorst* and *Gneisenau* had broken out into the North Atlantic where they caused havoc for a month and a half, disrupting the entire Atlantic convoy schedule and sinking twenty-two ships (115,622 tons) before heading into Brest on 22 March. There they had lain for ten months, demonstrating the humiliating inability of RAF Bomber Command to locate and destroy pinpoint targets, before their audacious race back to Germany through the English Channel in February 1942. Since then *Scharnhorst* had passed twenty-two months in thoroughly uncharacteristic inactivity, with the sole exception of the tip-and-run raid on Spitzbergen in early September 1943; and she was clearly being kept up at Altenfjord until the right opportunity for adding to her battle honours should present itself.

By December 1943 Fraser had gone over the problem countless times in his mind during those quiet afternoons of thought in Scapa Flow. He knew that no matter how sound the intelligence placed at his disposal, no matter how shrewd a plan he might devise, the natural conditions of the Arctic winter still favoured a German surface attack on a Russian convoy. The Barents Sea action of 31 December 1942 had opened with a near-perfect converging attack on convoy and escort by *Hipper* and *Lützow*; and the fact that the German commanders had thrown away a crushing victory because of their own hesitancy did not mean that a similar attack could never be made again. British escort tactics to counter such a formidable surface threat were cut and dried: move out aggressively and try to bluff the intruders into retiring by making simulated torpedo attacks. So far, on the Russian convoy route, the Germans had shown themselves unwilling to call this bluff. But it *had* been called elsewhere in northern waters – and by *Scharnhorst*. That had been back in June 1940, when she and *Gneisenau* had overwhelmed *Acasta* and *Ardent* before finishing off the helpless *Glorious*.

If *Scharnhorst* were to press an attack on a convoy instead of sheering off at the first contact with the escort forces, obviously the chances of a decisive action would be all the more improved. But Fraser could not forget that *Scharnhorst*'s most dangerous assets were her speed, her fire-power, and her armoured protection. Moreover, her sheer size made her a far more effective sea boat when it came to high-speed evolutions in heavy weather. The best chance of sinking *Scharnhorst* seemed to be a heavy-calibre gun action to neutralise or at least reduce her fire-power, get her on the run and hopefully slow her down enough for the cruisers and destroyers to finish the job with torpedoes if *Scharnhorst* had not run clear out of radar range after first contact had been made.

Fraser was sure that *Scharnhorst* would come out, and that his basic dispositions offered the best chance of bringing her to action. The decisive element was the battle group. If this were kept too far west the catch could easily be dropped, with disastrous results for both convoy and escort. With JW.54A and JW.54B Fraser delegated command of the distant covering force to his VA2: Vice-Admiral Sir Henry Moore, once Fraser's class captain at *Britannia*. But when JW.55A sailed on 12 December Fraser put to sea himself in *Duke of York*. As he saw it, if the Germans were going to commit *Scharnhorst* any of the next convoys could be the chosen victim.

From the moment they sailed on 12 December until their return to Scapa on the 31st Fraser and his battle group were to be almost constantly on the move, and those two and a half weeks were destined to write a new chapter of naval history. Captain Richard

Courage, then Fleet Signal Officer on Fraser's Staff, makes the point that:[17]

> One or two changes in the Home Fleet Staff had taken place. First, The CoS, Captain Michael Denny, had been relieved by Captain W. Slayter. Michael Denny was one of the first senior officers really to get down to the business of harnessing the rapid progress in surface radar detection to the tactics of war at sea. He also realised the need to enthuse and train operating, plotting, and maintenance teams in the use of this new and efficient tool of war. Except for maintenance he could do all these jobs himself, and he did them very well. Not for nothing did the Staff nickname him 'The Nugget'. It was descriptive of the concentrated energy he personally put into training.
>
> The Captain of the Fleet Flagship had also changed shortly before sailing. Captain the Hon. Guy Russell had assumed command of *Duke of York* in the role of Flag Captain. Guy Russell commanded HMS *Nelson* in the Mediterranean during the landings in Sicily and Italy. During these operations he had built up valuable experience in the use of a battleship's main armament at night and had developed advanced methods of blind firing and plotting procedures, plus the necessity for a proper eye drill to prevent temporary loss of vision when the big guns were fired at night. As soon as he took command of *Duke of York* he ensured that these lessons were put into effect, and organised his programme so that *Duke of York* had one final live full-calibre firing before leaving the Scapa area. His arrival on the scene paid a rich dividend and quickly filled the vacuum created when someone like 'The Nugget' leaves a team.
>
> One or two other members of the Staff were also away when *Duke of York* sailed from Scapa. One of them was the Fleet Gunnery Assistant Commander, Alan Campbell, and Lt-Cdr Michael Le Fanu. 'Lef', as Michael Le Fanu was always known, was away getting himself married. Needless to say he was hopping mad to miss what was to be the last battleship engagement in British naval history. . . . His flair and enthusiasm played a major part in all Home Fleet operations.

Fraser's readiness to break with standard operational procedure to bring *Scharnhorst* to action was soon demonstrated. Only two days out of Loch Ewe, JW.55A was detected by German air reconnaissance. He immediately decided on the unprecedented step of taking the battle group right through the Barents Sea to Murmansk, to give the convoy close cover. Though the voyage through the Barents Sea was uneventful this time, Fraser's first visit to North

Russia (16–18 December) enabled him to make personal contact with his Soviet opposite number: Admiral Arseni Golovko of the Soviet Northern Fleet.

Golovko's memoir, *With the Red Fleet*, is available in English and the book is a perfect reflection of the apprehension, suspicion and thorough-going wrinkled meanness with which the Stalinist regime regarded and treated its British ally. Golovko's reaction, on hearing that Fraser was on his way, was baffled distrust. 'For what purpose can Fraser be coming here?' he worried in his diary entry for 14 December.[18]

> 16 December. The *Duke of York*, *Jamaica* and four destroyers have arrived on time. A signal was immediately received from the British battleship asking when Admiral Fraser could pay a visit to the C-in-C, Northern Fleet. In reply I declared my readiness to call on him and requested a time to be fixed. An invitation followed at once and I set out for the battleship already in possession of all the necessary information about Fraser. He is a sea dog who has knocked about the world for a bit and is now one of the pillars of the British Admiralty.

Fraser had decided to exploit his only previous experience of Soviet hospitality – Baku – to melt the ice. Golovko records that he was 'really astonished' when Fraser jokingly expressed gratitude for the poverty of the jail diet in Baku, claiming that it was so meagre that it had helped him recover from digestive troubles. 'I had to own up that I did not know of this detail,' Golovko wrote heavily, 'indicating, as it did, a very peculiar form of appreciation of the Bolsheviks on the part of the Admiral.'[19]

Subsequent entries in *With the Red Fleet* are almost touching, with poor Golovko stoutly trying to maintain the safe, suspicious Party line without admitting to the warmth of the 'Fraser touch':[20]

> Like a good host Fraser showed me over the whole ship, which indeed made a powerful impression, and even invited me into the ship's bakery where we were regaled with some good newly baked buns. After eating one I praised both it and the bakers, little suspecting that this would lead to a surprise. When we had disembarked from the battleship a bulky sack was lowered on to the deck of the launch containing a vast quantity of buns. What you might call the acme of hospitality!
>
> At the same time I still do not grasp for what purpose the C-in-C of the British Home Fleet should have decided to visit us at the height of the polar night season.
>
> 17 December. Fraser and his staff have returned my visit. We

gave a dinner in their honour and after this our fleet choir put on a performance. . .

The visitors were delighted by the choir, and especially by the dances and the few songs sung in English. They even entreated me to let them take the choir to Scapa Flow for a fortnight. All in all we received our British visitors as true allies.

For his part, Fraser found Golovko easy enough to get on with, almost embarrassingly so. One of Lord Fraser's many souvenirs from the war years was a magnificent marble desk top, gleaming like a black mirror. 'I got that,' he told the author, 'from the Russian C-in-C's desk!'[21]

'I went into his room, and saw it sitting on his desk. I said, "That's very nice!" and he said, "Have it, take it away." So I said "Well, what will I do if you come on board and say you like the *Duke of York*?" And he said "Oh, I'd treat it as your wife." And he was very nice indeed, charming.

But our people stationed up there were being treated so badly – they had difficulties about mail, and so on. As soon as I got there, of course, everything changed right away, which is what the Russians do. They had their mail brought to them – everything. The moment I left, everything went back to the same as before.

In *With the Red Fleet* Golovko not only omits the desk-top incident but gives the impression that Fraser was deliberately keeping the Russians guessing:[22]

'19 December. Last night, after receiving a radio message of some sort from sea, the *Duke of York* and escorting ships weighed anchor and left the Kola Inlet in such haste that Fraser sent his apologies to the Mission, explaining that he was returning to England. A strange hurry. Where are the British racing off to now? To meet the convoy and support it?'

Of course they were, as Golovko knew very well: on 19 December the next convoy, JW.55B was scheduled to sail from Loch Ewe (though atrocious weather conditions forced a 24-hour postponement). Fraser was therefore 'racing off' to get back to Akureyri in Iceland, refuel his ships and sail again to take part in the double passage of JW.55B and the return convoy, RA.55A. There was no mystery about it at all. But if Golovko's uncertainties were stage-managed, Fraser's were very real. His biggest worry had been that the British battle group's passage through the Barents Sea – justified though it had been in ensuring the safety of JW.55A – would deter the Germans from sending out *Scharnhorst* against subsequent convoys. But he had scarcely left the Barents Sea when Admiralty Intelligence began to feed him portions of the most heartening information. From 20 December a sequence of intercepted and decoded German signals argued more and more strongly that the Germans thought the British would not send heavy ships into the Barents Sea a second time; that *Scharnhorst* was being readied for sea; and that she would probably sortie against the next convoy: JW.55B.

The first clutch of decrypts reached the British Admiralty shortly after midnight on the night of 19–20 December. Allowing for the time-lag required for decoding, they showed that *Scharnhorst* had been advanced from six to three hours' readiness for sea on the evening of the 18th. At the same time the *Luftwaffe* commander in the Lofotens area had been asked to provide air reconnaissance 'against convoy which is certainly to be assumed and against heavy group which is probably at sea'. On the 19th the *Luftwaffe* had reported that air reconnaissance was impossible because of bad weather – the same bad weather which had forced the 24 hours' delay in JW.55B's departure. On the 20th the British Admiralty also learned that German air reconnaissance had been cancelled for that day as well, but that *Scharnhorst* had been ordered to take 'preparatory measures so that departure would be possible at any time'.[23]

These were the pieces of the puzzle which, when laid before Fraser, confirmed his original belief that *Scharnhorst* would sortie against JW.55B. He was particularly cheered that the Germans, so far from being cowed into inactivity by the Home Fleet's recent voyage to Murmansk, were well aware that a British 'heavy group' was a force to be reckoned with. The 'ULTRA' decrypts had given Fraser a gleam of one-way vision through the fog of war in which the Germans were still groping for the two most important pieces in play: JW.55B and the British 'heavy group'. It was therefore highly unlikely that some miraculous combination of circumstances would suddenly alert *Scharnhorst* to the true positions of JW.55B and its escort, Fraser's 'Force 2' (HMS *Duke of York*, *Jamaica* and their four destroyers), RA.55A and its escort, and Burnett's 'Force 1' (the cruisers HMS *Belfast*, *Sheffield* and *Norfolk*). Nor was Fraser dismayed when he heard, late on the 21st, that *Scharnhorst* and her supporting destroyers had been 'stood down' from three hours' notice to six. It was not surprising, given the weather, that the Germans had not yet located the convoy, and if Fraser had been in the German admiral's place he would have done the same himself. It made no sense to keep ships' companies at short notice to sail when there was insufficient information on which to send them to sea. Better to give the men some rest until the situation became clearer, for which there was still ample time.

The mounting excitement among Fraser's Staff by 23 December, and the confidence radiated by Fraser, has been vividly captured by Richard Courage:[24]

It was on Wednesday 23 December that Force 2 arrived at Akureyri in Iceland. By that time we were aware that *Scharnhorst* was in the 'four day declarations' and was an almost certain runner for an attack on the convoy. Force 2, the heavy covering force, was at sea for one purpose only: to sink the *Scharnhorst*. The *Duke of York* had the only armament that could really make any impression on *Scharnhorst*'s armour. *Scharnhorst* being faster than any British ship, the intention was to slow her up with the *Duke of York*'s gunfire and so make it easier for the destroyers to intercept and sink her at close range with torpedoes. It is difficult to sink a heavily-armoured ship by gunfire alone, but torpedoes below the waterline are lethal.

Force 2's entry into Akureyri was at full speed in single line ahead up a long inlet in very poor visibility, so poor that it was a job for the destroyers to see their next ahead. *Duke of York* had the best radar in the Fleet and all on board had great confidence in its performance. Ships following astern of us were amazed and somewhat frightened by the speed at which we entered these hazardous waters.

The same day the C-in-C got the Captains of Force 2 and his own Staff together and told them what he had in mind about the part Force 2 should play in what he already regarded as a certain confrontation with *Scharnhorst*, probably accompanied by half a dozen destroyers.

I obtained permission to miss the briefing in order to conduct a lifelike signal exercise with our force on VHF/RT,[25] using the actual call signs and signals and codebooks that we would have to use in the action. There was some risk that this RT exercise would be heard by the Germans, but probably no more than the possibility of police radios in the Sussex countryside being heard in Glasgow. The risk had been considered and accepted. It meant the sealed operation orders had to be opened and the relevant parts shown to the signalmen. This sort of thing was very much encouraged by the C-in-C and was certainly not confined to putting signalmen in the know. For my part I felt it important that the signal ratings should be familiar with the race card before the actual race took place.

The signal exercise seemed to go well, with people entering

into the spirit of the thing and – even more important – they all seemed to have digested the sealed orders. Our own *Duke of York*'s internal coding exercise ended up with 'Make to Admiralty – SCHARNHORST SUNK'. I was somehow certain we should be making that signal in due course.

As the early winter night fell on 23 December, Fraser knew that there was little more he could do to ready his Fleet for battle. Admiralty Intelligence had told him that all the omens were good. *Scharnhorst* had not only been restored to three hours' notice on the 22nd, but had again been ordered to make preliminary preparations for sea. Certainly it would be an exaggeration to claim that Fraser's mind was at ease; there was always the chance, remote though it might be, that *Scharnhorst* would break with all German precedents, race confidently out to sea and strike at the convoy before either Fraser or Burnett could intervene. But until the ships of Force 2 had taken on all the fuel they could hold at Akureyri matters were, for the moment, out of Fraser's hands. And he chose to add to the Royal Navy's eve-of-battle tradition by taking a brief 'run ashore' with Captain Russell:[26]

> 'We went ashore for some Christmas shopping – clothing or something – and I walked back with the Captain. When we got back on board all the Icelanders ashore were skating, by light – we were in darkness, of course. I asked the band to come up on deck and play Christmas carols; and really, it almost brought tears to your eyes.'

They sailed from Akureyri at 23.00 hrs on 23 December, the 'box' of four destroyers (*Savage*, *Saumarez*, *Scorpion* and the Norwegian *Stord*) leading the flagship and *Jamaica* covering the group from astern. The friendly lights of Akureyri were abruptly lost, exchanged for the pitch darkness, gales and monstrous seas of the Arctic night.

. 18 .

Sinking the *Scharnhorst*
[23–26 December 1943]

When Fraser took Force 2 out of Akureyri on 23 December he knew well enough what he wanted to do with it, but he also knew that, as a fighting team, Force 2 had been together for less than a fortnight. His address to the captains of Force 2 on the 23rd had therefore stressed how vital it was that every officer and rating must be thoroughly familiar with his post and with his duties. If all went well Force 2 would be presented with a night action in which Fraser's stated prime objective was to close on radar to a range of 12,000 yards, before opening fire with star-shell to illuminate the enemy. As soon as the gun action began the four destroyers were to form sub-divisions and take up positions for torpedo attacks – but not to close until *Scharnhorst*'s fire-power had been reduced and Fraser gave the word for them to go in. As for *Jamaica*, Fraser wanted her to operate in close support of *Duke of York*, thus hopefully splitting the German fire, but if the cruiser should be heavily engaged she was to break away and open the range at once.

Such was Fraser's battle plan, as unfolded three days before its triumphant execution on 26 December 1943. It envisaged each type of warship (battleship, cruiser, destroyer), each type of equipment and weapon (search radar, gunnery radar, gun, torpedo) being used to maximum advantage at the appropriate moment, in the role for which it had been designed. The plan did not consist of a mass of precise details, all to be minutely fulfilled; nor did it, in any part, rely on the enemy doing what it was hoped he would do. Unforeseen contingencies would have to be tackled as they arose; there was, for instance, no way of estimating how many German destroyers (if any) might accompany *Scharnhorst*. The true genius of Fraser's battle plan lay in its flexibility. Fraser already had complete confidence in Burnett and Force 1; after the Akureyri conference on the 23rd, he knew that the men of Force 2 would be doing more than blindly following a string of orders from the flagship. He had told his captains all they needed to know about how he hoped to fight the battle, and what he wanted them to do in it. In all essentials, Fraser's preparation of his Fleet for battle was Nelsonic.

There have been many studies of the ensuing action, the Battle of the North Cape. By no means all of them – Roskill's highly-respected *The War At Sea* being a case in point – mention that Fraser's battle plan was given an invaluable rehearsal on the eve of action. As Richard Courage has put it:[1]

> In the small hours of the 24th the cruiser *Jamaica* was detached to represent *Scharnhorst* in yet another game of hide-and-seek, in the dark and appalling weather. This final gallop went well and the owner – the C-in-C – was satisfied. We proceeded to the battle area in the certain knowledge. . . that our own forces had been trained to the minute for their 'race'.

The most encouraging lesson of this last-minute practice interception was that *Duke of York*'s radar operators had no trouble in distinguishing between the modest radar echo of *Jamaica* and those of the even smaller destroyers. As *Jamaica* had only one-third of *Scharnhorst*'s displacement and was well over 200ft 'smaller' than *Scharnhorst* as a radar target, this was an excellent omen. For the radar men of Force 2 the exercise epitomised the great general Suvorov's famous maxim, 'Train hard, fight easy'. But nothing is more misleading than the apparent inevitability and ease with which Fraser's planning earned its just reward on 26 December. At any time in the tense 48 hours after Force 2's 'final gallop' early on the 24th, the whole plan could have gone disastrously wrong. By noon on the 24th Fraser already knew that he had a crisis on his hands. JW.55B was not only equidistant between *Scharnhorst* in Altenfjord (400 miles to the east) and Force 2 (400 miles to the south-west): the convoy was being shadowed by German aircraft. If *Scharnhorst* should seize this moment to strike at the convoy, both Fraser and Burnett would be too far away to intervene.

The recent unscheduled voyage to Murmansk – fully justified in that the safe passage of JW.55A had been guaranteed – had nevertheless put Force 2 three days behind the departure of JW.55B. Fraser's late start was made more problematical by the limited fuel endurance of his destroyers. To nurse this along he had planned a 15-knot approach to the anticipated battle area in the vicinity of Bear Island, where JW.55B and RA.55A were scheduled to 'cross'. Once RA.55A had safely passed to the west, its destroyer escort could join Burnett's Force 1 in ushering JW.55B through the Barents Sea. Fraser's 15-knot approach speed was intended to give the Force

2 destroyers an operating margin of 30 hours in the Bear Island battle zone. But JW.55B's dangerous isolation by noon on the 24th demanded prompt action, and for Force 2 to crack on speed to catch up with the convoy was not the answer: this would only cause the destroyers' fuel to be consumed all the faster. Yet somehow the gap between Force 2 and JW.55B had to be reduced.

Fraser now did what he had always planned to do in such an emergency: he broke radio silence to order a compromise. At 1325hrs he signalled to the convoy to reverse its course for three hours and not turn back to the east until 17.00hrs. At the same time he increased the speed of Force 2 from 15 to 19 knots. These complementary measures would, he hoped, at least halve the distance between JW.55B and Force 2, and make it impossible for *Scharnhorst* to find the convoy until the brief daylight period ('daylight' being a purely nominal term for Arctic latitudes in December) on the following day. By then both Force 1 and Force 2 would be in a much better position to intervene. As it happened, the violent weather had so disorganised the ships of JW.55B that the convoy Commodore (Rear-Admiral Boucher) and the close escort Commander (Captain McCoy) had already had to reduce speed to allow stragglers to regain station.

When Fraser's order came through, Boucher and McCoy agreed that to attempt a course reversal would be highly unwise in the prevailing conditions. At best it would be sure to dislocate the convoy even more; at worst, the plethora of coloured-light signals required to execute such a ticklish manoeuvre would act like a beacon to the prowling German aircraft. Agreeing that the convoy's estimated position by 17.00 hrs would have been about 20 miles closer to Force 2 than provided for in the original sailing schedule, Boucher and McCoy complied with the spirit rather than the letter of Fraser's order They maintained their course, but reduced the convoy's speed to 8 knots. This, it was hoped, would help Force 2 catch up while assisting the process of getting JW.55B back into an ordered cruising formation which the escorts could defend from chance U-boat attacks. Though not as effective as a course reversal would have been, it resulted in narrowing the gap by about 100 miles, a small enough contribution on the face of it, but one soon to prove vital.

To understand what was meanwhile happening on the Germans' side it is necessary to describe their lengthy, disjointed chain of command. Grand-Admiral Dönitz had persuaded a sceptical Hitler (19–20 December) that *Scharnhorst* should be used against these new Russian convoys, as the most effective way in which the German Navy could support the hard-pressed armies in Russia. This was a half-truth. Dönitz was just as keen to show Hitler that the surface fleet's reprieve after the Barents Sea fiasco had been justified. Moreover, if the German Navy could destroy or rout a Russian convoy, succeeding where the *Luftwaffe* was helpless, this would greatly strengthen Dönitz's hand in his eternal struggle with Göring for top place in Hitler's favour. Thus operation 'Ostfront' ('Eastern Front'), as the *Scharnhorst* sortie was code-named, was to no small extent an offshoot of Nazi court politics; and the way Dönitz acted was that of a politician rather than a naval strategist. He did not assume personal responsibility for the execution of 'Ostfront', nor did he leave matters entirely to the discretion of the commander afloat. Instead he turned operations over to the admirals in the chain of command.

From the *Marineamt*, the German Admiralty in Berlin, orders passed first to Naval Group North at Kiel. Here the Commander-in-Chief was Admiral Otto Schniewind, who 'doubled' as *Flottenchef* or Fleet Commander. Under Schniewind came the Admiral Commanding Northern Waters at Narvik, and finally the Admiral Commanding Battle Group in Altenfjord. In December 1943 the latter was not Admiral Kummetz, who had led the foray against JW.51B the year before: he was on leave, and had been temporarily replaced by the Flag Officer Destroyers, Rear-Admiral Erich Bey. Any interpretations of Bey's motives during these crucial days involve a good deal of speculation, because he never had the chance to put them on record. Suffice it to say that Bey was a 'destroyer man' rather than a 'big-ship man'. And if the shattering defeat of his destroyers by the British at Narvik in 1940 had clearly not ruined Bey's career, it is at least safe to assume that in December 1943 he was more keen to be remembered as the victor of the Arctic convoys than as the loser of Narvik.

Fraser's signal to JW.55B on 24 December *was* picked up by the German listening stations, and accurately pinpointed. The *Luftwaffe* commander in the Lofotens signalled his intention of sending out, on the 25th, air reconnaissance 'against what is thought to be a battle group approaching from the south-west which has been D/F'd [Direction Finding]'.[2] As it happened, the Commander of 'U-boats North', Rear-Admiral Kluber, was 'doubling' as Admiral Commanding Northern Waters at this time; he too suspected that the British had a battle group at sea, and had warned his U-boats accordingly on the 23rd. By the morning of the 25th both the *Luftwaffe* and Admiral Commanding Northern Waters had advised Bey that none of the preconditions for a sortie by *Scharnhorst* existed. But the Naval Staff in Berlin, and *Gruppe Nord* in Kiel, had both taken a very different view. They had decided to treat the pinpoint obtained from Fraser's signal as a 'poor fix', more likely originating from a straggler from the convoy than a British battle group. Thus by the morning of the 25th Berlin and Kiel held that if the *Luftwaffe* failed to detect a British battle group during the day it would be safe for *Scharnhorst* to put to sea – overruling the opinions to the contrary prevailing in Narvik and Altenfjord.

Fraser would, of course, have been immensely cheered if he could have had an inkling of the pit the Germans were digging for themselves. As it was, the early hours of the 25th found him worrying about the chances of RA.55A escaping safely to the west. It was now clear that because of JW.55B's speed reductions on the 24th, the two convoys would not now be crossing in the Bear Island battle area. Though the Germans had not yet detected RA.55A (and never did, as it turned out) the return convoy would therefore be passing through the battle area without any substantial heavy cover. Fraser therefore broke radio silence for the second time early on the 25th, ordering RA.55A to steer a northerly course heading safely out of the battle area. At the same time he asked RA.55A's escort commander to detach four destroyers – fleet destroyers, armed with torpedoes – to strengthen JW.55B's escort as the latter came up from the west. Fraser left the man on the spot, Captain Campbell, to choose which destroyers should be sent; and Campbell sensibly chose the four with the highest fuel reserves, the 36th Division: HMS *Musketeer*, *Matchless*, *Opportune* and *Virago*. This would raise the strength of JW.55B's escort to fourteen destroyers, enough, Fraser reckoned to help Burnett's cruisers 'see off' *Scharnhorst* and win time for Force 2 to arrive on the scene.

When the 36th Division took up its new position, fanned out 4 miles ahead of JW.55B at 12.55hrs on the 25th, the convoy had been shadowed for nearly four hours. At 09.01hrs JW.55B had been sighted by *U-601* as the convoy crossed the U-boat patrol line, and at 11.15hrs one of the convoy escorts sighted a shadowing Dornier Do-18 flying-boat. The latter was soon forced to return to base by the worsening weather but *U-601* stuck to the convoy throughout the morning and early afternoon of the 25th, and 'Huff-Duff' intercepts told the men of JW.55B that their course and position were being passed on.

Thus by the afternoon of the 25th Dönitz and the more sanguine German Naval Staff officers had convinced themselves that the omens were good for 'Ostfront'. The convoy had been located and shadowed (though *U-601* had not reported the full strength of the escort) and the initial sighting had been confirmed by the *Luftwaffe*. The only fly in the ointment was the continuing lack of information about the whereabouts of a possible British battle group. But Dönitz and the Naval Staff held to the view that no news was good news, and at 15.15hrs on the 25th the order '*OSTFRONT* – 17.00 – 25th' was sent to Bey in Altenfjord.

Bey had stayed in *Tirpitz* throughout the 25th, close to the German battle group's only telex receiver; the *Luftwaffe* and Flag Officer Northern Waters had briefed him that the worsening weather made further air reconnaissance that day extremely unlikely, and he seems to have been expecting a 'stand-down' order cancelling the sortie. Thus the 'Ostfront' executive order caught him by surprise and two more hours – 17.00–19.00hrs – passed before Bey had held a quick conference with his destroyer commanders and transferred himself, his flag and his staff to *Scharnhorst* in Langfjord. This delay dealt another vital card to Fraser; but at last, at 19.00hrs, *Scharnhorst* weighed anchor and headed for the open sea with the destroyers *Z-29, Z-34, Z-38, Z-30* and *Z-33*, preceded down Altenfjord by an arrowhead formation of three minesweepers.

Dönitz had got his way, and 25 minutes after the battle group had begun to move he sent a final admonitory signal to Bey:[3]

1. Enemy attempting to frustrate the heroic struggle of our Eastern Armies by sending valuable convoy of supplies to the Russians.
2. *Scharnhorst* and destroyers will attack convoy.
3. Tactical situation must be used skilfully and boldly. Engagement not to be broken off with only partial success achieved. Every advantage must be exploited. Best chance lies in *Scharnhorst*'s superior fire-power. Therefore endeavour to deploy her. Destroyers to operate as seems suitable.
4. Disengage at your discretion but without question if heavy forces encountered.
5. Inform crew accordingly. I rely on your offensive spirit.

On the face of it a delegation of responsibility to the commander afloat, this shows Dönitz 'passing the buck' with a politician's artfulness. He would now be covered no matter what happened. If *Scharnhorst* should return prematurely or empty-handed, Dönitz could censure Bey for lack of 'offensive spirit'. If *Scharnhorst* should be driven off, Dönitz could present it as a prudent withdrawal. Even if *Scharnhorst* should be overwhelmed and sunk, Dönitz could blame the weather for concealing – or better still Göring's *Luftwaffe* for not revealing the British battle group. In the last analysis, however, Dönitz in committing *Scharnhorst* was guilty of that notorious military sin denounced by Napoleon as 'making pictures'. As Dönitz claimed in his memoirs:[4]

Our reconnaissance had not discovered the presence of any
heavy enemy formation, though that, of course, did not mean
that no such force was at sea. But if it were it must have been a
long way from the convoy, and the *Scharnhorst* seemed to have
every chance of delivering a rapid and successful attack.

Here was another half-truth: Dönitz had *no* grounds for claiming
that any British heavy force 'must have been a long way from the
convoy'. Even six hours after *Scharnhorst* had sailed, all the *Luftwaffe* could report was that no British heavy force had been sighted
within an extremely modest, 80-kilometre radius of JW.55B. The
unfortunate Bey was not given this highly significant piece of information until the morning of the 26th. All he had on putting to sea
was Dönitz's valedictory signal with its emphasis on perseverance,
boldness and offensive spirit. Given Bey's record and natural anxiety
to prove himself, Dönitz could hardly have composed a more fateful
signal if he had known all the British positions to a 'T' and had been
deliberately trying to steer *Scharnhorst* to destruction.

By midnight on 25 December Fraser's personal conviction that
Scharnhorst was going to sortie against JW.55B, supported as this
had been by the earlier intelligence forwarded via Whitehall, had
been strengthened still further by the persistent shadowing of the
convoy throughout the day. During the last hours of the 25th he
was nevertheless nagged by fears that *Scharnhorst* was already at
sea, having sailed undetected – like every other German heavy warship to come out during the war. He had to assume that the German
commander had been accurately fed with information as to JW.55B's
position. As we have seen, Fraser's first suspicion was well-founded:
Scharnhorst was indeed at sea. But Fraser's second suspicion was
not. The most up-to-date information passed to Bey before the
morning of the 26th – fleeting *Luftwaffe* sightings of JW.55B on the
afternoon of the 25th – all failed to include the convoy's position.
The lack of this vital information therefore squandered the advantage unwittingly gained by *Scharnhorst*'s sailing, as Fraser had
always feared, while he and Burnett were still too far away to
intervene. Thus, instead of carrying out a precise 'smash and grab'
attack on JW.55B, Bey was forced to hunt for his victim first; while
all the time Burnett and Fraser were steadily reducing their distance
from the most likely scene of the crime.

Two overriding problems were common to both sides: the Arctic
darkness, and the appalling weather which continued to deteriorate
throughout Christmas Day, wind strength rising from Force 6 to 8
and scouring up a monstrous sea. The darkness had always meant
that this would be (in its preliminary stages at least) the first 'all-

radar' sea battle. Fraser was as confident as he could reasonably be in the British superiority in radar equipment and training. But the weather dealt out disadvantages to both sides. It helped the British by cutting German air reconnaissance to the minimum, thus shielding Force 2 from detection during its long approach. At the same time it helped the Germans, because the enormous following seas threatened the lightweight destroyers with the fate of broaching-to: being swept sideways-on to the waves, in peril of capsizing, unless speed was kept well down. Thus even without the worry over fuel consumption Fraser was obliged to keep Force 2's speed below 20 knots, despite the fact that this would take him all the longer to arrive in the battle area.

Previous British accounts of conditions in the ships have tended to understatement, from 'unpleasant' in Roskill's *The War At Sea* to 'most uncomfortable' in Fraser's own 'Despatch'. For the men in the ships conditions were wretched, and the lighter the ships the more hellish life was. As Richard Courage writes:[5]

> Our destroyers had a job to keep up with the *Duke of York*, which was plunging under the huge waves of a following sea which made her look like a submarine breaking surface. A number of anti-aircraft weapons for close-range work had been fitted on the fo'c'sle. All these were torn from their mountings, and water poured through the empty rivet holes on to the messdecks below.

If life was that bad aboard the 36,000-ton bulk of the flagship, the imagination recoils from what it was like in the flimsy destroyers, battling the giant waves with barely a twentieth the displacement and well over half the waterline length of *Duke of York*. And it was even worse in the German destroyers. Not only did the German destroyer men lack the seagoing experience of the British: in German destroyer design, seaworthiness had been sacrified to fire-power. The price German destroyers had to pay for carrying cruiser-sized 5.9-inch guns was a decided top-heaviness, imparting a built-in vicious roll. Even *Scharnhorst*, arguably the finest ocean-going capital ship ever built, was far from immune to the wildness of the sea, and her complement included forty hapless young officer cadets, who had had the bad luck to be assigned this as their first-ever operational sea cruise.

If *Scharnhorst* had sailed on her own, unimpeded by a clutch of labouring destroyers, it might have been a very different story. Bey found his destroyers were more of a hindrance than a help as soon as the German battle group reached the turmoil of the open sea. 'OFFENSIVE ACTION BY DESTROYERS GREATLY IMPAI-

RED', he signalled at 21.16hrs. 'SPEED RESTRICTION'.[6] As a former destroyer man Bey should have been the first to realise that his destroyers would never be able to keep up with *Scharnhorst* in the high-speed search-and-attack operation for which he had gone to sea. Already two hours late in sailing, he should have ordered his destroyers back to base and pressed on to search for the convoy at full speed. But it again seems most likely that Dönitz's last signal had had a mesmerising effect, inhibiting Bey rather than inspiring him. Ambiguous orders, especially orders drafted in ignorance of the situation prevailing at the recipient's end, can never be carried out in full, but that is what Bey tried to do. Unfortunately for Bey and his men, in Dönitz's signal '*Scharnhorst* AND DESTROYERS will attack convoy' came before 'Destroyers to operate AS SEEMS SUITABLE'. Though his motives for doing it will never be known, Bey kept the destroyers with him instead of sending them back to Altenfjord. It was the first of many fatal errors.

But for Fraser the night of 25–26 December seemed particularly long. At any minute, he believed, the escorts of JW.55B might signal that *Scharnhorst* was attacking; there would be nothing he could do about it if she did. And yet every hour that passed helped lessen the chance of failure. From 22.00hrs details of more 'ULTRA' decrypts began to reach him from the Admiralty. The German minesweeper *R-121* had been ordered to proceed to *Scharnhorst*'s anchorage at 11.58hrs that morning. At 14.21hrs, the *Luftwaffe* had reported that JW.55B had been located again. Then came the '*OSTFRONT – 17.00 – 25th*' signal of 15.25hrs, followed shortly by a signal from *Scharnhorst* to patrol boat *V-5903* that she would be passing 'outward-bound as from 6pm'.[7] Finally, at 03.19hrs on the 26th, Fraser received a curt Admiralty 'appreciation' that *Scharnhorst* was at sea. After that the Admiralty fell silent – and remained silent for the next 18 hours and 34 minutes. Admiral Cunningham in Whitehall knew far better than to saddle a commander at sea, on the eve of action, with a load of extraneous information and distracting orders. Admiralty Intelligence, superbly fed by the 'ULTRA' decoders, had passed all the known facts to Burnett and Fraser, with whom the chances of success or failure now rested.

Even as the electrifying news that 'ADMIRALTY APPRECIATES THAT *SCHARNHORST* IS AT SEA' was being transmitted and the men of Force 1 and Force 2 prepared to go to Action Stations, Fraser was preparing for his next two moves. The first, prompted by a most timely improvement in the weather, was an instant increase of Force 2's speed to 24 knots. The second was a third calculated breach of radio silence, regardless of whether the Germans listened in or not. At 04.01 hrs on 26 December 1943, Fraser issued the first in a series of taut, economical orders with which he took control of and directed the Battle of the North Cape.

Fraser's first signal of 04.01hrs was a three-item package:

> 1 McCoy was to swing JW.55B on to a northerly course. Wherever *Scharnhorst* was, this would make it harder for her to close the convoy;
>
> 2 Fraser stated his own position, course, and speed. This meant that both McCoy and Burnett knew precisely where he was;
>
> 3. McCoy and Burnett were ordered to state their own positions, courses and speeds. This meant that Force 1, Force 2 and the convoy escort each knew where they were in relation to the others.

The risk remained the same, that German D/F stations would pin-point Fraser's position, identify him correctly as the commander of a British battle group and alert *Scharnhorst* accordingly, but it was a well-calculated risk. The information Fraser wanted was essential, and he had already broken radio silence twice without stopping *Scharnhorst* from putting to sea; it was unlikely that anything dramatic would result from this third instance. Events were soon to prove Fraser absolutely right, but it must also be conceded that Bey was wretchedly served by U-boat, *Luftwaffe* and German shore intelligence. Lord Fraser always admitted as much; 'We had a lot of luck, really,' he would say in future years.[8] But there is a difference between gratuitous luck and made luck, and Fraser made plenty of his own good fortune that day.

When the positions of McCoy and Burnett were first added to the plot in *Duke of York*, however, the situation looked none too good. Still some 220 miles away to the south-west, Fraser learned that he was about 70 miles further away from the convoy than Burnett; and that although Burnett and JW.55B were on converging courses, the convoy was already being shadowed by a U-boat. As for *Scharnhorst*, she could be anywhere between the Norwegian coast and the convoy and was presumably waiting for the U-boat's signals to guide her in to the attack. About the only solid piece of good news was the heartening progress of RA.55A, now safely 'off the map' some 200 miles west of Bear Island and plodding on, still undetected, into the teeth of the gale at 8 knots.

At 04.00hrs on the 26th, *Scharnhorst* and her destroyers were actually about 100 miles south-east of the convoy, heading north at 25 knots (see Diagram 2). Bey and his staff, forced to work out their own estimate of the convoy's position because of the *Luftwaffe*'s

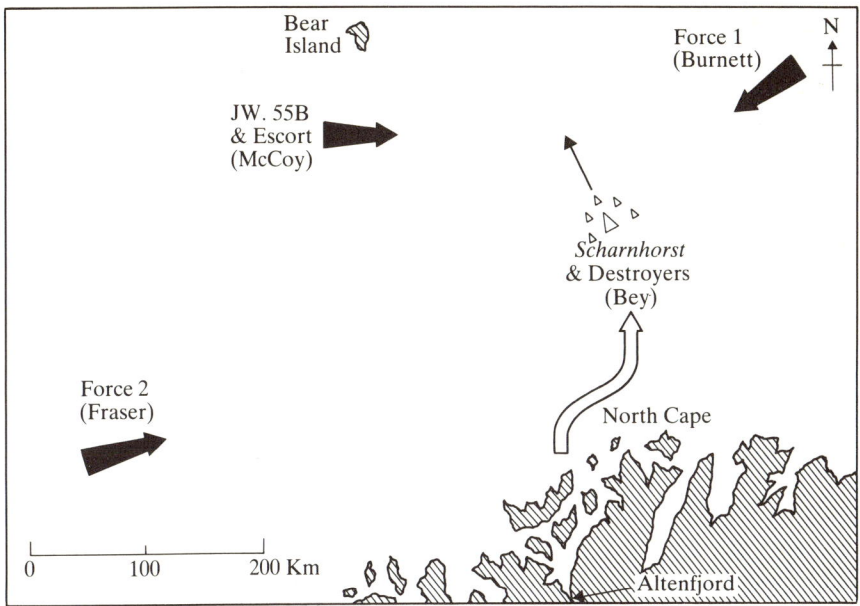

Diagram 2   The situation at 04.00hrs.

maddening failure to do so, believed JW.55B to be further east and further south than it actually was, an error which Fraser's convoy course alteration helped augment.

Reproducing the plot and describing it is an easy process, but a misleading one in that it suggests that Fraser's subsequent decisions were straightforward. This was not the case, because the only Home Fleet unit with which Fraser could communicate in 'real time' was his own Force 2. When it came to signalling orders to Force 1 and JW.55B's escort, Fraser had to work to a slow-motion time-scale: the result of the time it took his signals to reach their destination and be put into effect. Thus it was not until 05.46hrs that Fraser received Burnett's reply to his initial signal of 04.01hrs, while McCoy was unable to execute JW.55B's course correction until 06.05hrs. Nor was this slow-motion time-scale constant. It was subject to change with every fluky effect of atmospheric conditions on WT reception, and was dramatically reduced as the widely separated Home Fleet units converged. This intriguing aspect of Fraser's control of the battle has been all too often overlooked. It demanded the constant ability to think ahead and keep all possible combinations of ship positions in mind. To some extent Fraser's prewar experience of carrier work in *Glorious* helped; carrier command requires similar long-distance communications and allowance for where the aircraft will be at such-and-such a time in relation to the carrier. In any event, there can be no denying that the way Fraser coped with the communications problem in the North Cape action was masterly.

Having given JW.55B time to embark on its side-step to the north, Fraser sent out his second 'compound order' at 06.28hrs:

1 McCoy was ordered to turn JW.55B on to an easterly course to reduce the distance from Force 1;
2 Force 1 was ordered to close the convoy for mutual support.

Burnett received this order at 06.51hrs, McCoy 14 minutes later. Though it was easy enough for JW.55B to comply by turning 'down-wind' on to 045°, Burnett decided to approach the convoy on a dog-leg course, heading first south-west, then north-west as he closed. This would save Force 1 from having to slog head-on in to the heavy seas if *Scharnhorst* should put in an appearance.

Meanwhile, at 07.00hrs, Bey had decided that the German battle group was already astride the convoy's estimated line of advance. He therefore wheeled his force to 250° and ordered Captain Johannesson, in command of the destroyers, to deploy in line-abreast ahead of *Scharnhorst* and search for the convoy. Having thus committed himself to the wrong line of search – JW.55B meanwhile steaming away from *Scharnhorst* to the north and east – Bey thereby handed the British still more time in which to find him before he found the convoy.

By 07.30hrs, however, Fraser was for the moment obliged to wait upon the events he had set in motion. While Force 2 drove on to the north-east at 24 knots, he could do no more until his orders of 06.28hrs had run their course. Away to the east, Burnett at 07.42hrs swung Force 1 to starboard on a course of first 300°, then 305°: the last stage of his dog-leg approach to the convoy, working up to 24 knots by 08.15hrs. As *Scharnhorst* was now groping uncertainly to the eastward of her destroyers (all of which were heading in the opposite direction) with all the hesitancy of a burglar in a dark room wondering if this really *was* where the silver was kept, the waiting game was fast drawing to an end. It was now inevitable that Force 1 would encounter *Scharnhorst* on her own before the British cruisers could make rendezvous with JW.55B. The vital difference was that Burnett was ready for such an encounter and Bey was not.

First contact was made at 08.30hrs when *Norfolk*'s radar located *Scharnhorst* at a range of 33,000 yards, confirmed by *Belfast* at 08.40hrs and by *Sheffield* at 08.50hrs. Burnett immediately signalled 'UNIDENTIFIED RADAR CONTACT BEARING 295°, RANGE 16 MILES'; and McCoy ordered the 36th Destroyer Division to move out 6 miles ahead of the convoy and deploy in line-abreast.

Burnett's prime concern was to close the range. If, as seemed increasingly likely, this contact should be confirmed as *Scharnhorst*, he had to get within a range at which Force 1's twenty-four 6-inch guns (*Belfast* and *Sheffield*) and eight 8-inch guns (*Norfolk*) could hurt – to take as long a step as possible inside the superior reach of the battle-cruiser's 11-inch guns. The confrontation was uncomfortably reminiscent of the River Plate action in December 1939, when Commodore Harwood had engaged *Graf Spee* with one 8-inch gun cruiser and two 6-inch gun cruisers. Making ferocious play with her 11-inch guns, the pocket-battleship had battered the 8-inch gun cruiser *Exeter* into a defenceless wreck and badly damaged Harwood's flagship *Ajax*; if the German captain had pressed on with the action instead of running for Montevideo, *Ajax* and her consort *Achilles* could well have shared the fate of *Exeter*. This time a similar trio of British cruisers was up against an opponent which was not only much more heavily armoured than *Graf Spee* but which carried three more 11-inch guns and had the most formidable combat record in the German surface fleet. A premature engagement with *Scharnhorst* could be disastrous for the Force 1 cruisers, and the problem was quite tricky enough without the possibility of intervention by Johannesson's destroyers.

Johannesson, however, was having troubles of his own. At 08.55hrs he sent off an enemy sighting report and prepared to open fire – on a target which, in the nick of time, he identified as one of his own destroyers, Z-38, which was badly out of position. None of the German destroyers detected the cruisers of Force 1 approaching *Scharnhorst* from the eastward.

At 09.00hrs *Belfast*'s radar also located the straying Z-38, but by 09.15hrs it was obvious which of the two radar echoes was *Scharnhorst*. The range was now down to 13,000 yards and Burnett prepared to open fire. He decided to ignore the mysterious second contact, which was only moving at 8 knots and seemed to be a straggler from the convoy. So much for the deterrent value of the German destroyers!

At 09.21hrs *Sheffield* sighted *Scharnhorst* for the first time, and for the next 8 minutes Burnett's cruisers made successive fruitless attempts to illuminate *Scharnhorst* with star-shell at extreme range. Horrified at the thought that *Scharnhorst* might break off and escape unscathed, Burnett ordered Force 1 to open fire at 09.29hrs. *Norfolk* not only had the guns with the longest range: she was the best placed of the three cruisers and carried the brunt of this first action, firing six full 8-inch broadsides. Good shooting was rewarded with good luck. *Norfolk*'s second or third salvo landed fairly on *Scharnhorst*'s port high-angle director, wrecking it and destroying the main radar aerial. Though *Scharnhorst* still had a secondary radar aerial aft, the battle-cruiser's all-round fire-control was now reduced to visual and not radar guidance, a decisive advantage for the British.

As had always been expected, Bey's reaction was to take *Scharnhorst* out of action at her full speed of 30 knots, firing several blind salvoes from her after turret, but he was not running for base. Bey was determined to work his way round this unexpected opposition and keep trying to find and attack the convoy, this time after making an anti-clockwise detour to the south-east and north. With *Scharnhorst*'s clear 6-knot speed advantage over the British cruisers the range opened rapidly. *Norfolk* reluctantly ceased fire at 09.40hrs, and though Force 1 gave valiant chase *Scharnhorst* finally vanished off *Belfast*'s radar screen, still heading north-east, at 10.19hrs.

The news that Burnett's cruisers were in action prompted Fraser's next two orders. At 09.30hrs he ordered McCoy to turn JW.55B to the north, and then (09.37hrs) signalled McCoy to 'SEND FOUR DESTROYERS TO JOIN *BELFAST*'. Fraser did not then know that McCoy had anticipated him by two minutes, asking Burnett at 09.35hrs if Force 1 required destroyer assistance. This timely thinking by the convoy escort Commander cut to the minimum the transfer of 36th Destroyer Division to Force 1. By 10.50hrs Commander Fisher's four destroyers had formed a scouting formation ahead of the cruisers. Burnett meanwhile, confident that *Scharnhorst* would attempt a second thrust at the convoy, had placed his cruisers about 10 miles ahead of JW.55B: a blocking move as brilliant[9] as it was instinctive.

After vanishing off Force 1's radar screens at 10.19hrs, Bey found his problems multiplying rapidly. First, the brief cruiser action had effectively 'blinded' *Scharnhorst*'s radar. Second, his destroyers were clearly following the wrong scent; they were too far to the south-east; Johannesson was showing none of the intelligent co-operation and foresight of the British commanders, and the only information Bey could send Johannesson was the last convoy position reported by U-boat two hours before. Even more disquieting was a *Luftwaffe* message to the effect that one large and several smaller unidentified vessels had been located by airborne radar to the south-west. The *Luftwaffe* had found Force 2 at last, but Bey nevertheless believed that he would still have time to find and attack the convoy before these new British intruders could intervene.

Fraser's thoughts were running on very similar lines. Fuel was the crux: the ever-dwindling fuel of Force 2's destroyers. The time was steadily approaching when Fraser must make up his mind whether to turn back to Scapa Flow or carry on to Murmansk, regardless of what might be happening away to the north-east. He knew German aircraft had found Force 2, and could still only conclude that *Scharn-*

horst had been furnished with accurate information. At 11.03hrs, therefore, Fraser signalled to Burnett, 'UNLESS TOUCH CAN BE REGAINED BY SOME UNIT THERE IS NO CHANCE OF MY FINDING ENEMY'. But Burnett dared not leave his blocking position ahead of JW.55B and try to seek out the enemy: it would be only too easy to miss *Scharnhorst*, which would then have a comparatively easy time attacking the convoy. There was nothing for it but for Force 1 to sit tight, wait for *Scharnhorst* to try again – and hope she did it soon.

Fraser, however, dared not rely on such a waiting brief for Force 2. On his shoulders rested the responsibility not only for the protection of JW.55B, for which he had made every possible provision, but for the guarding of the entrances into the North Atlantic. Burnett's last signal to Fraser after the first cruiser action was 'HAVE LOST TOUCH WITH ENEMY WHO IS STEERING NORTH. AM CLOSING CONVOY' (10.44hrs). But over the 45 minutes after his bleak signal to Burnett of 11.03hrs, Fraser became increasingly haunted by a possibility which he had previously assessed as remote: that *Scharnhorst*, having been baulked of an easy strike at JW.55B, might now break first north, then west, and make a bid for the North Atlantic. Once at large there, she was the only German warship capable of catching the fast Allied liners – *Queen Mary, Queen Elizabeth, Aquitania, Mauretania, Ile de France, Nieuw Amsterdam* – speeding the American build-up in the UK with monster troop deliveries on each passage. The 'Queens' alone had been carrying no less than 15,000 soldiers on every transatlantic passage they had made since June 1942. If any one of these ships – which, as Fraser well knew, sailed unescorted, relying on their speed – should be caught by *Scharnhorst*, the result could only be a catastrophic loss of life, not to mention a serious disruption of the build-up for the cross-Channel invasion to which Britain and the United States were pledged. And if Fraser pressed on to the east, hoping to engage *Scharnhorst* when she might well already be racing west to the Denmark Strait, the blame would rest squarely on him and him alone.

It was therefore at 11.50hrs that Fraser ordered Force 2, by visual signals, to reverse course to the west. In the wild seas this was a major task for the destroyers, which took about 15 minutes to make the turn and required a reduction of speed to 18 knots to enable them to keep station. 'COURSE IS TO BE ALTERED IN SUCCESSION TO 260°, SHIPS TURNING TO STARBOARD', he signalled at 11.57hrs, having alerted *Jamaica* to the coming manoeuvre 6 minutes before. 'MEAN LINE OF ADVANCE FROM NOW IS TO BE 250° UNTIL FURTHER ORDERS', he added at 12.01hrs. If the worst came to the worst and *Scharnhorst was* heading for the North Atlantic, Force 2 was now positioned on a parallel course, ahead and to the south of the German. If not, the strengthened Force 1 still hovering in support of JW.55B should be able to 'see off' any further thrusts at the convoy until Force 2 had again reversed its tracks. But as it turned out Force 2 barely had time to settle on its new course of 250° before electrifying news came in from Burnett.

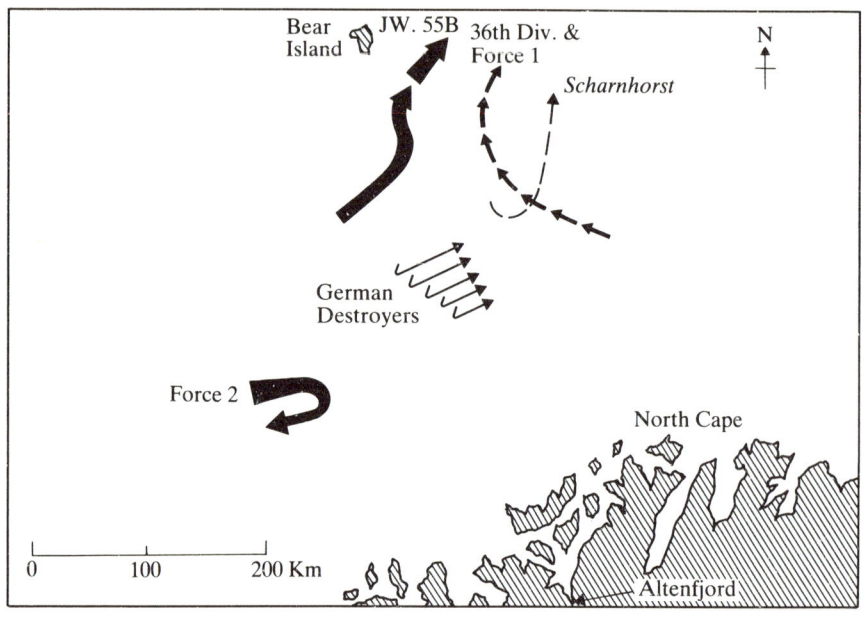

Diagram 3   The situation at 12.00 hrs.

At noon on the 26th *neither* of the two British admirals knew for sure where *Scharnhorst* actually was. At 11.35hrs *Norfolk*'s radar had made fleeting contact with an unidentified ship, but this had been lost at 11.50hrs. Fraser had meanwhile freed McCoy's hands, signalling 'USE YOUR DISCRETION REGARDING MEAN COURSE OF CONVOY'. There had been a 4-minute flurry of excitement when the destroyer *Onslaught* reported another unidentified contact, until at 11.35hrs Burnett in *Belfast* had coldly signalled 'ONSLAUGHT'S CONTACT IS ME'. Then, at 12.05hrs, *Belfast*'s radar made yet another contact. 'J 075–13', signalled Burnett to his cruisers, the code standing for 'RADAR CONTACT AT 075°13''. It was this signal, reported to Fraser at the very moment when Force 2 was completing its painful turn to the west, that induced Fraser immediately to turn back to the east. His instinct was right: this time it was the real thing. At 12.20hrs *Belfast* exultantly signalled 'ENEMY IN SIGHT BEARING 090°', with Burnett's order to open fire following at once.

The second cruiser action with *Scharnhorst* lasted twice as long as the first: 21 minutes in all, from 12.20 to 12.41 hrs. Taken completely by surprise for the second time, *Scharnhorst* hit back fiercely and concentrated her fire on *Norfolk*. This was not so much because *Norfolk* was the most powerful British cruiser: she had also had the bad luck not to have been supplied with flashless cordite charges, which made her gun flashes an easy target. At 12.27hrs *Norfolk* had her 'X' turret and radar put out of action by two direct hits from *Scharnhorst*, whereby one officer and six ratings were killed and another five ratings were badly wounded. *Sheffield* was also straddled by a German salvo and hit by shell splinters but suffered no casualties; *Belfast* escaped unscathed. Burnett's orders to 36th Destroyer division to close and attempt to launch torpedoes came to nothing. The destroyers passed ahead of Force 1 and both *Musketeer* and *Virago* came within gunnery range of *Scharnhorst*, but the target's energetic course changes to port and starboard made torpedo attacks impossible. By 13.00hrs the second cruiser action was over, with the British having had decidedly the worst of it. Bey was once again trying to shake off his pursuers, steaming at high speed to the south-east; and there seemed no good reason to believe that *Scharnhorst* would not vanish into the darkness for a second time – most likely for good.

All now turned on how Bey would react to the earlier warning of a British battle group to the south-west. One of *Scharnhorst*'s survivors, Petty Officer Willi Gödde, later made it clear that *Scharnhorst*'s company had been alerted to this threat by Captain Hintze between 11.00 and 11.30hrs, in the lull between the two cruiser actions. As Gödde recalled it, the announcement had said that, 'A British heavy battle group has been sighted 150 miles to the westward; I repeat 150 miles to the westward. That is to say, well out of our way. We are forging on towards the convoy. End of announcement!'[10] And two hours later, as Bey made off to the south-east, he seems to have been confident that his new course would keep the British battle group 'well out of his way'. What he had not taken into account was the fact that he had chosen a course which, in relation to the gale and the violence of the sea, allowed the pursuing cruisers (though not the destroyers) to remain in radar contact. Certainly the *Luftwaffe* report relayed to Bey at 13.06hrs conveyed no sense of urgency and was inexcusably vague, omitting as it did any reference to a British heavy unit. By 14.18hrs Bey had accepted that the vigilant British cruisers would prevent him from approaching the convoy again. He made the decision to abandon *Ostfront*,

ordering Johannesson's destroyers to return to base without rejoin-
ing, while *Scharnhorst* shaped a lone course for home.

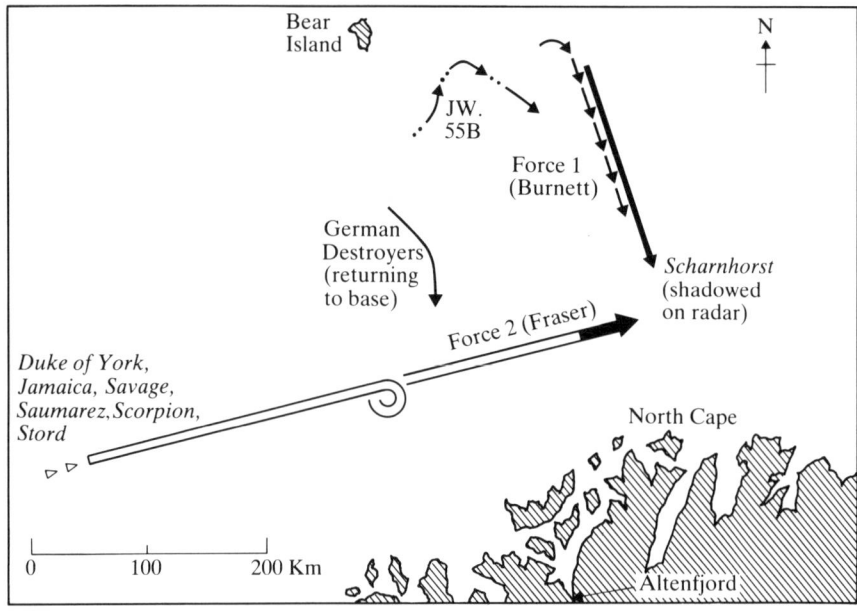

Diagram 4   The situation at 15.00hrs, with German destroyers returning independently, *Scharnhorst* shadowed by Burnett's Force 1 and Fraser's Force
2 closing from south-west.

It was therefore from 13.00hrs that it began to dawn on Fraser that
if the Force 1 cruisers kept in touch with *Scharnhorst*, and that if
Scharnhorst held to her course, Force 2 would still be in with a
chance of intercepting the retreating battle-cruiser. This dawning
awareness is reflected by the following exchange of signals (note the
steadily-decreasing time-scale) between Fraser and Burnett:

13.18hrs – C-in-C to *Belfast*: REPORT COMPOSITION OF
ENEMY
13.25hrs – *Belfast* to C-in-C: ONE HEAVY SHIP
14.35hrs – C-in-C to *Belfast*: HAVE YOU DESTROYERS IN
COMPANY
14.42hrs – *Belfast* to C-in-C: NO, THEY ARE FOLLOWING
14.49hrs – C-in-C to *Belfast*: IF PRACTICABLE INTEND TO
ENGAGE FROM THE WESTWARD ON A
SIMILAR COURSE

The next hour was vital because it saw Bey hold to his course, never even attempting a high-speed breakaway to shake off the radar 'grip' of Burnett's cruisers labouring in his rear. Had he succeeded in doing this, his chances of returning safely to Altenfjord would still have been high. But *Belfast* continued to feed Fraser with *Scharnhorst*'s course and speed as she stood on to the south-south-east, zig-zagging on a mean course of 160°. At 15.51hrs, his hopes rising fast, Fraser made another signal:

> 15.51hrs – C-in-C to Home Fleet in Company: THE ESTIMATED BEARING AND DISTANCE OF THE ENEMY FROM ME ARE 025°, 25 MILES

Then at last, at 16.17hrs, *Duke of York*'s Type 273 radar located *Scharnhorst* at a range of 45,000 yards. The battle-cruiser's inadequate after radar set failed to detect Force 2 as Fraser continued to narrow the range, while briefing his ships to prepare for the action for which he had waited so long:

> 16.35hrs – C-in-C to *Belfast*: PREPARE TO FIRE STARSHELL OVER ENEMY
>
> 16.40hrs – C-in-C to destroyers in Company: TAKE UP ADVANTAGEOUS POSITIONS FOR FIRING TORPEDOES BUT DO NOT ATTACK UNTIL ORDERED

At 16.44hrs Fraser swung Force 2 to starboard, opening the arcs of all the 14-inch turrets of *Duke of York* and ensuring that all his heavy guns would be bearing when the moment came – then:

> 16.46hrs – C-in-C to *Belfast*: OPEN FIRE WITH STARSHELL

Belfast's gunners, however, had no better luck in illuminating *Scharnhorst* than they had enjoyed earlier, and that honour fell to the flagship. Commander K. Wintle writes:[11]

> My place of duty was probably the coldest in the ship: the Air Defence and Illuminations position abaft the compass platform, and completely in the open. I was starshell control officer and opened the action with four 5.25-inch starshells.

The glare of the four star-shells, hung perfectly in the sky behind their target (see Diagram 5), revealed one of the most breathtaking sights of the war. There at last was *Scharnhorst*, caught completely by surprise for the third time that day, plumb in the centre of the stage and carving her way majestically through the blackness of the gale-driven sea. From the *Jamaica*, a junior officer later recalled, 'The *Scharnhorst* appeared on the horizon a black silhouette against

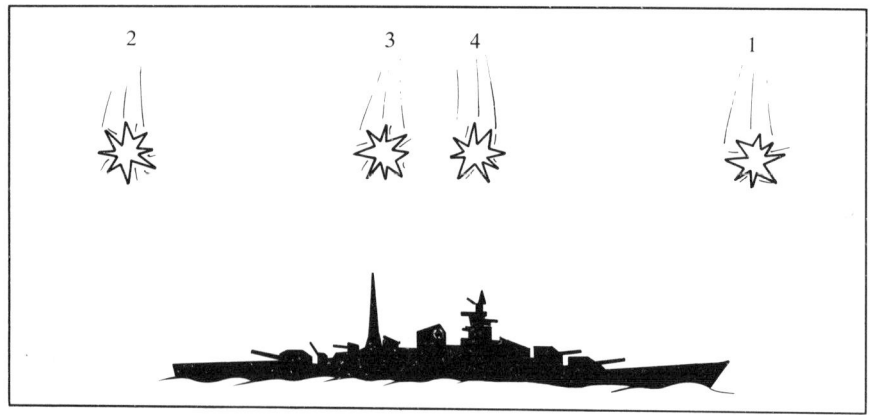

Diagram 5   The star-shell pattern over the *Scharnhorst*

the flickering candle-glow. Even at that distance the sheer of her bows was perfectly noticeable and she stood out clearly for an instant as if removed bodily from her page in "Jane's Fighting Ships".'[12] This, of course, was one of the supreme moments of Fraser's life, and it had obviously not dimmed an iota thirty-six years later. 'Four star-shell, and there she was, guns still fore-and-aft. *It was terrific* – I can still see that illumination now.'[13]

At 16.50hrs the Arctic night was split wide open by ten blinding 14-inch gun flashes as *Duke of York* opened fire, at the range which Fraser's planning had always envisaged: 12,000 yards. As Richard Courage recalls:[14]

> It was a dramatic moment – especially as it nearly made the C-in-C a casualty. A large sort of kitchen clock hung on the bulkhead of the Admiral's Bridge; it was essential to time changes of course when steaming a zig-zag in U-boat waters. Before practice in full-calibre firing such items are taken down and carefully stored away in a safe place, but in the long build-up to the action the clock had been overlooked. No one even had to look at the clock, as we were not working a zig-zag. But with the first salvo it fell with a loud crash between the C-in-C and me. That was our most dangerous moment, and also the only time either the C-in-C or I *saw* the *Scharnhorst*.

Fraser's ships made full use of the surprise they had achieved. *Duke of York* straddled *Scharnhorst* with her very first broadside, disabling the battle-cruiser's 'A' turret and causing a flash fire in the 'B' turret handling-room which came within an ace of blowing up the ship. Without the excellent anti-flash precautions maintained in the German Navy since Jutland, this would have brought the battle to a spectacular and early close, grim revenge for the shattering destruction of HMS *Hood* under *Bismarck*'s fifth salvo on 24 May 1941. The practice of *Jamaica*, playing the part of 'Little Sir Echo' astern of the flagship, was no less effective. *Jamaica* straddled *Scharnhorst* with her third salvo, and also scored a hit. Thus within the first few minutes of the battle *Scharnhorst*'s main armament had been reduced by one-third.

This gratifying but unexpected start highlighted the biggest 'missed opportunity' of the North Cape action: the inability of the closest destroyers to attack with torpedoes at the outset, because of Fraser's order to the destroyers to wait until so ordered. When Force 2 opened fire *Savage* was the leading destroyer, ahead and to port of the flagship; by 16.55 *Savage* was so close to *Scharnhorst* that *Duke of York*'s starshells were illuminating her as well as the enemy. After the battle Fraser was the first to concede that his order *had* cramped the style of the destroyers at this favourable if transient moment, and would good-naturedly feign annoyance that Commander Meyrick had not disobeyed orders and attacked all the same![15]

Roskill, in *The War At Sea*, does not fail to comment on Fraser's 'hold-your-fire' order to the destroyers, claiming that it 'resulted in the *Savage* and *Saumarez* losing a favourable opportunity, which was not to recur until one-and-a-half hours later'.[16] This can certainly not be accepted as the last word: far more was at risk than a wasted spread of destroyer torpedoes, and though Fraser was a master of the calculated risk he also knew where to draw the line. He did not want to risk driving *Scharnhorst* away to the north-east, which a premature failed torpedo attack would almost certainly have done, until the destroyers and cruisers of Force 1 had moved into position on *Scharnhorst*'s port quarter. Again, Fraser knew that *Duke of York*'s radars were far superior to those in the destroyers, which he was determined to spare from heroic but fruitless action based on inadequate data. *Scharnhorst* was able simultaneously to return the fire of *Duke of York* and *Jamaica* while reserving no less than six 5.9-inch guns (her starboard secondary broadside) to *Savage* and *Saumarez* alone. *Savage* drew secondary fire from *Scharnhorst* at once, with the German shells falling only 20–30 yards short of the dangerously exposed destroyers. If, therefore, Fraser had changed his original plan and ordered *Savage* and *Saumarez* to press a torpedo attack, they would most probably have achieved nothing and sustained heavy casualties and crippling damage. As it was the Force 2 destroyers prudently fell back, surviving to play a decisive role at a much more propitious later stage of the battle.

Scharnhorst's first reaction to the devastating shock of Force 2's opening fire was to swing sharply to the north. Then, as Force 1's leading ships crept up on her port quarter, she turned to the east and ran for it, working up to her full speed of 30 knots and maintaining an increasingly accurate fire on her pursuers. As Fraser had hoped, the German fire was split between *Duke of York* and *Jamaica*. From the viewpoint of the control officer in *Jamaica*'s port high-angle director:[17]

> Throughout the next few hours, although life was by no means quiet or safe, the *Scharnhorst*'s gunnery was concentrated mainly and accurately upon the flagship. We collected those not quite so well calculated, of which the majority arrived during the earlier part of the action. There was no mistaking the aim of two salvoes at least, though, one of which rumbled like an express train close overhead and the other pitched into the sea abreast and very near 'B' turret on the starboard side, without exploding but effectively drowning everyone on and around the bridge in a deluge of icy water. Many 11-inch shells burst on impact with the sea and disintegrated in a shower of splinters which droned unpleasantly near but luckily did no damage . . .
>
> In the fluorescent screen of the training tube I could watch not only the confused twelve-point blur of our own broadsides but, and much more alarmingly, the answering flicker of the 11-inch reply as it neared the ship.

Aboard *Duke of York*, as soon as the gun action started Fraser moved into the Plot (a makeshift operations room next door to the Bridge wireless officer on the Admiral's Bridge) to supervise the co-ordination of the attacks. Richard Courage's account continues:[18]

> I remained outside in the darkness, getting rather bored and seeing nothing except the splashes of *Scharnhorst*'s shells, which seemed much too close for comfort. In the dark I could see no damage – in fact the only thing I clearly remember seeing were our two great white Battle Ensigns which had been broken out at each masthead as the first salvo was fired, an inspiring sight when illuminated by the flash of our own guns. This practice goes back to days well before Trafalgar and had been remembered by Signal Boatswain Harold Kelly.
>
> At one moment there was a loud tinkle just aft of the Bridge structure, and I told Commander Peter Dawnay, Fleet Wireless Officer, that I thought some of his aerials had been shot away. His cheerful reply through the voicepipe was something like, 'Perhaps – but we're still on the blower to the Admiralty and everyone else.'
>
> The next day it was apparent that a shell had gone through

both masts and actually severed one of the mainmast's tripod legs. There were also one or two bits of German shell lying about the deck. That was *Duke of York*'s only damage – the near-miss from the clock being the worst as far as I was concerned.

This first battleship action lasted from 16.50hrs to 18.24hrs. Like the Battle of the Falkland Islands on 8 December 1914 in which the first *Scharnhorst* (a burly, sharp-shooting armoured cruiser of the Imperial Navy) had been sunk, it took the form of a chase. In this chase the British had the advantage in fire-power and gunnery range, but not, as at the Falklands in 1914, in speed. From the moment *Scharnhorst* turned east at 17.08hrs, it seemed increasingly likely that the quarry would outrun the hunt and get clean away.

As a gunnery specialist Fraser was perfectly familiar with the dilemma confronting him, but it was none the less intensely frustrating. With ten 14-inch guns against (after the silencing of 'A' turret) six 11-inch, *Duke of York* decisively out-gunned *Scharnhorst*. But *Scharnhorst*'s massive protection included a main armour belt of 12–13 inches, 12 inches on the turrets, 6 inches on the decks. When it came to penetrating armour of this quality, the range favouring sustained broadside fire at which Fraser opened the action was far from ideal: it was close enough for *Duke of York*'s shells to arrive on a comparatively flat trajectory. This meant that the shells hit the thin deck armour at a very low angle, reducing their penetrative power (an angle of 50° to the line of impact gives armour plate double the resistance without having to be twice as strong). As *Scharnhorst* drew away, as the range increased and the trajectory of *Duke of York*'s shells became higher and more plunging, the chances of landing a really damaging hit paradoxically increased, but so, of course, did the chances of *Scharnhorst* escaping out of effective range before such a hit could be inflicted. As things turned out, *Duke of York*'s gunners made it with barely four minutes to spare.

Force 1's share in the first battleship action was necessarily limited. Burnett's ships had become strung out during the long run south on *Scharnhorst*'s tail, first by an oil tank fire in *Norfolk*, then by a stripped shaft bearing in *Sheffield*. The latter fault forced *Sheffield* to cut her speed to 8 knots until the damaged shaft could be locked, straining Burnett's patience to the limit. 'COME ON', he urged *Sheffield* at 16.12hrs, to which *Sheffield* replied 8 minutes later, 'AM FOLLOWING YOU. MY MAXIMUM SPEED 23 KNOTS'. These untimely mishaps meant that Force 1 came up on *Scharnhorst*'s port quarter in 'dribs and drabs': first 36th Destroyer Division, then *Belfast* and *Norfolk*, with *Sheffield* valiantly bringing up the rear.

Force 1 was therefore only able to join in the first battleship action for 15 minutes – from 16.57 to 17.12hrs – before *Scharnhorst* drew ahead out of range of the cruisers. During those 15 minutes the joint contribution of *Norfolk* and *Belfast* was limited to two full broadsides apiece, with an additional five salvoes from *Belfast*'s forward turrets.

But what mattered was Burnett's instinctive positioning, superb as ever. Before he ceased fire at 17.12hrs he had headed Force 1 north-east, pre-empting any attempt *Scharnhorst* might make to escape in that direction or work back towards the convoy. For as Burnett knew without being reminded by Fraser, the latter possibility was the most dangerous of all. If *Scharnhorst* had broken away towards the north, *Duke of York* and the Force 2 destroyers would never have been able to keep pace with her against the force of the sea, and Fraser was to spell this out in his 'Despatch'. From start to finish, this battle's fortunes turned on modern electronic technology – yet the elemental forces of wind and weather retained the same dominant influence as in the classic days of fighting sail. Fraser and Burnett, no less than Hawke and Boscawen 200 years before, could only fight and defeat the enemy if they wrung the maximum advantage out of the weather. Their joint success in this battle was due very largely to the seamanship and tactical anticipation displayed throughout by Burnett. No commanding admiral in modern naval history was ever better served, or admitted as much so gratefully.

Certainly Fraser had hoped that Force 1 would encounter better luck as it joined the action, and that Burnett would be able to press ahead with a torpedo attack as well as gunfire. 'ANY FURTHER NEWS', he signalled to Burnett at 17.02hrs, but he soon learned that *Belfast* and *Norfolk* were already struggling to keep within gunnery range. At 17.13hrs, with *Savage* and *Saumarez* still dodging German shells and awaiting the order to attack, Fraser finally signalled 'DESTROYERS CLOSE AND ATTACK WITH TORPEDOES AS SOON AS POSSIBLE', uneasily aware that he might have left it too late. So indeed it proved. The fleeting opportunity prevailing at first contact had passed; the range was already at 1,900 yards and opening, and *Savage* and *Saumarez* were unable to attack. With Force 1 and Force 2 destroyers already out of the running, Fraser ordered Burnett at 17.23hrs to 'STEER SOUTH TO GET BETWEEN ENEMY AND HIS BASE', and a minute later 'STEER 140° AND JOIN ME'. Everything now turned on the heavy-calibre gunnery duel between *Duke of York* and *Scharnhorst*.

At 17.42hrs *Duke of York* was left as the only British ship still engaging *Scharnhorst* when *Jamaica* ceased fire, after a contribution of nineteen 6-inch broadsides. *Scharnhorst* had now crept so far ahead that *Duke of York*'s after 14-inch turret was trained as far forward as it would go in order to keep firing full broadsides. The blast from the after-guns soon found its way down the flagship's ventilation trunking, causing extensive damage in the Wardroom as well as wrecking the Admiral's Barge. By 18.08hrs the range had increased to 9 miles, too far to observe results from *Duke of York*, and Fraser asked his destroyers for help. *Scorpion* and *Stord* were now about 10 miles from the flagship on *Scharnhorst*'s starboard quarter.

18.10hrs – C-in-C to *Scorpion*: CAN YOU REPORT MY
FALL OF SHOT
18.13hrs – *Scorpion* to C-in-C: YOUR LAST SALVO 200
YARDS SHORT
18.16hrs – *Scorpion* to C-in-C: CAN ONLY SEE
OCCASIONAL SPLASHES DUE TO SMOKE

Ironically, much of the smoke now shrouding and helping protect *Scharnhorst* was the result of *Duke of York*'s own good shooting. During this stage of the action more hits were scored which not only caused extensive damage to *Scharnhorst*'s upperworks but lowered her fire-power still further. One 14-inch shell severed the ventilation trunking of *Scharnhorst*'s 'B' turret, which meant that each time the guns fired the turret was flooded with choking cordite fumes and smoke. By 18.20hrs 'B' turret had fallen silent, the second of *Scharn-horst*'s three 11-inch turrets to go. Another 14-inch shell wiped out *Scharnhorst*'s forward starboard 5.9-inch turret, killing all the turret and magazine crew. But her main armour held up stoutly, her engines remained intact, and by 18.20hrs *Scharnhorst* had opened the range to 20,000 yards from *Duke of York* – a clear gain of 4½ miles during the 1½ hours of the action.

The crisis of the battle had arrived, for *Scharnhorst* was now within minutes of winning clear from her lone tormentor: *Duke of York*, whose shooting was already beginning to suffer. But around 18.20hrs the two ships inflicted vital damage on each other virtually simultaneously. The 'loud tinkle' which Richard Courage heard abaft the flagship's Bridge was an 11-inch shell, the fragments of which not only punctured the mainmast tripod but severed the wires between the Type 284 gunnery radar scanner up the mast and the set. Several minutes passed before Lieutenant H. Bates climbed the mast, re-spliced the severed wires and restored the gunnery radar's 'vision',[19] during which time *Duke of York* was like a heavyweight boxer temporarily blinded by a bad cut over the eye. At 18.24hrs, with the Type 284 still blind, the range now up to 21,400 yards, the line of accuracy falling off badly and fifty-two broadsides having been fired with no apparent decisive results, *Duke of York* ceased fire.

Nearly 30 minutes passed before Fraser realised that *Duke of York* had, in fact, managed to land her own 'Sunday punch'. It happened at 18.20hrs, when a 14-inch shell burst in *Scharnhorst*'s No. 1 boiler room, cutting a pipe feeding steam to the turbines and dropping *Scharnhorst*'s speed to a limping 8 knots. The Chief Engineer, *Korvettenkapitän* Otto König (emulating Bates's feat up *Duke of York*'s mainmast) soon isolated and repaired the damage, restoring *Scharnhorst*'s speed to 22 knots. But the temporary loss of speed at last enabled the two British destroyer sub-divisions of Force 2 – the 1st (*Savage* and *Saumarez*) and 2nd (*Scorpion* and *Stord*) – to close in and launch the all-important torpedo attack.

Yet after *Duke of York*'s check of fire at 18.24hrs, Fraser suffered the blackest half-hour of his professional career. His spirits briefly slumped to a nadir of depression, for which he can hardly be blamed. Everything had seemed to be coming right at last. His strategic hunch about *Scharnhorst*'s sortie and his tactical planning had both been proven sound. Force 1 had ushered *Scharnhorst* into the arms of Force 2; all along the line the enemy had been out-thought. But now, after all, it seemed that the enemy could not be out-*fought*: that *Scharnhorst* was going to get clean away from a British concentration of overwhelming strength. Bitter though the pill was to swallow, there would soon be nothing more to do except pick up the pieces and at least take JW.55B safely through to Murmansk. And at 18.47hrs Burnett, in utter frustration, received Fraser's signal that, 'I SEE LITTLE HOPE OF CATCHING *SCHARNHORST* AND AM PROCEEDING TO SUPPORT CONVOY.'

Looking back across thirty-seven years to that dreadful moment, Lord Fraser was frank but unrepentant. 'Yes,' he told the author, 'I *did* give up hope then, for the moment. Of course, I can see *now* that I shouldn't have sent that signal – Admiral Burnett was furious – but what else could I think? We'd tried everything, and it wasn't enough.'[20] Lord Fraser added that he was already reproaching himself for not having ordered in the destroyers at the outset, and that he was trying, in all honesty, not to blame his destroyer captains for having failed to show a flash of the 'Nelson touch' and disobey their Commander-in-Chief's explicit order to wait. But the black moment soon passed. Fraser had in fact issued the most important order of the battle back at 17.13hrs: 'DESTROYERS CLOSE AND ATTACK WITH TORPEDOES *AS SOON AS POSSIBLE*.' Now *Scharnhorst*'s engine-room damage gave the destroyers their chance, and only 5 minutes after Fraser's despondent signal to Burnett the air waves were crackling with very different news:

18.52hrs – From *Savage*: AM PROCEEDING TO ATTACK
18.52hrs – From *Scorpion*: ATTACK COMPLETED
18.53hrs – From *Stord*: ATTACK COMPLETED
18.53hrs – From *Savage*: ATTACK COMPLETED

Though the transmission time-lapse was now down to between 5–10 minutes, the signal sequence quoted above does not reflect the actual sequence of the destroyers' attacks. When *Scharnhorst* lost speed Bey had ordered a change of course towards the Norwegian coast, which placed *Scorpion* and *Stord* ahead of *Scharnhorst* and *Savage* and *Saumarez* astern, to the south-east and north-west respectively. Commander M. D. G Meyrick co-ordinated the attacks of the two sub-divisions from *Savage*. First, *Savage* and *Saumarez* closed from the north-west, drawing *Scharnhorst*'s fire while *Stord* and *Scorpion* attacked from the south-east. The roles were then smoothly reversed, with *Stord* and *Scorpion* drawing the German fire while *Savage* and *Saumarez* attacked (see Diagram 6).

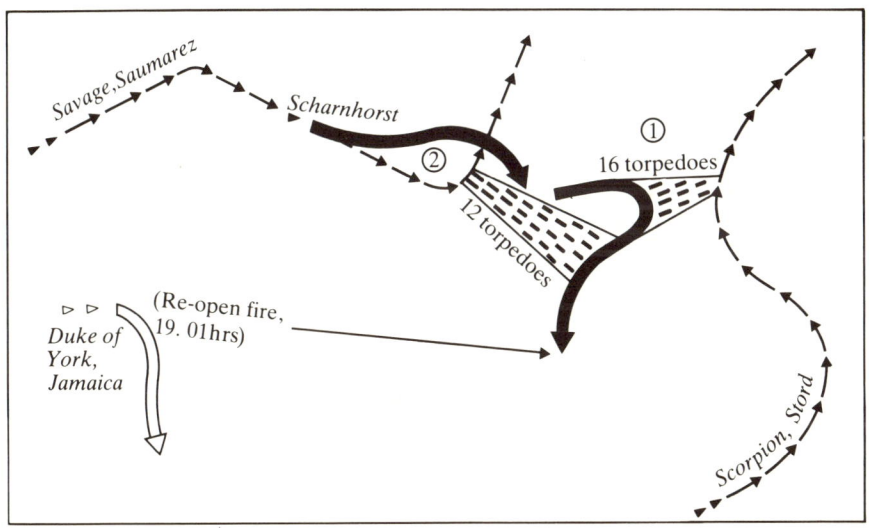

Diagram 6   The vital torpedo attacks by (1) *Scorpion* and *Stord*, (2) *Savage* and *Saumarez*, 18.52–18.55hrs.

It was a superb piece of teamwork, catching *Scharnhorst* from both sides and exposing her to maximum advantage. But it also demanded the traditional gallantry of the destroyer arm, for *Scharnhorst* still had her after 11-inch turret and enough secondary fire-power to blow all four destroyers out of the water. As Fraser stressed in this 'Despatch', this consideration failed to daunt the destroyers: 'they pressed on indomitably to fire their torpedoes point-blank'.[21] *Saumarez* paid the heaviest price for drawing the German fire in those hectic 4 minutes (16.52–16.55hrs). Eleven-inch shell splinters and the bursts of near-misses resulted in one officer and ten ratings killed and another eleven ratings injured, plus severe damage to her director, rangefinder and engine-room and a reduction of speed below 10 knots. But her work had been superbly done. The two sub-divisional attacks each prompted *Scharnhorst* to shy away to starboard in attempts to avoid the torpedoes, back to the westward, and directly towards *Duke of York*.

Scharnhorst's evasive tactics were good, but not good enough. Of the twenty-eight torpedoes launched at her it seems that four hit: one from *Scorpion* just forward of the bridge on the starboard side and three more from *Savage* and *Saumarez*, exploding in rapid succession on the port side. Of these hits the most fateful was the one which exploded beside a boiler room, damaging one of the port shafts and dropping *Scharnhorst*'s speed well below that of *Duke of York* – 22 knots and constantly falling as more and more compartments became flooded. From this moment, *Scharnhorst*'s fate was sealed. Less than 15 minutes had sufficed to snatch certain victory out of the jaws of failure.

With *Scharnhorst* already slowing and taking on an ominous list to starboard, Bey sent off a final message to Hitler:

> 19.00hrs – From *Scharnhorst* to the Führer: WE SHALL FIGHT TO THE LAST SHELL. *SCHARNHORST IMMER VORAN!* ['*Scharnhorst* ever onwards!']²²

At 19.01hrs, her Type 284 radar back in service at last, *Duke of York* reopened fire in company with *Jamaica* with the range at 10,400 yards and rapidly decreasing. Away to the north, *Norfolk* had caught up sufficiently to fire two broadsides as the Force 2 destroyers completed their attack, but soon ceased fire because of the 'clutter' on her radar screens and the difficulty of identifying friend from foe. As the last phase of the battle began, Fraser's only remaining problem was avoiding accidental damage to units of his Fleet as the ships of Force 1 and Force 2 came racing to the scene from all directions, fighting mad to be in at the death.

The last act amounted to a brutal execution, made necessary by the superb determination of the men of the *Scharnhorst* – no less gallant than the men of the *Bismarck* on 27 May 1941 – to fight their ship to the last. Their agony lasted as long as it did for two reasons: the bravery of *Scharnhorst*'s crew and the incredible toughness of her construction. Fraser re-entered the battle with broadside fire from the flagship and *Jamaica* to complete the obliteration of *Scharnhorst*'s remaining fire-power before ordering in his cruisers and destroyers for the final torpedo attacks. Of this second battleship action a revealing eye-witness account, hitherto unpublished, is that of the RAF Liaison Officer aboard *Duke of York*, Wing-Commander Robin Compston:[23]

> The enemy was now almost down to only a few shots – she was glowing on the bridge and quarterdeck but she continued to fire with all the guns she could bring to bear on us as well as using her secondary armament against the destroyers. Now was the time, as the Chief of Staff said, 'to slap her down': the *Duke of York* closed the range to give the *coup de grace*. It was a smashing blow. The tracer bands of her 14-inch shells enabled one to follow little circles of light thrown, like illuminated quoits, on to the glowing target now less than 3 miles away. As each salvo registered, flames and sparks flew up as high explosive disintegrated, piece by piece, the great structure that had been the *Scharnhorst* . . .
>
> In the intervals when the Admiral could leave his Bridge he went into the plotting room and I shall always remember this scene.
>
> This room some ten feet square contains two small plotting tables, one carrying the main and the other the large-scale action chart. The room is a veritable maze of telephones and voicepipes to various strategic points in the ship; these latter curl away into the roof, resembling great coiled pythons on the ceiling.
>
> Dials and gauges are on every hand and surrounding the action chart were the Chief of Staff and his officers, their gaze riveted on the development of the battle. The voicepipes were conveying vital information to the Staff; each voice was answered very quietly and distinctly by one or other of the officers concerned.
>
> In the short periods between our own broadsides and the enemy's salvoes, there was complete quiet in this little space high up in the superstructure – the cranium, as it were, of the brain behind the action. So quiet were the discussions that one might have imagined they were carrying out an ordinary practice shoot at the battle practice target. The question I have sometimes asked myself, and heard others ask, as to why boys were taken away from home at so young an age to be trained for the Royal Navy, was answered then.
>
> These men, controlling the destiny of some eighteen hundred souls, and in the act of writing a page in the annals of history, gave the impression that they were able to make time wait for them.

The Flag Captain was fighting and handling his ship superbly; he spoke frequently through his voicepipe on the Compass Platform to the Admiral on the Bridge, who replied in the same quiet conversational tone we all know so well.

I was deeply impressed by the wonderful co-ordination of forces and perfect timing of the whole action.

By 19.15hrs both Fraser and Burnett were steering south to keep the triangle formed by Force 2, Force 1 and *Scharnhorst* as wide as possible, and lessen the chances of accidental hits on the Force 2 warships as Force 1 re-entered the action. Commander Fisher's 36th Destroyer Division, which had pushed ahead of the Force 1 cruisers during the long chase to the east, was following suit about 8 miles east of Burnett. Shortly after Burnett in *Belfast* opened fire at 19.15hrs, *Scharnhorst*'s last 11-inch turret fell silent under the hail of shells tearing her upper hull apart; and Fraser ordered *Belfast* and *Jamaica* to 'FINISH HER OFF WITH TORPEDOES', checking fire at 19.30hrs as the cruisers went in to attack.

As with the first destroyer attack, this second torpedo attack by the cruisers caught *Scharnhorst* between two fires. *Jamaica* went in at 19.25, having fired twenty-two broadsides since 19.01hrs:[24]

As we closed to under 4,000 yards it was just possible to distinguish the *Scharnhorst*'s dim outline through the smoke of her innumerable fires. Her bridge area was faintly aflame. It may have been imagination, but some said they saw a glimpse of the camouflage and the indication of a steep list through the murk. At twenty-five past seven we fired three torpedoes to port just a minute or two before the *Belfast* did the same – as she was on a similar mission. No hits were secured, but the opportunity was taken to fire, at almost point-blank range, nearly every weapon from 6-inch to Oerlikon as rapidly as possible until we turned to allow the starboard tubes to bear. The *Scharnhorst* was then broadside on and practically stopped. Two heavy underwater explosions indicated hits but could not be observed because an impenetrable pall of smoke descended to cover the area. Before this the *Scharnhorst* had fired at us spasmodically but only with her 5.9s and close-range weapons, which were all ill-directed and of more pyrotechnic than lethal value.

Belfast's four torpedoes were launched at 19.26hrs and she, too, hauled round to describe a figure-eight course bringing her other (port) tubes to bear. But even light cruisers take up a lot of sea when turning at speed, and neither *Jamaica* nor *Belfast* had returned to fire their 'second barrel' before, shortly after 19.30hrs, the destroyers of the 36th Division went in to attack. By this time *Scharnhorst*'s starboard list, which seems to have been increased by at least two hits from the cruiser torpedo attacks, was so great that her last guns could no longer bear. As long as her devoted engine-room staff could deliver revolutions, *Scharnhorst* had feebly tried to dodge her attackers, turning first to the north and then to the south. But by 19.30hrs her speed had fallen off virtually to nothing. With his dying ship no longer able to defend herself or avoid further punishment, Captain Hintze ordered 'Abandon Ship' at about 19.30hrs.

It was, therefore, against an immobile and completely defenceless target that 36th Destroyer Division came boring in at 19.33hrs, splitting into two sub-divisions to catch *Scharnhorst* broadside-on from both port and starboard. *Musketeer* and *Matchless* went for the vulnerable port flank, the one highest out of the water due to *Scharnhorst*'s starboard list, and three of *Musketeer*'s four torpedoes hit between the funnel and the mainmast. *Matchless*, however, was unable to fire: a monstrous wave had smashed the destroyer amidships, cutting communications between bridge and tubes (a useful reminder of the still-formidable weather conditions). As a result the torpedo men of *Matchless* did not receive the order to train tubes to starboard and *Matchless*, having followed *Musketeer* in to attack, swung round to approach from the other side. Meanwhile, *Opportune* and *Virago* had attacked *Scharnhorst*'s starboard side. Each destroyer fired two salvoes between 19.31hrs and 19.34hrs, claiming a total of four hits out of the fifteen torpedoes fired.

By now *Belfast* and *Jamaica* had completed their turns and were ready to attack again with their remaining torpedoes, but Burnett held back in order to let *Opportune* and *Virago* complete their attacks and get clear. It therefore fell to *Jamaica* to deliver the last attack of the battle at 19.37hrs, firing three torpedoes of which two hit. The next attack would have been delivered by *Belfast* and *Matchless*; but when *Belfast* closed the area firing star-shells to illuminate her victim there was nothing to be found but smoke, wreckage and a handful of survivors in the sea.

The final scene was vividly described by Fraser in his 'Despatch':[25]

All that could be seen of *Scharnhorst* was a dull glow through a dense cloud of smoke which the star-shells and searchlights of the surrounding ships could not penetrate. No ship therefore saw the enemy sink, but it seems fairly certain that she sank after a heavy underwater explosion, which was heard and felt in several ships about 19.45.

With reference to Fraser's earlier moment of doubt over the outcome

217

of the battle, it is very noticeable that after *Scharnhorst* went down he fired off repeated signals requesting confirmation of the fact. He had already let slip one premature signal and was determined not to make the same error of judgment again:

19.54hrs – C-in-C to Home Fleet in Company: CLEAR THE AREA OF THE TARGET EXCEPT FOR THOSE SHIPS WITH TORPEDOES AND ONE DESTROYER WITH SEARCHLIGHT

19.56hrs – From *Scorpion*: A LOT OF WRECKAGE ON SEA, AM CLOSING NOW

20.12hrs – From *Scorpion*: AM PICKING UP GERMAN SURVIVORS

20.15hrs – From C-in-C PLEASE CONFIRM *SCHARNHORST* IS SUNK

20.18hrs – From *Scorpion*: SURVIVORS ARE FROM *SCHARNHORST*

20.19hrs – From C-in-C: HAS *SCHARNHORST* SUNK

20.32hrs – *Belfast* to C-in-C: SATISFIED THAT *SCHARNHORST* IS SUNK. WHERE SHALL I REJOIN YOU

It was therefore not until 21.00hrs that the triumphant signal went out from *Duke of York*:

21.00hrs – C-in-C Home Fleet to Admiralty: *SCHARNHORST* SUNK

to which the Admiralty replied at 21.53hrs, repeating the signal to Burnett in *Belfast*:[26]

GRAND. WELL DONE

Thirty-six *Scharnhorst* survivors, none of them officers, were picked up: thirty by *Scorpion*, six by *Matchless*. That was all, out of *Scharnhorst*'s complement of 1,803 officers and men. Both Captain Hintze and Rear-Admiral Bey were sighted in the water after abandoning ship, but died before they could be rescued. *Scharnhorst*'s Commander, *Fregattenkapitän* Dominik, lived long enough to grab at a life-line but died before he could be hauled from the water. This very high casualty list was mostly inflicted in *Scharnhorst*'s last hour, by gunfire from *Duke of York* and the cruisers; by torpedoes from the cruisers and destroyers; by the gunfire and small-calibre fire maintained during each torpedo attack; and of course by the heart-stopping cold of the sea on shocked, wounded and bone-weary men.

Aboard *Duke of York* the flush of victory produced a hilarious tail-piece to the battle. This has been omitted from all previous accounts of the North Cape action, though well enough known to Lord Fraser's former Staff officers. For the version which follows the author is indebted to Captain Richard Courage:[27]

As soon as the action was over, a situation arose that was dreaded by all properly trained signal officers of that generation. Admiral Fraser wished to speak to Admiral Burnett on the R/T. Neither Admiral had received any training about the personal use of this new method of communication.

When Peter Dawnay realised that he would be unable to dissuade the Admiral from embarking on this unwise venture he gave him his first lesson. After explaining that the Germans would be listening to every word, the instruction started.

'First, sir, you press this thing when you want to speak. When you have finished speaking, you say "Over", release it, and listen to what Admiral Burnett has to say. Finally, sir, you *must* use call signs, or you will make it easy for the Germans to make use of what you say.'

Peter Dawnay finished by saying:

'Your call sign, sir, is WIGLEY and Admiral Burnett's is REMBRANDT.'

Then the trouble started. '*Wiggly?*' exploded the Admiral; '*Wiggly?* Who gave me this ridiculous name? Did *you?*' Meanwhile Admiral Burnett was in happy ignorance of the fact that he was about to be summoned to the microphone, and had not had the benefit of expert instruction from the Fleet Wireless Officer. Peter Dawnay describes the ensuing conversation as 'frightfully unsuccessful'. This was probably an understatement – the only people who understood every word must have been the Germans! What we could hear went rather like this:

'Bob, is that you?'

'Bob, can you hear me?'

('Say "Over" and release that handle' – from Peter.)

'Bob, are you clutching your thing? I'll send you *Jamaica*; I'm off to Russia; follow me when you can. . .'

Peter seized the microphone and said 'Out', and we all breathed again. In fact the incident may have done more good than harm: it proved that even Very Senior Officers must be properly trained in the use of this double-edged means of rapid communication. It also made us all laugh, which is always a good thing.

Vernon Merry adds a second anecdote concerning the 'after-the-battle' sense of exhilaration shared by Fraser and his Staff:[28]

When the action was over the Admiral told me to go down to his Sea Cabin below the Admiral's Bridge to fetch an unopened bottle of whisky. Not only did he feel he deserved some: he wanted to pass it round among all the others on the Admiral's Bridge and the Admiral's Plot. I couldn't find the bottle anywhere, but there were two Paymaster Lieutenants RNVR sitting in the armchairs – it was their Action Station as an Emergency Cyphering Team in case other teams were killed. They had been closed up all day, unable to see anything. They hadn't heard anything all day except for the sound of the guns. Nobody had spoken to them, and of course the ship's broadcast system didn't extend to the Admiral's Cabin. So I twigged what had happened to the whisky, and accused them of scoffing the lot. They owned up, and offered to reimburse the Admiral. He was highly amused and of course refused to take their money. In the event the Ward Room Bar was, uniquely, opened for half an hour for a 'quick one' all round!

So ended the Battle of the North Cape – the last battleship action in the history of the Royal Navy, one of the first sea battles of the modern electronic era, and a resounding victory on both counts. The sinking of the *Scharnhorst* was, from the British point of view, a unique blend of shrewd planning, seamanship, endurance and technological skill. Yet there has been a distinct tendency on the part of British historians to 'write down' the battle as a perfectly planned and executed foregone conclusion which, as we have seen, was far from the case. Only an hour before *Scharnhorst* went down, Fraser was glumly convinced that he had lost her. The most recent manifestation of this 'inevitable victory' syndrome came with·the spate of publications after the lifting of security over the 'ULTRA' decrypts. Some of these, carried away by the undeniable drama of the 'ULTRA' story and the importance of its contribution, came close to suggesting that 'ULTRA'-based naval intelligence made the winning of sea battles child's play. Lord Fraser found this decidedly irritating. 'Well, of course,' he told the author, 'it *was* all very useful, as far as it went, but I still had to *find* the *Scharnhorst* and fight her!' In the last analysis it was Fraser's masterly use of the decoded clues passed to him by Admiralty Intelligence that mattered. At no stage could he afford to assume that German intelligence was as lamentable as subsequent enquiries revealed. Nor did he so assume. All the false assumptions were made on the German side.

Fraser's own *Scharnhorst* 'Despatch', as concise as it is lucid, remains the master-key to understanding the North Cape action. In it Fraser points to *Duke of York*'s gunnery as the decisive factor:

'She fought the *Scharnhorst* at night, and she won.' This would have been impossible without British advantage in search and gunnery radar, the brilliance of Burnett's initial cruiser manoeuvres, and the final teamwork of battleship, cruisers and destroyers. Once *Scharnhorst*'s speed had been beaten down to that of *Duke of York* by the vital combination of long-range heavy gunnery and destroyer torpedo attacks, the outcome of the battle was no longer in doubt.

When Fraser's 'Despatch' was published after the war (August 1947) the ensuing issue of the *Naval Review* (November 1947) featured a commentary from which the following points seem particularly worthy of note:

> However ill one may have thought of the Germans, however evil their design or poor their conduct of the action, there were brave men in the *Scharnhorst*. She went down into the Arctic Ocean a mass of scorched and twisted steel pounded to a standstill; but she took nearly all her crew with her and they fought her to the last chance. Of the larger ships in the German Navy she was reckoned to have been one of the happiest and, therefore, by our standards at least, one of the most efficient . . . .
>
> What of the conclusions to the action? I cannot add to those of a technical or tactical nature already so admirably expressed [in the 'Despatch'] but would wish at least one thought to the analyst. If he should size up the list of Allied ships pitted against the German, compare the relative superiority in gun-power, enumerate the torpedoes fired to effect disablement and even take into account the lack of German intelligence, let him be mindful of the enormous barren waste of the Arctic Ocean, the *Scharnhorst*'s advantage in speed and the mantle of the Arctic night. The reading and the analysing of Admiral Fraser's Despatch will then be the more remarkable and, in particular, the achievements of British radar. It was a masterpiece of science.

To which there *is*, in fact, one further point to be made. If Fraser had the advantage in numbers, he surely needed all of it to make certain of his victory because of the immense constructional strength of *Scharnhorst*. At the most modest estimate, she did not sink before taking at least thirteen direct hits from *Duke of York*'s 14-inch guns, about twelve 8-inch and 6-inch direct hits from the cruisers and eleven torpedo hits out of the fifty-five fired at her. It was very probably more. And if the concentration of warships which Fraser brought to bear against *Scharnhorst* had been any weaker, it could well have proved insufficient; as it was, she so nearly got away.

The *Naval Review* commentary did not close without making two interesting points on the battle in general. In 1914 and 1943 the two *Scharnhorsts* were sunk closer to the South and North Poles than any other capital ship sunk in the two world wars: and finally

> Nor are those memories [of the Falklands in 1914] unworthy to recall. Whereas the two actions in no way coincide tactically, there is one curious comparison. At seventeen minutes past four on the afternoon of the 26th December 1943, the *Duke of York*, whose gunnery is acknowledged the prime factor of the action, made her first radar contact with the *Scharnhorst* at a range of 45,500 yards. As had been told, the *Scharnhorst* was utterly surprised by her presence. Perhaps, though, if she had known, it might have struck a cord of premonition. For, on the afternoon of the 8th of December, 1914, off the Falkland Islands, her predecessor was caught, pounded to scrap, overturned and sunk with the loss of most of her company — at seventeen minutes past four.'

After the battle Fraser headed for Murmansk with his victorious Fleet, Burnett steering north to resume the cover of JW.55B. The British warships arrived on 27 December, the convoy on the following morning. Fraser stayed only for as long as it took to refuel his ships and receive the congratulations of the Soviet authorities. Before this could be done, he had the German survivors transferred from the cramped destroyers to the *Duke of York*. As the transfer was made in a Russian tug, it caused the Germans no little momentary panic until they realised that Fraser had no intention of handing them over to the Russians.

Golovko's congratulations to Fraser were cordial enough, but the Soviet admiral's memoirs did not fail to echo the correct Stalinist tone of curmudgeonly ingratitude. As with Fraser's first visit ten days before, Golovko privately accused the British of keeping important information from their Soviet allies:[29]

> 27 December. I have been with Fraser and congratulated him. He described the action briefly. The details are not yet complete, since not all the destroyers have arrived. This must be a pretext, as the British Admiral spoke mainly about his own losses and was very distressed about them . . .
>
> Only 38 (*sic*) men were picked up from the ship, none of whom according to Fraser was an officer. I did not raise the question of officers. In all probability the British Admiral mentioned this on the assumption that we should request the opportunity of talking to captured Nazis from the *Scharnhorst*'s crew.

Golovko also got in a grumble about the fuel oil required by the ships which had sunk *Scharnhorst* in his country's cause:[30]

> I have been told the fuel requirements of the British squadron – about 10,000 tons of fuel oil are needed for the whole of this 'armada'.
>
> 28 December. Details of the sinking of the *Scharnhorst* will no doubt be assembled in the British Admiralty. We are not being told anything more, although it must be clear to Admiral Fraser and his Staff that the information obtained from the Nazis fished out of the water interests us keenly – not, of course, the details of the action, but the situation at Altenfjord and Lang Fjord which form the pivot of the Nazi naval forces operating against us in the Northern theatre. Hence the annoyance caused by the way the allies on this occasion confined themselves to radiant smiles and lengthy declarations that they and we were allies.
>
> Never mind, we will manage on our own information.

Richard Courage recalls how the Russians chose to pay their respects in the most awkward manner – right in the middle of the night:[31]

> After arrival in Russia the next day the C-in-C gathered one or two Captains of ships that were available and gave a small celebration dinner party. Everyone was very tired and went to bed early. At about 02.00hrs I happened to be on the Quarterdeck, having just attended to some signal problems that had arisen, when I saw an enormous black motor-boat loom alongside the starboard gangway. Out stepped two Russians, carrying parcels. They told the Officer of the Watch that they wanted to see the Commander-in-Chief in person. Nothing the O.O.W. said would dissuade them so the poor Flag Lieutenant, Vernon Merry, was hauled out of bed to handle the matter. The Russians had express orders from the Supreme Soviet to present the Commander-in-Chief, in person, with two gifts: a large fur hat and an enormous fur coat. The Admiral had to turn out and drink a glass of whisky with them before returning to bed, while Vernon Merry conducted them round the *Duke of York* – at 04.00hrs!

Fraser, who would far rather have had the Soviet authorities start behaving in civilised fashion towards the British servicemen stationed in North Russia, was less than delighted with his fur coat. 'As I had no hope of wearing this at home I asked Gieves [the famous naval tailors] to sell it; and they said they were awfully sorry but it was such poor quality that they couldn't get rid of it!'[32]

By the 28th all due civilities had been exchanged; temporary repairs to battle damage and refuelling had been completed. For Fraser and his men it was a distinct relief to leave the cold comfort of Murmansk and embark on the voyage back to Scapa, where the Fleet arrived on 31 December:[33]

> The southward trip to Scapa was eventful only in the weather. A typical gale-force wind from the north-west set up heavy seas, and most of our seaboats on the boat deck were severely damaged. It was an uncomfortable journey and bitterly cold. Four days later we made Hoxa Gate and steamed slowly into the Flow, battle-ensigns flying, the *Duke of York* ahead and our destroyers astern. Despite its remoteness from civilized habitation it was an impressive and unforgettable experience passing through the Fleet to our anchorage, each ship's company massed on deck cheering as we came abreast of them. And then the flood of congratulatory telegrams and signals from all parts of the world, including one most dearly prized from Admiral Fraser's mother, who had launched the *Jamaica*.

It was a great homecoming.

· 19 ·

Last months with the Home Fleet

[January–June 1944]

As the victors of the North Cape action had missed their Christmas, Fraser's first order on returning to Scapa Flow was a general signal saying that New Year's Day 1944 would be Christmas Day routine for all Home Fleet ships involved in the battle. He himself was hard at work completing the despatches which, as tradition demanded, must be rushed to the Admiralty with all speed. For two of his officers there would be no 'Christmas' with the Fleet. Commander E. H. Thomas, Master of the Fleet, was entrusted with the task of delivering the despatches by air personally to the First Sea Lord in Whitehall. With Thomas went Richard Courage. 'I myself was due to go on leave,' he explained, 'and naturally cadged a lift with the Master. This would be much quicker than a train journey, still known by the First World War title of "The Jellicoe Express".'

But Courage was soon regretting his decision. During the long flight south in a light aircraft without radio, visibility steadily decreased and the young RNVR pilot got lost. They completely missed their destination, Hendon, and after a hair-raising circumnavigation of south London via Croydon, dodging barrage balloons, eventually landed at the RAF fighter airfield at Hornchurch, nearly 20 miles east of Hendon. ' "Despatches for the Admiralty" ', says Courage, 'did not cut much ice when the Master said it to the first person who met us. But the RAF came up trumps, and very soon I was handing the despatches to the Master over the tailboard of a 3-ton RAF truck, clambering in after them myself.' He went on:[1]

It must have been about 1900 by the time we drew up outside the Admiralty, full of importance, and demanded to see the First Sea Lord in person. A somewhat cross-looking 'ABC' [as Cunningham was known from his initials] came out of his office, took the Master inside and left me outside without even saying 'How do you do'. Very unlike the real 'ABC', I thought. I went in to have a chat with 'ABC's' Paymaster secretary and said, 'It seems a bit gloomy up here – something gone wrong?' The Secretary said, 'Yes, it has. It may be Christmas Day in Scapa but it certainly isn't in Archway Block North' [Cunningham's office].

He then told me what had been happening while the Master and I were battling our way south. The C-in-C had had a 'Christmas Day' lunch party in *Duke of York* and one enterprising guest had said, loud enough to be overheard, 'I think Dicky ought to arrive at the Admiralty carrying the despatches on a horse – it would make a wonderful photograph.' Apparently the C-in-C had lit up with that look which meant 'Good idea!' and contact had been made with the police, to accomplish the ride with the help of police horses. The police considered it too far to ride from where we were due to land at Hendon, so Charing Cross was mentioned as a suitable place to mount. But the C-in-C, apparently, disagreed: 'Much too close – the horses must arrive in a lather, *steaming*. Better pour some hot water over them.' But when we failed to arrive at Hendon on time enquiries started, and at this point 'ABC' heard what was going on in Scapa! No wonder we got rather a frigid reception, even though we were in complete ignorance of the whole affair. Anyhow, I was glad we ended up at Hornchuch – I'm sure I would have capsized on the way from Charing Cross to the Admiralty. I was in no state to ride a sharp two furlongs across Trafalgar Square in the dark, especially in the blackout with no light showing anywhere.

This short-lived burst of ill-temper on Cunningham's part was the first real manifestation of his chip on the shoulder towards Fraser, apparently caused (*see* Appendix 1) by Cunningham's sense of only having become First Sea Lord as 'second best' to Fraser. Though it would recur with subsequent peaks of 'ABC's' natural tendency to irascibility, happily both admirals had far too deep a professional respect for each other to let this develop into the sort of petty feud which had separated Fisher and Beresford earlier in the century.

The day after the 'Scharnhorst despatch' was so eventfully delivered to the Admiralty, Fraser heard that he had been awarded the Grand Cross of the Order of the Bath. But it was typical of the man that of all the congratulatory letters and telegrams he received, pride of place in his files at home went to a short but charming letter from Buckingham Palace. Fraser had had two sixpences from *Duke of York*'s Christmas puddings (veterans of the North Cape battle and duly consumed on New Year's Day) mounted in two presentation boxes made in the flagship as Christmas presents for the King's daughters. 'Dear Admiral', their letter began; 'My sister and I were delighted to receive the two beautiful boxes and we both send you our most grateful thanks for such a charming Christmas present.'[2]

> Will you please tell the makers of the boxes how much we admire their craftsmanship.
> Boxing Day was a wonderful day, for we heard during the evening of your great victory.
> We felt very proud of the Duke of York and her Ship's Company, and of all the other ships who took part in the action.
> Thanking you again so much for the lovely boxes.
> We both send you our best wishes for 1944.
> Yours very sincerely,
> Elizabeth and Margaret

But in January 1944 Fraser and his Fleet were given no time to rest on their laurels after their victory. The sinking of the *Scharnhorst* only removed the most urgent *surface* threat to the Russian convoys. Invaluable though this relief obviously was, the surface threat would materialise again as soon as *Tirpitz* was fit for sea. After eliminating *Scharnhorst* Fraser still had to contend with a triple enemy: the location of convoys by German long-range air reconnaissance; an Arctic U-boat force of between twenty-five and thirty boats; and unusually appalling Arctic winter weather as the 'JW' convoys continued to sail.

The combined deadliness of these three elements made itself felt as soon as the next convoy, JW.56A of twenty ships, sailed from Loch Ewe on 12 January 1944. Only three days out the convoy was blown to shreds by a shattering gale with five ships turning back, many damaged and what was left of the main body forced to run for shelter in Akureyri. It took until the 21st before repairs were completed and cargoes restowed, and when JW.56A set out again from Akureyri its departure was reported by a Nazi agent. As the sixteen ships of JW.56B sailed on time (22 January) and were scheduled to cross with the next return convoy, RA.56A, the delay suffered by JW.56A was a serious setback. To add to the troubles of the British escorts, overloaded as they now were by the disruption of the sailing pattern, the U-boats stationed in the Arctic were armed with the 'Gnat' acoustic homing torpedo. Fortunately for the British this had arrived too late for the climax of the Battle of the Atlantic in the spring of 1943; but it was now unleashed as the U-boats' main 'secret weapon' against the escorts on the Russian convoy route.

Fraser's countermeasures, based on a shrewd guess at what the Germans would do and on his own experience with JW.55B and RA.55A four weeks before, prevented what could easily have developed into another cruel mauling for the Arctic convoys. What he did was to capitalise on the fact that JW.56B was now hard on the heels of JW.56A; postpone the sailing of RA.56A; divert JW.56B to a more northerly course; and send what would have been RA.56A's escort to reinforce that of JW.56B, which he knew had been detected by the *Luftwaffe*.

Nothing could be done to prevent JW.56A from running into a waiting patrol line of ten U-boats, which attacked on 26 January and sank three ships from the convoy, also damaging the destroyer *Obdurate*. But as Fraser had anticipated the U-boats, instead of clinging to the flanks of JW.56A, moved west as soon as the *Luftwaffe* reported the approach of the weaker JW.56B. The final concentration of fifteen U-boats against the sixteen ships of JW.56B should have been decisive. Instead of swamping the convoy, however, the U-boats were themselves swamped by the reinforced escort contrived by Fraser, which forced the U-boats to remain submerged, harried them for hours with depth-charge attacks and sank *U-314* on 30 January. Not a ship of JW.56B was lost, though the destroyer *Hardy* had her stern blown off by an acoustic torpedo and had to be sunk by her own side. Thus the 'score' for the passage of JW.56A and JW.56B was one U-boat sunk against the safe arrival in Murmansk of thirty-three out of thirty-six merchant ships, one British destroyer sunk and another damaged. Fraser's first attempt to outthink the U-boats had produced a resounding success.

By the end of January 1944 there were so many empty merchant ships cramming the Kola Inlet that Fraser had no choice but to sail a return convoy. He decided to bring them all back in a single big convoy: RA.56, of thirty-seven ships. Thanks to the recent passage of JW.56A and JW.56B, RA.56 could be given a massive escort reinforced by three more destroyers sent out from Scapa for luck – twenty-six destroyers in all, plus sloops and corvettes. This would guarantee the 'swamping escort' which had paid such dividends with JW.56B – but Fraser's good judgment was again rewarded by a fortuitous piece of good luck. When the *Luftwaffe* spotted RA.56 four days out of Murmansk on 6 February, the sighting report was based on the classic error of a 'reciprocal bearing', announcing that the new convoy was steaming *east* instead of *west*. The ensuing total confusion at HQ U-boats North resulted in a wild-goose-chase which

RA.56 and its escort evaded with ease, reaching Loch Ewe intact on 11 February.

Fraser now decided that the time had come to revert to the original sailing of large single convoys protected by the strongest possible escort forces. As the next major Allied operation was to be no longer in the Mediterranean but the cross-Channel assault on Occupied Europe, the Home Fleet could now be assigned the ships it needed to get such large convoys through. Moreover, with the initiative in the North Atlantic firmly retained by the Royal and US Navies, the Home Fleet could also be assigned expert 'hunter-killer' groups and the inestimable boon of escort carrier air cover. Only one Russian convoy had ever sailed with an escort carrier: PQ.18 back in the desperate September of 1942. Now, seventeen months later, Fraser prepared the strongest convoy yet to sail to North Russia: JW.57, of forty-two ships and a tanker screened by four cruisers, seventeen destroyers, the escort carrier *Chaser*, and partial land-based air cover from Sullom Voe in the Shetlands. Sailing on 20 February, JW.57 reached Murmansk on the 28th without the loss of a single ship, while the Germans lost two U-boats – *U-601* sunk by a Catalina operating at its maximum range from Sullom Voe, and *U-713* sunk by the veteran destroyer *Keppel*. But these successes had to be paid for by the loss of the destroyer *Mahratta*, torpedoed and sunk with very heavy loss of life.

The return convoy, RA.57 of thirty-one ships, sailed from Murmansk on 2 March with the same big escort and the company of *Chaser*, with Fraser prudently ordering the convoy to steer a wide evasive course through the Barents Sea. Seldom had there been such a convincing demonstration of how far in the Allies' favour the U-boat war had swung since the previous year. Driven to the attack against these empty ships in a desperate effort to justify their existence, the U-boats lost three of their number in as many days (*U-472*, *U-336*, *U-973*), sinking only one ship, the *Empire Tourist* (4 March). It was all a far cry from the deadly summer and autumn of 1942; in fourteen days Fraser's Fleet had delivered forty-two laden merchant ships for the loss of one destroyer and one empty merchant-man, destroying five U-boats in the process. Fraser's dispositions had created a classic instance of the *offensive* value of convoy. (He was, alas, destined to live long enough to see British politicians of the postwar era forget just about every lesson he had helped to teach.)

By mid-March 1944 Fraser could look back on four months of unbroken success since the 'JW' convoys had been resumed in November 1943, but he was already working on the most complex operation undertaken by the Home Fleet since the hunting of the

Bismarck in May 1941. This was the simultaneous running of the biggest convoy ever sent to Russia – JW.58, of forty-nine ships – with the Home Fleet's first massed carrier strike at the Norwegian coast. The latter objective was of course *Tirpitz*, on which a close watch had been kept since the end of February by reconnaissance Spitfires based on Vaenga in North Russia, and which was now known to be approaching readiness for sea. Fraser's planning for the passage of JW.58 and Operation 'Tungsten' (as the strike at *Tirpitz* was code-named) epitomised his mastery of the subtle arts of delegation. He entrusted the detailed planning and the execution of 'Tungsten' to his VA2, Vice-Admiral Sir Henry Moore, flying his flag in *Anson*. Under Moore, command of the fleet carriers *Victorious* and *Furious*, seconded by the escort carriers *Emperor*, *Searcher* and *Pursuer*, was exercised by Rear-Admiral Bisset. This, the Royal Navy's first genuine attempt at a carrier strike force on the lines of the task forces perfected by the US Pacific Fleet, was escorted by four cruisers and fourteen destroyers. Rear-Admiral Dalrymple-Hamilton commanded JW.58's escort from the light cruiser *Diadem*: escort carriers *Activity* and *Tracker*, twenty destroyers, four corvettes and the five sloops of Captain F. J. Walker's 2nd Escort Group, hunter-killer 'aces' of the Western Approaches.

Despite the presence of two escort carriers with JW.58 there was always the chance that bad weather would make carrier flying operations impossible and favour a high-speed attack on the convoy by *Tirpitz*, which by the last week of March was preparing for her steaming trials in Altenfjord. Because of this possibility Fraser planned to sail the convoy first, then put to sea himself with *Duke of York*, *Anson*, and *Victorious* as distant battleship/carrier cover. Bisset would be the last to sail, heading for a prearranged launch-point for the air strike at Altenfjord. As soon as it became apparent that JW.58's penetration of the Barents Sea was progressing satisfactorily, Fraser and Moore would rendezvous with Bisset and Moore would assume command of the 'Tungsten' operation.

Mention has already been made of the apparent yet deceptive smoothness with which Fraser's plan to destroy *Scharnhorst* had unfolded back in December 1943. Precisely the same applies to the resounding success of JW.58 and 'Tungsten': *ars celare artem*. The convoy's story may be briefly told, at the admitted risk of injustice to the tenacity and professionalism of the escort forces. There was only one casualty to the convoy: one ship turned back, damaged by ice, but the remainder arrived intact. Fighters from *Tracker* and *Activity* hacked down a splendid total of six German reconnaissance aircraft and no less than four U-boats were sunk (*U-961*, *U-355*, *U-360*, and *U-288*). Early on the 30th, three days after JW.58 had sailed, Fraser and Moore put to sea from Scapa Flow with Bisset following that evening. 'Tungsten' had been scheduled for 4 April, but by the morning of the 1st two factors prompted Fraser to change the plan. First, JW.58 and its escort were clearly doing splendidly and needed no extra close support; second, the weather conditions, so liable as they were to instant change, were particularly favourable for the attack, which Fraser now advanced by 24 hours. Bisset's escort carriers had to steam flat out to make the rendezvous, which was nevertheless successfully accomplished on the afternoon of the 2nd. Fraser in *Duke of York* then withdrew 200 miles to the north, leaving Moore and Bisset to carry out the attack on the morning of the 3rd.

However 'Tungsten' is assessed it is hard to see how the Fleet Air Arm could have done more.[3] As *Tirpitz* lay within extensive net defences torpedoes could not be used; and the heaviest bombs which the strike aircraft could lift were incapable of doing serious damage at the height at which the aircraft had to bomb. Two striking forces were launched, each originally consisting of twenty-one Barracuda torpedo-bombers escorted by forty fighters. Though one Barracuda failed to start and another crashed into the sea on take-off with the loss of its crew, the first wave attacked at 05.29 hrs on the 3rd and the second just over an hour later. In each strike the Barracudas were preceded by the fighters making strafing attacks to suppress *Tirpitz*'s anti-aircraft fire. The two attacks were pressed with the greatest gallantry and *Tirpitz* was plastered with fourteen bomb hits (four 1,600lb armour-piercing, five 500lb semi-armour-piercing and five 500lb high-explosive). Though these hits inflicted widespread superficial damage on the battleship's upperworks, none penetrated her main armour. She was fit for sea again in three months, but those three months were enough to keep her from disrupting the Allied naval build-up for 'Neptune', the great cross-Channel assault. (As it happened, British intelligence over-estimated the damage inflicted and set *Tirpitz*'s repair-time at six months.) It was enough to enable 'Tungsten' to be viewed as a miniature 'repeat' of the 1940 Norwegian campaign. After the latter ordeal the German Navy had been incapable of playing a decisive role in the planned German invasion of Britain. After 'Tungsten' four years later, *Tirpitz* was incapable of impeding the planned Allied invasion of Normandy.

For Fraser, 'Tungsten' had a particularly disagreeable aftermath because of a resounding difference of opinion with Cunningham in Whitehall. Cunningham wanted a repeat attack to be hurled at *Tirpitz* at the earliest opportunity. No sooner had *Duke of York* returned to the telephone buoy in Scapa Flow than Cunningham was on the line to Fraser, demanding a second attack. But Fraser, while thoroughly endorsing the principle that a battered enemy should be aggressively kept on the ropes whenever possible, demurred in this case. He took the view that the Home Fleet had made the most of a unique opportunity: weather conditions so ideal that they could not be encountered again, and German defences which had been caught by surprise once but which would be alert and ready for a second attack. Fraser insisted that a second attack would only mean the sacrifice of much-needed aircraft and air-crew, and the stubbornness with which he held to his view prompted Cunningham to some splenetic accusations in the First Sea Lord's private diary (*see* Appendix 1). Not until November 1977, after the publication of Roskill's *Churchill and the Admirals*, did an incredulous Lord Fraser learn that Cunningham had privately accused him of what would have been a monumental act of indiscipline: threatening to haul down his flag rather than repeat 'Tungsten'.[4]

For his part Fraser argued that in the weeks before the cross-Channel assault the Home Fleet would be far better employed beating up German convoys in Norwegian coastal waters. In the end Cunningham and Fraser resolved their differences in a compromise which proved Fraser to have been right all along. On 21 April Fraser sent Moore out again to attempt a second strike at *Tirpitz*, but with a strike on Bodö harbour and its adjacent sea-lanes as a secondary objective. Operating in weather so bad as to rule an attack on *Tirpitz* out of the question, Moore's carriers lost six aircraft in return for three ships sunk out of a German convoy south of Bodö. Over the following weeks down to D-Day the Home Fleet's carriers and submarines, together with RAF Coastal Command, raised their efforts in Norwegian inshore waters to a pitch not seen since the ill-fated campaign of 1940.

Fraser's disagreement with Cunningham over the repeating of 'Tungsten' was still working to its climax, when on 7 April, RA.58 (thirty-six ships) sailed from Murmansk. None of the sixteen U-boats on patrol in the Barents Sea made touch with the convoy, which arrived intact on 14 April. The last Russian convoy to sail under Fraser's direction was RA.59, which sailed on 28 April. This convoy of forty-five ships was carrying Admiral Levchenko, his staff, and 2,300 men of the Soviet Navy to take over the battleship *Royal Sovereign* from the Royal Navy. Also in transit with RA.59 was the crew of the American cruiser *Milwaukee*, which had also been transferred to the Soviet Navy after going out with JW.58. To cover their passage Fraser sent out an escort force consisting of sixteen destroyers and the escort carriers *Fencer* and *Activity*. In atrocious weather, a symbolic accompaniment to this the last convoy of the current cycle, a patrol-line of twelve U-boats made contact and sank one ship from the convoy on 30 April, but they paid dearly for it. Aircraft from the *Fencer* sank *U-277*, *U-674* and *U-959* in the space of 48 hours. No further losses were suffered by the convoy, which arrived on 6 May. Fraser's last Russian convoy had ended with another jarring tactical defeat for the U-boats.

Quite apart from the undertaking of the complex operations outlined above, March, April and May 1944 were hectic months at Scapa. Once again, as the 'count-down' to D-Day proceeded, the Home Fleet base had to accommodate an unending stream of warships training for their part in securing a beach-head in Normandy and supporting the troops once ashore. For Fraser, 'this was the attack as it should have been delivered' at Gallipoli in 1915: ship-to-shore radio communication, radar-controlled gunnery, minutely-prepared fire plans, and maps of the enemy positions accurate to the last machine-gun position. 'In April and May,' writes Roskill, 'four battleships, twenty cruisers, two monitors and many destroyers were given special "working-up" practices. Even these great bases [Scapa Flow and the Clyde], which had played such an important part in both World Wars, can rarely have been more busy.'[5]

So good was the practice provided that during the battle of Normandy in June–July 1944 Allied warships found themselves not merely annihilating coastal targets, but confidently joining the land battle to 'take out' pinpoint targets many miles inland. On 16 June the commander of the SS Panzer Division *Hitlerjugend* was killed 20 miles inland by a timely 16-inch shell from *Rodney*, while the Chief Operations Officer of 9th SS *Panzergrenadier* Division later wrote that:[6]

> Our counter-offensive broke down under air attack and artillery fire, particularly the heavy guns of the battleships. They were devastating. . . . It was these broadsides from the warships, more than the defensive fighting of the enemy's troops, which halted our division's Panzer Regiment.

Finally there was a procession of VIP visitors to the Home Fleet in Scapa, of which the most exciting – his presence indicative of the imminence of the invasion – was General Montgomery in early May:[7]

Headquarters
21 Army Group
9-5-44

My dear Admiral,

I would like to thank you for your kind hospitality and to say how very much I enjoyed my visit to the Home Fleet. It was a great thing for me to be able to pay my respects in person to the Navy, and to thank the Navy for what it has done for the Army. Also, I feel that we now know each other and our co-operation in the battle will be all the more close.

It was a great thrill to meet so many fine officers and men, and I learnt what a very highly efficient Service you are. Thank you again for letting me come,
Yrs sincerely,
B.L. Montgomery

It would be impossible to find two British commanders who, in their dealings with their American allies, were more completely different than Fraser and Montgomery. Even after he had come to know Montgomery better during their postwar relationship, Fraser always believed that 'Monty's' brusque tactlessness towards the Americans was easily his biggest fault. Interestingly enough, Lord Fraser opined to the author that Montgomery was 'a wonderful leader but quite hopeless as an administrator'[8] – as revealing a comment as Fraser ever made on the delegation of authority. The refusal to get bogged down in detail should not, Fraser considered, relieve the commander of *concern* for detail. Reliance on one's staff, as with confidence in oneself, could be taken too far, and Fraser noted both in Montgomery. Nor was Montgomery's tactlessness reserved for Americans, although when he personally encountered it Fraser found it more amusing than offensive:[9]

'Actually, it was Tedder who first drew my attention to it. He said once, "Watch when we leave Downing Street: you'll see that Monty'll either stop behind or go out first." And sure enough, we waited to look – and he lagged behind and waited until we'd all gone, and then came out and everybody cheered him. And when he came down to visit me at Portsmouth we had to walk along to some place or other, and I couldn't think why he wouldn't come up to walk with me – he just lagged behind and took the cheers of the multitude . . .

He *was* a great leader, no question about it; though how anybody could sleep through the great Battle of Alamein in his caravan just baffles me!'

The programme prepared for Montgomery was in fact a useful dress-rehearsal for another visit to the Fleet by King George VI, which took place a week later:[10]

BUCKINGHAM PALACE
May 14th 1944

My dear Fraser,
Once again I am writing to thank you for having arranged such a varied programme for my visit to the Home Fleet. The weather was really kind which made my stay with you such a comfortable one. I was greatly impressed by the spirit which permeates all the ships under your command, a spirit which I know you have carefully fostered during the past year, & I could see what good relations exist between you & the officers & men.

I also thank you for your kind hospitality to me on board the 'Duke of York'.

I shall be very anxious to learn of the result of your coming 'operation'[11] whch I trust will be very successful.

Believe me
Yours very sincerely
George R.I.

To Fraser, not the least important of the VIP visitors were the show business stars and musicians whom he invited north to entertain the men of his Fleet, another legacy of his dreary Scapa months in *Resolution* during the First World War. These guests ranged from Yehudi Menuhin to Flanagan and Allen, Will Hay, Bernard Miles and John Mills. In the opinion of the latter actor, 'Bruce Fraser was one of the best hosts I have ever met in my life. Judging by the remarks we heard during our six-week tour he appeared to be the most popular and admired sailor in the entire Navy.'[12]

Still touring the Home Fleet at the time of the king's visit, Sir John was particularly impressed by what had become Fraser's own *tour de force*. This was the imposing spectacle of the Navy's 'Sunset' parade, constantly improved by Fraser and raised at his direction to the level of a thrilling work of art:[13]

The Fleet lay at anchor, the ships dressed from stem to stern and the ships' companies lined up on deck. The weather that evening was perfect; the sea was calm and still, the giant ships standing out against the skyline. The massed bands of the Marines on the quarterdeck played the national anthem, during which a flag was slowly hoist to the top mast; as the last note died away over the water and the flag reached the top, a single shot was fired from a musket. The C-in-C raised his cap and called for three cheers for the King. His Majesty then walked to the rail, took out a white handkerchief and waved to all his ships. It was an unforgettable moment.

A moment rather more ridiculous than sublime came on another occasion, as Fraser was preparing to welcome a party of Cabinet ministers:[14]

> 'It was very funny when Alexander came on board with three other ministers. Bevin was one, and he was senior to Alexander, but Alexander was determined to show his authority. I heard him solemnly telling the others, "I am going to get out first. I am First Lord of the Admiralty, and you've all got to get out after me. And when we go ashore you all get into the boat first, and I come last. So that's settled." It was a very funny moment, hearing him lecturing the others like that.'

From March 1944, amid all these duties, Fraser already knew that he would not be serving out his full time as Commander-in-Chief, Home Fleet. He had been chosen as the next commander of the Eastern Fleet, due for a steady build-up throughout 1944 in preparation for the Royal Navy's hoped-for participation in the Pacific War. Hence Fraser's consistent entrusting of Home Fleet combat operations to his eventual successor, Admiral Moore. It was by no means easy to have, as it were, a foot in each command, and Fraser was still in command of the Home Fleet when the liberation of Europe began on 6 June 1944. It had been expected that the German naval reaction to the invasion would be vigorous, including at least a diversionary sortie by the surviving units of the German surface fleet. But as soon as it was clear that no such challenge was impending, a week after D-Day with the Normandy beach-head established and its reinforcement proceeding unchecked, the Admiralty decided that Fraser could safely be spared. On 16 June 1944 he hauled down his flag and handed over the Home Fleet to Admiral Moore, leaving as goodly a heritage as Tovey had passed to Fraser in May 1943. Now a victorious Fleet commander in his own right, having added mightily to his laurels in the most demanding naval theatre of the European war, Fraser bent his mind towards the new challenge of the Far East and the war against Japan.

Part Four

The British Pacific Fleet
[1944–6]

. 20 .

The Eastern Fleet
[June–November 1944]

The most obvious reason for Fraser's transfer to command the Eastern Fleet was his excellent performance as Commander-in-Chief, Home Fleet which, together with his seniority, eminently qualified him for a leading role in the Royal Navy's new concentration of effort against Japan. But though Fraser was always to deprecate the fact out of loyalty to his former colleagues and brother-officers, there was another, scarcely less urgent reason for his new appointment. By the second half of 1944 Fraser's genius for tactful co-operation was needed as never before to resolve a most unfortunate clash of personalities in the Far Eastern high command. Preparing to carry the war to the Japanese was really a secondary objective for Fraser: his immediate task was to restore harmonious relations between the Eastern Fleet and Admiral Lord Mountbatten's South-East Asia Command.

Since the hard spring of 1942, Admiral Somerville had manfully striven to make bricks without straw as Commander of the Eastern Fleet, based on Ceylon. Throughout 1942 and 1943, the overriding demands of Home Waters and the Mediterranean had combined to keep the Eastern Fleet at the bottom of the list of priorities for reinforcement. Not that it had been much to write home about when Somerville took command in March 1942. 'SO THIS IS THE EASTERN FLEET', he signalled to his new command; 'WELL NEVER MIND. THERE'S MANY A GOOD TUNE PLAYED ON AN OLD FIDDLE'.[1] But it was a rag-bag of a fleet, built round five old battleships of Jutland vintage, the no less obsolete light carrier *Hermes*, and a scratch collection of seven cruisers. Somerville's 'old fiddle' would have passed muster twenty years before, but it was no answer to the Japanese Combined Fleet in the spring of 1942 — out-paced and out-gunned on the surface, completely outmatched in the air. Even with the temporary loan of the modern fleet carriers

Indomitable and *Formidable*, Somerville knew that he had no choice but to refuse battle and try to keep the Eastern Fleet in being. He achieved this by withdrawing the Fleet from Trincomalee to Addu Atoll in the Maldives when it became clear that the Japanese Combined Fleet was heading west. Even so, when Admiral Nagumo's Fast Carrier Striking Force burst briefly into the Indian Ocean at the beginning of April 1942, the victors of Pearl Harbor caught and sank the carrier *Hermes*, the cruisers *Cornwall* and *Dorsetshire*, the destroyer *Vampire*, a corvette and two tankers.

No British admiral of the Second World War had to begin his command in a crisis of this magnitude. If the Japanese had continued to operate in the Indian Ocean, they could have driven the rump of the Eastern Fleet west to the African coast, as they had already driven the surviving heavy units of the US Pacific Fleet east to the American coast. By the middle of April, however, Nagumo's carriers were on their way back to the Pacific and the crisis in the Indian Ocean had eased sufficiently for the Eastern Fleet to participate in the capture of Madagascar in the following month. This at least offered the Eastern Fleet a new base in the south-west Indian Ocean, should the worst come to the worst. But the annihilation of Japanese carrier supremacy at Midway (June 1942) and the continued attrition of the Japanese Combined Fleet off Guadalcanal (August 1942-February 1943) did not mean that the British Admiralty was able to recoup Somerville's earlier losses and restore the strength of the Eastern Fleet. On the contrary: the demands of other theatres meant that the Eastern Fleet continued to shrink. By January 1943 Somerville had been deprived of his last modern carrier. By April his battleship strength had been reduced to three. By September 1943 Somerville was left with only one old battleship (*Ramillies*) and four modern cruisers; his other five old cruisers and handful of destroyers were all required as escorts for the vital convoys running between India and the Suez Canal. Not only was the Eastern Fleet completely incapable of offensive operations: it was stretched to the limit by convoy escort duties. As we have seen, under Tovey and Fraser the British Home Fleet was in similar straits during these months; but at least the Home Fleet could receive sporadic reinforcement from the American Atlantic Fleet. Such help was out of the question for the Eastern Fleet.

The strength of the Eastern Fleet was therefore at rock bottom when on 31 August 1943 Lord Louis Mountbatten was appointed Allied Supreme Commander of the newly designated South-East Asia Command (SEAC). South-East Asia had been an Allied theatre since the outbreak of the war with Japan, as American lend-lease commitments to China required an American presence in Burma. Mountbatten's job as Supreme Commander was to co-ordinate the incongruent strategies of securing land communications with China and reconquering Burma and Malaya from the Japanese. The base for both these operations was Manipur province in north-east India, whither the survivors of the Burma campaign had retreated in May 1942.

From the outset, a major problem was the integration of the Eastern Fleet within the command structure and requirements of SEAC, for the command areas of the Eastern Fleet and of SEAC overlapped alarmingly. Whereas SEAC's south-western boundary stopped at the coastline of India and Ceylon, the Eastern Fleet's domain – just as in Fraser's prewar years with the East Indies Squadron – included the entire western Indian Ocean, the Persian Gulf, the convoy route to the Red Sea via Aden to Suez, and all the east African coast down to the Mozambique frontier. Given the Eastern Fleet's lack of resources and its inescapable commitments outside the SEAC area, it was plain to see that the Eastern Fleet's new subordination to the strategic requirements of SEAC was a recipe for trouble. In Whitehall, Cunningham hoped that 'elasticity and good will' would suffice to prevent friction between Mountbatten and Somerville. It was not to be.

Trouble, when it came, stemmed from Somerville's failure to overcome his resentment at being subordinate to Mountbatten. It was not that Somerville coveted Mountbatten's job, nor even that Somerville had been commanding a fleet when Mountbatten was only a destroyer flotilla commander. But Somerville was eighteen years older than Mountbatten and a substantive admiral. Mountbatten, only forty-four years old, with the rank of captain (and only halfway up the Captain's List at that) had been shot to the rank of acting admiral to give him the seniority required as SEAC 'supremo'. For his part Mountbatten, acutely aware of his juniority and consequent vulnerability, had only agreed to go to South-East Asia on condition that he be given full powers (extending to American as well as British commanding officers) to run his own show, including the issuing of directives to the Eastern Fleet. Such was the underlying irritant behind the practical incompatibilities between the Eastern Fleet and SEAC command areas.

This is not the place to follow the ups and downs of the Somerville-Mountbatten clash; suffice it to say that by the spring of 1944 it was still going strong and it was obvious that a decision would have to be taken soon, in Whitehall, before Mountbatten took the step of asking for Somerville's removal. Cunningham and Alexander, the First Lord, decided to resolve the dilemma by bringing home Admiral Noble, head of the British Naval Mission in

Washington, and replacing Noble with Somerville. But this decision (March 1944) coincided with the arrival of substantial reinforcements for the Eastern Fleet: two British battleships and a battle-cruiser, the British fleet carrier *Illustrious* and the American carrier *Saratoga* ('on loan' to the Eastern Fleet, pending her return to the United States for refit), and two escort carriers. With these forces Somerville took the offensive for the first time since the Eastern Fleet had been formed two years before, launching carrier strikes at Sabang in Sumatra (19 April) and Surabaya (17 May).

The relevance of these events to Fraser's take-over of the Eastern Fleet is threefold. First, Somerville's operations in April and May 1944 prompted Churchill to intervene, and object to the takeover being made at all: he argued that both admirals should be left where they were, regardless of the Somerville-Mountbatten difficulty and the genuine need for a forceful British Admiral in Washington. The result was prolonged argument between Alexander, Cunningham and Churchill before Churchill finally agreed, in early June, that Fraser should replace Somerville after all. Second, the decision once taken meant that the Eastern Fleet would be losing the commander who had borne the burden and heat of the day for the past two years. Just when Somerville had been given the force with which to show his mettle, he was to be whisked away to a shore appointment, and this was bound to cause resentment. Third, Fraser was only to be a 'caretaker' Commander-in-Chief for the Eastern Fleet, whose future role in the Japanese war was still far from clear. All these considerations made Fraser's new command a total contrast to his straightforward assumption of the Home Fleet from Tovey in May 1943. It was a prospect befogged with difficulties at every turn.

Lord Fraser's loyal reluctance to imply criticism of either Mountbatten or Somerville caused him to lapse into reticence when questioned on these points by the author. Readers with particular interest in the topic are recommended to other recent works;[2] this author is indebted to Fraser's then Flag Lieutenant, Vernon Merry, for 'filling out the picture'. On one point Fraser had no doubts at all. 'He felt that before he went out to the East he ought to go and see something of the situation in Normandy. He realised that he'd be talking with the Americans out East, and felt that he should visit Normandy so that he could talk fairly knowledgeably about it all.'[3]

Though Montgomery (during the repeated crises of the Normandy fighting throughout June) was rationing beach-head visits by VIPs, there was no objection to Fraser's visit, which took place at the end of June. 'He [Fraser] took the staff who'd be going with him to the East, and we went off in a destroyer and had more or less a full day in Normandy. We saw Monty in his caravan and had a good ride all round; saw the beaches, and came back in the same destroyer that night. The Admiral had insisted on taking back a bottle of brandy from France. I remember driving through the main gate of Portsmouth Dockyard at dawn, with the Admiral absolutely refusing to declare his brandy – not for anyone! But he regarded that visit to Normandy as very necessary preparation.'[4]

At long last the date of Somerville's replacement by Fraser was settled for the last week in August; and Fraser and his staff set out for Ceylon on the 17th of that month. Their aircraft was an Avro York, crewed by former heroes of the famous 'Dambusters' Squadron. The route was via Maison Blanche in Algeria to Cairo, where Fraser breakfasted with the man destined to become his second-in-command in the Pacific, Vice Admiral Sir Bernard Rawlings (then commanding in the eastern Mediterranean). Incorrigible sightseer that he was, Fraser refused to leave Egypt before he had travelled out to Giza to see the Pyramids and the Sphinx. Then it was on again by air from Cairo to the RAF base at Habbaniyah in Iraq. Here Fraser made another brief detour, to Baghdad in a Rapide. In November 1943, he had entertained Emir Abdul Illah, Regent of Iraq, aboard *Duke of York*; his departing guest had politely invited Fraser to be *his* guest should he ever be travelling through Iraq, and Fraser had no intention of passing up this open invitation now he had the chance.

Fraser's reception by the Regent of Iraq was princely: he was cordially invited to a banquet with other British service chiefs in Iraq. But his visit had a sequel as unexpected as it was disconcerting. As the Regent and his guests feasted in luxury beneath the stars, Vernon Merry made some comment to his neighbour about the beauty and tranquillity of the surroundings, only to learn that the situation was very far from tranquil. The Regent had just signed the death warrants of four political prisoners, whose executions at dawn were expected to trigger an insurrection. When Fraser and his staff officers returned to their guest house after the banquet, they opened the door and found themselves looking down the barrel of an emplaced machine-gun, crew at the ready for trouble. As if this were not enough, the Regent then appeared, airily informing his guests that if they had no objection he would spend the night under the same roof!

Though dawn brought no rising of the masses, it was a distinct relief to fly back to Habbaniyah from Baghdad and re-embark in the York for the flight to Karachi, where they dined that night with the Governor of Sind. On the 20th, having moved on to Delhi, Fraser stayed with Field-Marshal Wavell, the Viceroy, also visiting the headquarters of the Royal Indian Navy. Finally, on the following day, came the long flight south across India to Ceylon. And on the next day, 23 August 1944, Fraser formally relieved Somerville as Commander-in-Chief, Eastern Fleet.

In this his second fleet command, as with the first in May 1943, Fraser also took over his predecessor's staff, only to find that this time he had a far bigger problem on his hands. Even after the departure of Somerville, echoes of the Somerville-Mountbatten clash threatened to rumble on. 'It wasn't just the two admirals who couldn't get on,' recalls Vernon Merry. 'It went *right the way down* the two staffs (Eastern Fleet and SEAC). There was very, very little communication between them and a lot of bad blood.' He continued,[5]

> 'And of course, when Fraser arrived in Ceylon, Somerville's staff didn't like losing their admiral; they were very fond of Somerville. But they soon got the message from Fraser. As ever, he was very good at giving people his "party line", and letting them know that that's the way I want it, and if you don't want to play it my way there's always a job at sea for you, my lad. . . .That was the reason he went East so early – he didn't *mind*, though I'm sure he felt he'd have been of more use working and planning ahead for the entry into the Pacific – to patch up the rift. And he did it wonderfully well.'

The most notable point about this victory of personality was that Fraser was completely uninterested in the 'points of principle' which had exacerbated relations between Somerville and Mountbatten. Fraser's prime concern was straightening out the attitude of his own staff before making any move towards establishing a formal *rapport* with Mountbatten. A lesser man would probably have taken the easy way out and executed a purge, making a clean sweep of Somerville's discontented staff officers and replacing them with 'his' men. But Fraser made a point of arriving in Ceylon with only the smallest personal staff, deliberately retaining every officer of Somerville's staff willing to accept his *modus operandi*.

Once he was satisfied that the Eastern Fleet staff had indeed 'got the message', Fraser hoisted his flag in the battle-cruiser *Renown* and sailed round to Trincomalee to meet the ships and men of the Fleet. Even with the substantial reinforcements which had joined since January 1944, the Eastern Fleet had retained a distinctive multi-national patchwork, but to Fraser, lacking as he did the faintest taint of chauvinism, this was no problem at all. There were old friends in the Eastern Fleet, most notably the superb French battleship *Richelieu* which had served under Fraser's command in the Home Fleet. He won the hearts of the Royal Netherlands Navy by throwing a special party for the Dutch on Queen Wilhelmina's birthday. As Vernon Merry comments, 'He got on terribly well with *all* foreigners.'

Having 'made his number' with his new staff and with his Fleet, Fraser had no intention of hastening back to Colombo and immuring himself in his office. After a leisurely drive back to Colombo, looking up favourite haunts from *Effingham* days along the way, Fraser finally drove up to Kandy to meet Mountbatten on 5 September. The staff he took with him was a carefully ostentatious mix of 'new men' and 'Somerville men', the latter being officers who, Fraser knew, Mountbatten would want to be weeded out after the unhappy experiences of the past year. It was an obvious symbol of the way Fraser intended to operate in his dealings with the 'Supremo': the sinking of past grievances with no witch-hunts.[6]

> 'He and Mountbatten always got along absolutely splendidly. But, you see – that was Fraser. There was no pomposity to him at all. With *anyone* who shared an existence in the Royal Navy, they were partners. It didn't matter if it was a chief stoker or an ordinary signalman: they were all privileged to be in the Royal Navy, which was the finest Service in the world. And the fact that he was an admiral and they weren't even officers made no difference to him. So it was with his attitude to Mountbatten. He knew Mountbatten's history from his time on the Board, and Mountbatten's meteoric rise to fame didn't worry him at all. Fraser could *never* join a faction (though he might favour Gunnery officers – he was naturally fond of Gunnery officers); and Mountbatten had a job to do, *he* had a job to do, and the factors of age or seniority didn't worry him at all. And this was plain for all to see. Mind you, it was funny to watch it working, as the two staffs got the message. The Supremo's staff were all on edge at first, wondering what we chaps were going to be like, but Fraser was so charming and friendly – irresistible. But Fraser *always* knew what he was doing: he always let it be known to his staff that they either accepted his line, or they were out. And in no time that whole terrible atmosphere of tension and hostility between the staffs just melted away.'

This, then, was Fraser's major achievement during his first brief spell with the Eastern Fleet, which lasted just over a month (August-September 1944). As Commander-in-Chief he followed the same basic round of regular visits to ships and shore establishments which he had developed with the Home Fleet. By no means all of these visits passed off in 'sweetness and light'. Fraser's first inspection of 'The Racecourse', nothing to do with the sport of kings, but a naval shore establishment, produced one of those celebrated Fraser phenomena referred to by the initials JGSU – a Jolly Good Shake-Up (the problem was aircraft maintenance). As in his last months with the Home Fleet Fraser, looking keenly to the future, left the seagoing command of the Eastern Fleet to his VA2, Vice-Admiral Sir Arthur Power (who had also been VA2 to Somerville) and to force commanders like Rear-Admiral Moody, Flag Officer Aircraft-Carriers. During Fraser's first sojourn in Ceylon, Moody took the carriers *Victorious* and *Indomitable* on two strikes at Japanese targets in Sumatra. Apart from being heartening demonstrations of the Eastern Fleet's retention of the tactical initiative in the Indian Ocean, such operations continued to yield invaluable experience. But they also demonstrated that the naval aircrews of the Eastern Fleet had a long way to go before they could match the expertise of the American carrier task forces in the Pacific.

September 1944 was, however, a decisive month in Fraser's career. It saw the 'Octagon' conference in Quebec between Churchill and Roosevelt, during which Churchill formally offered the services of a British squadron in the Pacific and Roosevelt accepted the offer 'with both hands'. This was the true genesis of the British Pacific Fleet, and at the end of September Fraser returned to Kandy to discuss the decisions of 'Octagon' with Mountbatten. Though all but prostrated by a virus infection, Fraser insisted on being 'dosed up' so that he could go through with this most important conference; but the inevitable reaction obliged him to undergo a couple of days' convalescence in his bungalow at Kandy. And almost immediately after his return to Colombo on 3 October Fraser was summoned back to London to receive his briefing for the Pacific from Churchill and the Admiralty.

There was no time for leisurely stops and visits during this trip: it was made at top speed with the shortest of breaks for refuelling, and with the last leg cutting across barely liberated France. This breathless return was particularly memorable for Vernon Merry, because Fraser's baggage included a gigantic stalk of bananas. 'It had about four or five hundred bananas on it,' recalls Merry, 'and it was damned heavy. And when we clocked in at the Admiralty, *I* was the one who had to carry the bananas. Remember that they hadn't been known in England for so long; I was practically lynched. But I carried out the Admiral's order that so many were to go to each of his particular friends in the Admiralty – people like Renée Nash' [who had been Fraser's secretary during his time as Controller, and was to remain a devoted friend for the rest of his life].[7]

During the ensuing ten hectic days in Whitehall, Fraser was informed that his days with the Eastern Fleet would be brief. From the moment of his return East, Ceylon would serve as a temporary base for the nucleus Pacific Force, to be moulded around a task force of the most modern British fleet carriers. The Eastern Fleet would then be split to form a permanent East Indies Fleet commanded by Power, which would remain at Ceylon to work with SEAC. From December 1944, however, an entirely new entity – the British Pacific Fleet under Fraser's command – would move to Australia to work up efficiency before reporting for duty with the Americans in the Pacific.

There was, however, one familiar obstacle to the formation of the new Pacific Fleet, and it lay far to the north-east in a Norwegian fjord. Battered and warped though she was by repeated British attacks, unable now to cruise the high seas, *Tirpitz* was still able to float and shoot; and as long as the German battleship survived the Admiralty dared not finalise plans for wide-ranging capital ship transfers from Home Waters to the Pacific. But on 12 November 1944 the luck of the *Tirpitz* ran out at last when the Lancasters of the 'Dambusters' caught her at her anchorage in Tromsö Fjord, unprotected by smoke-screens or fighters, in perfect visibility. A devastating cascade of 6-ton 'Tallboy' streamlined bombs sealed *Tirpitz*'s fate, capsizing and sinking her where she lay.

Ten days later, in Ceylon, Fraser hoisted his flag as Commander-in-Chief, British Pacific Fleet, a command still non-existent, but for all that faced by more apparently insurmountable problems than had confronted any admiral in the entire history of the Royal Navy.

. 21 .

Building the British
Pacific Fleet

[December 1944-March 1945]

The creation of a British Pacific Fleet able to participate in the final defeat of Japan was Fraser's last and surely greatest achievement in the Second World War. It was an achievement dominated by paradox. Though Fraser was Britain's most eminent serving practitioner of the most finely calculated naval science of them all – gunnery – he was now forced to create a modern carrier-oriented striking force, virtually from nothing. Naval aviation had changed considerably since Fraser's prewar command of *Glorious*, though the basic principles remained the same and he remained for ever grateful for having had that experience. (It was also a useful asset when talking to Fleet Air Arm aircrew, who could appreciate that their C-in-C was a former carrier captain as well as a Gunnery Officer.) But on Fraser's shoulders now rested Britain's chances of claiming a share in arbitration over the postwar fortunes of South-East Asia, China, and the Pacific; and this vital objective had to be pursued hand-to-mouth at breakneck speed, in the most frantic, improvised 'lash-up' in Royal Naval history.

Roskill's summary of the tasks confronting Fraser in December 1944, as Commander-in-Chief of a non-existent Fleet, provides a forbidding list:[1]

The problems which faced Admiral Fraser were extremely complex, and his position was probably unique in the long annals of the Royal Navy; for while he was under Admiral Nimitz for operational purposes, he was responsible to the Admiralty for the maintenance of his ships and the welfare of their crews; and the governments of Australia and New Zealand owned the rearward bases and shore installations on which he depended. Lastly nearly all his supplies had to be transported across some 12,000 miles of sea from the British Isles.

Yet these were the least of Fraser's problems at the beginning of December 1944. A triple dilemma was staring him in the face, with no immediate prospect of resolution. The Fleet Train of supply ships, without which the British Pacific Fleet would be shackled to the Australian coast and of no use to the Americans, did not exist. Despite this glaring inadequacy, Fraser would nevertheless have to 'sell' the Royal Navy to the Americans not as a limping, demanding passenger but as a fully effective, self-sufficient partner. And this he had to do in the teeth of stubborn Admiralty insistence that the British Pacific Fleet must retain its autonomy and not function as an integrated task force of the US Pacific Fleet.

The extent to which Admiralty obduracy complicated Fraser's already monumental task has always tended to be underrated, though Lord Fraser himself was to look back on it with more amusement than bitterness, at least in its more trivial aspects. One such was Fraser's proposal for the British Pacific Fleet to adopt khaki uniform (as worn by the US Navy) in place of the traditional Royal Naval 'tropical whites' – shirts, shorts and knee-socks. 'Cunningham was very insistent that we should stick to whites,' said Lord Fraser, 'but I told him we might have to change to khaki in the end. Which we did.'[2] Fraser's predilection for khaki stemmed more from psychology than practicality or comfort. If the fleet kept to its 'whites', quaint as these were to American eyes, every officer and rating so attired would be a walking demonstration that the British were set on doing things *their* way, instead of taking useful tips from the US Navy whose achievements had already made Japan's defeat certain. Going into khaki was the most obvious courtesy gesture which the British, 'new boys' of the Pacific War, could make; and as the photographs show, Fraser's own choice of dress when dealing directly with his American colleagues was always most carefully calculated.

Far more serious than the 'whites or khaki?' question was the initial Admiralty ban on the Fleet's adoption of American signalling codes and techniques. The winning of this particular battle was a source of enduring gratification to Lord Fraser and he was never reticent in stressing its vital importance (*see above*, p.167). As recorded by Richard Courage, chosen by Fraser to be Fleet Communications Officer of the British Pacific Fleet, this was how Fraser tackled the problem:[3]

> As Bruce Fraser put it to me, it was our job to get the British Pacific Fleet to the right place at the right time, and talking the right language.
> My half-hour interview with Fraser in his Admiralty office

proved to be revolutionary as far as the world of signals was concerned. Fraser handed me a voluminous Admiralty docket with various 'appreciations' and 'opinions' on how the British Fleet should cope with the signal problem – at sea, from bases in Australia, from advance base at as yet unknown locations, and from a special communication ship (as yet unfinished) to be put to the sole task of handling signal traffic in advance anchorages.

What language were we to talk – that of the US Navy or Royal Navy? This was the vital question Bruce Fraser asked me after I had sat in a corner of his office, studying the docket. For its final minute read something like this:

'The Board is strongly of the opinion that on no account should the British Fleet use the American system of signalling. The British method is superior.'

There was really no need for me to comment: Bruce Fraser read my thoughts and I read his. The US Navy had lent us a squadron to serve under Fraser when I was with him in the Home Fleet. They had willingly used our books, and I had gone to sea once or twice in their ships to help them with the language problem.

My reply was, 'They won't accept us unless we use their signal books; it won't work.' Fraser agreed, and said so on the docket. He then said, 'I leave in a few days to go and see Admiral Nimitz in Pearl Harbor. Have a look at this communication ship being built at Glasgow; go to Washington, see the Americans there; then go to Pearl Harbor and meet the signal staff of Admiral Nimitz; have a look at Manus in the Admiralty Islands, if you can get there, and join me in Sydney, Australia by about January 1st.'

It was then mid-December and time was short, but I had the authority of Bruce Fraser behind me. I quickly wrote out my own 'authority', got it typed on the best Admiralty notepaper I could find, and persuaded some unsuspecting person to sign and rubber-stamp it. Then I nipped up to Glasgow. The Admiralty's idea of a suitable communication ship for advanced bases was not mine, and I had to say so in no uncertain terms. As a result the Director of the Signal Division at the Admiralty sent for me: how dare I say such a thing? I explained that I was responsible to Bruce Fraser and no one else, and that what he wanted had got to be done. After this somewhat stormy start to the interview, we parted on the best of terms.

All in all, this was a perfect example of how Fraser expected his

Staff to operate when the pressure was on. By the time Courage reached Hawaii on 26 December after an odyssey via Montreal, Washington and San Francisco, Fraser had already taken the vital first trick by his historic flying visit to Pearl Harbor (15–24 December). This visit was the opening move in his plan of campaign to ensure the American acceptance of the British Pacific Fleet in the theatre that really mattered: the Central Pacific, axis of the final American drive on Japan. Having mulled over the problem for the past nine months, Fraser needed no reminding that the formidable anglophobe Fleet Admiral 'Ernie' King, US Chief of Naval Operations, would do everything he could to 'keep the Limeys from muscling in' on the defeat of Japan. King was already trying to dump the British Pacific Fleet on General MacArthur's South-West Pacific Area, still, in December 1944, the centre of action in the Pacific, but scheduled to become a secondary theatre after the conquest of Luzon in the Philippines was launched in January 1945. Unless Fraser moved fast, it would be easy for King to arrange for the British Pacific Fleet to be attached to Admiral Kinkaid's 7th Fleet, under MacArthur's command – and end the war in the comparative backwater of the Philippines and Borneo. Hence Fraser's determination to 'make his number' at the earliest opportunity with Admiral Chester Nimitz, Commander-in-Chief Pacific Fleet (CINCPAC), and Commander of the Central Pacific Area. Nimitz's support would be essential to secure the British Pacific Fleet assignation to the final drive on Japan via Iwo Jima and Okinawa.

The little band that flew from Colombo to Pearl Harbor via Perth and Sydney consisted of Fraser, Flag Lieutenant Vernon Merry, Fraser's Chief of Staff and his Assistant Chief of Staff (Plans) – Commodore Evans-Lombe and Captain Brown – and Intelligence Officer, Lt Commander Charles Sheppard and Group Captain Kearey, RAF. Fraser's Secretary, Captain Allfrey, was assisted by Wren Secretaries Second Officer Nancy Bond and Stella Brown (the latter making history as the first Wrens to serve in the Pacific during the war). It was in every sense an historic trip, starting with the first-ever flight by a land-based aircraft (a Civil Airways Liberator) from Colombo to Perth. From Australia to Pearl Harbor – via Espiritu Santo in the New Hebrides and Canton Island in the Phoenix Islands – the party was in the capable hands of NATS, the US Naval Air Transportation Service. Though the long hours in the air were devoured by the drafting and typing of agenda for the coming discussions, Fraser found time to chat with the American crewmen, commenting in mock indignation to Vernon Merry, after talking with an American Master Sergeant, 'He earns more than I do!'[4]

The arrival at Pearl was a dazzling experience, the dazzle being provided first by the myriad lights of Honolulu and then by a barrage of photographers' flashlights as the party disembarked from the flying-boat at the jetty. Every member of the party had been assigned an officer or rating of equivalent rank as host and guide, from Admiral Nimitz himself for Fraser to a 'Wave' rating for Wren Brown. Fraser had made it clear that the object of the exercise was to show that the British meant business as well as being easy to get on with, but the warmth of the American reception was genuine and unmistakable. By striking up an instant and lasting friendship with Admiral Nimitz, Fraser won the British Pacific Fleet's vital 'first victory'. 'There was no doubt,' writes Commander Sheppard, 'that the US command in the Pacific wanted the B.P.F., and from the moment of the arrival of the party at Pearl Harbor we had the maximum co-operation from Admiral Nimitz down to individual staff officers;[5]

I think the basis of the friendship between Admiral Fraser and Admiral Nimitz lay in the similarities of their characters. Both were 'quiet' men, both had a good sense of humour – Admiral Fraser's of an impish variety – and both were easily approachable. (Later, in Guam, I found it as easy to go and see Admiral Nimitz about something as it was to see Admiral Fraser.) My main memory of the Pearl Harbor visit is that it was like a family party, rather than an Admiral and Staff, visiting little-known relations and finding them friendly and likable, and returning with a feeling that it had been a most successful visit in every way.

One small incident illustrates the family feeling. One night we had gone to a large, 'officers only' party given by CINCPAC at which there was hula dancing, and Admirals Nimitz and Fraser were both given *leis* of flowers. Admiral Nimitz gallantly presented his *lei* to Second Officer Bond with a kiss, but Wren Stella Brown, as a rating and not an officer, could not attend. The next morning, at our Staff meeting before starting discussions with the Americans at 0830, Admiral Fraser arrived carrying his *lei*. He went up to Stella, put it round her neck and kissed her as a consolation for missing the party. Somewhat startled, Stella called out 'Ooh, sir!', threw her arms round his neck, and kissed him back.

But the visit was certainly not all hula parties and flowery compliments: there was a lot of hard bargaining, too. The Americans were determined to retain for themselves all the credit for avenging Pearl Harbor (1941) by sinking all remaining heavy units of the Japanese Fleet. They therefore rejected the British offer of specialist anti-shipping forces – the RAF's 'Dambusters' and the Royal Navy's X-craft flotilla. For all that, Fraser gained his main objective. The offer of a British carrier force for the Pacific was accepted, and immensely valuable foundations had been laid by the time Fraser and his party arrived back in Australia on 24 December to set about establishing the British Pacific Fleet's HQ and main base facilities. When, two days later, Richard Courage arrived at Pearl Harbor from San Francisco:[6]

> The welcome I received from Admiral Nimitz's Signal Officer could not have been more encouraging. Plans were soon made for complete sets of American signal books to be sent to Sydney for distribution to HM Ships as they passed through Australia from the UK. A liaison team was promised for every ship to help us learn the language. Most important of all, he got his hands on some air transport to cope with the vast quantities of signal books that were eventually to be sent.
>
> This done, he made it clear to me that our telegraphists would have to learn to type morse. American broadcasts were too fast to be copied by 'stick' (pencil). He said, 'My advice is, put it on a sexual basis. Get a pretty girl to teach them and in no time they'll be typing letters to their girlfriends in England. Typing from morse signals soon becomes natural.' This was to prove a most valuable piece of advice. No RN telegraphist had ever been taught to type during training. There were a lot of other professional signal matters to be fixed up: call signs, crystals, radio frequencies, radar organisation, recognition signals, the provision of American cyphering machines, and the like.

Back in Australia, the task of establishing a working base for the Fleet had barely got under way before Fraser was on his travels again. At Pearl Harbor he had expressed his anxiety to witness in person the next major American amphibious landing: MacArthur's invasion of Luzon, set for the first half of January 1945. This was to be the greatest amphibious armada yet unleashed in the Pacific War, and the major question-mark was how it would stand up to the punishing Japanese suicide (*kamikaze*) air attacks, first used in mass against MacArthur's forces during the invasion of Leyte in October 1944.

To the Royal Navy, in which memories of the loss of *Repulse* and *Prince of Wales* to conventional Japanese attacks three years before were still vivid, the question of whether a modern fleet could beat off *kamikazes* and attain its objective was of more than academic interest. But Fraser's latest determination to 'see for himself' came within an inch of costing him his life. After a 'most cordial' visit to General MacArthur and Admiral Kinkaid at Leyte, Fraser embarked in the battleship *New Mexico* to witness the coming bombardment and landings at Lingayen Gulf in northern Luzon. Accompanied by General Sir Herbert Lumsden, recently sent out as Churchill's special representative to MacArthur, Fraser took with him Vernon Merry, Sub-Lieutenant Morton and David Barnwell (personal steward and valet). Commanded by Vice-Admiral Jesse B. Oldendorf, the bombardment force sailed from Leyte Gulf on 2 January and the first big *kamikaze* attacks began to come in from the 4th.[7]

'On January 4, 1945 the escort carrier *Ommaney Bay* was so seriously damaged that she had to be abandoned and sunk. The luckless (cruiser) *Australia* was hit six times between January 6 and 9; although 44 men were killed and 72 wounded she was able to remain in action. During the landing the battleships *New Mexico* and *Colorado*, cruisers *Columbia* and *Louisville*, and 21 other vessels were hit.

To maintain this level of attack the Japanese set up a training base on Formosa where crews received a seven-day course in *kamikaze* tactics before being flown to the Philippines. Attack methods had been standardised using two main approaches: either at high altitude to about five miles from the target followed by an ever-steepening dive, or a low level approach at about 30 feet above the sea followed by a climb to about 1,000 feet close to the target and a near-vertical dive.'

New Mexico's turn came on the morning of 6 January:[8]

'The bombardment started on the 6th from the line of battleships and cruisers, going dead slow – and *that* was the day when the escort carriers had to withdraw to refuel. Air cover that day was to be provided by the Army Air Force, and it didn't materialise. No one was sunk, but the *New Mexico* was hit on the port side of the bridge.'

Vernon Merry's escape was no less providential than that of Fraser himself:[9]

'I had been talking with General Lumsden up to 10 minutes before on the starboard wing of the bridge. Having finished that conversation I went inside to read the signals in the Admiral's Plot. As the attack developed, I gathered, Fraser just happened to go to the starboard side; Lumsden moved across to the port side. And then this thing came in and hit us. General Lumsden and young Morton, whom Fraser had taken as his travelling secretary, were both killed instantly. The Captain was killed, too – it hit between the Captain's Bridge and the Admiral's Bridge. I was knocked flat, only 14 feet from the point of impact, but I was all right behind the armour; the C-in-C was on the other side. I tried to fight my way out of the Plot; it was difficult to get out in the chaos, with fire and dead bodies everywhere outside. I found him at the side: he'd been worrying about me, knowing that the others were dead.'

Unbelievably, Fraser had escaped without a scratch, but he was not unnaturally dazed and in momentary shock from the colossal blast of the explosion. For all that, until the American 'corpsmen' arrived on the scene, he and Merry tried to make themselves useful amid the carnage, while the ship's 'Con' was switched from the Bridge to the lower control position and effective command restored:[10]

'They were marvellous, the Americans: it took only a few minutes to switch the "Con" and restore control. The C-in-C meanwhile was upset by the procedure of the "medics", who left the obviously serious cases and concentrated on the ones who were only slightly wounded. After about half an hour the Exec., who had taken over, asked me to get Admiral Fraser below. They were appalled at having lost a Limey three-star general and didn't want to lose a four-star admiral, too. They were all the more embarrassed because Fraser was easily the most senior officer in the ship. But of course – he didn't want anybody to think he was chicken. He didn't want to go below at all. But people kept coming to me, and in the end I had to say "Come on, sir; you're really embarrassing our hosts." He *was* in shock, more than I was; but the real trouble was that he didn't have anything genuinely useful to do – by this time the attacks were over, and there wasn't much going on. I told him, "Look, sir, you can always blame me later; but why don't we go below for a bit and let them get on with it." In the end I got him below to the alternative Con, and he found that interesting; then the Main Battery Plot, where he could talk gunnery. But that night, after we'd secured from battle stations, we went on deck, and stumbled into the burial party. His main concern was to report what had happened, and we got off a signal as soon as we could.'

Merry adds that apart from giving him an autographed photograph in thanks for 'your services on 6th January 1945', Fraser never referred to the ordeal again, other than to reiterate his grief at the loss of General Lumsden and young Morton. Nor was Lord Fraser any more forthcoming in his brief allusions to the incident in conversations with the author. My own conclusion is that Fraser was never quite able to excuse himself from blame for the deaths of Lumsden and Morton – a high price to pay for personal experience of the *kamikaze* menace. Yet Fraser never made any secret of the fact that he considered this experience essential, because of the extraordinary nature of his new command. His seniority made it impossible for him to command the British Pacific Fleet at sea, descending in status to that of a task force commander under an American fleet commander. Like Nimitz in Pearl Harbor, therefore, Fraser would command from ashore, in Sydney. The vital difference was that, being the man he was, Fraser could not order the British Pacific Fleet to brave the *kamikaze* menace without having experienced the same danger himself.

The ordeal of the Lingayen trip did not end with the *kamikaze* attack of 6 January. When Fraser, Merry and Barnwell left Lingayen after the landings on the 9th had swept inland against negligible opposition, they heard gunfire ahead of them as they were taken out to their PBY flying-boat. Two Japanese were killed in the water, trying to swim away, and Fraser's PBY was found wired up with explosives After another aircraft had ferried them down to Mindoro to pick up the Liberator for the flight back to Australia, Fraser's aircraft was accidentally given take-off clearance down a runway on which a flight of American fighters was already coming in to land. Only another miracle avoided a fatal collision and the chance of American aircraft succeeding where the *kamikazes* had failed. After all these dangers a moment of comic relief after touchdown at Tacloban Field, Leyte, imparted a warming sense of being 'on the team':[11]

> 'The airfield dispersal areas were packed, as usual, and there
> was only one space in which we could park; our pilot taxied
> straight into it. And hordes of Americans rushed out, screaming
> "Hey, no, you can't park there – that's reserved for the
> General!" Our pilot wasn't "fazed" at all. He just cranked open
> his window, leaned out and said:
> "How many stars has your General got?"
> "Three!"
> "Waal. . ." (*jerk of thumb towards Fraser*) "MY guy's got
> FOUR stars!" '

The importance of Fraser's trip to Lingayen was conveyed to the Admiralty in a quadruple signal on 17 January. First, the trip had built on the foundation laid at Pearl Harbor in the previous month, extending Fraser's outflanking move to avoid the British Pacific Fleet being assigned to the South-West Pacific. To this end Fraser had enlisted the unwitting help of MacArthur himself:[12]

> The General said that he would welcome the British Fleet in his area but indicated a probable intention of turning South to North Borneo at the same time as Admiral Nimitz was pressing north.
>
> I stated that we were already committed to Admiral Nimitz and could not do both at the same time, but if it was possible to do so we would always consider assistance in bombardment support. In such a case it would be necessary for him to provide logistics which he quite understood. He said I could write my own ticket concerning command, but in viewing the situation it would obviously be impracticable for a British Admiral to take over the area bound up as it is with American supply, transport, amphibious forces and air.
>
> I emphasized the reason for the delay in arrival of our forces necessitated by Admiral Nimitz's wish to strike at Sumatra and he seemed fully to understand and agreed with the project.

(Note how artfully Fraser had used his by no means finalised 'commitment' to Nimitz, the embarrassing fact of his own seniority, and the need for the British Pacific Fleet to 'get its hand in' with preliminary strikes at Sumatra, all politely leading MacArthur to decide against acceptance of the British Pacific Fleet in his area.)

The second and third sections of Fraser's post-Lingayen report dealt with the bombardment-and-landing programme and with the damage done by the *kamikazes*. Referring to the latter, he reported that: 'In no case did the damage prevent ships from carrying out their tasks although casualties were fairly heavy, e.g. in battleships 1 suicide bomber usually averaged 30 to 40 killed and 100 wounded.'[13] He reported accurately on the two main *kamikaze* approach tactics, and while noting the effectiveness of 'saturation' AA fire observed that on the first day the Americans had had too many fighters in the air to permit accurate direction; reducing the number led to much better results. And he summed up:[14]

> The following points need again emphasizing during air attacks:
> (a) Unnecessary personnel must not be on upper deck or concentrate on bridges;
> (b) Alternative positions for controlling the ship must be permanently manned;
> (c) Arrangements for fire fighting and dealing with wounded on upper deck and bridges must be frequently practised.

A fourth section, 'Fleet Tactics And General Remarks' was used to highlight some crucial deficiencies which were clearly going to add to the British Pacific Fleet difficulties:

> The Navy's own Catalinas arriving on S-Day (9 January, the day of the landings) for immediate reconnaissance, courier service, and transport, makes one envious of the American Naval Air Service after the difficulties experienced in finding one of our own aircraft to take one about.
>
> Such operations involve a considerable strain on personnel principally because of the suicide bomber. Everyone however seemed cheery although in the *New Mexico* no one had been ashore since the 20th November.
>
> The provision of amenities on board is of great importance, soda water fountains, ice, ice-cream, water coolers and movies are all in abundance together with much literature and a mail was delivered at sea on S minus 5. There seemed to be ample resources.

Concluding 'Altogether a well planned operation and carried out with determination, boldness and courage', Fraser appended a bleak, economical account of the fatal *kamikaze* attack of the 6th, asking for his personal sympathy to be forwarded to the families of General Lumsden and Sub-Lieutenant Morton. His signal to the Admiralty 'crossed' with a 'Personal and Private' signal from Churchill: 'Mrs Churchill and I have just read in paper of your narrow escape at the time Major General Lumsden [sic] was killed. We feel his loss deeply and are thankful that you escaped. All best wishes for future.'[15]

Two days later, Cunningham's reply left Whitehall and it contained little of immediate comfort to Fraser. Cunningham pointed out that the German counter-offensive in the Ardennes (December 1944) had completed the wreck of the over-confident Allied forecast that the German war would be over by the New Year of 1945. On that forecast, industrial manpower and supply allocation had been reduced and the Navy's manpower reduced by 20,000 to keep the Army up to strength. Moreover, the new generation of *schnorchel* U-boats, able to operate for long periods, was already causing serious alarm in home waters and there was no prospect of the British Pacific Fleet's escort forces being released *en masse* before the summer. Cunningham added that he hoped major units earmarked for Fraser's command would not be so delayed, but admitted that dockyard problems had already put some ships behind schedule in their departure for the Pacific.

On one vital point Cunningham expressed complete agreement with Fraser: the crying need for the Fleet to secure an advanced base to which, hopefully, ships and supplies could be sailed direct from the UK:[16]

> I feel there is a great danger that we may dig ourselves in too
> deeply in Australia. What one would like – and I think you will
> agree – is that we should get a base as far forward as possible,
> if necessary sharing it with the U.S., and ship all our stores,
> aircraft, etc., direct there from the U.K., using the Torres Straits
> or perhaps later going up the west side of New Guinea. This
> would mean an immense saving in shipping, which is going to
> be the bottleneck in all operations this next year, especially if
> the new enemy submarines really get busy.

As was his wont, Cunningham added a longhand postscript: 'I hope the above will keep you to some extent in the picture as we see it here & which is so necessary for you to have. Don't you go pushing yourself too much into the forefront of the battle – leave that to the more easily spared', and signed off 'All the best, Andrew Cunningham'.

This letter is of great importance because it shows the gulf between Admiralty thinking as personified by Cunningham and the realities of the Pacific War. 'We have been trying,' commented Cunningham, 'to think out the answer to the suicide chap. Flame throwers are no good, and it looks as if plenty of close-range weapons is as far as we can get at present. The Seafire fighter may also do good work.' (In fact its weak undercarriage and low endurance made the Seafire, naval version of the Spitfire, unsuited to carrier work and the best carrier fighters turned out to be the latest American models, the Hellcat and Wildcat.) Far more serious, however, was Cunningham's apparent reluctance to grasp – as Fraser had already grasped – the need to improve endurance on prolonged operations at sea by a proper attention to shipboard amenities:

> I hope our people will not get too blinded by American
> lavishness. We cannot compete with them in either personnel or
> material, nor do I think we should train our men to expect the
> same waste as is practised in the American Navy. I am sure that
> soda fountains, etc., are very good things in the right place, but
> we have done without them for some hundreds of years and I
> daresay can for another year or two.

Cunningham's crushing dismissal of American 'waste' and 'lavishness' shows his loyalty to the old brigade, resting on centuries of Royal Naval laurels instead of accepting, as Fraser did, that the Americans in the Pacific had changed the nature of 'sailoring' for ever. Fraser had seen for himself the immense psychological value of shipboard amenities on long cruising, reducing strain and fatigue and making the sailor more efficient. Fraser saw this as perfectly compatible with the long tradition of the Service, for which no one had a higher regard than himself. In this he was a 'modern': the first British naval Commander-in-Chief to campaign successfully for a modicum of the myriad amenities taken for granted in the Royal Navy of the 1980s. Knowing that he was right Fraser stuck to his guns, refusing to be browbeaten by Cunningham's impatience, encouraging his Staff to go on finding out all they could about what made service in the US Navy more attractive, more endurable, and above all more efficient with regard to this new form of warfare than in the Royal Navy.

By the beginning of February 1945, however, Fraser was no nearer to solving his most urgent problem: the creation of efficient base facilities for the British Pacific Fleet. This was primarily geographical, caused by Sydney lying as far south of the Equator as Japan lies north. Over 4,000 miles of sea separated Sydney from the Fleet's hoped-for combat zone south of the Ryukyus; and the shared use of American facilities at Manus in the Admiralty Islands, freely offered by Nimitz at Pearl Harbor, would reduce that distance by less than half. At first Fraser hoped that the British could imitate American practice and build their own advanced bases; but the British services lacked anything to rival the magnificent American Construction Battalions (CBs, or 'Seabees') who could create a fleet base or bomber field from a coral atoll virtually overnight. As a second best, Fraser hoped that the Americans would grant the British Pacific Fleet base facilities in the Philippines. But the battle for Luzon dragged on until the end of June, American fleet base facilities in the lesser Philippine islands were severely restricted, and this project also came to nothing. If the British Pacific Fleet was to fulfil its pledge to share in the softening-up of the Japanese home islands, it would have to operate from Manus.

Fraser's other overriding problem lay on the political front. His initial impression of Australia had been encouraging: the Australian people and press were genuinely delighted to welcome back the Royal Navy after a two-year monopoly of their goodwill by the Americans. But the attitude of Prime Minister John Curtin's Labour Government was that Australia had already done more than her share in the war. As for the dockers' and shipwrights' unions, on whose exertions the smooth turn-around of the British Fleet would depend their attitude was positively hostile to the new burden imposed by the build-up of the Fleet. Strikes and stoppages plagued the British Pacific Fleet throughout its time in Australia, and for a while – until the familiar geographical problem ruled such a step out of the question – Fraser seriously considered transferring the British Pacific Fleet from Australia to New Zealand. Shaw's Burgoyne, in *The Devil's Disciple*, lets slip the immortal *bon mot* that 'the British soldier can stand up to anything except the British War Office'. Fraser might easily have said the same about the BPF and the Australian trade unions – and shattered the goodwill which meant so much to the BPF's fortunes and morale. Not the least of his many achievements was his resounding personal success in Australia, not merely as a lion in Australian high society (which he certainly was) but as a respected and much-loved 'ambassador in uniform', even when it came to unseaming union disputes.

February 1945 was the month in which the first heavy units of the British Pacific Fleet reached Australia from Ceylon, whence they had been 'blooding' themselves since December with strikes at the Japanese East Indies. Rear-Admiral Sir Philip Vian, commanding the First Aircraft Carrier Squadron, arrived at Fremantle on 4 February with the fleet carriers *Indomitable*, *Victorious*, *Indefatigable* and *Illustrious*, battleship *King George V*, cruisers *Euryalus*, *Argonaut* and *Black Prince*, and ten destroyers. This force was met at Fremantle by Vice-Admiral Sir Bernard Rawlings, who hoisted his flag as VA2, British Pacific Fleet in *King George V* and brought the fleet in to a tumultuous welcome at Sydney on 10 February. Less than three months after Fraser had assumed command of a then nonexistent fleet, the nucleus of the British Pacific Fleet was in being and concentrated at its main base.

Nine days later, 4,000 miles to the north, the Americans launched the invasion of Iwo Jima in the Bonin Islands. This new invasion was, as ever, conveyed and covered by the main body of the US Pacific Fleet, designated 5th Fleet when, as now, it was commanded by Admiral Raymond A. Spruance, and 3rd Fleet when commanded by Admiral William F. Halsey. The latter had been commanding 3rd Fleet off the Philippines when Fraser went to Pearl Harbor in December 1944. Fraser had, however, met Spruance, the reserved, silent mastermind of the decisive American carrier victories at Midway (June 1942) and the Philippine Sea (June 1944): 'a great commander – but very austere. He gave me lunch; I think we had a couple of lettuces, or something.'[18] The provisional agreement reached between Fraser, Nimitz and Spruance at Pearl Harbor was that if the British Pacific Fleet could be got ready in time Nimitz would be happy for it to serve with the 5th Fleet during Spruance's next spell of command. After witnessing the Lingayen landings for himself, Fraser had appointed his former Home Fleet staff officer, Commander Michael Le Fanu, to serve as liaison officer afloat in USS *Indianapolis*, Spruance's flagship.

The necessarily delayed start of the British Pacific Fleet's formation ruled out any chance of its participation in the Iwo Jima operations. By mid-February 1945 it remained to be seen whether the Fleet could be made ready in time for 'Iceberg', the invasion of Okinawa scheduled for the month after Iwo had been declared secure (which, due to fanatical Japanese resistance, did not occur until 25 March). But as desks in the ships of the Fleet vanished beneath the mountains of forms, manuals, and the infinitely variable 'bumf' required for the change-over to American signalling, the prospect of attaining combat readiness by the end of March seemed remote in the extreme. Even with the lavish aid generously provided by the US Navy's signal department (every British warship was provided with an American signal liaison team) it would be weeks before Rawlings's warships could make sense to each other, let alone to the US 5th Fleet. The British Pacific Fleet was chronically short of spares, particularly in radar parts and aircraft. Radar parts had to come from the UK, and the fact that the Fleet Air Arm operated American aircraft was not much of a help: the Fleet's nominal independence of the Americans created a situation akin to 'Catch-22'. Admittedly, once the captains of the British Pacific Fleet had actually made first contact with the American depot commanders, matters eased considerably. As Fraser put it:[19]

> 'At one moment we were short of three Avenger aircraft. I made a signal to Admiral Nimitz to ask if he could lend us three Avengers, and the reply came back, no. I sent for my American liaison officer: he couldn't understand this at first. And then he said, "Ah, it has to go through Washington! I think you'll find that they'll provide you with some." Sure enough, when we got up to Manus, the American CO there said, "I'm sorry, but we don't issue less than six – and if you've got a bottle of whisky you can have a dozen!" '

But this was of little help in February 1945, in the frantic days when it seemed that not enough of anything was there *now*. Only the rudiments of the Fleet Train had been scraped together, nothing like enough fast tankers and storeships to support even the modest force under Rawlings's command. And over all there hung the demoralising knowledge that the British Pacific Fleet's eventual combat destination still had to be confirmed, thanks to the persistent delaying tactics of Fleet Admiral King in Washington.

Despite all these setbacks, Fraser took the considerable risk of sending the British Pacific Fleet up to Manus, knowing full well that the outcome could well be an early, humiliating failure for the Royal Navy in its first test in the Pacific. As ever, though, it was a well-calculated gamble. Fraser had no doubt that the British Pacific Fleet would perform creditably enough once in action. The difficulty would be getting it there and keeping it there, and Fraser sensed that American goodwill, essential at this early stage, would help the Fleet over its first hurdle. As Fraser had already reported to the Admiralty, 'the American logistic authorities have interpreted self-sufficiency in a very liberal sense.'[20] When Admiral Rawlings sailed for Manus on 28 February, therefore, fingers remained firmly crossed: there could be no ignoring the Fleet's rampant problems, yet hope and confidence were high.

This positive mood was momentarily depressed when the Fleet reached Manus on 7 March. Admiral Rawlings proudly signalled to Nimitz that 'I HEREBY REPORT TASK FORCES 113 and 112' (the British Pacific Fleet warships and Admiral D. B. Fisher's Fleet Train) 'IN ACCORDANCE WITH ORDERS RECEIVED FROM C-IN-C, B.P.F.' Rawlings did not fail to add that 'IT IS WITH A FEELING OF GREAT PRIDE AND PLEASURE THAT THE B.P.F. JOINS THE U.S. NAVAL FORCES UNDER YOUR COMMAND.' With equal courtesy, Nimitz replied that, 'THE U.S. PACIFIC FLEET WELCOMES THE BRITISH CARRIER TASK FORCE AND ATTACHED UNITS WHICH WILL GREATLY ADD TO OUR POWER TO STRIKE THE ENEMY AND WILL ALSO SHOW OUR UNITY OF PURPOSE IN THE WAR AGAINST JAPAN.'[21] But, wrote Admiral Vian:[22]

> Manus itself, and the facilities we found waiting for us, were our first disappointment. Only twenty-seven of the sixty-nine ships of all types earmarked for the Fleet Train had as yet been assembled, many having been held up by the incessant labour strikes of the Sydney waterfront. One of the missing vessels was a water-boat, so that our ships, dependent on their own condensing plants, were permanently short of water in the tropical heat. A long swell running through the great expanse of the harbour made fuelling from the tankers an uncomfortable and damaging process, in the absence of catamarans to hold the ships apart. Long journeys by boat were necessary to get from ship to ship or from ship to shore, and a chronic shortage of harbour craft, owing to lack of shipping in which to transport them from Sydney to Manus, made for a chaotic situation.
>
> Over all lay the humid heat of a climate for which our ships were ill-adapted.

The British Pacific Fleet was left to sweat at Manus in the equatorial heat and humidity for ten miserable and debilitating days, with officers and men erupting in an epidemic of boils and prickly heat, while Admiral King fought his last battle to shuffle off the British Pacific Fleet on to MacArthur's command. But this wretched interlude was mercifully brief. On 17 March 1945 the long-awaited order came through for the Fleet, subject to withdrawal at seven days' notice, to put to sea and join the US 5th Fleet.

. 22 .

The defeat of Japan
[March-September 1945]

After leaving Manus on 18 March, Admiral Rawlings's 'British Strik-ing Force' moved up to the American base at Ulithi in the western Carolines, where it refuelled and received its final orders for 'Ice-berg'. On the 23rd, redesignated 'Task Force 57' – 5 for the US 5th Fleet, 7 for itself – the spearhead of the British Pacific Fleet sailed from Ulithi to play its part in the bombardment and conquest of Okinawa.

The British Pacific Fleet's brief combat life – March-August 1945 – may be summarised as follows. From 26 March to 20 April, operating on the south-western flank of the US 5th Fleet, Task Force 57 bombarded the island airfields of the Sakishima Gunto, the archi-pelago between Okinawa and Formosa. Its task in this period was to make it impossible for the Japanese to maintain regular air sup-port for Okinawa from Formosa, using the Sakishima Gunto air-fields as stepping-stones. So successful was the Fleet's debut that Admiral King's last attempt to divert the British to Borneo, made while the British Pacific Fleet was replenishing at Leyte, was over-come on the direct insistence of Nimitz as CINCPAC. Sailing on 1 May from Leyte, Task Force 57 rejoined the US 5th Fleet for its second operational 'tour', resuming strikes at the Sakishima Gunto from 4 May to 25 May.

After this second 'tour' the Fleet's participation in the Okinawa operations came to an end, withdrawing for major repairs and re-plenishment in Australian waters (5–28 June). But it was by no means idle in this period, mounting Operation 'Inmate', an air/sea bombardment of Truk in the eastern Carolines, on 14–16 June. The British Pacific Fleet's final return north was under the new designa-tion 'Task Force 37' serving now with the US 3rd Fleet under Admiral Halsey. The Fleet's new objective, in notable contrast to its necessarily belated participation in 'Iceberg' was to join in the pre-

265

liminary strikes heralding the invasion of the Japanese home island of Kyushu: Operation 'Olympic', scheduled for the beginning of November. The Fleet's share in these initial bombardments lasted from 17 July to 10 August. Though the dropping of atomic bombs on Hiroshima (6 August) and Nagasaki (9 August) barely anticipated the Fleet's scheduled disengagement for replenishment in Australia, Admiral Rawlings had no trouble in persuading Admiral Halsey that a token British force should remain with the 3rd Fleet until the Japanese made their formal surrender.

Such in outline was the combat record of the British Pacific Fleet, Fraser's last and greatest wartime command. When the Fleet went to war at the end of March 1945 its combat strength was less than 30 per cent of the majestic armada assembled under Fraser's command by VJ-Day (15 August), as Tables 22.1 and 22.2 show.

Table 22.1 *BPF actual operational strength, March-September 1945*

	Battleships	Fleet carriers	Escort carriers	Cruisers	Destroyers
'Iceberg 1' (26 March-20 April)	2	4	0	5	11
'Iceberg 2' (4-25 May)	2	4	0	5	14
'Inmate' (10-16 June)	0	1	1	5	5
'Olympic 1' (17 July-10 August)	1	3	0	6	15
Token force, Surrender of Japan (10 August-2 September)	1	1	0	2	10

Table 22.2 *BPF nominal strength, VJ-Day, 15 August 1945*

Battleships	Fleet carriers	Escort carriers	Cruisers	Destroyers
4	10	9	11	40

(plus 18 sloops, 13 frigates, 29 submarines and 33 minesweepers)

It therefore fell to Fraser, who had already fought and won the Royal Navy's last battleship-*v*-battleship action, to command the greatest concentration of seaborne striking power assembled in the Navy's history. Yet a unique concentration of circumstances – the protraction of the German war into the spring of 1945, and the early Japanese surrender in August 1945, both contrary to the original expectations of the Allied Joint Chiefs-of-Staff – made it inevitable that only a fraction of the British Pacific Fleet's eventual strength ever saw action. The Fleet was still expanding when the war ended and did not reach its maximum strength until the autumn of 1945. But even if this could have been achieved six months earlier, it would have been quite impossible for Fraser to deploy his maximum strength beside the Americans. With the patchwork logistic resources at his disposal, it was little short of miraculous that Fraser managed to deploy as big a fighting force as he did.

For the US Navy, necessity had indeed proved the mother of invention; in over three years of Pacific campaigning the Americans had developed the finest supply fleet in the world, with fast tankers and storeships custom-built for the speedy replenishment of carrier fleets at sea. But the British, whose wartime Home, Mediterranean and Eastern Fleets all operated from shore bases because of the far smaller distances involved, had never been required to amass such resources. Moreover, with a shipbuilding capacity dwarfed by that of the United States, Britain had no prospect of creating such a fleet, and because of the ravages of the U-boat war (in which tankers had always been prime targets) the British Merchant Navy had lost 54 per cent of its prewar tonnage (11,455,906 tons out of 21,215,261 tons). The tankers assembled in the Pacific to service the British Pacific Fleet were therefore old, slow, and designed for the leisurely transportation of fuels from port to port. Unlike the US Pacific Fleet Train, which went to its warships and kept up with them as required, the British Fleet Train was from start to finish the cannon-ball shackled to the British Pacific Fleet's ankle.

Fraser's first situation report to the Admiralty from Australia (December 1944) had stated that supply was easily the Fleet's greatest problem. Though a subsequent revised Admiralty estimate had allotted the British Fleet Train an ideal strength of eighteen fast tankers, only ten were actually on station at the Fleet's disposal during its Okinawa debut in March-May 1945. By VJ-Day the Fleet Train's strength in oilers (nominally all fast tankers) had risen to twenty-four, but of these only thirteen were Royal Fleet Auxiliary (RFA) vessels, and only four of the total were capable of 15 knots. The remaining 83 per cent of the supply ships carrying the British Pacific Fleet's life-blood – fuel oil – had a beggarly maximum speed of 11 knots. This was far too slow for the breathtaking fleet manoeuvres executed by Spruance and Halsey, which required the US

Fleet Train to swop from one flank of the fleet to the other, taking up widely separated replenishment areas at top speed as a matter of course. Such virtuosity was never within the British Pacific Fleet's grasp; indeed, as Commander Sheppard writes:[1]

> I particularly remember one period when the ability of the B.P.F. to take part in an air operation against Japan depended on three tankers arriving on time on the refuelling area. Every day, at the morning Staff meeting, we watched the progress of these tankers plotted on the Operations wall chart; one was coming up from the South Pacific, one from the west coast of the USA and one, I think, from Panama. They did arrive on the day, and the Fleet was refuelled, but our dependence on three ships from such widely separated and distant places illustrates the precarious nature of our supplies.

As if the limited numbers and low speeds of the ships available were not sufficient problems, the polyglot nature of the growing Fleet Train was another headache manfully surmounted by Admiral Fisher under Fraser's aegis. Whereas the American Fleet Train was naturally homogeneous, the British Fleet Train was virtually a prototype of the postwar multi-national fleets, served as it was by British, Australian, New Zealand, Dutch, Danish, Norwegian, Belgian, Lascars, Goanese, Chinese and Papuan crews. This mixture of nationalities and races produced a rich crop of supplementary problems over religion, customs and food, quite apart from the fact that each ship in the Fleet Train tended to be supplied and manned with differing articles of agreement and charter parties. A tendency by ill-informed Americans (whose merchant navy had never taken the beating suffered by the British) to express surprise that the British should deliberately saddle themselves with such additional difficulties, was another irritant to be endured and overcome.

But the logistics of the British Pacific Fleet were not furnished by the Fleet Train alone. Fraser was also making history as the first British Fleet Commander to have an RAF Transport Command Group under his command, operating what amounted to a global air service. This was No. 300 Wing (later 300 Group), established at the close of 1944 with its HQ at Melbourne to ensure close liaison with the Royal Australian Air Force. The airfields of Mascot and Camden, both of them close to the British Pacific Fleet's headquarters in Sydney, became the terminus not only for supply flights up to the Fleet at Manus and Leyte, but for the thrice-weekly service across the Pacific via New Zealand to San Diego in California, across the USA to Dorval Airport, Montreal, and across the Atlantic back to the UK. As summarised by Arthur Pearcy, historian for the immortal Dakota transport:[2]

> Great difficulty was experienced in obtaining adequate housing facilities for No. 300 Wing in Australia, but after the first six Dakotas had arrived in February 1945, accommodation was found at Camden, near Sydney, in spite of the hangars there being too small to take the aircraft. By February 26 a regular service had commenced between Sydney and Manus. . . . Subsequently this service was a daily one, and in addition a thrice-weekly service between Sydney and Perth, Western Australia, had been started, in addition to many special *ad hoc* services for the Royal Navy.
>
> Between February 26 and May 28 a total of 1,251 passengers, 117,650 lb of freight, and 383,200 lb of mail were carried between Sydney, Manus and Leyte, the total mileage flown being 90,662 miles. By this service mail could be delivered to the Fleet at Leyte in an average time of three weeks from posting in London, a very important factor in maintaining morale in the combat area. Many tons of urgent operational stores were also delivered to the Fleet without which it might have been impossible to maintain the offensive.

The latter comment was putting it mildly. When Richard Courage paid his first flying visit up to the Fleet on the eve of its departure from Manus (16–18 March) he reported back to Fraser that:[3]

> The radar stores are living a hand-to-mouth existence. One ship swaps a transformer for a couple of valves from another ship. It is vital we get some stores into the store-issuing ships. Combined Cypher Machines are giving a lot of trouble, chiefly due to extreme humidity and tropical conditions. Lieutenant Pleass who has returned with me is organizing what he can to meet the situation. It will also be necessary to inform Admiralty of their unsatisfactory performance. T.B.S. sets, on which the Fleet largely relies, are breaking down largely through unskilled operating and teething troubles. The repair teams in *Tyne* [*destroyer depot ship*] have done wonders, but we must get some more spares and sets up to the Fleet.

Courage was forced to add to Fraser's worries by reporting that the British Pacific Fleet's shore base at Manus was 'entirely dependent on American goodwill for transport and many other matters. It has been provided with a will,' he commented, 'but I think we may well see signs of "killing the goose that lays the golden egg".'[4] Two weeks later, however, Courage flew to Leyte via Guam in the Marianas to report on the British Pacific Fleet's first stint in 'Iceberg', and when he returned at the end of the first week in April the news was much more cheering:[5]

> I think the most valuable report comes from the Leading Coder who came up with me, and was therefore able to get a much more true 'Gallup Poll' impression of the effect of the arrival of the B.P.F. in the Pacific. This man Lee found everywhere he went that ordinary folk made a point of coming up to him and saying how very glad they were to have the B.P.F. fighting in the Pacific and helping them out – they liked the look of our Carriers, and thought it rather sporting to respond so quickly when we had been at it so long. Little kindnesses were showered on him. . . . The other side of the story comes from Williams who said we were not really wanted – I believe this is also Sheppard's opinion. I must say I certainly got the impression the Fleet was looked upon as a welcome and essential help rather than an unwanted guest. The difference of opinion over this matter may possibly be accounted for by the fact that the people who have formed the 'unwanted' impression have only come into contact with those desk-ridden Staff officers who have had to amend their plans because of our arrival. I personally am more than ever convinced that the Americans of the Fleet and a large part of those ashore are damn glad we are with them and rather admire us for it.

To add to these heartening impressions, the news Courage brought of the Fleet's performance was of rapid adjustment to its shortcomings and challenges. The state of affairs at Manus was much better: 'The Americans continue to be of the greatest assistance. *Formidable* was supplied at short notice with essential radio spares. S.B.N.O. [*Senior British Naval Officer*] is now self-supporting in both land and water transport – in fact he has more than he wants for his present needs.'[6]

At Guam, so far from American complaints about British inadequacy during 'Iceberg 1', Courage found that:[7]

> The thing that has really gone down with a swing is the B.P.F. adoption of American phrases. *Illustrious*'s requests for 'Life Guard' submarines, Admiral Rawlings's summaries and intentions, and the use of the word 'splashed' [for aircraft crashes in the sea]. An all-time high was reached when a message from CTF 57 (*Rawlings*) was passed by V.H.F. to the 'Life Guard' submarine for onward despatch in due course. The full details I don't know, nor do I know if it was really worth

it, but it scored ten out of ten. . . . No trouble was experienced in the Fleet with handling the American books – they still prefer the British books, but consider there are several matters which we have learnt from the Americans which must be adopted in our books.

On the debit side of the ledger, though the British Pacific Fleet's internal communications had held up well, its external communications were still 50 per cent below par; and, as expected, refuelling at sea with insufficient tankers and obsolescent equipment had taken far too long. But even here there was confidence of improved performance next time. 'The timely arrival of the fuel hose in the special Dakota,' reported Courage, 'has eased the situation. It caught the third tanker group which sailed with *Whirlwind*, *Redpole* and others [*destroyer/sloop escort*] on 4th April. I also believe R.A.F.T. [*Rear-Admiral Commanding, Fleet Train*] has borrowed some hose from American sources.'⁸ He added that Rear-Admiral Edelsten, commanding the Fleet's destroyer flotillas, 'has discovered a great friend in the U.S. Navy at Leyte, and regardless of what the official regulations may say on the subject, his destroyers will have every assistance in stores and equipment that the U.S.N. can provide. A special team of U.S. staff officers were instructed to report on board *Tyne* to take particulars.'⁹ In other words God, through the medium of American goodwill and munificence, was proving happy to help those who had showed themselves so determined to help themselves.

And this all-important latter factor represents Fraser's greatest achievement as Commander-in-Chief, British Pacific Fleet, for without spontaneous American assistance the Fleet could have achieved nothing. It went to war at the end of March 1945 dependent on American goodwill and active help in everything, from signal liaison to supply and replenishment. And it was Fraser, building on the personal contacts with Nimitz made at Pearl Harbor in December 1944, who ensured that this goodwill and help never faltered, from Nimitz down to the commanders at sea and in the American shore bases. Fraser knew how vulnerable the American benevolence would quickly become if he stayed aloof in Sydney. Without his keeping the vital personal contacts alive by frequent visits to the Americans at Guam and Leyte, the goodwill he had nurtured could swiftly falter and die – Courage's 'goose-that-lays-the-golden-egg' syndrome. It was thanks to Fraser that the British Pacific Fleet had been accepted as a probationary member of the American team for 'Iceberg'; it was largely thanks to him that the Fleet stayed that way.

Thus apart from his official burden as Commander-in-Chief, British Pacific Fleet, Fraser scored another resounding success in the parallel role of British supreme liaison officer with the US Pacific Fleet. At all times, however, he found dealing with the Americans far easier than persuading the Australian Government to take more energetic action in furnishing the British Pacific Fleet's needs. In this he was hampered by the fact that Prime Minister John Curtin was a mortally sick man, effective power being exercised by Acting Prime Minister Joseph B. Chifley. The latter replaced Curtin after Curtin's death on 5 July. But throughout May, as the men of the British Pacific Fleet struggled to keep pace with their American allies in the Okinawa battle, Fraser was obliged to deal with an Australian care-taker government lacking a chief executive with orthodox freedom of action. Though it was as vital to avoid a breach with this Labour Government as it was vital to supply the Fleet, Fraser nevertheless had no hesitation in roundly condemning the dilatory performance of the Australian labour unions. He was fully prepared to enlist Australian public goodwill towards the presence of the British Pacific Fleet in doing this, but had to walk a tight-rope between the urgency of the problem on the one hand, and the danger of putting the government in an impossible position on the other.

Fraser started by publicising the shocking fact that because of strikes, ships of the British Pacific Fleet had had to be sent out to fight without the prior completion of long-overdue repairs. This is how he notified the British Admiralty on 11 May:[10]

> Owing to waterfront disputes, it has been necessary to send ships forward foregoing docking as follows:–
> (A) *Troubridge* and *Tenacious* [destroyers] – routine dockings due.
> (B) *Newfoundland* [cruiser] – docking to complete work of stiffening plating.
> (C) *Maidstone* [submarine depot ship] routine docking which by reason of her employment was very overdue and for which another opportunity is unlikely to occur in the near future.
> Matter has been vigorously pressed with Australian Government with no practical result.
> Without mentioning names, I said at the opening of the British Centre in Sydney, on 8th May, that I had had to send ships forward improperly maintained for the causes stated, and that I did not think that people in Australia could realise that this was happening, since in every other way they had been so co-operative. Reactions on the whole have been favourable.
> I have arranged for an interview with the [Acting] Prime

Minister on Tuesday 15 May to keep him in touch with our various problems, and shall discuss this among them.

Fraser did not mince his words when he met the Australian politicians at Canberra on 15 May. He made it clear that he believed the time had come for the Australian Government to state plainly whether or not it was capable of fulfilling its commitment to support the British Pacific Fleet. Fraser was asking for frankness and for immediate action, overlooking the fact that neither forms part of the normal stock-in-trade of politicians. Chifley and his colleagues were left in no doubt that Fraser meant what he said about making the problem a public issue, and if necessary asking for a uniformed work force to be sent out from the UK. Not satisfied with the good intentions expressed on the 15th, Fraser kept up the pressure over the next week. The upshot was that on the 23rd Chifley's Government cabled the British Foreign Office to protest that the British Pacific Fleet's needs were fully appreciated and that the Australian Government was doing all it could. This in turn prompted a sharp Admiralty signal to Fraser, asking what he was up to. His crisp *résumé* of the facts on the 31st included the all-important news that his initiative (having prompted emergency meetings between government representatives and union bosses) had achieved its aim:[11]

Background briefly as follows.

There were a number of questions affecting the British Pacific Fleet within Australia which had been raised through the usual channels, but which were not progressing. So as to expedite progress by bringing them to a higher level, I wrote to Mr Curtin asking him if he would see me and enclosing an 'aide memoire' of the matters which I wished to discuss.

The meeting took place on the 15th May at Canberra with Mr Chifley, Acting Prime Minister during the sickness of Mr Curtin. Several members of the Cabinet were present.

No new requirements were put forward and the following were the chief subjects discussed:—

(a) *Provision of R.A.A.F. Pilots for Royal Navy.*
(b) Development of airfield at Sydney [Mascot] for use by Transport aircraft.
(c) Provision of additional airfields for Fleet Air Arm.
(d) Strikes: in my 'aide memoire' I mentioned that the strikes at Sydney were affecting the loading and repair of ships. See my 110306 May [*quoted above*]. Between my writing to the Prime Minister and the meeting, further strikes developed at Sydney and the subject naturally became of immediate practical importance.

Since the meeting a large number have gone back to work [Author's italics].

(e) Man Power:

A request for additional man power to complete the R.N. Programme was considered to be extremely difficult. I therefore made it clear that the Australian Government must come into the open and decide whether or not they could support the British Pacific Fleet. If not, then they must either provide more Australian man power or ask for men from United Kingdom. The Acting Prime Minister agreed to go into the matter with Vice-Admiral (Q) and decide on the course of action.

Apart from the fact that it got him what he most wanted – the unplugging of the dockyard labour bottleneck – this episode shows Fraser's invaluable talent for getting on with people, even politicians. At all times his personal credo was plain speaking delivered with courtesy and persistence. This had stood him in good stead when dealing with the ministers of Churchill's War Cabinet when Controller, in 1940–2. In 1945 it prevented his dealings with the Australian Government from developing the counter-productive taint of mutual antagonism, hostility and resentment, which could easily have set in if the British Pacific Fleet had had a more abrasive Commander-in-Chief. As it was, direct access to the Acting Prime Minister at any time over any problem, actual or potential, was cordially offered, and Fraser readily accepted that the government must not be pressurised by direct appeals to the Australian people. Both parties emerged from the exchanges of May 1945 with a relationship strengthened by heightened mutual regard.

Fraser's complete lack of political guile showed through on the visit to Canberra when, driving through the capital, he lost his way and stopped to ask directions from a gentleman walking his dog. The gentleman turned out to be Opposition leader Sir Robert Menzies, who recognised Fraser instantly and offered his services as guide. 'I said to Menzies, "I'm not sure whether I ought to have a former Prime Minister as my guide!", and he said, "Oh, well – I'm unemployed at present." '[12] But as Captain Merry recalls while this cheery exchange was taking place,[13]

'I sat there in the front, *willing* the C-in-C not to ask him in, but in vain. I knew that with these Government talks going on, all hell could break loose if word got out that he'd been seen hobnobbing in private with the Leader of the Opposition. But that was Fraser for you: it never even crossed his mind. Luckily, nothing came of it, either.'

But despite Fraser's successful maintenance of an amicable working relationship with the Australian Government, nothing could reduce the fundamental problem to manageable proportions. In this summer of 1945 Australia could not afford the massive outlay of money, manpower and material to create the extensive land, sea, and air facilities required for the British Pacific Fleet. And in the United Kingdom there was even less political will to find a way round the problem than there was in Australia. By June and July 1945, the refusal of Attlee's Labour Party to extend the wartime Coalition until the defeat of Japan had precipitated the first General Election since 1935. From Fraser's point of view it was enough to try the patience of a saint: no sooner had the Australian political scene clarified with Curtin's death and formal replacement by Chifley than the British political scene clouded over with the General Election campaign. As if this were not enough, the Election coincided with the vital Potsdam Conference (17 July–August 2), at which haggling over Europe's postwar frontiers came in an easy winner over the tactical difficulties of beating Japan. Thus by the second half of July Fraser was putting his case against a background of political distraction in Britain, where no major decisions were going to be taken until after the Election.

Nor was Election fever solely to blame. The Potsdam Conference had not got fairly down to business when Churchill and Truman heard that the first atomic explosion had been successfully accomplished at Alamogordo in New Mexico. That was on 17 July, the day Rawlings's British Pacific Fleet joined Halsey's 3rd Fleet as Task Force 37. As shown above (p.266) the British Pacific Fleet had sailed for the opening phase of 'Olympic' weaker in battleships and carriers, despite considerable interim reinforcement, than it had been in March. Unaware of the impending decision to use atomic weapons against Japan, determined that the British Pacific Fleet's precarious logistic base should hold up throughout 'Olympic', Fraser spent the last fortnight of July doggedly urging a new compromise between the British and Australian Governments. He now proposed the redeployment of 3,000 Royal Marine Engineers (RMEs) to British Pacific Fleet construction works in Australia, which would appreciably help the Australians in their current manpower crisis. At the same time he besought the British Government to help by making a token gift of building materials to Australia, deploring proposals to make such assistance a straight commercial transaction for which Australia must pay. 'If a gift of say 1 cargo of timber and 1 cargo of corrugated iron could be made to the Australian Government now,' he signalled on 29 July, 'I feel it would make all the difference.'[14]

As a Fleet Commander immediately responsible to the Admiralty, Fraser was therefore immersed during these thankless weeks in dealings far more appropriate to a trade secretary or ambassador extraordinary than to an admiral with a fleet to command and a war to fight. No other British Commander-in-Chief of the Second World War was ever dropped into such a political morass and left to find his own way out, with no other 'navigational aids' than his own reserves of pragmatism, persistence, and unshakable faith in the right and decent thing to do. One of the first decisions of Attlee's Labour Government, triumphantly returned to power on 26 July with a record overall majority of 146 seats, was to reject Fraser's plea for a cargo of timber and a cargo of corrugated iron 'in view of acute housing problem here [in the UK] and shortage of materials.'[15]

His one consolation was the superb performance of the British Pacific Fleet during the first phase of 'Olympic'. Though deliberately assigned non-naval targets in the Japanese homeland by Halsey, the Fleet had nevertheless got in its first blow against the Tokyo district on 17 July and had gone on to sink three Japanese frigates, also damaging a Japanese escort carrier. Meanwhile, far to the south, the British X-craft spurned by the Americans had demonstrated their versatility by sinking the cruiser *Takao* at Singapore and cutting the submarine cables between Singapore, Saigon and Hong Kong. By 3 August the British Pacific Fleet had completed replenishment despite delays imposed by bad weather and was ready for another week's operations with the 3rd Fleet; but the weather was still imposing a suspension of operations on the fateful 6 August, when the first atomic bomb burst over Hiroshima.

The date of the Hiroshima attack found Fraser visiting Nimitz at Guam. *Duke of York* had arrived at Sydney in the first week of July and Fraser had sailed in her for Guam via Manus on the 31st. His immediate duty on this visit was the pleasant task of investing Nimitz with the Order of the Bath, the ceremony being followed with due celebrations aboard the British flagship and a typical Fraser 'leg-pull':[16]

'When Nimitz wanted to leave after the investiture, he said, "Can I have a barge now?" I said, "No, you've got to taste a bit of grog out of our grog-tub." So he did that; then he said, "Can I have my barge now?", and I said, "No, you've got to visit the Wardroom, I'm afraid, and have a drink there." And when we'd visited the Wardroom, he said, "Can I have my barge now?" and I said, "No, I'm sorry, you've got to come down to the Gunroom." And after the visit to the Gunroom he said, "Can I have my barge *now*?" – getting a little bit heated – but I said, "No, you've got to visit the Warrant Officers' Mess". . . . We went through the lot, and finally, quite red-faced, he went over the side. He never forgave me for that, he said – a wonderful man.'

Also at Guam was General Carl Spaatz, Supreme Commander of the US Strategic Bombing Forces in the Pacific. It was from Nimitz and Spaatz that Fraser was made party to the biggest Allied secret of the war, and, with a necessarily baffled Vernon Merry, was roused early on the 6th to watch a lone B-29 take off for Hiroshima.

The Hiroshima raid, the Soviet invasion of Japanese-held Manchuria two days later and the Nagasaki raid on the 9th were followed with stunning speed by Japan's suing for peace. Rawlings's British Pacific Fleet had been due to retire to Sydney on the 10th, but Halsey readily agreed that a token British task force should remain with the US 3rd Fleet to receive Japan's formal surrender. On Fraser's orders this force consisted of *King George V*, *Indefatigable*, two cruisers and ten destroyers; he himself set off from Guam to join Rawlings in *Duke of York*. In the last tense five days before the surrender *Indefatigable* carried out two final strikes, as Halsey kept up the pressure on Japan until his immortal signal:

C-in-C 3rd Fleet to 3rd Fleet Pacific
THE WAR WITH JAPAN WILL END AT 1200 ON 15TH
AUGUST. IT IS LIKELY THAT KAMIKAZES WILL
ATTACK THE FLEET AFTER THIS TIME AS A FINAL
FLING. ANY EX-ENEMY AIRCRAFT ATTACKING THE
FLEET IS TO BE SHOT DOWN IN A FRIENDLY
MANNER.

Duke of York joined the 3rd Fleet and the British Pacific Fleet on the 16th, Fraser's first act being to visit Halsey aboard his flagship USS *Missouri* and present him with the KBE. When Halsey's armada surged into Tokyo Bay on 27 August, *Duke of York* anchored close astern of *King George V*. Three years and ten days after the Americans had launched their Pacific counter-offensive with the landings on Guadalcanal, the men of the US Pacific Fleet watched the sun set over Mount Fujiyama with their British allies at their side. Against all expectations less than six months before, the mission of Fraser and the British Pacific Fleet was thus triumphantly accomplished.

Ponderously directed by General MacArthur, the Japanese made their formal surrender aboard USS *Missouri* on the morning of 2

September 1945. If the stage-management was American the central furniture 'props' were British, the signatories using chairs from *Duke of York*. Fraser signed for the United Kingdom, the proudest moment of his life; and none of the dignity of the occasion could suppress the grin of honest gratification as he did so. Among his most treasured possessions in later life was one of the six copies of the surrender instrument and a copy of the 'Mighty Mo's' deck log for that historic morning, the latter autographed 'with warmest regards and best wishes' from his friend and colleague Nimitz:[17]

> 0856, Japanese representatives came aboard. At 0902 the ceremony commenced and the 'Instrument of Surrender' was presented to all parties. 0904, Mamoru Shigemitsu, Japanese Foreign Minister, signed for Japan. 0906, General Yoshijiro Umezu, Chief of Staff, Japanese Army Headquarters, signed for Japan. 0908, General of the Army Douglas Mac Arthur [*sic*], the Supreme Commander for the Allied Powers, signed for all nations. 0912, Fleet Admiral C. W. Nimitz signed for the United States. 0913, General Hsu Yung-Chang signed for China. 0914, Admiral Sir Bruce Fraser signed for the United Kingdom. 0916, Lt. General Kuzma Nikolaevish Derevyanko signed for the United Soviet Socialist Republic. 0917, General Sir Thomas Blamey signed for Australia. 0918, Colonel L. Moore Cosgrave signed for Canada. 0920, General LeClerc signed for France. 0921, Admiral Helfrich signed for the Netherlands. 0922, Air Vice Marshall Isitt signed for New Zealand. 0925, ceremony completed. 0926, U.S.S. TAYLOR (DD468) came alongside to port to embark correspondents and photographers. 0929, Japanese representatives left the ship. 0940, U.S.S. NICHOLAS (DD449) came alongside to port to embark General of the Army Douglas MacArthur. 0958, General of the Army Douglas MacArthur left the ship and his personal flag was hauled down. 1003, U.S.S. NICHOLAS cast off. 1005, U.S.S. BUCHANAN (DD484) came alongside to port to embark allied representatives. 1027, U.S.S. BUCHANAN cast off. 1044, Fleet Admiral C. W. Nimitz left the ship. 1052, secured the crew from quarters. 1059, CincPac's flag was broken in the U.S.S. SOUTH DAKOTA (BB57). Hauled down Cincpac's flag; broke flag of Commander Third Fleet.

Though the Americans naturally dominated the impressive massed fly-past which followed the surrender ceremony, the British had the last word on 2 September with a special 'Fraser Sunset' parade which left some very high-ranking American officers unashamedly in tears. Despite MacArthur's attempts to retrieve all the pens used in the signing of the surrender for an all-American distribution, Fraser managed to keep his. Apart from its obvious souvenir value there was a special letter he wanted to write with it, which earned a special reply:[18]

SECRET
PERSONAL TO BE DECYPHERED BY AN OFFICER
SPECIALLY DETAILED BY YOU
PRIVATE FROM MR CHURCHILL
TO ADMIRAL FRASER
Begins
>I am most grateful to you for your very kind letter of September 5th written on the date and with the pen of the unconditional surrender of JAPAN. Your work during the war has always commanded my highest respect and admiration.
>Not once or twice in our rough island story
>The path of duty was the path of glory [*sic*]

Ends.

· 23 ·

'Thank you, Australia'
[September 1945-June 1946]

The defeat of Japan was by no means the end of the road for the British Pacific Fleet. It had always been as much a political weapon as a naval one, the political aim being nothing less than the speedy restoration of British colonial power in the Far East. But the Fleet's political role was matched by a no less urgent humanitarian one. After Japan's surrender the Allied navies in the Pacific, with their logistic air forces, were the only instruments whereby millions could be reprieved from the ravages of disease and starvation. Great though the problems of peace had been after the Armistice in November 1918, they were dwarfed by those of September 1945.

Amid the swarming difficulties of keeping the British Pacific Fleet at sea, Fraser's efforts to concentrate on the primary aim of defeating Japan had earned him reproof from his masters in Whitehall. 'You appear to consider a short term policy the most advisable,' Cunningham had written to Fraser on 5 July,[1]

> bringing the greatest force possible to bear during OLYMPIC and CORONET but not really taking much thought for the morrow after these operations. We, on the other hand, while fully agreeing with your views about bringing the greatest force possible to bear in the two operational periods, can find no evidence either in Washington or London which leads us to conclude that all will be over as far as the British Pacific Fleet is concerned even if CORONET went according to plan and met with the fullest success.

When the 'Coronet' invasion of Japan was rendered unnecessary by the epoch-making events of 6-10 August, the unconditional surrender of Japan at American dictation was to be only the prelude. Mountbatten in South-East Asia and Fraser in the Pacific were ordered not to waste an hour in restoring British 'face' by procuring the surrender of Singapore and Hong Kong to British forces. In 1941-2 the Japanese had dealt such shattering blows to British prestige east of Suez that in August and September 1945 far more importance was attached to the liberation of Singapore and Hong Kong than had been the case with the British Channel Islands back in April and May.

On 13 August the Admiralty informed Fraser that the reoccupation of Hong Kong must be his first priority after the Japanese surrender. This was inhibited by MacArthur's order that no preliminary landings were to be made on Japanese-held territory until the instrument of Japan's unconditional surrender had been signed; Chiang Kai-shek's vacillating approval also had to be solicited. The delay gave Fraser time to arrange a special force for Hong Kong. Had the Japanese war continued, Rear-Admiral C. H. J. Harcourt's light carrier task force (*Vengeance*, *Venerable*, *Glory* and *Colossus*) would have moved up from Australia to reinforce the British Pacific Fleet. Fraser now ordered Harcourt (27 August) to proceed to Hong Kong with the cruiser *Euryalus*, auxiliary AA ship *Prince Robert* and flotilla craft. This force entered Hong Kong harbour without incident on 30 August and the Japanese surrender of the colony was signed on 16 September with Harcourt, in his new capacity as Commander-in-Chief, Hong Kong and Head of Administration, signing for both Britain and China. Fraser attended the ceremony, but merely as an observer.

Meanwhile Lord Mountbatten had received the surrender of Singapore on the 12th; and six days before that the 140,000-odd by-passed Japanese troops still holding out in the Australian dependencies (New Guinea, the Solomons and the Bismarcks) had surrendered to General Sturdee of the Australian Army. The latter event was one of the happiest instances of ready collaboration between the British Pacific Fleet and the Australian Government, which had asked Fraser to provide a suitable warship. Fraser obliged by detaching the light fleet carrier *Glory* and two sloops, General Sturdee receiving the Japanese surrender aboard *Glory* at Rabaul on 6 September.

Thus by the middle of September 1945 Mountbatten and Fraser had carried out their orders and the Union Jack again flew over Singapore and Hong Kong, the brightest luminaries of the British Empire in the Far East. But this was a paltry task compared with the immense humanitarian labour which now confronted the two commanders-in-chief: repatriating former British prisoners-of-war and succouring the populations of the liberated territories. In this Fraser certainly had the easiest share, for Mountbatten's SEAC area had been expanded to include Indo-China. This meant that until the

THE BRITISH PACIFIC FLEET, 1944–6

Dutch and French colonial authorities could take over, Mountbatten had the colossal job of acting as caretaker in Indo-China as well as in the East Indies. He was also saddled with the administrative support of Hong Kong, although the latter was kept in Fraser's sphere of command. Mountbatten never really forgave the Admiralty for this. But the situation was made far more tolerable than it might have been by the readiness and courtesy of Fraser's collaboration, which Mountbatten was to acknowledge in a special note of thanks on Lord Fraser's 90th birthday (see below, pp.337–8).

For the British Pacific Fleet the prisoner-of-war problem had raised its head as soon as the Fleet arrived off the Japanese coast in the last week of August. Almost crazy with joy at seeing HM Ships lying offshore, scores of wasted prisoners had struggled out to the Fleet, some commandeering boats, the stronger even swimming. 'It was deeply moving; they came on board in scraps of uniform they'd managed to keep, many weeping, some even kissing the deck.'[2] In nearly every case prompt medical treatment was essential, followed by a spell in rehabilitation centres before ships could be found for the long voyage home. In this task the supply net of No. 300 Group proved invaluable for airlifting Red Cross medical aid from the UK.

As the merchant shipping crisis was as bad as ever, Fraser's solution was to use the carriers of the British Pacific Fleet for the repatriation of ex-POWs. As most of the camps had been situated in Malaya and Siam, the result was an improvised repatriation-route from South-East Asia across the Pacific to Vancouver, the men then being transferred to the Atlantic coast by special trains. So effective were the measures contrived by Fraser in collaboration with Mountbatten that as early as 6 October Cunningham was writing approvingly that:[3]

> The prisoner of war situation appears to be clearing up and I cordially agree with the use of the carriers to carry them about. We are going to turn Victorious round quickly and use her and two light fleets for trooping; also we hope to have 6 [escort carriers] and 2 more 8″ cruisers in the trooping fleet in a few weeks.

The laborious repatriation of the ex-POWs – some 127,000 of them from the SEAC area alone – naturally took precedence over the return of servicemen scheduled for early demobilisation to relieve the acute manpower crisis in the UK. 'The pressure to bring home men is intense,' added Cunningham in his letter of 6 October, 'but the personnel lift just does not exist to keep up with political desires, so we are doing all we can to lift our own and leave the liners for the Army and R.A.F.'[4]

Despite these successes in these trying weeks, Fraser also met with what he always considered a major setback. This was his failure to persuade the Admiralty that the postwar Royal Navy must preserve as much as possible of the close wartime bond established with the US Navy. It was only to be expected that the dwindling peacetime British Pacific Fleet would be brought (in Cunningham's own words) 'out from under' the US Pacific Fleet at the earliest opportunity. The wartime standardisation of equipment, most notably with aircraft, was also bound to change. But, urged Fraser in a deeply-felt signal to the Admiralty:[5]

> I am sure that you fully appreciate that the lessons learnt during the time the BPF has used USN signal systems and doctrines must not be forgotten but in view of their importance to the future of the Navy I make the following observations.
> The British Signal Publications must be rewritten to incorporate the best US doctrines and methods and this must be started now and finished by the end of 1946.
> The committee to undertake this should be presided over by an Officer who has had combat experience with the US Fleet and contain a proportion of signal officers with the same experience. If you agree, I would suggest a president from this Fleet and would regard the matter of sufficient importance to justify asking for him to be relieved in his present appointment.

Cunningham, however, would have none of it. 'Delay of re-embarkation of Brit. Signal Books cannot be accepted,' was the Admiralty's cold reply. 'Transferring to British Signal Publications.'[6] The ungracious speed with which the British Pacific Fleet resumed British signalling practice was a churlish treatment of the lessons of the past eight months. Moreover, though the peacetime CINCPAC offered the British a permanent liaison officer's berth with the US Pacific Fleet, this invaluable post was allowed to lapse within weeks of Le Fanu's relief in early December. In the immediate aftermath of the war, Fraser was the only senior British admiral to sense intuitively that the future of his Service would best be served by the closest possible alignment with the development of the US Navy. Though by a unique stroke of fortune he would get the chance to do what he could when he finally became First Sea Lord in 1948, many invaluable opportunities had been lost for ever over the preceding three years.

Before returning to Australia after the Japanese surrender, Fraser visited both Tokyo and Hong Kong. His Intelligence Officer, Commander Sheppard, had years of prewar service experience in the Far East and was to remain in Tokyo as British Naval Liaison Officer to MacArthur. Sheppard was guide to Fraser's small party which drove up to Tokyo on 5 September. As Captain Merry recalls: 'It was creepy. There we were, only six of us, and *hundreds* of able-bodied Japanese soldiers all over the place. They could have massacred us with ease if they'd a mind to. And then our car broke down. But Sheppard was marvellous: he bellowed orders at the nearest Jap soldiers and they all fell in behind to give us a push.'[7] Sheppard took Fraser to the British Embassy, which had been excellently preserved through the war years by the Swiss. The visitors' book still lay on the hall table, the last entry dated 5 December 1941. Fraser symbolically reopened the book on a clean sheet, signing with the rest of the party.

The visit to Hong Kong a few days later was attended by an unpleasant incident to which Fraser reacted in typical fashion. There was, unhappily, a feeling in the British Pacific Fleet that *Duke of York*'s belated arrival in Tokyo Bay for the surrender had poached on honours which should have been reserved for *King George V* and her consorts, which had done all the fighting. Perhaps this might have been mitigated if Fraser had given Rawlings any other flagship than *King George V*, for there was undeniable hostility between the 'KG Five' and the 'Duke' which had been known to result in brawls when men of the two ships' companies met ashore; this animosity dated back to Home Fleet days at Scapa. Though Fraser was a widely respected and loved Commander-in-Chief, this resentment towards his flagship was shared by other units of the British Pacific Fleet, and when the *Duke of York* passed the cruiser *Euryalus* on entering Hong Kong harbour the flagship was booed.

Vernon Merry's friend John Uniacke (later Colonel J. A. C. Uniacke, RM) had served in *Duke of York* with the Home Fleet. As commander of the Royal Marine Detachment from *Euryalus* at Hong Kong, he saw Fraser's reaction at close quarters:[8]

> The Admiral took it that these remarks [the booing] had been directed at him personally and was furious, as I learned when I called on *Duke of York* that evening. I took care to make the point to Vernon Merry that the RM Detachment was ashore and had not been involved in the incident.
>
> The following Sunday was to be *Euryalus'* last in Hong Kong before she went down to Sydney for leave, and when I re-embarked on the Saturday with the Detachment we learned that the C-in-C was to inspect the ship on the next day before deciding whether the conduct of the ships' company had been such that the ship's departure was to be delayed or even cancelled. On his arrival on board the Admiral was greeted by a

Guard of Honour from the Detachment, and the only remark he passed to me was to comment that my newly grown moustache made me look older. This was his way of letting me know that he knew that the Marines had not been involved in the incident, for he really waded in to the sailors, and only just relented sufficiently to let the ship proceed to Sydney as planned. I think this illustrates Lord Fraser's ability to communicate with the young and junior.

Some 18 months afterwards I met him in London at Vernon Merry's wedding. He told me, with relish, that when he had visited Gibraltar a few months beforehand, *Euryalus* had entered harbour on her way back to the UK from the Far East. 'And she didn't boo me this time, Uniacke,' was his final comment.

Though he never made a major issue of the fact, Fraser could certainly have coped more easily with this tension in the Fleet if he had had more effective support from Admirals Rawlings and Vian. The two officers did not get on, and Fraser had to blend tact and firmness in replying to the confidential letters each was wont to send him about the other. Fraser had nothing but praise for Rawlings's handling of the British Pacific Fleet since March, but the experience had left Rawlings very tired and under strain. Of Vian, Lord Fraser commented briefly to the author that 'he could be a very difficult fellow to deal with, really, but charming when you got to know him. He was frightfully good – a great admiral.'[9] But by the end of September 1945 Fraser was obliged to mention his difficulties to a sympathetic Cunningham at the Admiralty. 'I am not clear,' wrote Cunningham in a longhand postscript to his letter to Fraser of 6 October,[10]

> if Rawlings is just tired. His family have been a bit worried about the tone of his letters. He will anyway get a good rest when he returns, there is nothing for him at present. Later there will be C in C South Africa – West Indies or he might go to Chatham. What do you think?
> Why don't you like Vian as No 2?

The situation was soon eased by Vian succeeding Rawlings as second-in-command, Rawlings returning to the UK for a well-earned rest. And when Fraser himself came home six months later, Rawlings was the first to greet him and, in a heart-to-heart talk, make full amends by apologising to Fraser for not having made his job easier in the Pacific. It was a generous gesture, a happy ending for which Fraser was deeply appreciative.

October and November 1945 were crammed with preparations for the British Pacific Fleet's scheduled transfer of base from Sydney to Hong Kong. Fraser's earlier difficulties with the Australian Government were forgotten in the round of official and unofficial farewells, voicing the Fleet's gratitude for the boundless Australian hospitality over the past months. The replies to Fraser's letters of thanks amounted to a stream of testimonials for the man and his Fleet. Journalists, for instance, are not generally renowned for sentimentality, but this was how the President of the New South Wales Institute of Journalists wrote to Fraser on 16 November:[11]

> We are most anxious, before you leave Sydney, for an opportunity to express to you our feelings after this, the most notable visit ever paid by the Royal Navy to Australia; to let you know our appreciation of the attitude of yourself & of all under you while in our country; but especially to tell you publicly that though in wealth, material force, & military power the old country comes out of this war no longer first among the nations, yet in the admiration, affection & pride of her daughter nations she has certainly never stood so high at any time in our history.

The Managing Director of the Cockatoo Docks wrote that: 'The uniform courtesy that we have received from the officers and men under your command in all classes of ships that we have taken care of has made it a pleasure for this dockyard to carry out the various types of work entrusted to its care.' The Secretary of the British Centre added that: 'it has been a pleasure to work for the men under your command. They have been a credit first to you as their Commander, and to the Country they represent.' The Sydney Commissioner of Police assured Fraser that: 'at all times, it was the aim of the Police Authorities of this State to afford the maximum co-operation and assistance to the British Navy personnel, and the fact that this was successfully accomplished is largely due to the splendid bearing and orderly conduct of the men under your command.' The Federal Administrator of the Australian Comforts Fund affirmed that: 'The presence of the Navy in our waters gave us all new heart. The boys at all times conducted themselves in such a manner as to receive the approbation of all members of the community. We have all taken them into our homes and by this means have created friendships which we think will last for all time. . .the presence of the Fleet in these waters has created a feeling of friendship and understanding, the result of which can never be truly measured.'[12]

Though carefully drafted and re-drafted, Fraser's own farewell to Australia came straight from the heart:[13]

In a few days I shall be leaving Australia for Hong Kong. Many of my ships will be coming back to Australia at intervals, but for many of us it is farewell for the time being.

In a Naval life one should get accustomed to farewells, but in my experience from a Midshipman, aged 15, to an Admiral it is always a very sad occasion when parting with friends whom one has grown to know so well.

One stands on the ship's deck watching the hawsers cast off, the waving handkerchiefs growing smaller and smaller and then at last ship and shore fade in the distance, but just the sky and sea with us. The memories will not fade, we hope it will be the same with you.

We sailors may be happy-go-lucky people by reputation and to a point it is probably true. The long periods at sea battling with the elements, and the somewhat brief spells on shore all make for a natural inclination to get the best out of life when opportunity offers. But deep down, sailors are the most sentimental people on earth, and they will always have the deepest appreciation for the little things which count, the friendships, the kindnesses, the laughs, and in these ways how wonderfully Australia has shown the genuineness of her welcome. . .

As Commander-in-Chief, much of one's time is taken up with official duties and functions where, under the scrutiny of many thousands of eyes, one's personal fancies must be sacrificed for what one represents. One's uniform inevitably makes one conspicuous and one cannot wander freely about. But in Australia I have occasionally managed to slip into a civilian suit and mix for a time unknown amongst you and see some of your character.

In such a manner I walked to a little Newsreel Theatre in Kings Cross and took my place in the queue. A long one, and it seemed doubtful if I should get in. Presently I was joined by a young Australian pilot and we started talking about Australia; then we talked of England – I suppose he had discovered by that time that I was a 'Pommie', although I don't know how! Then he started to look at me rather intently and I knew my number was up. For he said, 'I believe you are Admiral Fraser', and I said, 'Yes'. He then said, 'But sir, you should not be standing here, let me take you straight in past the queue.' I said, 'I don't think I can do that. They might take me for an arrogant Englishman!' He thought a moment and said, 'Sir, I would like to pay for your seat.' The value of the gift was a shilling, the value of the thought and deed was, to me, infinite. Then he said, 'Could you help me to join the Fleet Air Arm?' which thrilled me even more. Today there are 20 Australian pilots serving in my carriers, and there would have been many more if the war had not ceased. . .

This has been a year of much anxiety to me. I knew that the Fleet would distinguish itself in whatever activity it was engaged, but with the vast distances involved, should we be able to supply them, give them the provisions, replace casualties, get up the mail to them – and it is these human things which are so important. With the co-operation of the Australian people and the Americans, we just managed it with the barest margin. We got through with very few casualties, but let no one ever forget that for the men at sea it was a tough war, and I am very proud of them.

Since the peace, the human side becomes even more complicated, the compassionate cases to deal with, the demobilisation, the resettling in civil life. At the same time the work of the Navy, which never ceases, must go on. In these difficulties, in a world still unsettled with many internal conflicts, let us remain cool, calm and collected, whatever disappointments or setbacks we may have. The stabilising influence of the British Commonwealth of Nations is very great – we must keep strife and suspicion away from our doors, and preserve that integrity on which the world so much relies. . .

And now the year draws to a close. I feel more and more convinced, as time goes by, that the ties which have been cemented in Australia between you and us, will never be severed however many thousands of miles we are away.

For our part we are deeply conscious of the great work of the Australian Navy, and of the gallantry of the Australian Army and Air Force. From the days of ANZAC, we shall always remember them. We are sincerely grateful to you for the homes you have thrown open to us, and in which you have made us feel one of the family.

There is a favourite tune of mine, of which many of us will be wistfully thinking, should we again head towards Australia – 'I'll be seeing you in all the old familiar places'; and finally we shall ever remember what you have done for us, the Voluntary Workers who have given their services for so long, the Australian Comforts and Red Cross organisations, the British Centre and Anzac Buffet, the food gifts for Britain, and many others.

For all these things, for all your good wishes, for all your kindnesses, thank you so much Australia.

Fraser's arrival in Hong Kong coincided with a letter from the Prime Minister, asking for his name to be included in 'a short list of outstanding war leaders for Peerages in the New Year list'. Attlee wrote that, 'It would be a special satisfaction to me to include in this list your name for the honour of a Barony in recognition of the notable contribution you have made to the winning of the war.'[14] When it came to choosing a name for his peerage Fraser decided, after much hesitation, to name his barony after 'his' battle: North Cape. As Cunningham and Tovey both chose the names of their homes, this made Fraser the last upholder of a Service tradition followed by ennobled British admirals since the time of St Vincent and Nelson.

But the new peerage was still *sub rosa* at Christmas 1945, which Fraser spent with his men in Hong Kong. The first peacetime Christmas for seven years was particularly emotive for the thousands of men and women serving with the British Pacific Fleet on the wrong side of the world from home. At this uniquely family time the 'Fraser touch' was very much in evidence in the surrogate role of *paterfamilias*; and it left signalmen Geoff Race and Gerry Penn with an unforgettable Christmas memory:[15]

I served under Lord Fraser when he was C-in-C, B.P.F. in 1944–45. I was serving in *King George V* at the time, and I can remember the deep respect and affection we had for this indomitable man. However, it was after the war, when serving in HMS *Moon*, an Algerine minesweeper, that I had the opportunity of actually meeting him.

Sir Bruce was aboard his flagship *Duke of York*, lying in Hong Kong on Christmas Day 1945. *Moon* and another sweeper were lying alongside *Duke of York*, dwarfed by her size: we only weighed about 1/45 her weight! On Xmas morning Sir Bruce came aboard *Moon* and visited our Mess, wishing us all the festive greetings – we were all bucked at seeing him at close quarters. The next night I went ashore with a signalman 'oppo' of mine, Gerry Penn, and we decided to go up to the Fleet Club for a drink. On entering the bar we were surprised to see Sir Bruce, surrounded by his Staff officers.

Turning to Gerry, I suggested it would be a nice gesture to ask the C-in-C if he'd have a drink with us. Gerry was horrified, muttering something about 'You can't just go up like that.' I replied, 'We'll never know if we don't try,' and approached Sir Bruce, followed by one terrified signalman. He turned towards us as we arrived and smiled. I greeted him by saying, 'Good evening, sir, may I ask you a question?' 'By all means,' he replied. I introduced myself and Gerry as ratings off the minesweeper alongside the flagship and asked whether we might buy him a drink.

'Thank you, I'd like that; a small beer, please.'

'With respect, sir, we'd like to buy you a large Scotch.'

He laughed and accepted it, and we then spent a pleasant ten minutes answering his questions on what ships we had both served in, etc.; then he bought us both a drink. On our return to the ship with a memory of meeting a very great man who had great humanity, none of our shipmates would believe the story until Gerry confirmed it.

When I next wrote home I told my mother of the meeting and his kindness to us. To my astonishment, Mother wrote in her next letter that *she* had written to *him*; and in due course a further letter from her informed that she had had the following reply from Sir Bruce.

Commander-in-Chief,
British Pacific Fleet
8th February 1946

Dear Mrs Race,

Thank you very much for your very nice letter of 16th January, which I greatly appreciated.

I enjoyed hearing from the mother of one of my sailors. I am very proud of the way they behave in these difficult times.

Yours sincerely,
Bruce Fraser

And that, in a nutshell, was the sort of commander Fraser was: a Commander-in-Chief whose men felt impelled to walk up and buy him a drink, not a small beer either, but a large Scotch. His men looked up to him without the crick in the neck required for other wartime heroes, no less senior, famous or respected, but far more Olympian. Natural, unforced, irresistible, it was – for an officer of Fraser's seniority in any of the three services – a very rare attribute indeed.

With the New Year came the announcement of Fraser's peerage and another flood of congratulatory mail. 'My dear Ali Baba,' wrote Lord Beaverbrook, 'I rejoice at the news that they have made you a baron. And the country rejoices as well at this public recognition of the part you played as an architect of victory. I am bound to tell you also that my pleasure is increased by the thought that we shall in future be colleagues in the House of Lords. For you will add fire and vigour to that assembly even as you have done to the Navy.' In his reply to Beaverbrook Fraser, keeping alive the old joke, wrote that: 'it is going to be a great pleasure to join you and all the other Lords, though I hope I shall not arrive there with the reputation of a Robber Baron!' And a former colleague of the 'boilermakers', General 'Tim' Pile, wrote affectionately, 'My dear Bruce, I was delighted to read of your elevation to the Peerage. God Help the House of Lords! Best wishes to you, and many congratulations on all you have done in this war.'[16]

Fraser's last five months with the British Pacific Fleet based on Hong Kong, saw him revert to the quasi-diplomatic role in which he had excelled in Australia. His task now was to help restore British influence and prestige in China to its prewar status. To a large extent, of course, this was another 'mission impossible' after the upheavals of the past decade. Postwar China, unlike postwar Germany or Japan, had not been reduced to exhausted acquiescence by the end of the war. It was clear that Chiang Kai-shek's Nationalists, for whom the United States and not Britain had been both paymaster and quartermaster in the war with Japan, were now spoiling for a showdown with Mao tse-Tung's Communists. In December 1945 President Truman had sent General George C. Marshall to China, hopefully to negotiate a settlement between Chiang and Mao. Without distracting from these negotiations, Fraser's task was to assist the restoration of British diplomatic representation in China, at the same time demonstrating, by showing the Flag along the China coast, that the British were returning to China by virtue of having shared in the defeat of China's major enemy Japan.

With the British Pacific Fleet already a shadow of its strength on VJ-Day and continuing to diminish weekly as demobilisation ran its course, Fraser was lucky in that the full fury of the Chinese civil war did not break out until after he had left for home. A Nationalist-Communist truce was negotiated on 10 January 1946 and lasted until 14 April; during the subsequent outbreak of hostilities the Nationalist capital was moved from Chungking to Nanking before another uneasy truce was established, this one lasting from 12 May to 30 June. After three months of local cruises and visits while life in the Crown Colony of Hong Kong began to struggle back towards normal, Fraser embarked on a month's cruise (15 April-18 May) to Shanghai, Chinwangtao and up the Yangtse to Nanking, where he conferred with General Marshall. Fraser then crossed to Japan where he visited Kure, Yokohama and Tokyo before returning to Hong Kong, his last major cruise as Commander-in-Chief, British Pacific Fleet before leaving Hong Kong on 6 June.

This was the Royal Navy's first important postwar goodwill cruise and Fraser was naturally anxious to make it a success as such. But he knew that it would also be the British Pacific Fleet finale, the last chance to demonstrate the sophistication his creation had acquired since its unpropitious beginning back in December 1944. Fraser's objective was therefore to impress the Americans in China as much as the Chinese themselves. The British Pacific Fleet squadron, which left Hong Kong on 15 April with Fraser's flag flying in the cruiser *Swiftsure*, included the fleet amenities ship *Menestheus*. The latter prodigy could brew beer with distilled seawater and lay on practically every form of entertainment from an ENSA or film show (her film library included Olivier's brand-new *Henry V*) to a gala reception of prewar lavishness. Compared to the spartan facilities to be found on the Chinese mainland at this time, *Menestheus* was a floating cornucopia, and her finest hour was the great party thrown by Fraser at Shanghai on Easter Sunday 1946.

'On board there came a constant succession of distinguished local residents,' states the official record of *Swiftsure*'s British Pacific Fleet commission – her first:[17]

> There came Admiral Chow, Senior Chinese Naval Officer in Shanghai; General Maddocks, the Senior United States Army Officer; the British Consul-General, the French Naval Attaché, the Russian Military Attaché, and a host of other people. . . .On board [*Menestheus*] Admiral Lord Fraser held a huge party, at which there were over three hundred guests, mainly of a buffet supper (and when it comes to drinks and buffet suppers the *Menestheus* knows exactly what is wanted).

Captain P. Purkis of *Menestheus* recorded his ship's triumph in his diary:[18]

> There were cards out for 400, but as usual a small number of gatecrashers turned up and brought the total number of guests up to 460. We had the ship nice and sweet for the reception and built a fairly substantial platform gangway from pontoon to ship. The C-in-C came on board at 5.15 pm with his Staff and after introductions were made, he made an inspection of the ship and was acutely interested in everything. We finished rounds at 6 pm and he immediately took up station just inside of the cafeteria and welcomed his guests.
>
> This Admiral is a man of great charm and personality. He is a strong man, with a strong character, a red tanned face, and steely blue eyes, which never seem to move in their sockets, and yet are watchful at all angles at the same time. This I found out on two separate occasions when I was passing him, & although he was already in conversation with someone else and his back

almost turned away from me, I was amazed to hear him addressing me with a remark without even turning his head. I saw the same thing with other people during the evening. Admiral Lord Fraser is, I am informed, idolised in the Fleet, not only for what he has done, but for what he is, so extremely informal in all his ways. . . asks the right brand of pertinent questions to the right people, at the right time, and in consequence gets the right answers.

And yet Lord Fraser never found it possible to look back on this undoubted triumph with anything but mixed feelings:[19]

'This party in Shanghai cost a fortune, and I asked the Admiralty to pay for it, and they refused. I said well, it was given on behalf of the Americans, and I can't afford it, so you've got to pay for it! The *stupid* thing was that the Americans, whom we'd given this party *for*, were so thrilled with *Menestheus* that they wanted to buy her – they offered the Admiralty a million pounds for her. And the Admiralty refused. The Americans were very upset, they thought highly of her, didn't have anything like her at all. But she was just brought home and broken up.'

After Shanghai the squadron's next destination was Nanking, and the voyage up the Yangste to Nanking was a definite case of 'from the sublime to the ridiculous':[20]

'When the Admiral went up the Yangtse to Nanking he flew his flag in *Newfoundland*; and just before she sailed the Chief Pilot came out – the only English pilot on the river – and with much pomposity presented signed copies of his book on how to navigate the Yangtse. He went on at great length about how useless the Chinese pilots were – how the fellows could never judge their distance off the bank, and so forth. Now during the war the Yangste navigation had changed a lot, and although the Americans were running LSTs up to Nanking we were one of the first big ships to go up. And the inevitable happened. We came to a stretch where the Chief Pilot said, "This is the easy bit, Captain, you can make speed here"; and no sooner had we done so than *wummmmpphh* – brought up all standing, and one of the accompanying destroyers, too. We finally got her off after a lot of hard work, shifting the crew aft, but not before a little Chinese motor boat came out to present its compliments and ask, most politely, if we'd be staying the night. That provoked some ribald answers. . .

On the very first day in Nanking the British Ambassador's

wife took the C-in-C for a walk in the garden after lunch, and said, "You must tell me what you really want to achieve while you're here, Admiral, so I can hot up Horace." He found this very funny, and "hotting up Horace" became one of his favourite in-jokes.'

After talks in Nanking with General Marshall on the dubious chances of negotiating a genuine settlement between the Nationalist and Communist Chinese, Fraser took the British Pacific Fleet on to its 'furthest north': Chinwangtao on the Gulf of Chihli, 1,200 miles north of Hong Kong. From here he insisted on visiting Peking, where he smilingly posed with the glamorous Mayor of Peking wearing his 'brass hat' at a fetching angle. But the tenuous peace between the rival Chinese was fast breaking down, and Fraser's party got back to Chinwangtao on one of the last trains to leave Peking before the Communists cut the line.

At last, after a farewell visit to General MacArthur in Tokyo, Fraser's Fleet headed back to Hong Kong, arriving on 17 May. He celebrated the end of this highly successful cruise with a 'social' for the men of the Fleet in *Menestheus* before the round of official farewell functions began. The last of these, at Government House, unfortunately prostrated Fraser with food poisoning (the result of a malignant fish course), but this rare gastronomic mishap only delayed *Duke of York*'s sailing from Hong Kong until 6 June. Five days later, at Singapore, Fraser was relieved as Commander-in-Chief, British Pacific Fleet by Admiral Sir Denis Boyd. A smooth passage home in *Duke of York* ended at Plymouth on 11 July 1946; and on the following day Fraser struck his flag.

There is no better summary of Fraser's achievement with the British Pacific Fleet than the Admiralty signal to him on that day in July 1946:[21]

TO: DUKE OF YORK   FROM: ADMIRALTY
                        UNCLASSIFIED
PERSONAL FOR ADMIRAL LORD FRASER
    On the occasion of your return to the United Kingdom and hauling down your flag, the Board of Admiralty wish to express to you their high appreciation of your services as Commander-in-Chief of the Eastern Fleet and British Pacific Fleet.
    My Lords recall that you assumed command of the Eastern Fleet at a time when it was building up in order to strike in increasing strength against the enemy. Upon the formation of the British Fleet to operate in the Pacific you were selected for the high responsibility of commanding it, and My Lords appreciate the fine spirit, high standard of efficiency and eager

desire to come to close grips with the enemy which under your outstanding leadership pervaded the whole Fleet.

They know how much your personal example and inspiration contributed to the success of the many and gallant operations conducted by the ships and aircraft under your command.

They recognise that there were great technical and strategical problems to be solved before the success which was achieved could be guaranteed and in this connection your great experience was of outstanding value.

The Board are happy to feel that your services to the Royal Navy continue.

Part Five

*First Sea Lord
and
Admiral of the Fleet*
[1946–81]

· 24 ·

Commander-in-Chief, Portsmouth

[June 1946-September 1948]

Fraser's return to Britain in summer 1946 was a climacteric in his life. His mother, who had been at the hub of his private life and for whom he had patiently borne much responsibility, had died when he was still with the British Pacific Fleet in Hong Kong. 'The news had a great effect on him,' affirms Vernon Merry; 'he didn't want to talk about it, but quietly arranged things so he could be alone for a few days – sent us all away. This I remember particularly well, because it was while I was away from him that I met my future wife! We all knew how much his mother meant to him; it was a very great blow indeed. Yet I think I knew him well enough to sense that during those few days he was reflecting that he was not only alone: he was, in a way, *free*, having had to look after her affairs all those years.'[1]

Mrs Fraser's death was rapidly followed by the biggest disappointment of Fraser's entire professional career. When Admiral Lord Cunningham retired as First Sea Lord in June 1946, Fraser – the man who had loyally stepped aside for Cunningham three years earlier – was not appointed as Cunningham's successor. Instead the new First Sea Lord was Admiral Sir John Cunningham (no relation to 'ABC'). Sir John's advancement in preference to Fraser rested on a couple of years' seniority; he had been Vice-Admiral Commanding First Cruiser Squadron at the outbreak of the war, when Fraser was still a Rear-Admiral. Sir John had taken over the Mediterranean Fleet when 'ABC' became First Sea Lord, with subsequent responsibility for the 1944 landings at Anzio and in Provence. Apart from a spell as Fourth Sea Lord (when Fraser was Third Sea Lord and Controller), Sir John's other wartime distinction was having commanded the task force which failed to take Dakar from the Vichy French in September 1940.

To many in the Navy the choice of Sir John as 'ABC's' successor in June 1946 occasioned considerable surprise. 'It was well known on my level,' writes Captain G. D. Coney, Fraser's ex-FGO of Home Fleet days, 'that [ABC] was only holding the fort for Fraser to suceed him later.'[2] Fraser would have been less than human if he had not been downcast by Sir John's preferment, though his immense resilience helped him to adjust to the decision better than most would have done. But historians of the modern Navy may well speculate that the Service was the real loser. If Fraser had taken over as First Sea Lord in late 1945 instead of three years later – after three years of withering demobilisation and economies imposed by Governmental 'austerity' – it is certain that the postwar Navy would have retained far more of the tangible benefits and heightened efficiency so painfully acquired in the war years.

These two blows, both intensely personal, both suffered with dignity in private, hit all the harder because in June 1946 Fraser was tired after the strain of the British Pacific Fleet command. He was looking forward to a good long rest, which was highlighted by two trips abroad, one to Spain and one to Russia. One of Fraser's most rewarding diversions had always been simply to take off by himself on lone motoring tours, going where he liked, meeting and talking with everyone he came across. As Vernon Merry recalled, 'In Spain he bought some lottery tickets, and his number came up. He won a packet, and left it banked in Spain to draw on for future holidays.' Fraser's visit to the Soviet Union, however, was the result of an official invitation for which he had 'fished', in a social chat with the Soviet Military Attaché at Nanking. This was the last major occasion on which Vernon Merry accompanied his chief as flag lieutenant:[3]

'The Russian trip was a lot of fun; it was just before the Iron Curtain came down with a vengeance. In Leningrad the Admiral was asked to address some very senior Russian naval officers on the lessons of the war and the need for good relations in peacetime. He spoke for about 50 minutes, and then asked if there were any questions. "Yes," said one of the Russian admirals solemnly; "Can you explain why it is that in London the Naval Board wears plain clothes?"

We had a special train for the trip down to Moscow, with a coach on the end laden with "Intourist" goodies; we ate and drank the whole of the way there. Our escorting officer was a senior captain, Hero of the Soviet Union and a prominent submariner. We taught him to play Liar Dice, and played all night. At one stage I saw him deliberately fumbling the dice over after a throw. I said in a loud voice, so that everyone could hear, "Comrade Captain, that is cheating! You are not allowed to turn the dice over!" "Ah, Comrade Lieutenant, I know," he said; *"but you get a better hand that way!"* '

While in Russia, Fraser had hoped to renew acquaintance with Admiral Golovko. 'When I got to know Moscow I asked to see Golovko, but I was told he was in hospital. So I said I'd ring up the hospital, and they told me I wasn't allowed to do that. But he did come and see me later on, at Portsmouth. He came in the *Suvorov* – the same thing I've got the Order of. They had their Bolshevik choir, and all the rest of it, but it was just the same lunch as we'd had in Moscow!'[4] This minor disappointment was effaced with interest when Fraser exercised his privilege, as a holder of the Order of Suvorov, of travelling free on the Moscow Metro. He took an impish delight in insisting that the British *and* Soviet officers accompanying him should stick to the rules and pay their own fares.

Back at home in East Molesey, Fraser realised that his swelling collection of gifts and souvenirs from his travels was steadily converting 'Moorcroft' into a miniature museum. These included an impressive German Admiralty model of *Scharnhorst* (acquired by the Army during the occupation of Germany) and the beautiful silken Confederate Battle Flag which he hung in the hall. The latter was the result of a chance conversation with an American seaman during Home Fleet days in 1943. 'He was from the South, and when he heard I'd never seen the "Stars and Bar" flag he pulled one out from under his shirt to show me! This got into the American papers, and the ladies of Richmond embroidered this flag for me.'[5] Fraser conceived the typical idea of holding a party for his local tradespeople – milkman, postman, baker, etc. – and showing them the collection. He wanted to include the switchboard girls of his local telephone exchange. But when he rang the exchange, awkwardly identifying himself as 'the Lord Fraser' and asking if any of the girls would like to come to a party, Chief Supervisor Miss F. Scales sharply informed him that her operators were not allowed to visit public houses on request. A somewhat confused conversation ended with 'the Lord Fraser' establishing his *bona fides* and Miss Scales apologising for having subconsciously linked her caller with the 'Lord Nelson', her local pub in Twickenham. This ludicrous incident remained one of the favourite jokes Fraser loved to tell against himself, both in private company and when speaking in public.

But the Britain of late 1946 – exhausted, penurious, beset with strikes, shortages, rationing and endless queues – was very far from the 'New Jerusalem' image which had swept Labour to power in July 1945. And the serious side of the man may be judged from a letter Fraser felt impelled to write to *The Times* on 5 December 1946. It bears comparison with his far-seeing 'War with Germany, Italy and Japan' of eight years before; and it is quoted here for the benefit of all who have expressed regret that Fraser never chose to enter politics after the war:[6]

I think that most of us on our arrival home are appalled at the restrictions, the coupons, the rationing & the difficulties in which we live.

Some of us will immediately blame the Government but in reality we ourselves can produce the answer by hard work.

In Russia there was a potato shortage. The Govt. asked citizens to plant the verges of the roads with potatoes & when I drove out 25 miles from Moscow there were 25 miles of roadside potatoes. The potato shortage was averted but only by hard work. In Spain the population were toiling at the harvest, a bumper one, & were still working man woman & child up to 10 o'clock at night.

I stayed a Saturday in Salamanca. The shops were full of goods at reasonable prices; in the middle of the day there was a band playing in the square with peasants dancing in their country costumes & bullock carts in their best turn out. At 5 p.m. a bullfight with 10,000 people to watch & in the evening peasants & farmers from miles around crowded the streets & cafés sipping their refreshments. The trams & buses & theatres were running until 2 a.m. As I saw it everyone seemed to be enjoying themselves.

Some people will say not by the Govt. was this achieved, most people will say it was by hard work.

In this country we do not yet seem to have realized our object. In the Service we are taught that a definition of the object & then sticking to it is the only means of success.

Then you set about finding the method of obtaining it. The object I think is quite certain, namely prosperity.

The only method of obtaining it is by production, & full production can only be achieved by hard work.

The British people must realize this since in my experience they are second to none in education & common sense.

So why do we find go slow movements, stoppages of work, etc, which are definitely preventing the attainment of our object?

Again my experience tells me there are three reasons:
(1) A failure to declare our object & the method of obtaining it.
(2) Lack of good leadership.

(3) [Refusal to accept that] a rise of wages is of no value unless it is coupled with increased production.

I have already outlined the factors in (1).

As regards (2) knowledge of the Service has always shown that whenever and wherever there is trouble you will generally find that some leader is to blame. In the 6th Century the Emperor Maurice said:—

"If a soldier disobeys his instructions he shall suffer punishment; but if he fail through misunderstanding of the orders the non-commissioned officer shall suffer punishment for having failed to instruct him properly."

In the regrettable disputes that are occurring (& they are not only regrettable but grave at this juncture) I cannot take sides; it may be that the management display crass stupidity; it may be that the labour leader seeks cheap notoriety or neglects to lead. Whichever it is a very grave responsibility rests on these men, in fact the prosperity of the British nation.

As regards (3) everyone knows that on a desert island money is of no avail.

In our case the only object we should have in mind is to increase production & so reduce the cost of living.

An increase in wages has a negligible & short-lived effect on our lives compared with some permanent reduction in the cost of living; moreover every increase in the cost of production makes it more difficult to sell our goods abroad.

So, if we go on as we are going now, bickerings, disputes, stoppages & lack of thought of one's fellow citizens, the day will come when we shall find it too late & we shall have no money to buy our food.

Therefore I make these points:—

(A) What is our object – Prosperity.

(B) How do we attain our object – Hard Work.

(C) Everything else such as nationalisation, closed shops, private enterprise may affect the issue in a minor degree but must not divert us from the main object & the method of attaining it.

Mr Churchill once promised us nothing but Blood, Sweat, Toil & Tears & after 7 years we won the war.

Some great leader is now required or it may be two – a leader of management & a leader of labour – to say, "We promise you nothing for the next two years but Sweat and Toil".

Then I think our troubles would cease.

Yours faithfully

Fraser of North Cape

In January 1947 Fraser was appointed First and Principal Aide-de-Camp to King George VI. Though Fraser was naturally deeply appreciative of the honour, it was an ideal appointment only in that nothing relaxed the king more than 'being treated as a sailor' (*see above*, p.174), and Fraser was just the man for this. But, though Fraser always insisted on the highest standards in turnout, drill and execution where naval ceremonial was concerned, the minutiae of Court protocol were another matter, and he found them somewhat of a strain. So much of Fraser's unpretentious nature made an ADC's job alien to him.

There was, for instance, his blind spot towards medals and decorations. It was only after insistent coaching by Vernon Merry that Fraser had learned to 'read' medal ribbons adequately, often very necessary for a courteous reference in conversation, when visiting or receiving highly decorated officers. Apart from the use of the Order of Suvorov for the free Moscow Metro trip, Merry only heard Fraser discuss his own decorations but once. This was after the North Cape battle, when he expressed regret that he had never won a decoration in action, and wished that it could have been possible to make him a special award of the DSO for sinking the *Scharnhorst*. Long after the war, during an attic tidy-up at 'Moorcroft', Fraser's forgotten *Légion d'Honneur* and *Croix de Guerre* came to light at the bottom of a trunk. It had simply never occurred to Fraser that he might cause offence by not wearing these decorations, especially when meeting Frenchmen. Nor did Fraser ever bother to catalogue his full collection of decorations and honours for *Who's Who* or the Navy List.

Lord Fraser recalled the occasion when an American naval squadron visited Portsmouth and was honoured by a royal visit:[7]

'We were on our way to Portsmouth to have lunch with the American Admiral Conway. The weather changed, so I said "I don't think we can stand greatcoats, sir." The King agreed, but then he said, "Well, but surely my Guard of Honour will be in greatcoats?" I said I thought that would be difficult to change; he agreed. Then I said, "I never take my gloves with me because I always leave them behind somewhere and they get lost; do you think we could leave our gloves?" The King said he thought that'd be all right, but then he thought again and said, "If the Queen sees me in a photograph without my gloves, she'll be so angry!" But he finally agreed, and we did leave our gloves behind; he arrived without a greatcoat, and the Guard sweating like *hell*!

The American Admiral was very keen to give the King lunch,

but very fussed because they couldn't have any drink on board. He asked if he could take the King to an hotel to have a drink beforehand. I said he certainly couldn't, but we could have a drink in Admiralty House. But the Admiral didn't want that, because he was to be host. So I told him the King would be quite all right with a tomato cocktail, or whatever they had; so that was settled.

When we sat down to lunch, the first course was soup; and the King said, "Admiral, there's sherry in this soup!" And the Admiral said, "*Cooking* sherry, Your Majesty." That amused the King. Later, in came a plum pudding *blazing* with brandy; and the Admiral got his say in first. "*Cooking* brandy, Your Majesty. . .".'

At the other end of the scale, Fraser's most important duties as the King's ADC in 1947 were connected with the coming marriage of one of his former officers to the heir to the throne. The engagement of Lieutenant Philip Mountbatten and HRH Princess Elizabeth was announced in July 1947, Prince Philip having become a naturalised British citizen in February. Prince Philip had first met Fraser in Home Fleet days, and had served in the British Pacific Fleet as First lieutenant of the destroyer *Whelp*. On the voyage up to Guam in *Duke of York*, escorted by *Whelp* and *Wager*, Fraser had had occasion to give Prince Philip and the First Lieutenant of *Wager* a good-natured joint 'bottle', or admonition, for wearing 'non-regulation headgear'. Now, two years on, Fraser found himself involuntarily committing a similar offence on the day of the Royal Wedding, 20 November 1947:[8]

'I was placed in the Abbey Chancel, opposite the King. It had started such a cold day that the occasion was made "Greatcoats", but then it got milder, and the order was changed to "Off Greatcoats". Now you can't wear aiguillettes with a greatcoat, and when I took it off I hadn't got them on. My Flag Lieutenant had forgotten to bring them; so I had to go in without them on, and I saw the King look at me right away. I knew I'd hear more about it, and sure enough I did. He said to me afterwards, "I think you were incorrectly dressed!" '

Fraser's time as the King's ADC overlapped with his seventh Service appointment since reaching flag rank nine years before. He now took on the Navy's senior shore command in the United Kingdom, with Nelson's *Victory* as his dry-docked flagship: Commander-in-Chief, Portsmouth (15 May 1947). Cunningham, Tovey and Somerville had all 'gone ashore'; Mountbatten had gone to India as the last Viceroy, charged with bringing about Indian independence; Vian had gone to the Admiralty as Fifth Sea Lord. Fraser was thus left in harness as the foremost admiral of the war years, for whom none of the fleet commands offered sufficient eminence after the British Pacific Fleet. Though Fraser's proven administrative and diplomatic abilities were of the highest order, and his popularity in the Dominions was never in doubt, it was true that none of the Commonwealth Governor-Generalships was really suited to a confirmed bachelor without a wife to act as 'first lady'. For an officer of Fraser's seniority and achievements, the Portsmouth command was therefore the only post suitable for him bar one; and it was most welcome confirmation that he was being retained in active service as a future First Sea Lord.

There was an air of 'going home' in taking over the Portsmouth command. It included the gunnery specialists' *alma mater*: HMS *Excellent* at Whale Island, with *Vernon* (mines and torpedoes) alongside the Dockyard and *Dolphin* (submarines) at Gosport. Fraser's main job as Commander-in-Chief was to assist the stringent contraction of the wartime Navy from a manpower strength of 863,000 in August 1945 to 147,000 in April 1948. The process of demobilisation was well advanced when Fraser went to Portsmouth and he inherited an established routine. This left him largely free to concentrate on what was, to him, the all-important side of the job: seeing to it that the Navy's surviving warships and shore establishments were kept up to the highest pitch of efficiency.

For Fraser the formal parades and inspections had always been secondary to talking with the men on the job and listening to their problems. As likely as not the process involved meeting old shipmates of whatever rank. At the Royal Naval Barracks, he was introduced to Marine Bandmaster Alfred Howard. 'As we shook hands he said, "Where were we?" I answered, "HMS *Resolution*, 1916–20." His eyes lit up as he said, "Ah, happy days," and passed along the line of some hundred or so other ratings who were proud and honoured to have served with him.'[9] For Lt-Commander Peter Tunbridge, a dreary vigil in one of Haslar Hospital's more funereal waiting-rooms was transformed by Fraser's arrival on Commander-in-Chief's inspection. 'What's your trouble, laddie?' – then a disapproving glance round the room. 'I would have thought, Matron, that you might have had some flowers in here to cheer the place up.' Pause. 'But I expect you do usually.'[10] His eye missed nothing, and he was the first to spot an untimely outbreak of fire while inspecting the Galley at HMS *Hawke*, the Upper Yardmen's Training College at Southampton. Lightning work with the fire extinguisher by the Supply Officer, Commander Beckwith, over-zealously ruined Fraser's uniform with a blast of foam. But this apparent disaster did not prevent Beckwith's department from receiving the prize for the best department, or Beckwith himself, on two separate occasions many years later, from being jovially hailed as, 'Ah – the officer who covered me in foam!'[11]

Even on less congenial occasions he usually managed to introduce a special note into the proceedings:[12]

> In 1947 I was Correspondence Officer of HMS *Helmsdale*, a 'River' class frigate of the 13th Escort Flotilla. We had an ERA & a leading stoker on charges of indecent exposure, for which the punishment warrants needed the signature of the C-in-C, Portsmouth.
>
> After the second occasion the signed warrant was returned with a letter saying:
>
> 'I note with concern two cases of indecent exposure from one ship's company in a three week period. I hope this will not assume epidemic proportions.'

But Fraser was never content merely to concentrate on the men, the ships and the shore establishments under his command. He also looked outwards, working, as he had done in Australia, for the closest possible relationship between the Navy and the civilian community. He became a familiar figure at civilian functions such as the Portsmouth and Gosport Gas Company's sports day, at which he gladly accepted the manager's invitation to tour the Milsea Gasworks, to the delight of the many ex-Navy employees. 'He had a most marked appreciation of his place in local affairs and was indefatigable in representing the Navy at all times,' writes W. K. Tate, his host that day. 'He did much to maintain the prestige of the Navy in the inevitable reaction from the War.'[13] And it went without saying that civilian hospitality was readily reciprocated:[14]

> 'I was very great friends with the Lord Mayors of both Portsmouth and Gosport, and I asked them both to come out with me one day in a submarine. (Didn't know much about it myself!) So we went out, and they gave us a bump on the sea bottom, which frightened the two Lord Mayors a bit; then we came up in the middle of the harbour, and I brought the Lord Mayors up and said, "Now, whose water am I in?" – and neither of them could tell.'

Among all the invigorating memories of Fraser's fifteen months as Commander-in-Chief, Portsmouth, perhaps the most prominent is that of his arrival to take the King's Birthday Parade of 1947 on horseback, complete with *Excellent* gaiters. Impressive innovation though this was, the dignity of the occasion was threatened by his horse depositing an unceremonious mound during the proceedings, practical jokers afterwards marking the spot with an appropriate 'Foul Ground Buoy'. For the next year's parade he chose to arrive by helicopter, thus helping stimulate public interest in an aircraft still novel in Britain, but which he knew was going to be an inestimable boon to the Navy of the future.

In February 1948 came the official confirmation that Fraser would be Sir John Cunningham's successor as First Sea Lord. Long before he finally left Portsmouth, it was obvious that the new job was certainly not going to be peacetime routine. The massive reduction of British naval strength since the end of the war was already attracting adverse comment in the House of Lords and the press, at a time when Stalin had announced the creation of a Soviet ocean-going fleet and Western relations with the Soviet Union were going from bad to worse with the commencement of the Berlin Blockade (July 1948). None of this had any novelty for Fraser: making bricks without straw had been the story of his life since his appointment as Controller ten years before. And for this, the supreme challenge, Fraser was again cheered by the good wishes of the man he admired above all others, now Leader of the Opposition. 'My dear Fraser,' wrote Winston Churchill on 25 February 1948,[15]

> I have been meaning to write for some days to send you my congratulations on your appointment as First Sea Lord. I am very glad indeed that the choice has fallen upon you. I thought it right to bring to the notice of the First Lord the fact that I offered you this great position in the war and that you declined it in so becoming a manner.
>
> I look forward to your arrival at the Admiralty where I am quite sure you are greatly needed. I am far from satisfied with the manner in which the very large funds and manpower, hitherto at the disposal of the Navy, have been employed. Never was there so little to show in fighting value for the men and money Parliament has voted. Moreover this condition has been accompanied by what I feel sure is a deliberate writing-down of our real strength, which has already produced damage to our prestige all over the world. . . .
>
> When we look back through our experiences in the last war, when the fifty aged American destroyers became one of our main objects of desire, and remember how even the old *Centurion* was ready to play her part in the invasion crisis, it is I am sure a very great mistake to cast all this latent and undefined strength away. My experience, which is unique, is

that the moment war is declared every ship in the basins is a factor of value. . . .

I only trouble you with all this because I shall be making very serious criticism of the Admiralty when the vote comes on in the near future. I am glad you have no responsibility for all this, and of course I wish you all success when you take over, I believe, in August.

In his sixty-first year, forty-four years after joining *Hannibal* as a midshipman, Bruce Austin Fraser reached the peak of his career. On 6 September 1948 he took up the supreme naval appointment, that of First Sea Lord and Chief of Naval Staff, followed on 22 October by his promotion to Admiral of the Fleet.

· 25 ·

First Sea Lord:
the birth of NATO

[1948–50]

Fraser took up his duties as First Sea Lord at a time of considerable upheaval in defence priorities at home and abroad. Vociferous complaints had already been made about the pace of postwar demobilisation and the state of readiness of the armed forces. The rupture between the Western democracies and the Soviet Union had just been completed by the Berlin Blockade; the spectre of a Third World War was looming. In Whitehall there was much disagreement over Britain's defence structure between the Army and Air Force Chiefs-of-Staff and the government. And the negotiations which were to lead to the North Atlantic Treaty in the following year were already under way, pointing towards a revolutionary new basis of Britain's defence: that of a defensive peacetime alliance.

Quite apart from speaking for the Royal Navy during the genesis of NATO – no mean task in its own right – Fraser as First Sea Lord also had to cope with the biggest localised shooting war in which Britain had been involved since the Boer War fifty years before. But at least the Boer War had been fought as a *war*, with appropriate commitment. Korea was kept in a low key by the politicians, categorised more as a heavy-duty international police action, mere hostilities-in-peacetime, to be fought with peacetime resources.

All these complications meant that Fraser's penultimate Admiralty appointment, as Third Sea Lord and Controller back in 1939, had been a picnic compared with his time as First Sea Lord. The advent of war with Nazi Germany had marvellously simplified the Navy's priorities: 'The enemy at last was plain in view, huge and hateful, all disguise cast off,' as Evelyn Waugh has put it.[1] But no such simplification prevailed in 1948, and Fraser had to bring his main armament, pragmatism and experience, to bear on a swarm of problems all on conflicting courses.

Fraser's first week as First Sea Lord saw him plunged willy-nilly into a conflict which had been rumbling since July 1946, when Field-Marshal Montgomery had taken over as professional head of the British Army: Chief of the Imperial General Staff (CIGS).

Montgomery had begun as CIGS by making what amounted to a world tour, dropping in on the Army Commands overseas to assess their problems in a series of flying visits. These left him horrified at the Attlee Government's persistence with reductions in the British armed forces in a world which was patently unsafe and becoming more so as the months went by. Despite considerable shilly-shallying by Attlee's Minister of Defence, A. V Alexander, Montgomery succeeded in enlisting the support of his Navy and Air Force colleagues (Sir John Cunningham and Lord Tedder) in demanding legislation for peacetime conscription to keep up Service manpower. But the resultant National Service Act of July 1947 was only a partial solution. The real problem was the government's failure to encourage voluntary recruitment for long-term service in the armed forces, while continuing to make arbitrary reductions in defence expenditure and assign 'priorities' to the three Services. Alexander defined these in October 1947 in a particularly infuriating manner:[2]

> The first priority, which must not be interfered with, is defence research. The second, in the light of the present developing situation, must be to maintain the structure of the Royal Air Force, and its initial striking power. The third priority is for the maintenance of our sea communications, and, therefore, for the most efficient Navy we can get in the circumstances, and then we will do the best we can for the Army.

Montgomery never forgave Alexander for this 'writing-down' of the Army; and matters were not improved by the January 1948 Defence White Paper dropping total defence spending for 1949–50 to a limit of £600 million. But then came the Soviet imposition of the Berlin Blockade in July 1948. Montgomery, Tedder and Cunningham were further exasperated by Alexander's vacillation as to whether or not Britain was prepared to go to war over Berlin. But Montgomery's attempt to 'unstick' Alexander as Defence Minister, by a vote of no confidence made to the Prime Minister by all three Chiefs-of-Staff, came to nothing. (Tedder and Cunningham agreed that such a move would be unconstitutional.) By the late summer of 1948, when Fraser took over from Cunningham, it was war to the knife between Alexander and Montgomery. The latter seemed bent on extracting the last ounce of nuisance value from his last weeks as CIGS, and in his *Memoirs* records Fraser's first session with the Chiefs-of-Staff – 10 September 1948 – as 'a first-class row':[3]

Mr Alexander wanted to discuss a statement about release from the Services which was to be made in Parliament on the 14th September. Tedder at once asked that reference should be made in the statement to the need for giving every possible encouragement to regular recruiting, as it was the 'regular content' of the Services which was the hard core of our efficiency. . . . But Mr Alexander informed him that he was not prepared, for political reasons, to do this.

Tedder then got very angry and said that the Government had never given the Services any help in this very difficult matter, and had given no lead to the nation about the importance of a good response for regular recruitment in the fighting Services. This upset the Minister of Defence. He said that no Government in British history had ever done so much for the Services as had the present Labour Government. . . . I then said that I agreed entirely with the views of the Chief of the Air Staff about the need to encourage regular enlistment and to give the reasons. I said I could not understand the refusal to include this in the statement to be made in Parliament. Was the Government afraid to do so?

Mr Alexander was now getting really angry. He said the Government were frightened of nothing. The real trouble was that we were making a mountain out of a molehill. To this Tedder made a very neat *riposte*, saying that the Minister was using the molehill in his statement and was refusing to recognise the mountain; the crying need today was a better 'regular content' in each Service, and this was not going to be mentioned in the statement. I chuckled (audibly I fear!) at this *riposte* and chipped in again, saying that I agreed entirely with Tedder. I then said that I had been forty years in the Army and I had *never* known the Services reduced to such a parlous condition in relation to their commitments. I said we had sunk to the lowest depths.

This fairly put the cat among the canaries. Mr Alexander was so angry he could not speak for several seconds. He then said that statements had been made which would have to be taken up again in another place. I said I would gladly repeat my statement in *any* place and in *any* society – in the House of Lords if he liked.

The First Sea Lord (Lord Fraser) said practically nothing. He had only just taken over at the Admiralty. . . . The proceedings seemed to astonish him – as well they might!

Of course Fraser was no stranger to conflict with politicians, which he had experienced both as Controller and as Commander-in-Chief, British Pacific Fleet, in Australia. He could also live with Montgomery's abrasive manner and unashamed use of the cult of personality. But Fraser never sought conflict for conflict's sake; and the deliberate baiting of Crown ministers, let alone caballing against them as Montgomery had sought to do against Alexander, was anathema to him. Montgomery's replacement as CIGS by Slim at the end of October 1948 brought calmer counsels to Whitehall and a more balanced relationship between the Chiefs-of-Staff and Minister of Defence. But the fundamental problem, which Montgomery had tried to reduce with both enfilade and frontal assault, would not go away.

That problem was manifold, and did not consist solely of the inevitable ousting of defence as the prime national consideration after the end of the war. Attlee's Labour rank and file saw no threat in the massive Soviet military domination of the European states over which Hitler had held sway throughout the war. At the same time, the Attlee Cabinet continued to approve further defence cuts based on completely unwarranted forecasts that Britain's overseas land, sea and air commitments would diminish in proportion. 'The Service Estimates for 1948–49,' the Defence White Paper of March 1948 blandly announced, 'have been prepared on the assumption that no unforeseen requirements are likely to arise during the year.' But the flimsiness of this assumption was exposed only three months later by the Soviet imposition of the Berlin Blockade. Not surprisingly, Alexander's embarrassment over this crucial miscalculation was hardly soothed by the tauntings of Montgomery.

Yet as Montgomery himself was readily to admit,[4] the politicians were not solely to blame. How could the Cabinet decide on a sound defence policy without a concerted brief from the Army, Navy and Air Force Chiefs? On the other hand, how could such a concerted brief ever see the light of day so long as the Cabinet continued to lay down invidious Service 'priorities', compelling each Service to clamour for a bigger slice of the shrinking financial cake than the other two? The Navy's share, in 1948–49, was only £153 million out of £692.6 million, or 22 per cent of the total financial provision for the three Services; the Royal Air Force had 25 per cent and the Army 44 per cent. The picture was no brighter with regard to manpower reductions, still the government's main obsession in order to haul as much manpower as possible out of the Services and into the factories. The March 1948 Defence Statement contained little of comfort for Fraser as incoming First Sea Lord: 'It was found preferable to bring down the Navy [in manpower] as rapidly as possible during the current financial year, *and to accept a temporary measure of disorganisation and immobility* [author's italics]. No further reduction is planned during 1948–49.' The target figure for the Navy's manpower was set at 145,000, amounting to a reduction of 83 per cent in the first three years of peace. And further reductions were to be encouraged by natural wastage. National Service intake for all three services in 1948–9 was set at 150,000, of which the Navy's share was a mere 2,000.

The ships of the Fleet had suffered similar depletion. By the time Fraser took over as First Sea Lord the Fleet had lost ten old battleships and the battle-cruiser *Renown*, and twenty cruisers of pre-1935 vintage. No less than thirty-seven escort-carriers, built or converted for Royal Naval service in American yards during the war, had been handed back under the terms of lend-lease. Only HMS *Campania* had survived out of the five British-built escort-carriers; three others had been converted back to merchant ships and one handed over to the Royal Netherlands Navy. As for the escort warships which had been Fraser's overriding preoccupation when Controller, only nine years before, seventy-seven 'Flower' class corvettes and sixty-one pre-1937 destroyers had already been sold or scrapped.

Of course there were good *short-term* reasons for the frantic pace of the Navy's postwar shrinking. The country was near-bankrupt, utterly dependent on American dollar loans, desperate to revive domestic industry and exports. For all that, much permanent damage suffered by the postwar Navy was inflicted between 1945 and 1948, and it could have been avoided. There would have been no churlish severance of the wartime ties with the US Navy if Fraser had gone straight from the Pacific to the Admiralty as First Sea Lord. As the *Menestheus* incident shows (*see* pp.292–3) the British and American navies had much to offer each other, and this could have saved the postwar Royal Navy millions. For it was after 1945 that the US Navy broke all records in modernising, reconstructing and prolonging the active lives of warships rather than selling or scrapping them unnecessarily early, as the British did. By the time Fraser took over in 1948 the unique opportunities of 1945 were long past.

Again in the purely short-term view these early warship disposals were justified, in that the Fleet had plenty of new warships left over from the war. But it was not until Fraser took over at the Admiralty that a real effort was made to plan a long-term peacetime Fleet, a Fleet including the newest classes which had been under construction at the end of the war, but on which work had been subsequently halted. His predecessor Sir John Cunningham had been unable to reprieve the three planned 'Gibraltar' class heavy fleet carriers, all of which had been cancelled before the ink on the Japanese surrender documents was fairly dry. These big carriers would have been comparable with the three American 'Midways', completed just too late for wartime service. They would have enabled the British Fleet Air Arm to make a comparatively painless transition to the postwar jet age, which with its faster, heavier aircraft made impossible demands on the lightweight carriers of the 'Colossus' class. Two of the four projected 'Audacious' class carriers had also been cancelled. Under Fraser's aegis, however, work was at last pushed ahead on the other two: HMS *Eagle* and *Ark Royal*, the Royal Navy's last generation of fleet carriers. Work on *Eagle* was virtually complete by the time Fraser left the Admiralty in 1951.

Fraser's tenure of office also produced the first generation of postwar destroyers: the 'Daring' class, eight ships in all, of which seven had been launched by the time Fraser left the Admiralty. In their day the biggest destroyers built for the Royal Navy, the 'Darings' carried the unmistakable stamp of the experience gained under Fraser in the Pacific: high endurance and the best facilities money could buy to improve living and working conditions on board. The 'Darings' took British destroyer development to the highest level possible before the replacement of the gun by the guided missile from the late 1950s on. Ten years separated the laying-down of the last 'Daring' from that of the first 'County' class guided missile destroyer (March 1949–March 1959). In that decade the prompt completion of the 'Darings' and their excellent service were of the greatest benefit to the Fleet. *Eagle*, *Ark Royal* and the 'Darings' may therefore be seen as the last of Fraser's many contributions to the Navy's *matériel*, which had begun with the fire control table back in the early 1920s.

Lord Fraser was quick to point out that he owed much of this success in getting new construction moving again to his wartime association with the Labour leaders. This was particularly valuable with regard to the Prime Minister. When he chose, Attlee could treat Service chiefs with a calculated and devastating ruthlessness. There had, for instance, been the occasion when Sir John Cunningham had voiced perfectly reasonable doubts about the feasibility of Lord Mountbatten's return to active naval service after serving as the last Viceroy of India. In the presence of Mountbatten (Cunningham's junior) Attlee had given Cunningham a typically cutting rebuke: 'I am not asking for your comments; I am giving you an order.' Fraser, however, found Attlee 'a very good little man', courteous and much easier to work with than Churchill. The Foreign Secretary and his wife were also good friends, with Mrs Bevin more than once embarrassing the redoubtable 'Ernie' by referring to Fraser as her 'Little Boy Blue'!

As First Sea Lord, Fraser at last had the authority with which to work towards the closer inter-Service collaboration which he had always deemed essential. One of the first fruits of this conviction was the imaginative 'Exercise Trident', held at Greenwich in April 1949. 'Trident' was an inter-Service seminar aimed at relating the lessons of the past (predominantly of the Second World War) to the challenge of a future war. Two days were given to Part 1 – 'The Situation on the Outbreak of War'; a day and a half to Part 2 – 'Tactical and Strategical Operations in the Future'; and the final half-day was devoted to Part 3 – 'Scientific Progress'.

For Fraser, 'Trident' was a twenty-year-old dream come true: the sort of exercise which, if it had been held in the 1920s, could well have helped avert the humiliations which the Second World War had in store. His idea was not so much to lay down a fixed schedule of topics, as to offer a framework on which stimulating topics could be displayed and debated. Thus Part 3 included the startling notion that enemy ships might be sunk by reducing the water density below them, which could be done in the laboratory, instead of the tedious traditional method of puncturing the enemy ships and letting the sea in. If ideas like this were half tongue-in-cheek they were half serious, too. The decade which had produced such devices as the degaussing coil to counter magnetic mines, not to mention the atomic bomb, was no time in which to scoff at new scientific possibilities. During 'Trident' Fraser's readiness to accept new technology, rather than cling in crusty nostalgia to the traditional tools of the Navy's trade, was never displayed to better advantage.

In one important respect 'Trident' was a failure: not a single Cabinet Minister nor Member of Parliament chose to attend, the absence of the politicians being sourly noted by the servicemen. But in general the exercise was a resounding success. Though held under Navy auspices, it attracted unexpectedly high contingents from the other two Services. It was another masterpiece of delegation by Fraser, whose 'starring' role was to introduce and sum up the proceedings, turning the main burden of the exercise over to the specialists. But one RAF observer paid tribute to Fraser's unobtrusive direction: 'It was interesting to watch those present, rather hesitant at first, quickly settling down to get the most out of such discussions under the able helmsmanship of the First Sea Lord.' And the same officer concluded: 'We should like to think that the Navy will now join with the other two Services in making such an Exercise an annual event.'[5] There could be little doubt that Fraser's objective of inter-Service harmony had, with 'Trident', been well and truly gained.

'Trident' claims one other distinction: it was the first Anglo-American strategic study made after the signing of the North Atlantic Treaty. As the NATO Treaty was not signed in Washington until 4 April, American representation at 'Trident' merely a week later was of course arranged in advance. For all that, many were the surprised comments on the strength of the American representation at Greenwich, which must in every way be regarded as the shape of things to come.

'Trident' took place amid stirring events on the far side of the world. On 20 April 1949 the British frigate *Amethyst*, following the same route as Fraser on his visit to Nanking only three years before, was battered immobile by Communist Chinese gunfire and trapped 150 miles up the Yangtse. The ensuing game of bluff, with the Communists trying to bully the British into admitting culpability for the incident, dragged on through May, June and July in conditions of increasing physical hardship and mental stress for the men in *Amethyst*. Finally Lt-Commander Kerans made his famous decision to break out down-river by night, running the gauntlet of the Chinese guns to rejoin the Far East Fleet at sea. Fraser was on leave at the time, but of course knew that the breakout attempt was imminent. For him the drama of *Amethyst*'s escape was enhanced by the tense exchange of signals between *Amethyst* and the Far East Fleet, relayed to him by telephone from the Admiralty:[6]

Amethyst to C-in-C: HALF WAY
Amethyst to C-in-C: HUNDRED UP (miles)
C-in-C to *Amethyst*: A MAGNIFICENT CENTURY
Concord (waiting offshore) to *Amethyst*: FANCY MEETING YOU AGAIN
Amethyst to *Concord*: NEVER NEVER HAS A SHIP BEEN MORE WELCOME

Then, finally, Kerans's immortal conclusion:

Amethyst to C-in-C: HAVE REJOINED FLEET SOUTH OF WOO SUNG. NO DAMAGE OR CASUALTIES. GOD SAVE THE KING.

Lord Fraser later admitted to the author that hearing *Amethyst*'s 'HUNDRED UP' was one of the biggest moments of his later career; 'I somehow knew she'd be all right, then.'[7] He was particularly elated by the escape because, at Baku, he and his men had also spent frustrating months as political hostages to fortune, but without an escape route and a ship able to make steam! From his proximity to the Cabinet in summer 1949, Fraser could readily appreciate the Attlee government's refusal to extend its unwilling involvement in the Chinese Civil War. The escape of the *Amethyst* was the best solution all round – even for the Chinese, who could represent it as clemency.

Thus by the end of his first year as professional head of the Royal Navy, Fraser had made another excellent beginning. Ably assisted by Field-Marshal Slim, he had restored smooth relations between the armed Services and the Ministry of Defence. After the inevitable postwar 'freeze', new warship construction was moving ahead. Fraser's crusade for closer inter-Service collaboration seemed well launched; and he was planning to strengthen the Board of Admiralty by inviting Lord Mountbatten, whom Fraser had admired ever since taking over the Eastern Fleet in 1944, to accept the post of Fourth Sea Lord. Fraser now looked forward to a task for which, after the experience of the British Pacific Fleet, he was supremely well qualified: hammering out the new naval command areas of NATO with his American and European colleagues.

In his last eighteen months at the Admiralty Fraser would achieve all this, while coping with war in Korea, a Persian Gulf oil crisis, and unlooked-for friction in Whitehall: from Mountbatten below and Churchill above.

. 26 .

Goodbye to the Admiralty
[1950–1]

Contrary to popular mythology (in particular the brand consistently put out by Soviet and pro-Soviet propagandists) NATO did not spring into being like Athene, fully armed and looking for trouble. Many years passed before the political commitment signed in April 1949 acquired anything like the military structure familiar in the 1980s. (West Germany, NATO's 'front-line' state in Europe, did not attain full sovereign status, join NATO and set about the formation of her own armed forces until May 1955.)

The omens for NATO were far from promising, with no indication that a peacetime military alliance, to be upheld and equipped for collective security by pooled land, sea, and air forces, was likely to endure. Every historical precedent was against NATO, in particular the speed at which the wartime Anglo-Soviet-American 'Grand Alliance' had fallen apart after 1945. A strong current of conservatism and misplaced chauvinism ran against the idea of Britain's commitment to NATO. It was vehemently argued that Britain's best policy, as a world imperial power, should be the good old Galsworthian maxim: 'Keep clear and hold the ring.' But it was always far easier for Service chiefs like Fraser to adjust to the new policy than it was for civilians. In its crucial early years, NATO's biggest asset was the experience in operating multi-national forces gained during the Second World War. And of all the Allied Service chiefs who formed NATO's original land, sea, and air command structures, probably only Eisenhower could claim more experience in commanding multi-national forces than Fraser.

In his wartime fleet commands, Fraser had won the unqualified respect of all leading naval powers of the new NATO alliance: French, Dutch, Norwegian, Canadian, and above all American. He was in every sense the ideal 'link man' to superimpose the new demands of NATO on Britain's traditional relationship to the Commonwealth navies. There was, for instance, the immensely important question of Norway's new role as the northernmost linchpin of the Alliance, and the integration of the Norwegian Navy into the joint NATO naval command structure. In this, the uniquely high regard in which Fraser was held by the Norwegian Crown and Navy – in 1948 King Haakon had decorated him with the Grand Cross of the Royal Order of St Olaf for his services to the Norwegian Navy during the war – was of the highest value.

In partnership with Field-Marshal Slim, Fraser made an excellent start in the long negotiations with the American Chiefs-of-Staff over the future structure of NATO. The British Chiefs travelled to the United States in the liner *Queen Mary*, by 1950 restored to her full glory after serving as the biggest troopship of the Second World War. When it came to picking a Flag Captain for the trip, Fraser had no hesitation in borrowing the Naval Assistant to the Third Sea Lord (the latter being Sir Michael Denny, Fraser's former Chief of Staff in the Home Fleet). Fraser's new Flag Captain was the newly promoted Captain Michael Le Fanu, who had performed excellently in the Home and British Pacific Fleets and won great respect from the Americans as Fraser's Liaison Officer with the 3rd and 5th Fleets in the Pacific. It was during the voyage in *Queen Mary* that Fraser – not Le Fanu, as stated in Le Fanu's biography *Dry Ginger* – noticed a dignified but lonely young African in beautiful robes, sitting apart from the uproarious Bingo game in progress at the British officers' table. This was Dr Busia of the Gold Coast (afterwards Prime Minister of independent Ghana); and Le Fanu was at once despatched to invite him to join the game. 'I don't know what he made of our Bingo, with £5 notes flying about the table,' recalled Lord Fraser, 'but anyway our Navy team won, and he wrote me such a nice letter to say how much he'd enjoyed himself!'[1]

The NATO talks had barely got under way when they were suspended by an unforeseen crisis in Far Eastern waters. On 25 June 1950, Communist North Korean troops surged across the 38th Parallel into South Korea. The United Nations Security Council called on the North Koreans to withdraw; the North Koreans refused to oblige and kept coming; and on the 27th the Security Council summoned member states of the United Nations to come to the aid of the American-backed Republic of Korea.

The Royal Navy's consequent participation in the Korean War, serving with Commonwealth contingents alongside the US Navy off Korea, proved of the first importance in enhancing the British naval role in NATO. Above all, to Fraser's immense satisfaction, Korea re-stated the ancient truth that sea power is Britain's most timely gift to her allies in time of war. Without her ocean-going Navy,

Britain would have been reduced to making noises on the touchline during the only joint military intervention against naked aggression ever ordered by the UN Security Council. Fraser's pride in the speedy and effective commitment of the British Far East Fleet was all the greater because Commander-in-Chief Admiral Brind and his second-in-command, Rear-Admiral Andrewes, were both former members of Fraser's British Pacific Fleet team. (Brind had commanded the 4th Cruiser Squadron and Andrewes the fleet carrier *Formidable*). The British response came all the earlier because units of the Far East Fleet (based on Hong Kong) were currently engaged in the Fleet's summer cruise up to Japanese waters. Andrewes, commanding at sea, had actually arrived at Hakodate, in the northern Japanese island of Hokkaido, when news of the North Korean invasion came through. He anticipated Brind's order to concentrate the Fleet, the services of which Brind immediately offered to COM-NAVFE, the American Commander-in-Chief Naval Forces, Far East, who was based in Tokyo.

When the crisis broke HMS *Triumph*, the Far East Fleet's only aircraft-carrier, was heading for Hong Kong. Brind at once sent her back north to join Andrewes's cruisers (the veteran team of *Belfast* and *Jamaica*, with destroyers *Cossack* and *Consort*) off southern Japan. COMNAVFE's first request to the British was for *Jamaica* to proceed to the east Korean coast and assist in shelling North Korean forces advancing down the coast, while the other British warships headed for Okinawa to join a task force of Admiral Struble's US 7th Fleet. By 4 July 1950, within a week of the UN Security Council's appeal, the Royal Navy was back in action at the side of the US Navy. This time, of course, it was with a fraction of the wartime British Pacific Fleet's strength; moreover, Brind's fleet was not required to operate from a base 4,500 miles from the combat theatre but from American-occupied Japan, less than 200 miles from Korea. What gave Fraser the greatest satisfaction, however, was the immediate vindication of everything he had sought to achieve with the British Pacific Fleet, in the teeth of Cunningham's displeasure. This time co-ordination between British and American naval forces came naturally. HM Ships all carried the American signalling books and soon readjusted to American usage. In the summer of 1950 Anglo-American communication at sea was never the headache it had been only five years before, thanks to the revolution in signalling practice which Fraser had wrought in the wartime British Pacific Fleet.

In stark contrast to the *kamikaze*-ridden weeks off Okinawa in the spring of 1945, the Navy's initiation to war in Korean waters was deceptively gentle. After a brief conference with Andrewes off Okinawa, Admiral Struble led the Anglo-American fleet up the Yellow Sea for preliminary carrier strikes at airfield targets behind the North Korean lines. The opposition encountered during this initial foray was negligible. Over on the east coast *Jamaica* encountered three torpedo-boats in the early morning of 7 July; she sank two and drove off the third. This was the Royal Navy's only direct encounter with Communist naval surface forces.

But the unchallenged supremacy at sea of the UN forces was of no avail until the land and land-based air forces arrived in strength. By 5 September the North Koreans had penned the South Koreans and UN troops into an ominously small perimeter around Pusan, at the southern tip of the peninsula; but here, hammered by carrier air strikes, the North Koreans stuck, and on 13 September General MacArthur, the UN supreme commander, went over to the offensive. UN sea power was brilliantly exploited with an amphibious landing at Inchon, 200 miles up the west coast behind the North Korean lines. Supported by warships off the west and east coasts the UN forces advanced and were back on the 38th Parallel by the end of the month. As the North Koreans ignored MacArthur's demand for surrender he ordered the crossing of the 38th Parallel on 9 October. He repeated the tactic of an amphibious hook, withdrawing his 10th Corps from Inchon, shipping it right round the Korean peninsula and landing it again at Wonsan. The objective now was the Yalu River and the Korean-Manchurian frontier, which had been reached at several points by the end of October.

By this time the British and Commonwealth naval forces had settled into their role, concentrated mainly off the west coast while the bulk of the American fleet operated off the east. To Fraser, with his eye on NATO's future, the most welcome surprise was the ease with which the multi-national armada functioned: American, British, Canadian, Australian, New Zealand, French and Dutch. In October 1950 the British carrier *Theseus* relieved *Triumph*. Despite appalling weather in the worst three months of the year, *Theseus* nevertheless flew a superb total of 1,500 sorties – combat air patrol over the fleet, strikes at North Korean coastal shipping, and attacks on ground targets in support of the troops.

The Royal Navy maintained its contribution to the UN fleet off Korea throughout the winter crisis of 1950–1, when the second North Korean offensive – massively supported, from the end of November, by Communist Chinese forces – forced the UN troops to retreat south of the 38th Parallel. Seoul, the South Korean capital, fell to the Communists on 4 January 1951; a UN counter-offensive recovered the city on 14 March, but it was becoming increasingly clear that neither side had any real prospect of outright victory. When MacArthur prepared for a second advance north of the 38th

Parallel, President Truman replaced him with General Ridgway (4 April). By the end of May, in which another Communist assault was repelled, both sides were ready to begin armistice talks and these finally got under way at Kaesong in July 1951.

Though the armistice was not finally signed until July 1953 at Panmunjom, Fraser could rest easy in the knowledge that the Royal Navy, despite the withering effects of postwar shrinkage, had risen magnificently to the challenge of Korea. Unlike the British Pacific Fleet in 1945, the British Far East Fleet in 1950–1 had a First Sea Lord acutely aware, from his personal experience in the theatre, of the morale problems attendant on difficult service so far from home. 'He was determined,' writes Vice-Admiral Sir Peter Gretton, then Fraser's Naval Assistant, 'that the men serving in Korea should not think themselves the "Forgotten Army", as might easily happen. He maintained morale well by personal messages.'[2]

Fraser's last months as First Sea Lord, however, were far from carefree. No sooner had the Korean War been stabilised than the Middle East, source of Britain's oil fuel lifeline, began to crackle with tension. In July 1950 an imminent war between two feuding sheiks at Sha'am in the Persian Gulf had been quashed by the prompt despatch of the British frigate *Flamingo*. Her captain was Commander Godden, who had served in *Duke of York* in the Pacific. Godden tackled the problem by summoning both sheiks aboard *Flamingo* and dictating a peace treaty for them both to sign. This they did, and peace in the Gulf was maintained amid appropriate gifts of sheep and goats. When he heard of Godden's decidedly unorthodox action, Fraser heartily approved – and found the time, amid the demands of Korea, to send another of his personal 'specials' to *Flamingo*: 'WHAT A PITY THAT ALL PEACE TREATIES CAN-NOT BE MADE AS QUICKLY AND EFFECTIVELY AS SEEMS TO HAVE BEEN DONE BY *FLAMINGO*.'[3] The unsung story of the 'Sha'am Incident' immediately became part of Fraser's repertoire when speeches had to be made; it was, for him, a perfect example of the Royal Navy at work.

But the Sha'am squabble was as nothing to the full-dress crisis which blew up in May 1951. In Iran the extreme nationalist regime of Mohammed Mossadeq announced the cancellation of the Anglo-Iranian oil concession treaty and the nationalisation of the Iranian oil industry. This high-handed act abruptly ended eighteen years of cheap British oil imports from Abadan, the biggest oil-producing centre in the world; given the still-parlous state of the British economy, it was a crisis of the first magnitude. By the end of June all shipments of oil from Abadan to Britain had ceased, in defiance of the International Court of Justice ruling in favour of the dispossessed Anglo-Iranian Oil Company. All this presented Attlee's struggling government (its majority slashed from 148 to 7 by the February 1950 General Election) with an immensely complex problem. Here, it seemed, was another instance of direct force pre-empting peaceful discussion. There was much popular demand for resolute counter-action of the sort which had frustrated the Berlin Blockade and repelled the Communist invasion of South Korea. This was even favoured by Attlee's new Foreign Secretary. (A month before his death in April 1951, 'Ernie' Bevin had been replaced by Herbert Morrison.) But given the nationalist fervour whipped up in Iran by Mossadeq's policy, such intervention would most likely have resulted in war between Britain and Iran – a war in which, as the United States made very clear, Britain would be on her own. To add to their dilemma, the British had no sizable forces in the Gulf capable of pulling off a combined operation against Abadan; and with no end to the Korean imbroglio in sight, there could be no prospect of assembling such a force.

In such a crisis, with clear-headed pragmatism at a premium, Britain was lucky to have both a First Sea Lord ready to place unpalatable facts before the Cabinet, and a Prime Minister ready to listen. Overruling his more 'hawkish' Cabinet colleagues, Attlee made it clear that armed intervention was out: Britain's interests would be defended by the use of diplomatic and economic weapons against Iran, not military and naval ones. The most immediate worry was the safety of British personnel in Abadan, and with this end in view Fraser had no objection to sending the cruiser *Mauritius* up the Gulf to provide a naval presence. This assisted the safe evacuation of British personnel (4 October) the week after Mossadeq's nationalist takeover of Abadan. It soon became clear that there was in fact no danger of an 'oil famine' in Britain: BP immediately doubled its oil production in Kuwait, Saudi Arabia, and Iraq. The subsequent British 'oil blockade' of Iran wrought havoc on the Iranian economy; Iranian oil production slumped from 241.4 million barrels in 1950 to a pitiful 10.6 million in 1952, though it took until August 1953 before Mossadeq's regime was forcibly ousted.

Thanks to his fine working relationship with Attlee, Fraser had saved the Navy from possible humiliation in Iranian waters; but it was not given to him to bow out as First Sea Lord at the end of 1951 without suffering further strain from two sources at home. The first of these was the performance of Fraser's former superior Lord Mountbatten, the last Viceroy of India, now back in the Navy with the substantive rank of Vice-Admiral, on the Board of Admiralty. Fraser had developed a great respect for Mountbatten and had looked forward to his joining the Board as soon as his tour of duty in command of the 1st Cruiser Squadron was completed. Having, on Fraser's request, returned to the Admiralty as Fourth Sea Lord in 1950, Mountbatten soon began to attempt to intervene outside his department (stores and victualling). He believed that the Fourth Sea Lord's department should include ammunition; Fraser was obliged to correct this misapprehension. But when Richard Hough published his *Mountbatten: Hero of Our Time* in 1980, Lord Fraser was incensed when the following passage was brought to his attention:[4]

> Lord Longford recalls a brief exchange, typical of many at meetings of the Board. Mountbatten had intervened again outside his department. 'You leave me, young fellow me lad, to run my department, and I'll leave you to run yours.' Mountbatten responded at once in proper quarterdeck manner, 'Well, sir, if that's how you put it, I must bow to your superior stripes.' Fraser, much chastened replied, 'No, no, my dear boy. We are all equal on the Board of Admiralty.'
>
> It was not a very comfortable time.

While heartily agreeing with the last sentence, Lord Fraser could hardly believe his ears when this passage was read to him in December 1980. 'Pity he didn't ask me,' he told this author; 'the whole thing's absolute rubbish. We never spoke to each other like that in our lives. But we *did* disagree about the ammunition thing. I had to tell him he was wrong.'[5] Lord Fraser was also shocked by Lt-Commander Peter Kemp's assertion, also quoted by Hough, that 'there was very strong prejudice against Mountbatten by hard core professionals like Bruce Fraser.'[6] Quietly but emphatically, Lord Fraser rejected this as 'completely untrue'.

The second source of tension, all the sadder because of their excellent working relationship in the war years, came from Winston Churchill. For months before his triumphant return to power with the General Election victory of October 1951, Churchill had vehemently condemned the NATO naval command arrangements with the Americans. These arrangements provided for an American Supreme Commander, Atlantic (SACLANT), with command in the eastern Atlantic and Mediterranean being retained by the British; they were eminently sensible in view of the huge size of the peacetime US Navy and the role of the United States in NATO. Churchill, however, regarded the new arrangements as detrimental to British prestige and could not understand the readiness of the British Service Chiefs to approve them. In March 1951 Churchill most unfairly rebuked Fraser for publicly speaking in praise of the new command structure, and relations between them were never the same again.

The offending speech resulted from Fraser's acceptance of an invitation by Admiral Vian to visit Gibraltar, where the British Home and Mediterranean Fleets were serving together, and address the assembled ships' companies. In Sir Peter Gretton's words:[7]

> I wrote the first draft of Fraser's speech to the ships' companies of the Home and Med. Fleets at Gibraltar, and he delivered several talks to several assemblies of sailors. He was anxious to reassure the sailors about the future, and said that having an American as SACLANT was all right *so long as* there was a British officer as commander in the Eastern Atlantic. The Fleet would be in good hands, he said, and he also added that there were some good American admirals.
>
> At one of the speeches, to an assembly of the destroyer commands at the seaplane base in Gib., the Rear-Admiral (Destroyers), William-Powlett, had invited the journalist of the local *Gibraltar Chronicle* to attend what was essentially a private talk by the First Sea Lord to his sailors. Fraser had no idea that a journalist was present. A most distorted and offensive despatch was sent to London, which ignored the speech's accent on the need for a British commander in the Eastern Atlantic and stressed Fraser's remarks that American admirals would be all right.

This was how Fraser unwittingly incurred Churchill's wrath. Attlee, still Prime Minister, fully supported Fraser who tried to amend matters by explaining the 'leak' to Churchill. 'My dear Fraser,' replied Churchill on 19 March 1951,[8]

> I am very glad to have heard from you that you did not intend to make any public pronouncement on the Command arrangements, and to have had your explanation of how the leakage occurred. It is most important that Ministers, who can be criticised, should deal with these controversial matters, and that the Service Chiefs should not be involved.
>
> Thank you very much for what you say at the end of your letter. I look back with pleasure on our work together during so many years.
> > Yours sincerely,
> > Winston S. Churchill

But, insists Sir Peter Gretton,[9]

> Whatever he may have said in writing, W.S.C. did not forgive Fraser and he never realised how wrong he had been over the whole matter. In the last few weeks of Fraser's period as 1.S.L.,

W.S.C. treated him very off-handedly and failed to consult him on key issues. . . the command structure in the Mediterranean was discussed at a NATO meeting in Rome which Fraser was not allowed by W.S.C. to attend. As a result of his absence a stupid maritime air command structure was set up, owing to the refusal of Slessor, the Chief of Air Staff, to agree with his 'air' coming under US Naval command.

The Rome meeting from which Fraser was barred by Churchill would have rounded out the work of the big NATO Council talks (15–20 September 1951) for which Fraser again crossed the Atlantic in *Queen Mary*. At this exhaustive review of Western Europe's defence problems the admission of Greece and Turkey to NATO was agreed. By now Fraser was one of the most popular and respected Service Chiefs in the whole Alliance; he was held in warm regard by General Eisenhower, who was appointed as the first SACEUR (Supreme Allied Commander, Europe) in December 1951. Before returning home Fraser visited the Pentagon, and lectured at the US Naval War College.

Though Fraser's last two months in office would certainly have been far happier without Churchill's active resentment, Fraser was not a man who ever cried over spilt milk. By the time he left the Admiralty at the end of 1951 he already knew that all his work for 'Britain in NATO' had not been in vain; Churchill and Truman agreed on the appointment of an American SACLANT within weeks (18 January 1952). He could pride himself on a fitting conclusion to his long active career in the Service, now, he knew, at an end – a career majestically summed up by the Admiralty in mid-April 1952:[10]

ADMIRALTY

WHITEHALL   15th April 1952

Sir,

I am commanded by My Lords Commissioners of the Admiralty to inform you that there being no further appointment appropriate to your rank and seniority, they greatly regret the time has come for you to be placed on the half-pay list.

My Lords desire me to take this opportunity of conveying to you an expression of their high appreciation of the outstanding services which you have rendered to the Royal Navy and to the country during a long and brilliant career. They recall your excellent service during the First World War and in the period between the Wars: particularly your three years as Director of Naval Ordnance when considerable

327

advances were made in the development of naval guns such as the 14-inch and 5.25-inch guns, which were in later years to play such an invaluable part in the successful prosecution of the War at sea.

Just before the outbreak of the Second World War you were called upon at short notice to assume the important duties of Controller of the Navy. During the three critical years in which you held this office, you successfully inaugurated the very large warship building programme, while at the same time all available resources had to be used to effect the repair of ships damaged by enemy action. It would be difficult to over-emphasize the contribution to the War effort which, by your sound judgment, untiring energy and ready appreciation of essentials, you made in this appointment.

After a short period as Vice Admiral Second Battle Squadron, and Second in Command of the Home Fleet, you became Commander-in-Chief, Home Fleet in May, 1943. My Lords recall with admiration the brilliant manner in which the Home Fleet, trained as it was to a very high pitch of efficiency and under your inspiring leadership, sought out and destroyed the enemy battleship 'Scharnhorst' It was also in accordance with your plan that the successful attack by the Naval Air Arm was carried out on the 'Tirpitz' in Alten Fjord.

In 1944 you became Commander-in-Chief, Eastern Fleet and, when later in that year it was decided to form a British Fleet to fight alongside our American allies in the Pacific, you were selected to command it. Not only was this the biggest British Fleet assembled during the Second World War, but there was also the unique difficulty that it was required to operate some thousands of miles away from its main base and under a foreign Supreme Commander. You dealt with all the operational and administrative problems involved in this situation in a manner which earned the lasting respect and confidence of our American allies.

Your next appointment was as Commander-in-Chief, Portsmouth, the most important of the Naval shore commands, where your understanding coupled with your great professional knowledge and experience, endeared you alike to the Navy and to the civilian population of this great port. During your appointment at Portsmouth His late Majesty[11] also accorded you the honour of appointing you to be his First and Principal Aide-de-Camp.

In your last appointment, as First Sea Lord and Chief of

Naval Staff, you devoted all your energy, ability and exceptional personal qualities to the well-being and efficiency of the Royal Navy, which you have unhesitatingly put before all personal considerations during the whole of your career. It was during the time you were a member of the Chiefs of Staff Committee that the North Atlantic Treaty Organisation was brought into being and your work in this field has done much to ensure world peace.

My Lords are pleased to recall the many high honours which were so deservedly bestowed on you, principal among which were the barony which His late Majesty was graciously pleased to grant you in the New Year Honours List 1946, your creation to be Knight Grand Cross of the Most Honourable Order of the Bath for your services in the pursuit and destruction of the 'Scharnhorst', and your creation to be a Knight Commander of the Most Excellent Order of the British Empire in the Birthday Honours List 1941. You also received many foreign decorations including American, Dutch and Russian.

Finally, My Lords were particularly pleased when His late Majesty approved your promotion to the highest rank in the Royal Navy in October 1948, and they are happy in the knowledge that you will continue to take an active interest in the Service which is honoured to count you as one of its members, and to whose name you have added an abiding lustre.

· 27 ·

Sunset
[1952–81]

Lord Fraser's long and happy retirement – though technically, as he would remark with a laugh, 'an Admiral of the Fleet never retires' – illustrates the personal enigma of Fraser the man. As the Navy's 'senior bachelor' he had chosen to go down the quiet years of retirement without wife, children, or grandchildren around him, a prospect unenviable for any man without such a paradoxical character.

There never was a more gregarious or approachable loner than Fraser: qualities which meant that he would never become a misanthrope or recluse in retirement. Though he would have probably denied the suggestion in acute embarrassment, his inner strength owed much to Kipling's 'If–':

> If you can talk with crowds and keep your virtue,
> Or walk with Kings – nor lose the common touch,
> If neither foes nor loving friends can hurt you
> If all men count with you, but none too much. . .

All these undoubted attributes helped make him a Peer of the Realm and national figure whose annual parties in thanks for the services of his local tradesmen – postman, milkman, butcher, baker *et al.* – were eagerly anticipated events in the small community of East Molesey. A confirmed bachelor, Fraser was no misogynist: he was completely at ease, and an invariable charmer, in the company of women. Lacking children of his own, he showed a sympathy and courtesy towards the young which many a family man might envy. In the last analysis it might be said that Fraser was the friendliest and least self-centred of men, to whom no man could, in all honesty, claim intimate friendship. Even Renée Duncan, the close and trusted friend whom he chose as his executrix, admits that 'there were many

330

things which he simply treated as private, which he'd never talk about.'

Fraser never defined or proclaimed this private code, but would from time to time let it be known, from quietly disapproving comments, precisely where he stood. For example, he never fully approved of the high-ranking Army, Navy and Air Force memoirs and biographies which poured from the presses throughout the 1950s and 1960s, works obviously based on private diaries which, being contrary to regulations, should in Fraser's view never have been kept. This was a stream which he was determined not to follow. Content to stand on the record and let his achievements speak for themselves, he had no grievances to air or excuses to make. Here was a rare and enviable serenity of mind. It will be noted that very few of his contemporaries felt the same; the most notable exception was Field-Marshal Sir Claude Auchinleck. Fraser's sensitivity on this point was not prompted solely by modesty; it stemmed rather from his point-blank refusal to say or do anything which knaves might interpret to the Navy's discredit, or as disloyalty on his part towards former colleagues and shipmates living or dead. As for making money by writing his memoirs (self-advertisement aside) the thought never entered his head.

The same caution applied when Fraser considered taking on a modicum of work as a diversion in early retirement. Any retiring general, admiral or air marshal has always been able to take his pick of civilian directorships, and even build up a considerable income by taking on a number of 'sleeping' posts on different boards. Not so Fraser; he could never tackle any job in a token or figurehead role, and turned down a host of invitations until he found one in which he felt he would genuinely earn a director's fees. Mr Thomas Wallas, then General Manager of the London & Lancashire Insurance Company, recalls the circumstances:[1]

We had an affiliated company – the Standard Marine of Liverpool – and I suggested it would be appropriate that Lord Fraser should join the Board of the Standard Marine. The Board meetings were held in Liverpool once a month and another Director (Mr Plowden Roberts, Managing Director of Cox & Kings) Lord Fraser and myself travelled to Liverpool together. Mr Plowden Roberts arranged a private compartment for us, so we had every chance of getting to know Lord Fraser well. He was, in the true sense of the word, a humble man and never talked of his own career or successes, but was keen to know about insurance – particularly marine insurance.

After one of our Board Meetings in London, I asked him if he would like to meet some of the staff who had served in the Navy. He jumped at the idea so I arranged to get the boys into the Board Room for tea after the next Board Meeting. It was a great success and they all gathered round the end of the table exchanging naval gossip and he was just one of themselves, asking them about their ships and officers. I repeated the invitation to the small Standard staff in Liverpool but there was only one young lady who had been in the WRNS. On our visits to the Marine Board in Liverpool he never failed to look into the typists' room and have a word with Miss Bull.

Later he asked my wife and myself to lunch at the House of Lords. We found he had also asked a young lady, a buyer in Harrods, who had been on his staff in Hong Kong. He was the most 'human' man one could hope to meet. We always exchanged cards and friendly messages at Christmas and I shall always cherish my friendship with him.

There are still many who lament that more public use was not made of Fraser's talents after he left the Admiralty at the end of 1951. But it is easier to list and pay tribute to those talents than it is to identify suitable channels for their exploitation. As mentioned above (p.306), Fraser would have been a *succès fou* as a Governor-General anywhere in the Commonwealth. But he believed that his lack of a wife to act as 'first lady' in the social round was a severe handicap, and in any case Governor-Generalships seldom fall vacant to order. He was never attracted by active politics, which would in any event have meant resigning the peerage which he regarded as a mark of honour to the Navy as much as to himself. After the planned Royal Visit to South Africa was so sadly cancelled by the King's death in early 1952, Fraser was the man chosen to visit South Africa in the *Arundel Castle* as his country's representative, bearing good wishes to the South African people. The role as envoy of goodwill was one in which Fraser always excelled, but this visit was necessarily a 'one-off'; Britain's imperial and Commonwealth system, and British diplomacy in general, has never offered much scope to globe-trotting special envoys on the American model.

In retirement as in active service, Fraser never shirked what he had always considered a paramount duty: acting as ambassador for the Royal Navy in public appearances. He was in constant demand for school prize-givings and as guest of honour at both Service and civilian dinners and banquets. At all such functions, while putting over his enduring creed that the Royal Navy was the finest Service in the world, he could be relied upon to shun pomp and show the human touch. This left an ineradicable memory with one prize-winning Clifton College schoolboy:[2]

'I had won a very minor prize known as the E.F.C. Moore Prize for Reading, and duly marched up to the platform to be presented with three books previously chosen by me. As I stood before Lord Fraser my books were nowhere to be found, but without batting an eyelid he removed his gold watch from his waistcoat and gave it to me. I was, I remember, most put out when I had to give it back to him afterwards!

Again, many regret that Fraser never gave fuller scope to his undoubted fluency with the pen, despite his personal reasons given above. One notable exception was the chapter he wrote for the anthology *Winston Churchill: A Tribute* (Cassell, 1954). Apart from its inherent merit the generosity of this offering, given Churchill's behaviour to Fraser in 1951, moved Churchill to the following letter of 4 November 1954:[3]

My dear Fraser,
I feel greatly indebted to you for the delightful chapter about my connection with the Royal Navy which you have contributed to the book Cassells are publishing about me on my Birthday. I am touched by the trouble you have taken and gratified by the story which you tell.
  Yours sincerely,
  Winston S. Churchill

When Churchill resigned as Prime Minister in April 1955, Fraser joined the host of well-wishers who paid verbal tribute to Churchill over the air, and this prompted another grateful note (19 April 1955). 'My dear Fraser,' wrote Churchill, 'I am so much obliged to you for the kind remarks you made on the B.B.C.'[4]

Fraser's reticence and deliberate shunning of the limelight in retirement meant that no shower of civic and academic honours came his way, which suited him perfectly well. He did, however, accept an honorary Doctorate of Law from the University of Wales in November 1955. There was only one arena in which he had no hesitation in referring to his own successes. This arena was the House of Lords during the heated Defence debates of the early 1950s, with the Royal Air Force making its latest bid to usurp the Navy as prime strategic service (the RAF then being the sole delivery vehicle for the British 'nuclear deterrent'). When it came to contesting the persistent RAF claim that the land-based RAF could do anything in the power of the seaborne Fleet Air Arm, Fraser was prepared to come out with all guns blazing. Here he is in action during the 1953 debate on the Naval Estimates:[5]

Admiral of the fleet Lord Fraser of North Cape reinforced many of these arguments. He uttered 'a plaintive wish' that Lord Trenchard and Lord Tedder 'would not make so continuously strong attacks on the requirements of another Service, and I would ask them if they cannot make their minds a little less rigid against argument.' The Air Force sometimes seemed to him to think that work over the sea came as a matter of course and needs no training. 'When the war came the operations of Coastal Command were not successful. The Air Ministry decided to put Coastal Command under the operational control of the Admiralty. For the remainder of the war the co-operation was superb.' Lord Fraser would 'be very strongly against the Navy starting an argument with the idea of taking back Coastal Command. It would just start the old bitterness all over again.' He then asked Lord Trenchard a question: 'If you take over the air cover for the Navy and Convoys, would you abolish carriers?' Lord Trenchard: 'I recommended (in my speech) that the large carriers should not be built. I suggested that they would not be usable. I still hold that opinion.' This did not answer Lord Fraser's question – was Lord Trenchard prepared to abolish *all* carriers? Apparently he wants the small aircraft carriers which 'would make the position ten times worse, the small carrier is an unsteady platform; it cannot operate in a seaway; its runway is smaller; it does not give the height to stow aircraft, and it has less protection. So that Lord Trenchard is just accentuating the insecurity of naval aircraft.' Lord Fraser drew on his experience as C in C, Home Fleet. 'We were getting great opposition by air and submarine to our Russian convoys. We had no air cover, and in the summer months we had to stop the convoys. About October we had the good fortune to have a spare [escort] carrier available. I sent the carrier with a convoy. The effect was terrific. On the first night that carrier sank two submarines. And so it went on. . . . The case for the necessity of aircraft carriers has been absolutely proved in the last war. The Americans and ourselves are unanimous in that requirement.

It was with these short, emphatic sentences straight from the heart that Fraser fought his last battles on behalf of the Royal Navy in the House of Lords. Perhaps his most effective speech in the Lords was that in the debate of 2 December 1954, delivered in vehement harmony with Lords Chatfield and Cunningham:[6]

There is only one point which has not been mentioned, and that is that in about six or seven years' time we shall not have any cruisers. I am sure that the public do not realise that. That is the situation. The Fleet is running down to that extent. . . .The noble Lord, Lord Teynham, I think, mentioned the position of aircraft carriers and cruisers – they were not alternative – and that is why I [bring] in the weather so strongly. It depends entirely on the weather which type of vessel is used. In my *Scharnhorst* battle in the North, the wintry dark weather made use of the air by either side impossible. We could not have used an aircraft carrier, and the result is that three cruisers saved that big convoy of thirty ships. It was lucky that we had the three cruisers there, as well as the normal escort against submarines. Subsequently, other surface forces destroyed the *Scharnhorst*, but if we had not had those three cruisers there, that convoy of thirty ships would have gone, with no help, or possibility of help, or search from the air. . .

The question of aircraft carriers is a debatable point, and always has been; but in my view one has to look upon the aircraft carrier as an advance base near to the point of danger. That is what the carrier really is. It is capable of attacking in places which are 'un-get-at-able' by other means. The Fleet Air Arm was the only force, except our midget submarines, able to immobilise the *Tirpitz* for something like three months. That emphasizes once again the offensive character of our Navy: it is an *offensive* service.

Before the decade was out Fraser could look back with satisfaction on his joint orations with his fellow Admirals of the Fleet. The 'cruiser rot' had been halted with the completion of *Blake*, *Lion* and *Tiger*, and planning had begun on a new heavy aircraft-carrier – 'CVA01'. Fraser shared the widespread naval dismay at the Labour Defence White Paper of February 1966 in which 'CVA01' was cancelled, and it was announced that *Ark Royal* and *Eagle*, the Navy's last two fleet carriers, would not be replaced. By this time, however, Fraser's voice was no longer heard in the Lords; the 1966 Defence Review coincided with his seventy-eighth birthday, and he had accepted that 'front-line' defence of the Navy's interests had passed to younger colleagues. His last ceremonial role in the Lords was the honour of carrying the Sword of State before Her Majesty at the 1964 Opening of Parliament.

While vigour remained to him, Lord Fraser pursued his favourite relaxation: lone motor-car touring, going anywhere, meeting anyone. This he managed to include in the event which he unhesitatingly described as the crowning honour of his retirement: accompanying HRH Prince Philip on his world tour in the new Royal Yacht *Britannia* in 1958–9. Fraser joined *Britannia* at Vizagapatam on the east coast of India on 15 February 1959, after a leisurely journey out via Naples and Aden (where Vernon Merry, now Commander, organised a splendid reunion party), Karachi, Bombay and Colombo. By January 1959 he had hired a Morris car and happily 'taken off' to visit his old haunts in Ceylon, based at the Rest House at Matara on the south coast and sending back a delightful sequence of letters to Renée Duncan and her husband.

At Hambantota, 'a little place on the S.E. coast' of Ceylon, Fraser was obliged to attend the primitive local hospital when an untimely rash broke out on his arms and body. Ordered to the dispensary to receive medication for a virus infection, Fraser took his place in a queue 'of about 30 people carrying cigarette tins, jam jars, beer bottles for their medicine'. The dispenser, Fraser noted:[7]

> had about 4 large bottles from which he did a mixture rather like mixing a cocktail & poured it down a funnel into the cig. tins or jam jars or whatnot. . . . Thus armed & with 2 little bottles of penicillin (made in Germany) I repaired to the ward where the nurse was inoculating a soldier for tick bites & I hoped I should get another needle. She did take another from the tray & with pigeons flying about the ward & nesting in the roof I received quite a painless injection. It was now kill or cure! the final result after 3 days was a cure, & except for slight irritation never felt ill. I was very grateful, & all with no charge.

Such was Fraser's personal farewell to the East which he loved so much – no mean performance, be it noted, for a man just turned seventy-one. There could hardly have been a greater contrast between the primitive facilities of Hambantota and the air-conditioned luxury of *Britannia*, with the long days of cruising interspersed with full-dress ceremony at Rangoon (where he was promised that the name of Fraser Street would not be changed), Singapore, North Borneo, Hong Kong, the Gilbert Islands and the Solomon Islands. For Fraser the tour ended with the Pacific crossing, passage of the Panama Canal and return to England from the West Indies, having arranged two tickets for the airport Royal Enclosure for the Duncans, who met him at the airport.

Lord Fraser's long resistance to the compilation of his biography finally gave way in the autumn of 1977, his cautious agreement to the project finally being won by the gentle but persistent urgings of Renée Duncan. In November 1977 Lord Fraser granted me the first of an unforgettable series of interviews at 'Moorcroft'. His twenty-five-year distrust of any 'scurrilous journalism' was not easily relaxed. Many weeks passed before Lord Fraser accepted that we would draft and re-draft until he was fully satisfied with the results; but from our very first meeting he extended to me, 'non-Navy' outsider that I was, his inimitable courtesy and warmth. This was, as ever, blended with sly humour. 'Ah, it's the scurrilous journalist!' was the stock greeting I received until well into the spring of 1978. This gave place to 'Ah, the great historian!' and finally, via 'Humble', to 'Richard'.

It was a source of unalloyed pleasure to watch Lord Fraser warming to the job as the chapters of this book took shape. He gave his incredible memory no rest as the work progressed, and his unimpaired mental faculties rose shining and triumphant above his increasing physical frailty. When, in the summer of 1980, the time came for him to leave 'Moorcroft' and move to Tara House Nursing Home (close to the Duncans' home in Ealing) it was done, as ever, without fuss or regrets.

Our last session together was at Tara House in the first week of December 1980, when Lord Fraser made no secret of his gratification at having out-lived Grand-Admiral Dönitz (who had just died at the age of 89). We then went through the final draft of Chapter 18 which, being 'the *Scharnhorst* chapter', had naturally earned an even more exacting scrutiny than usual. But on this occasion it was painful to observe the grief and resentment which the recent BBC-TV broadcasts of Lord Mountbatten's filmed reminiscences had caused him. Mountbatten's comments (particularly on his time as Fourth Sea Lord under Fraser) were in brutal contrast to the friendliness which Mountbatten had always professed towards his senior former colleague. 'My dear Bruce,' he had written on the occasion of Lord Fraser's 90th birthday in February 1978,[8]

> I can hardly believe that you have reached the magnificent age of four score years and ten on the 5th February as you always seemed so very young and vigorous to me.
>
> I send you my very warmest good wishes on this great occasion.
>
> We had such a strange relationship in the higher ranks of the Service when you served under me while I was Supremo and I served under you as First Sea Lord.
>
> I will never forget the breath of fresh air you brought to the Fleet and to the relationship with Supreme Headquarters when you arrived out in command of the Eastern Fleet.
>
> Although 12½ years older than me and therefore many

years senior to me in substantive rank, you treated me so very kindly and correctly and in such a friendly heartwarming way that I have never forgotten it.

Nor will I forget the remarkable way you dealt with ABC's decision to separate the British Pacific Fleet from the South East Asia Command after the war and to take away Hong Kong from my Operational Command but leaving me responsible for its administrative support.

I remember so clearly your saying to me that I could ask for anything from the Fleet I wanted but instead of issuing an order you said that if I put it in the form of a request, perhaps adding 'if possible' in the signal, you would treat it, as far as possible, as if it were an order.

I was most honoured that you should have kept me in your confidence about your relations with ABC. What a remarkable old man he was. I thought that his attitude to me was fairly difficult but I had no idea that you had the same difficulties and that made me feel a closer bond of affection than ever with you.

I know how much Prince Philip enjoyed having you as a guest onboard the *BRITANNIA* and he was quite amazed when I told him the story that Winston and the Chiefs of Staff had decided that you should be offered the post of First Sea Lord in succession to Dudley Pound and had turned it down in favour of ABC. This was a very well guarded secret but I am afraid was the cause of a psychological upset that ABC suffered from in relation to you.

In my case it was much simpler, it was his strong disapproval of youngsters like me being given temporary acting high rank. At all events, ABC made real friends with me when I became First Sea Lord and was very helpful. So we ended up in good friendship. I hope you did too.

The country and, indeed, the world know too little about your great achievements in the war but I am sure the Service recognise all you have done to the full and we all share a great admiration, affection and appreciation of all you have done and this appears to be the right opportunity in which to express it.

I do so now with great affection and friendship.
>   Yours ever
>   Dickie

This 'affection and friendship' had always seemed genuine enough, with Mountbatten motoring over from 'Broadlands' on the occasions when Lord Fraser, in his latter years, visited Haslar Naval Hospital for observation or treatment. Only the week before Mountbatten's assassination in August 1979, the last of these meetings had taken place in Haslar on the friendliest of terms. But now, in December 1980, Lord Fraser was cut to the heart by the dismissive comments about him which Lord Mountbatten's image had posthumously – and unanswerably – broadcast to an audience of millions. 'The feller,' Lord Fraser told me – and *never* had I heard him use such a term for a fellow naval officer of any rank – 'the feller might have said that *I* was the one who asked for him to join the Board of Admiralty. When he was Fourth Sea Lord he *did* try to take over ammunition, which wasn't his job, and I had to tell him so.' He then told me, very firmly, 'I don't want this dealt with separately, Richard' (as we had agreed to do in the case of *Churchill and the Admirals* – see Appendix 1); 'I want this *in the book!*'

But to the last, Lord Fraser remained a man to whom sustained bitterness was a stranger; and his undoubted unhappiness over the Mountbatten broadcasts had already abated before his last illness set in as the New Year of 1981 opened. Though Lord Fraser expressed his usual eagerness to see the spring flowers again, it was not to be. As the end peacefully approached in the afternoon of 12 February 1981 Renée Duncan was at his side.

On 8 April 1981, a beautiful day of spring sunshine, the nation bade its formal farewell to one of its greatest sailors with a Memorial and Thanksgiving Service in Westminster Abbey. HRH Prince Philip, with representatives of the Royal, Commonwealth, United States and NATO navies, were in glittering attendance. In his Address (see Appendix 2) Sir Henry Leach, the First Sea Lord, paid tribute to 'Bruce Fraser the man', who 'made no great mistakes nor great enemies, and was loved and respected by all with whom he came in contact'. Sir Henry concluded by quoting from Captain Ronald Hopwood's poem of homage to the Navy's tradition, 'Our Fathers':

'Then if still we dare to argue that we're just as good as they,
We can seek the God of Battles on our knees, and humbly pray
That the work we leave behind us, when our earthly race is run,
May be half as well completed as our Fathers' work was done.'

As the Abbey thrillingly resounded to 'Reveille' from the Royal Marine buglers, my mind cast back to Lord Fraser in his armchair at 'Moorcroft', stirring in mild protest as I read him one of the many affectionate reminiscences which had reached me from his former sailors. 'Yes,' he said, 'yes – they're all very kind. It's very good of them. But you know, Richard, in the end it isn't words that matter – it's *deeds*.'

Appendix 1
Points arising from
Churchill and the Admirals
by Captain S. W. Roskill

I had only just started research on Lord Fraser's biography when Captain Roskill published his book *Churchill and the Admirals* (Collins, 1977). Naturally I bought a copy hot from the press, eager to see what Roskill might have to say in amplification of his many generous references to Lord Fraser in *The War at Sea*. At once, however, I realised that I had a serious problem on my hands. The picture of Lord Fraser painted in *Churchill and the Admirals* was, in my view, severely lop-sided, the result of a puzzling series of 'sins of omission'. Worst of all, from my point of view, Roskill's version of the relationship between Fraser and Cunningham demanded a reply which, if not made with care, could well turn out as an equally one-sided criticism of Cunningham – a wholly undesirable distraction from the basic objective of presenting Lord Fraser's life story to the public.

I had learned enough about Lord Fraser at our first meeting to appreciate his emphatic distaste for irrelevant or sensational controversy – 'journalists trying to make a story out of nothing', as he would put it. Lord Fraser's own wishes apart, it seemed to me that his biography was no place for a wrangle between historians, yet, at the same time, *Churchill and the Admirals* had to be answered. Happily, a solution to the problem was reached at a very early stage. Lord Fraser readily agreed to my suggestion that *Churchill and the Admirals* should be dealt with in detail in a separate appendix. Two or three discussion sessions sufficed to establish Lord Fraser's point of view; the text of this Appendix was drafted and approved; and we thankfully returned to the preparation of *Fraser of North Cape*.

Having used the phrase 'sins of omission' I propose to list these in the order in which they appear in *Churchill and the Admirals*, from which the page numbers quoted below refer to the first edition by Collins in 1977.

1 Footnote, p.158: the bombardment of the French fleet at Oran in July 1940

Roskill writes:

> None of them [Admirals Cunningham, Somerville and North] ever budged from the view that, given more time for negotiation, the tragedy could have been averted. On 9 January 1950 Cunningham wrote to Admiral Lord Fraser, then First Sea Lord, that '90 per cent of senior naval officers, including myself, thought Oran was a ghastly error and still do.'

However, Roskill does not quote Fraser's reply, nor Fraser's opinion, vehemently maintained, that Admiral Somerville was largely to blame for having presented the British ultimatum to Admiral Gensoul via a subordinate instead of going to see Gensoul himself.

2 P.165: Fraser's letter to Cunningham of 5 January 1950 in defence of Pound

Roskill makes no mention of the fact that Fraser, as Pound's former Chief of Staff in the Mediterranean, certainly understood Pound far better than Cunningham could have done. In view of Roskill's extensive criticism of Pound, his omission of this fact is unfortunate.

3 P.234: Fraser's appointment as C-in-C, Home Fleet

Somewhat surprisingly, apart from the fleeting references quoted above, this is the first real mention of Fraser in *Churchill and the Admirals* Roskill writes: 'Churchill had entertained a strong admiration, even affection for Fraser ever since he had proved a patient, adaptable and very successful Controller of the Navy during Churchill's tenure as First Lord. Towards Tovey he felt, as was mentioned earlier, much less warmly.'

Though essentially accurate this sketch is incomplete, suggesting that Fraser's wagon was hitched to Churchill's star. Fraser, of course, was Controller from March 1939 to June 1942, when he went to the Home Fleet as VA2.

In *Churchill and the Admirals* there is no mention at all of Fraser's prewar achievements as DNO and the way in which they were, in a sense, crowned by his time as Controller. It would have been charitable to point out that by 3 September 1939 Fraser already had a track record of solid achievement in updating the Navy to make it fit for another war; and it was to Fraser that Churchill turned on his very first day back at the Admiralty (*see above*, p.132).

Roskill also fails to mention either Fraser's eleven months as VA2 Home Fleet, or his 'incognito' passage with the appalling 'Pedestal' convoy to Malta in August 1942. To any reader without the proper background knowledge, Roskill's version in *Churchill and the Admirals* suggests that Fraser went straight from the Controller's office to the Home Fleet command: a Court appointment made less on Fraser's professional merits than Churchill's preference for tractable subordinates.

4. PP. 236–7: The resignation and death of Sir Dudley Pound, and Churchill's offer of the post of First Sea Lord to Fraser

This whole passage again implies that Churchill wanted Fraser to succeed Pound because Fraser was a compliant admiral to whom Churchill could dictate at will. Having already omitted any mention of the way in which Fraser had stood up to Churchill in Cabinet (see above, p.142), Roskill asserts that 'from the beginning of the war he [Churchill] was determined not to have strong men as First Lord and First Sea Lord'. Moreover, fond though he is of quoting 'off-the-record' discussions between Churchill and other Admirals, Roskill fails to spell out the way in which Fraser declined the offer and urged Churchill to send for Cunningham – 'Cunningham has the confidence of the Navy' – which Churchill himself was moved to quote in his own memoirs (*The Second World War*, Vol. 5, p.146).

5 Fraser's record as C-in-C, Home Fleet

Having warmly written up Fraser's predecessors, Admirals Forbes and Tovey, and the problems both had had with Churchill and the Admiralty, Roskill makes no mention at all of Fraser's impressive record as C-in-C, Home Fleet. This included widening and deepening the collaboration with the US Navy begun while Fraser was still Controller, and, by taking the Fleet through to Murmansk, attempting to establish some genuine rapport with the Russian naval authorities as well. All of this proved that Fraser was a promising diplomat as well as a most able fleet commander (the *Scharnhorst* action is not even mentioned in *Churchill and the Admirals*), which added mightily to Fraser's qualifications for the command of the BPF.

6 PP. 237–8: Cunningham's diary assertions that Fraser threatened to haul down his flag rather than repeat the 'Tungsten' air strike on *Tirpitz*

Roskill's absolute reliance on Cunningham's vitriolic diary entries for 13–14 April 1944, with no attempt to obtain Fraser's side of the story, is hard to accept. It suggests an unqualified hero-worship of Cunningham which, for once, cannot be wholly justified.

Having admitted that the Fleet Air Arm lacked the weapons with which 'to do lethal damage to the very stoutly built and heavily protected battleship', Roskill does not go on to point out that a second strike could only court unnecessary losses in aircrew and aircraft. Fraser was fully aware of this, also of the luck the Home Fleet had had in being granted a brief spell of fine weather in which to launch the first strike. And Cunningham, who had suffered more than most fleet commanders from peremptory Admiralty directives issued in ignorance of the situation on the spot, should certainly have respected Fraser's objections to a second strike.

Roskill's unqualified acceptance of Cunningham's diary entries is, in my submission, quite untenable. Just how high can double standards be hoisted when judging the worth of historical evidence? On p.283 Roskill admits that 'interviews can certainly be valuable; but such evidence must none the less be treated with caution – especially if the person interviewed has an interest, even perhaps a sub-conscious one, in propagating some particular point of view, or if he is speaking from memory of distant events'. Fair enough, but this does not explain why Roskill made no attempt to obtain the reply of Fraser to this charge of monumental indiscipline. Fraser was, after all, the man on the other end of the 'phone! Nor am I convinced that a choleric diary entry (and Cunningham could be extremely choleric when crossed!), made in the heat of exasperation, deserves to be treated as holy writ simply because it is 'a document'.

Captain G. Coney, at the time FGO on Fraser's staff, wrote to the author that 'Fraser in my experience never raised his voice or lost his temper, and if there was a "row" I suspect it was A.B.C. who did most of the shouting!' Lord Fraser himself remained adamant that he never threatened to haul down his flag, and he was always noted for his excellent memory and his readiness to admit to mistakes. He stated that he hung up on the First Sea Lord when Cunningham began to act as though Fraser had given in – 'He said, "I'm so glad you agree", when I hadn't done anything of the kind.' Negotiations between Scapa and Whitehall were then taken up by the staffs; and it was at this point that the 'threat' may have been used metaphorically by one of the Scapa staff officers to stress how dead set Fraser was against attempting a second strike.

As Fraser never kept a diary of his own, the documentary evidence for this episode is therefore incomplete, and Roskill should have said so. Roskill's version repeats an extremely serious accusation against Fraser, made by Cunningham in a flash of bad temper, though soon dispelled by events proving Fraser to have been absolutely right. And

Cunningham's over-reaction to Fraser's refusal to be brow-beaten brings us to the most serious of all the omissions in *Churchill and the Admirals.*

7 Cunningham's resentment of Fraser, and its reasons

Concluding his account of the 'Tungsten' affair, Roskill had this to say:

> It is difficult to assess the rights and wrongs of this squall at the top of the naval hierarchy. Perhaps it was merely a case, in Kipling's words, 'where two strong men stand face to face, though they come from the ends of the earth', but it does remind one of the rows between admirals earlier in the twentieth century, some of which have been mentioned here, but which did not, fortunately, often recur during World War II.

Unfortunately this is not good enough, ignoring as it does Cunningham's undoubted resentment at only becoming First Sea Lord as 'second best' to Fraser.

'It was well known at my level,' Captain Coney wrote to the author, 'that Cunningham was only holding the fort for Fraser to succeed him later' – and if this was so 'well known' at Coney's level then Commander Roskill, as he then was, must have caught echoes of it too. Much more important, the 'Tungsten' disagreement occurred when Cunningham had been at the Admiralty for six months: ample time for him to pick up the appropriate vibrations from the Admiralty grapevine and become thoroughly irked by them.

The whole subject can surely be laid to rest now by quoting from Lord Mountbatten's letter to Fraser on the latter's 90th birthday (February 1978) in which Mountbatten wrote:

> I know how much Prince Philip enjoyed having you as a shipmate aboard the *Britannia,* and he was quite amazed when I told him the story that Winston and the Chiefs of Staff had decided that you should be offered the post of First Sea Lord in succession to Dudley Pound, and then turned it down in favour of A.B.C. *This was a very well-guarded secret but, I'm afraid, was the cause of a psychological upset that A.B.C. suffered from in relation to you* (Author's italics).

The essential point, which supersedes all else, is that whatever friction existed between Cunningham and Fraser was, in the long run, irrelevant, never once threatening to becoming an all-out feud on the scale of that, say, between Admirals Fisher and Beresford before the First World War. Both Fraser and Cunningham were far too practical, and had too much common sense, to let their differences affect their necessary collaboration in the task of winning the war.

8 Fraser's insistence that the British Pacific Fleet adopt American signalling

Admiralty reluctance to allow the British Pacific Fleet to go over to the American system threatened to cripple the Fleet's chances at birth. This was averted by Fraser's insistence that the British Pacific Fleet *must* adopt American signalling if it were to be accepted as a useful ally – as American warships had already adopted British signalling when serving under British auspices – but Roskill makes no mention of this at all.

9 P.276: How Fraser reacted to Churchill's 'love-hate relationship' with the admirals

According to Roskill, 'Churchill never took kindly to servicemen who opposed him on any score.' This is clearly an exaggeration; Montgomery was an outstanding example of a senior officer who repeatedly put Churchill in check when circumstances demanded, and got away with it. Apart from the argument over merchant shipping (*see below*), Fraser joined forces with Pound to block Churchill's plan to send old battleships into the Baltic ('Catherine'); and it was Fraser who refused to overturn the building programme to build the new battleship *Vanguard*, insisting that no battleship could be built in a year.

10 P.280: Churchill's accusation that Fraser 'disobeyed orders' over the priority of merchant shipping repairs in 1940

This, admits Roskill, 'was especially absurd in the case of Fraser, who was always very attentive to Churchill's ideas and wishes'; yet Roskill's failure to quote Fraser's spirited rebuttal leaves the reader with the impression that Fraser swallowed Churchill's accusation without further demur.

11 P.281: Fraser's claim that Churchill did listen to hostile criticism
Roskill writes:

> Lord Fraser has remarked that 'He [Churchill] rarely pressed his case if sound arguments were put up against it'; but the despatch of the *Prince of Wales* and *Repulse* to Singapore in 1941 and the Aegean fiasco of 1943 surely lay that opinion open to challenge.

Lord Fraser's reply to this statement came straight from the shoulder:

'Yes. Well, of course, it doesn't at all. What happened there was that Dudley Pound agreed to *Prince of Wales* and *Repulse* going out if they were accompanied by an aircraft-carrier; and then the aircraft-carrier (*Indomitable*) went aground, and Dudley Pound said he couldn't send the ships out without a carrier. Churchill realised, when there wasn't an aircraft-carrier, that he'd have to make a change. He did. He said, "I want the two ships" – and these were his own words – "I want the two ships to go out there, *based on Australia, under Australian air cover*, and be a thorn in the side of the Japanese." ' (Author's italics)

Appendix 2
In memoriam
Address delivered by the First Sea Lord, Admiral Sir Henry Leach, GCB, ADC, at the Service of Thanksgiving, Westminster Abbey, 8 April 1981

We are gathered here today to pay tribute to a great sailor, a great gentleman and a great friend.

It is difficult to do adequate justice to an Admiral of the Fleet who was born nearly a century ago and whose life covered such a tremendous range: at sea in the pre-Dreadnought Navy; served in both World Wars; designed, put into production and fought a successful major sea action with the most advanced naval weapon of the age; who spent eight months in a Bolshevik prison but 25 years later received the Order of Suvorov, 1st Class, at the hand of Stalin himself; who commanded three Fleets in war; was Controller of the Navy and First Sea Lord; a member of the House of Lords; made no great mistakes nor great enemies; and was loved and respected by all with whom he came in contact. His career has been extensively covered in obituaries; I will try to concentrate on Bruce Fraser the man.

Highly intelligent, he obtained first-class certificates in all subjects as a Sub-Lieutenant. He specialised in Gunnery and was awarded the Egerton Memorial Prize for the best all-round student, subsequently undergoing the advanced course; throughout this period he demonstrated that he was a brilliant mathematician with a scientific turn of mind. His brain was matched by his ingenuity and pragmatism; at Gallipoli, for example, he increased the firepower of the elderly cruiser in which he was then serving in his first job at sea as a Gunnery Officer by acquiring an Army field gun and mounting it on the capstan. These attributes were nowhere put to better use than in the design of the highly successful 14-inch turrets for the ultimate in the Royal Navy's battleships.

His was also an acutely inquisitive mind, taking nothing for granted but fascinated by technicalities, the essentials of which he quickly grasped. Yet he never boasted of his achievements in technical innovation and the closest he ever came to admitting personal involvement was to give that gentle chuckle which those close to him came to know so well and quietly remark, 'We tried it, and it worked.' Indeed he never boasted of anything and it would be hard to find a man of his talents and position so totally devoid of pretension or pomposity, so unconscious of rank or position, and so very human and endowed with the common touch. He never sought publicity but when it came his way he would use it to promote the Navy, not himself.

The Navy was his whole life. He was a true professional whose particular brand of leadership was by example. He set himself standards of loyalty and integrity which can seldom have been surpassed and I doubt have often been equalled. This was infectious and an inspiration to all: you knew he would never let you down. No one appreciated this more than his fellow-prisoners in Bolshevik captivity. When released in 1920 they clubbed together and bought him a dress sword which he thereafter always used; it was a treasured possession which only last year he presented to the Naval Museum at Portsmouth. In return he demanded that no one should let *him* down, and he was ruthless over negligence or slipshod inefficiency – there was the case of an officer ordered to leave his ship within half an hour and of a member of his personal retinue sacked on the spot – but always with scrupulous fairness and due attention to the other view. He never raised his voice but the quiet, cold statement 'That's bad' was reproof enough for most.

He had a keen sense of humour and an enormous sense of fun. Like all great leaders he had a streak of independence, a touch of the rebel, backed by a dogged determination from which he would not be deflected so long as he was convinced he was right. This attitude was epitomised in his favourite few lines of verse on which he often drew and which ran:

Life is a voyage,

The winds of life blow strong from every point,
But each will speed thy way along
If thou with steady hand while tempests blow
Wilt set thy course aright, and never once let go.

He was forever encouraging initiative and practising decentralisation. A disciple of flexibility, he knew in his wisdom that in war things seldom go as planned or as previously envisaged. Totally unflappable in a crisis, he was invariably courteous and expected others to display good manners, sincerity and straightness.

He was never happier than when surrounded by people. He adored the young and would do anything for them. On a certain speech day at a school of which he was a Governor a youngster came up to the platform for his special prize, but the prize had got mislaid and could not be found; seeing the boy's disappointment, Bruce Fraser unhesitatingly took his gold watch out of his waistcoat pocket and handed it over.

Long after he left active service he used to remark that the event which gave him the greatest pleasure since retirement was the personal invitation from Prince Philip to accompany the Royal Family in *Britannia*. Apart from travelling abroad in his small car he had few hobbies or pastimes, but he continued to delight in meeting and talking with ordinary people. Every year at Christmas he would invite his local tradesmen – the milkman, dustman, shopkeeper, etc. – to a special party, an event which was much looked forward to in the neighbourhood.

Though his body became increasingly frail, his mind remained active and alert to the end, and he retained astonishing windows of memory. When the time came, he died as he had lived, quietly and without fuss. His devoted friend and ever-ready help, Renée Duncan, was with him only a quarter of an hour before.

In ending these few and very inadequate words I can do no better than draw on Captain Ronald Hopwood's well-known lines:

Then if still we dare to argue that we're just as good as they,
We can seek the God of Battles on our knees, and humbly pray
That the work we leave behind us, when our earthly race is run,
May be half as well completed as our Fathers' work was done.

Notes

Unpublished sources referred to in Notes

1 *Fraser Papers* (FP): Lord Fraser granted me unrestricted access to this fascinating collection, now in the charge of his executrix, Mrs Renée Duncan, for collating and cataloguing. Alas for historians, private diaries or journals are conspicuous by their absence, for Lord Fraser kept none. ('Well', he told me in mild reproof, 'We weren't supposed to.') The corpus of papers is replete with such gems as the epistolary account of the High Seas Fleet's surrender and internment (pp.55–61), and the purloined Admiralty Docket S.D.O. 2247/40 in which the 'Ali Baba and the thieves' joke with Lord Beaverbrook took root (p.144).

2 *Fraser Interview Tapes* (FIT): These consist of cassette recordings in the author's possession, made between November 1977 and December 1980 in a series of never-to-be-forgotten afternoon visits to Lord Fraser's home in East Molesey. The interviews ranged over widely differing topics prompted by the author and developed by Lord Fraser from his illimitable memory. I would then transcribe the tapes and submit typescripts of the most promising passages to Lord Fraser for his confirmation and approval. Though a lengthy process, it had the advantage of saving 'live' interview time and allowing both parties to double-check dates and other points of fact.

3 *Fraser Memoir Tape* (FMT): I use this term for a reel of selected recordings made by Lord Fraser on the encouragement of Mrs Renée Duncan. These reminiscences of Lord Fraser's early career were made several years before he gave permission for work on his biography to begin. The tape remains with the Fraser Papers.

1 'A most promising boy', 1888–1904
1 Fraser Interview Tapes (FIT).
2 Mason, Philip, *A Matter of Honour* (Jonathan Cape, London, 1974), p. 147.
3 FIT.
4 Letter to General Fraser, Fraser Papers (FP).
5 Ibid.
6 FP.
7 Ibid.
8 FIT.
9 *Daily Telegraph*, Tuesday, 2 November 1903.
10 Ibid.

2 Sea legs: *Hannibal* and *Prince George*, 1904–7

1 Fraser Memoir Tape (FMT).
2 FIT.
3 FMT.
4 Ibid.
5 Ibid.
6 FIT.
7 FMT.

8 Log of HMS *Prince George*, Public Record Office (ADM.53/24984).
9 Author's translation from M. Novince's *Ode* in FP.
10 *The Times*, 28 September 1906.

3 The Dreadnought Navy, 1907–12

1 *cf* Marder, Arthur J., *From the Dreadnought to Scapa Flow*, Vol. 1 (Oxford University Press, 1961), p. 11.
2 Ibid., pp. 38–43, 52–6.
3 Ibid., pp. 43–5, 56–70.

4 FIT.
5 Ibid.
6 Marder, *From the Dreadnought to Scapa Flow*, Vol. 1, p. 206.
7 FIT.
8 Ibid.

4 HMS *Excellent*, 1912–14

1 FIT.
2 Ibid.
3 Ibid.
4 Ibid.
5 *cf* Broome, Jack, *Make Another Signal*, William Kimber, London, 1973, 'A Signal Which Exploded'; also Marder, *From the*

Dreadnought to Scapa Flow, Vol. 1, pp. 97–100.
6 FIT.
7 FP.
8 FIT.
9 Ibid.
10 FP.

5 The old *Minerva*, 1914–15

1 Log of HMS *Minerva*, Public Record Office (ADM. 53/49449).
2 Letter of Lt Colonel G. R. Hawkins, OBE, RM, to author, 24.2.78.
3 Churchill, W. S., *The World Crisis* (Macmillan, London, 1931), 'Ireland and the European Balance'.
4 FIT.
5 FMT.
6 Lawrence, T.E., *Seven Pillars of Wisdom* (Penguin Books ed., Harmondsworth, 1964), Ch.LV,

p. 322.
7 FIT.
8 Log of HMS *Minerva*, Public Record Office (ADM.53/49449).
9 FIT.
10 Letter of Lt Colonel Hawkins to author, 24.2.78.
11 FIT.
12 Ibid.
13 Ibid.
14 Log of HMS *Minerva*, Public Record Office (ADM.53/49449).
15 FMT.
16 Ibid.

6 Gallipoli, 1915–16

1 FMT.
2 Log of HMS *Minerva*, March 1915, Public Record Office (ADM.53/49450).
3 Ibid., April 1915 (ADM.53/49451).
4 FIT.
5 FMT.

6 Diary of Air Vice-Marshal Sir Geoffrey Bromet (in May 1915 Sub-Lieutenant, RNAS); quoted in Liddle, Peter, *Men of Gallipoli* (Allen Lane, London, 1976), p. 163.
7 FMT.
8 FIT.

9 Log of HMS *Minerva*, July 1915, Public Record Office (ADM.53/49454).

7 Battleship *Resolution*, 1916–19
1 FIT.
2 Letter of Alfred H. Howard, LRAM Bandmaster, RM (retired) to author, 22.2.78.
3 FIT.
4 Letter of Alfred H. Howard to

8 Prisoner of the Bolsheviks, 1920
1 FIT.
2 Fraser's report, 'Enzeli Expedition', dated 12.11.20 and drafted for Commander-in-Chief, Mediterranean, while on passage to Constantinople in HMS *Centurion*; copy in FP.
3, 4, 5, 6, 7, 8, 9 Ibid.

9 Fleet Gunnery Officer, 1921–9
1 FIT.
2 FP.
3 Letter of Commander R. B. Chandler, OBE, RN, to author 1.3.78.
4 Ibid.
5 FIT. For full technical details *see* 1927 report on Fire Control

10 Captain of the *Effingham*, 1929–32
1 FIT.
2 For the most comprehensive account of the East Indies Squadron's 'beat' *see* log of HMS *Effingham* (1929–31), Public Record Office, ADM.53/76629–44.
3 Letter to Mrs Fraser, 5.1.30, FP.
4 Ibid.
5 Ibid.
6 Undated letter to Mrs Fraser, January 1930, FP.
7 Ibid.
8 Letter to Mrs Fraser, 1.6.30. FP.
9 Letter to Mrs Fraser, 23.6.30, FP.

11 Birth of the 'KG Vs', 1933–5
1 Churchill, W. S., *The Gathering Storm* (Cassell, London 1948).
2 Ibid.
3 FIT.

10 FMT.
11 FP.

author, 22.2.78.
5 Churchill, *The World Crisis*, 'Jutland: the Preliminaries'.
6 FP.
7 Ibid.
8 FIT.

10 FIT.
11 Fraser's report, *op.cit*
12, 13, 14, 15, 16, 17, 18, 19 Ibid.
20 FMT.
21 Fraser's report, *op.cit*
22 Ibid.
23 FIT.
24 Fraser's report, *op.cit*.

Table, Public Record Office, ADM.186/273, 275.
6 FIT.
7 Ibid.
8 FP.
9 FIT.
10 Ibid.

10 Letter to Cecil Fraser, 26.7.30, FP.
11 Letter to Mrs Fraser, 2.10.30, FP.
12 Letter to Mrs Fraser, 28.4.31. FP.
13 Ibid.
14 Ibid.
15 FMT.
16 Ibid.
17 FIT.
18 Ibid.
19 Letter to Mrs Fraser, 7.2.32, FP.
20 Ibid.
21 Letter to Mrs Fraser, 10.6.32, FP.
22 FMT.

4 Ibid.
5 Ibid.
6 Ibid.

12 Carrier *Glorious*, 1935–7

1 Letter of Frank Hague, FSCTE, to author, 19.2.78.
2 Ibid.
3 Letter of J. H. McCahon to author, 7.8.78.
4 Ibid.
5 FIT.
6 I am indebted to J. H. McCahon for his concise account of this incident.
7 FIT.
8 Ibid.
9 Letter of Frank Hague to author, 19.2.78.

13 Rear-Admiral and Chief of Staff, 1938

1 FP.
2 This and all subsequent quotations are from the original draft of 'War with Germany, Italy and Japan' in FP.

14 Third Sea Lord and Controller, 1939–40

1 Roskill, S. W., *The War at Sea*, Vol. 1 (Her Majesty's Stationery Office, London, 1954) p. 26.
2 FIT.
3 Churchill, *The Gathering Storm*, 'War'.
4 Ibid., 'The Admiralty Task'.
5 FIT.
6 Ibid.
7 Churchill, *The Gathering Storm*, 'The Admiralty Task'.
8 FIT.
9 Churchill, W. S. *Their Finest Hour* (Cassell, London, 1949), 'The National Coalition'.
10 FIT.
11 Churchill, *The Gathering Storm*, 'Appendix II: First Lord's Minutes'.
12 Ibid., 'Appendix G, Plan "Catherine".'
13 Ibid., 'Appendix H, New Construction and Reconstruction'.
14 FIT.
15 Churchill, *The Gathering Storm*, 'The Combat Deepens'.

15 The years of crisis, 1940–2

1 Churchill, *The Gathering Storm*, 'Appendix II: First Lord's Minutes'.
2 Ibid.
3 FIT. The VT ('Variable Time') or proximity fuse detonated shells passing close enough to a target, without the need for a direct hit. A British idea, taken as far as Lindemann's demonstration model as early as February 1940, the VT fuse was perfected and mass-produced by the Americans, with their enormous lead in miniaturised technology.
4 Ibid.
5 Churchill, *Their Finest Hour*, 'The National Coalition'.
6 Macmillan, Harold, *The Blast of War* (Macmillan, London, 1967). 'Arming the Nation', p. 98.
7 Another well-known 'boilermaker' was General Sir Frederick ('Tim') Pile, mastermind of Britain's AA-gun defences – the Air Defence Artillery.
8 From original S.D.O.2247/40, with annotations, FP.
9 Ibid.
10 FP.
11 Churchill, *The Gathering Storm*, 'Appendix II: First Lord's Minutes'.
12 FIT.
13 Ibid.
14 Roskill, *The War at Sea*, Vol. 1, 'American assistance extended', p. 455.
15 Added by Lord Fraser during drafting of chapter.

16 Second-In-Command, June 1942–May 1943

1 Admiralty 'HUSH' to C-in-C HF, 27 June 1942 (0157B/27). This vital 'where it all started to go wrong' signal is quoted in full in what must surely be the definitive analysis of the PQ.17 tragedy: Broome, Jack, *Convoy is to Scatter* (William Kimber, London, 1972).
2 Schofield, B. B., *The Russian Convoys* (Batsford, London, 1964), 'The Ill-Starred Convoys', p. 94.
3 Admiral of the Fleet Lord Tovey of Langton Matravers, *London Gazette*, 18 October 1950.
4 FIT.
5 Letter of Commander J. G Forbes, RN (retired) to author, 22.2.78.
6 FIT.
7 Ibid.
8 Ibid.
9 Letter of Commander Forbes to author, 22.2.78.
10 Churchill, W. S., *The Hinge of Fate* (Cassell, London, 1952).
11 Courage, Captain Richard, unpublished memoirs.
12 *cf* Schofield, *The Russian Convoys*, 'To the Sound of the Guns'; and Pope, Dudley, *73 North* (Weidenfeld & Nicolson, London, 1958).
13 Letter of R. C. Freaker to author, 20.2.78.
14 Letter of Commander C. J. Eliot, RN (retired) to author, 28.2.78.
15 Letter of B. L. Hall to author, 7.4.78.
16 FP.

17 Commander-in-Chief, Home Fleet, May-December 1943

1 Broome, *Convoy is to Scatter*, pp. 210–11.
2 Roskill, *The War at Sea*, Vol. 3, Part 1 (1960), p. 57.
3 Letter of Lt Commander Selwyn Powell, RNVR (retired) to author, 13.4.78.
4 FIT.
5 Ibid.
6 Ibid.
7 Letter of Captain P. H. E. Welby-Everard, RN to author, 1.3.78.
8 Captain Vernon Merry, RN (retired) to author, recorded 9.1.79.
9 Letter of Lieutenant J. D'a Nesbit, RNR, to author 27.2.78.
10 Ibid.
11 FIT.
12 FP.
13 Churchill, W. S., *Closing the Ring* (Cassell, London, 1954), 'A Spell at Home'.
14 FIT.
15 Churchill, *Closing the Ring*, 'A Spell at Home'.
16 FP.
17 Courage, Captain Richard, unpublished memoirs.
18 Golovko, Admiral Arseni, *With* the Red Fleet (Putnam, London, 1965), 'The End of the Scharnhorst', pp. 179–87.
19 Ibid.
20 Ibid.
21 FIT.
22 Golovko, *With the Red Fleet*.
23 Beesly, Patrick, 'Special Intelligence and Convoy Routing: JW.55B and the destruction of *Scharnhorst*' (with Dr Jürgen Rohwer). Translation from original German edition of *Marine Rundschau* (Oct. 1977), most kindly loaned to this author. *See also* Patrick Beesly's excellent book *Very Special Intelligence: the story of the Admiralty's Operational Intelligence Centre, 1939–45* (Hamish Hamilton, London, 1977).
24 Courage, Captain Richard, unpublished memoirs.
25 RT refers to radiotelephone, better known as 'TBS' – 'Talk Between Ships.' For Fraser's introduction to RT, *see below*, p.219.
26 FIT.

18 Sinking the *Scharnhorst*, 23–26 December 1943

1 Courage, Captain Richard, unpublished memoirs.
2 Beesly, *Very Special Intelligence*. 'D/F' is Direction finding (from intercepted radio transmissions).
3 Ibid.
4 Dönitz, Grand-Admiral Karl, *Memoirs: Ten Years and Twenty Days* (Weidenfeld & Nicolson, London, 1959).
5 Courage, Captain Richard, unpublished memoirs.
6 Beesly, *Very Special Intelligence*.
7 Ibid.
8 FIT.
9 Lord Fraser's own choice of adjective, substituted during drafting. I had written 'admirable' but this was rejected. 'No,' he quietly but firmly interjected: 'it wasn't admirable. It was *brilliant*.'
10 Busch, Korvettenkapitän Fritz-Otto, *The Drama of the Scharnhorst* (Robert Hale, London, 1956), p. 114.
11 Wintle, Commander K., letter to author 2.3.78, from whose invaluable sketch the diagram of the star-shell pattern is reproduced.
12 *The Naval Review*, No. 4, Vol. XXXV, November 1947: 'Sinking of the German Battle-cruiser *Scharnhorst* on the 26th December 1943', p. 311.
13 FIT.
14 Courage, Captain Richard, unpublished memoirs.
15 FIT.
16 Roskill, *The War at Sea*, Vol. 3, Part 1, p. 86.
17 *The Naval Review*, No. 4, Vol. XXXV.
18 Courage, Captain Richard, unpublished memoirs.
19 Lieutenant Bates received a richly deserved DSC and the nickname of 'Bare-hand Bates' for this feat.
20 FIT.
21 Fraser, Admiral Lord, '*Scharnhorst* Despatch', Supplement to *The London Gazette*, August 1947.
22 Scharnhorst *immer Voran!* (*Scharnhorst* ever onwards!) was the ship's motto and was also broadcast by Captain Hintze to urge on his men in their last fight.
23 Copy of Wing Commander Compston's report most kindly loaned to author by Captain Richard Courage.
24 *The Naval Review*, No. 4, Vol. XXXV.
25 Fraser, Admiral Lord, *op.cit.*
26 For the most succinctly presented 'edition' of key signals in the North Cape action *see* Broome, *Make Another Signal*.
27 Courage, Captain Richard, unpublished memoirs.
28 Merry, Captain Vernon, letter to author, 18.1.81.
29 Golovko, *With the Red Fleet*, pp. 186–7.
30 Ibid.
31 Courage, Captain Richard, unpublished memoirs.
32 FIT.
33 *The Naval Review*, No. 4, Vol. XXXV.

19 Last months with the Home Fleet, January–June 1944

1 Courage, Captain Richard, unpublished memoirs.
2 FP.
3 *See* the account of 'Tungsten' in Roskill, *The War at Sea*, Vol. 3, Part 1, pp. 273–8.
4 *cf* Roskill, S. W., *Churchill and the Admirals* (Collins, London, 1977), pp. 237–8.
5 Roskill, *The War at Sea*, Vol. 3, Part 1, p. 281.
6 Quoted in Bauer, Eddy, *World War 2*, Vol. 5 (Orbis, London, 1973) p. 1,687.
7 FP.

8 FIT.
9 Ibid.
10 FP.
11 Another attempt to repeat 'Tungsten' was foiled by *Tirpitz* being totally obscured by low cloud. A third attempt at the end of May, equally unsuccessful, was switched to anti-shipping attacks, north of Stadtlandet.
12 Mills, Sir John, *Up in the Clouds, Gentlemen Please* (Weidenfeld & Nicholson, London 1980), p. 192.
13 Ibid.
14 FIT.

20 The Eastern Fleet, June–November, 1944

1 Quoted in Broome, *Make Another Signal.*
2 *cf* Hough, Richard, *Mountbatten: Hero of Our Time* (Weidenfeld and Nicholson, London, 1980), pp. 165, 171; and Roskill, *Churchill and the Admirals*, pp. 251–5.
3 Captain Vernon Merry to author, recorded 9–10.1.79.
4 Ibid.
5 Ibid.
6 Ibid.
7 Ibid. For the unique debt owed to Renée Nash (afterwards Mrs Renée Duncan) in the compilation of this biography, *see* 'Acknowledgments'.

21 Building the British Pacific Fleet, December 1944–March 1945

1 Roskill, *The War At Sea*, Vol. 3, Part 2 (Her Majesty's Stationery Office, 1961), p. 203.
2 FIT.
3 Courage, Captain Richard, unpublished memoirs.
4 Captain Vernon Merry to author, recorded 9–10.1.79.
5 Letter of Commander Charles Sheppard to author, 2.4.78. I am also indebted to 2nd Officer Bond, WRNS (now Mrs Nancy Chaplin) for the loan of her article 'Blue Braid in the Pacific', giving the 'Wren's eye view' of the Pearl Harbor visit.
6 Courage, Captain Richard, unpublished memoirs.
7 Martin, Jonathan, 'Kamikaze: the "divine wind" ', *World War 2*, Vol. 7 (Orbis, London, 1973), Ch. 166, pp., 2,776–7.
8 Captain Vernon Merry to author, recorded 9–10.1.79.
9 Ibid.
10 Ibid.
11 Ibid.
12 'Top Secret' from Fraser to Admiralty, DTG.170619z/Jan/45.
13 Ibid. DTG.170633z/Jan/45.
14 Ibid. DTG.170651z/Jan/45.
15 FP.
16 Letter of Cunningham to Fraser, 19.1.45, FP.
17 Ibid.
18 FIT.
19 Ibid.
20 Quoted by Roskill, *The War at Sea*, Vol. 3, Part 2, p. 334.
21 Ibid.
22 Vian, Admiral of the Fleet Sir Philip, *Action This Day* (Frederick Muller, London, 1960), 'Operations off Sumatra', pp. 170–1.

22 The Defeat of Japan, March–September 1945

1 Letter of Commander Charles Sheppard to author, 2.4.78.
2 Pearcy, Arthur, Jnr, *The Dakota* (Ian Allan, Shepperton, 1972), 'British Pacific Fleet and the Dakota', pp. 132–42.
3 BPF Staff Minute Sheet from FCO: 'Visit to Manus 16th to 18th March 1945,' by courtesy of Captain Richard Courage.
4 Ibid.

5 BPF Staff Minute Sheet from FCO: 'Easter trip to the Tropics' (5.4.45), by courtesy of Captain Richard Courage.
6 Ibid.
7 Ibid.
8 Ibid.
9 Ibid.
10 Fraser to Admiralty: VA(Q), 11.5.45, in FP.
11 Fraser to Admiralty: DTG.310801z May 1945, in FP.
12 FIT.
13 Captain Vernon Merry to author, recorded 9–10.1.79.
14 Fraser to Admiralty: VA(Q), DTG.290248z July 1945, in FP.
15 Admiralty to Fraser, 1/241/2 0200z, in FP.
16 FIT.
17 Presentation copy of USS *Missouri*'s Deck Log, forenoon 2.9.45, autographed by Fleet Admiral Nimitz, in FP.
18 FP.

23 **'Thank you, Australia', September 1945–June 1946**
1 Cunningham to Fraser, 5 July 1945, FP.
2 Captain Vernon Merry to author, recorded 9–10.1.79.
3 Cunningham to Fraser, 6 October 1945, FP.
4 Ibid.
5 Fraser to Admiralty, transcript (undated), FP.
6 Ibid.
7 Captain Vernon Merry to author, recorded 9–10.1.79.
8 Letter of Col. J. A. C. Uniacke, RM, to author, 1.6.78.
9 FIT.
10 Cunningham to Fraser (longhand postscript), 6 October 1945, FP.
11, 12, 13 FP.
14 Letter of Attlee to Fraser, 16.12.45, FP.
15 Letter of ex-L/Tel. G. B. Race to author, 24.2.78.
16 FP.
17 Quoted from 'HMS *Swiftsure*' (ship's history of first commission).
18 I am indebted to Mrs Olga Parkes, daughter of Captain Purkis, for supplying me with extracts from her father's diary in *Menestheus*.
19 FIT.
20 Captain Vernon Merry to author, recorded 9–10.1.79.
21 Admiralty to Fraser, 12.7.46, FP.

24 **Commander-in-Chief, Portsmouth, June 1946–September 1948**
1 Captain Vernon Merry to author, recorded 9–10.1.79.
2 Letter of Captain G. D. Conley to author, 28.2.78.
3 Captain Vernon Merry to author, recorded 9–10.1.79.
4 FIT.
5 Ibid.
6 Letter of Lord Fraser to Editor of *The Times*, 5.12.46, copy in FP.
7 FIT.
8 Ibid.
9 Letter of Alfred H. Howard, LRAM Bandmaster, RM (retired) to author, 22.2.78.
10 Letter of Lt Commander Peter Tunbridge, RN (retired) to author, 22.2.78.
11 Letter of Commander C. E. Beckwith, RN (retired) to author, 23.2.78
12 Letter of Lieutenant David Hill, RNVR, to author, 20.2.78.
13 Letter of W. K. Tate to author, 22.2.78.
14 FIT.
15 Churchill to Fraser, 25.2.48.

25 First Sea Lord: the birth of NATO, 1948–50

1 Waugh, Evelyn, *Men At Arms* (Penguin Books, Harmondsworth, 1964), p. 12.
2 *cf* Montgomery of Alamein, *Memoirs* (Collins, London, 1958), 'I Make Myself a Nuisance in Whitehall', p. 481.
3 Ibid., pp. 484–6.

4 Ibid., 'Beginnings in Whitehall', pp. 436–7.
5 *The Naval Review*, No. 4, Vol. XXXVII, November 1949: 'Exercise *Trident*, An R.A.F. Comment', p. 239.
6 *cf* Broome, *Make Another Signal*, 'Naval History by Signal'.
7 FIT.

26 Goodbye to the Admiralty, 1950–1

1 FIT.
2 Letter of Vice-Admiral Sir Peter Gretton to author, 10.6.82.
3 FP.
4 Hough, *Mountbatten: Hero of Our Time*, p. 234.
5 FIT.
6 Hough, *Mountbatten: Hero of Our Time*, p. 238.

7 Letter of Vice-Admiral Sir Peter Gretton to author, 10.6.82.
8 FP.
9 Letter of Vice-Admiral Sir Peter Gretton to author, 10.6.82.
10 Admiralty to Fraser, 15.4.52, FP.
11 King George VI had died on 6 February 1952.

27 Sunset, 1952–81

1 Letter of Mr Thomas Wallas to author, 21.2.78.
2 Letter of Mr H. W. Gawthrop to author, 18.2.78.
3 FP.
4 Ibid.
5 *Hansard* summary in *The Naval Review*, No. 4, Vol. XLI, November 1953, 'Naval Estimate in the House of Lords, 1953', pp.

451–2.
6 *The Naval Review*, No. 1, Vol. XLIII, February 1955, 'Speeches by Naval Peers in the Debate on the Address', pp. 94–5.
7 Letter to Mrs Renée Duncan from HMY *Britannia*, 15.2.59, FP.
8 'For the 5th February', Lord Mountbatten to Lord Fraser, FP.

Select Bibliography

BAKER, RICHARD, *Dry Ginger* (W. H. Allen, London, 1977).

BROOME, JACK, *Make Another Signal* (William Kimber, London 1973); *Convoy is to Scatter* (William Kimber, London, 1972).

BUSCH, FRITZ-OTTO, *The Drama of the Scharnhorst* (Robert Hale, London, 1956).

CHURCHILL, WINSTON S., *The World Crisis* (Macmillan, London, 1931).

CHURCHILL, WINSTON S., *The Second World War*, 6 vols (Cassell, London, 1948–54): Volume 1, *The Gathering Storm* (1948); Volume 2, *Their Finest Hour* (1949); Volume 4, *The Hinge of Fate* (1952); Volume 5, *Closing the Ring* (1954).

GOLOVKO, ADMIRAL ARSENI G., *With the Red Fleet* (Putnam, 1965).

HOUGH, RICHARD, *Mountbatten: Hero of Our Time* (Weidenfeld & Nicolson, London, 1980).

LIDDLE, PETER, *Men of Gallipoli* (Allen Lane, London, 1976).

MARDER, ARTHUR J., *From the Dreadnought to Scapa Flow*, 5 vols. (Oxford University Press, 1961, 1965, 1966, 1969, 1970).

PEARCY, ARTHUR, JNR, ARAeS, *The Dakota* (Ian Allan, Shepperton, 1972).

POPE, DUDLEY, *73 North* (Weidenfeld & Nicolson, London, 1958).

RAVEN, ALAN, *King George the Fifth Class Battleships*, Ensign 1 series (Bivouac Books, 1972).

ROSKILL, S. W., *The War at Sea*, 3 vols (Her Majesty's Stationery Office, London, 1954–61); *Churchill and the Admirals*, (Collins, London, 1977).

SCHOFIELD, B. B., *The Russian Convoys* (Batsford, London, 1964).

VIAN, ADMIRAL of the Fleet SIR PHILIP, *Action This Day* (Frederick Muller, London, 1960).

WATTS, A. J., *Loss of the Scharnhorst* (Ian Allan, Shepperton, 1970).

WOODWARD, DAVID, *The Tirpitz* (William Kimber, London, 1953).

Index

Abadan: Fraser visits, in *Effingham* (1929–32), 88, 94; and Mossadeq oil crisis (1951), 323–4

Abdul Illah, Emir, Regent of Iraq, 243

Abyssinia, *see* Ethiopia

Achi Baba, Gallipoli, 44–5

Addiscombe College, 3–4

Addu Atoll: Fraser visits, in *Effingham* (1930), 93; Eastern Fleet withdrawn to (1942), 240; 336

Aden: and Fraser's time in *Effingham* (1929–32), 88, 91, 94, 97–8; and Eastern Fleet (1942), 241; 336

ADMIRALTY, BRITISH: praises Fraser's work on Director Firing Handbook (1914), 31; Fraser's work at, on Fire Control Table (1922–5), 82, 84; Fraser's work at, in Tactical Division (1926–9), 85–6; Fraser's work at, as DNO (1933–5), 100–6, 107; and RAF control of Fleet Air Arm (1918–37), 110–11; and Munich Crisis (1938), 117–18; war plans of, and Fraser's appointment as Controller (1939), 123, 127–9; Fraser's work at, as Controller (1939–42), 127–39, 140–50; and PQ.17 fiasco, 151–3; and first JW convoys, 158–60; and North Cape battle, 184–6, 187–95, 218; reluctance of, to adopt US practice in BPF, 249–50,

258–60; and Pacific Fleet Train, 267; and Australian Govt, 273; and postwar tasks of BPF, 280–2; breaks wartime links with US Navy, 283; blocks sale of *Menestheus* to US Navy, 293; thanks of, to Fraser (1946), 294–5; Fraser's work at, as 1st Sea Lord (1948–51), 310–18, 329; thanks of, on Fraser's retirement, 327–9

Admiralty Is, 250

Africa, East, and Fraser's time in *Effingham* (1929–32), 88, 92–3, 95, 98; and Eastern Fleet (1942), 240–1

Africa, French North, and 'Torch' (1942), 158

AIRCRAFT: *British* – Avro Lancaster, 247; Avro York, 243; Bristol Beaufighter, 175; Fairey Barracuda, 163, 231; Fairey Swordfish, 158; De Havilland Rapide, 243; Hawker Hurricane, 146, 157, 158; Sopwith Pup, '1½-Strutter', 54; Sopwith Camel, 55; Supermarine Spitfire, 230; Supermarine Seafire, 259; *German* – Dornier Do-18, 191; Focke-Wulf Fw.200 Condor, 145–6; Junkers JU-87 Stuka, 156; *American* – Consolidated B-24 Liberator, 251, 256; Consolidated PBY Catalina, 256, 258; Grumman Avenger, 262; Hellcat, 259; Wildcat (Martlet),

cripple *Tirpitz* (Sept. 1943), 174–5; rejected by Americans in Pacific, 253; successes of, with BPF, 276
Xeros (Saros), Gulf of, 42–3, 45, 47–8

Yalu River, 322
Yangtse-kiang, 291, 293, 317.
Yellow Sea, 321–2

Yemen, 94
Yokohama, 291

Zanzibar, 93
Zeebrugge Raid (April 1918), 60–1
Zeppelins: British naval aviation developed to counter; destruction of *L.23, L.54, L.60*, 54–5

Index of Ships

BRITISH AND COMMONWEALTH

INDEX OF SHIPS